The Body and the Self

The Body and the Self

edited by José Luis Bermúdez, Anthony Marcel, and
Naomi Eilan

A Bradford Book
The MIT Press
Cambridge, Massachusetts
London, England

First MIT Press paperback edition, 1998

This book was set in Bembo by Compset, Inc., and was printed and bound in the United States of America.

Second printing, 1998

Library of Congress Cataloging-in-Publication Data

The body and the self / edited by José Luis Bermúdez, Anthony Marcel, and Naomi Eilan.
     p.   cm.
"A Bradford book."
Includes bibliographical references and index.
ISBN 0-262-02386-5 (HB), 0-262-52248-9 (PB)
   1. Body image. 2. Body schema. 3. Self-perception. I. Bermúdez, José Luis. II. Marcel, A. J. (Anthony J.) III. Eilan, Naomi.
BF697.5.B63B6   1995
128—dc20   94-33975
                                                                              CIP

Contents

Acknowledgments

Approximately half of the contributions to this volume were specially commissioned for it. The other half had their origin in presentations to the workshop The Perception of Subjects and Objects, held by the Spatial Representation Project at the King's College Research Centre, Cambridge, in September 1992. For reasons of length and cohesion, we have focused on a limited set of issues raised in that workshop. But we speak on behalf of all workshop contributors to this volume in expressing our gratitude to all the participants in the workshop for their presentations and for the constructive discussions they provided, which had a significant effect both on the versions of the papers presented here and on our approach to introducing them.

The workshop came toward the end of the four-year joint philosophy and psychology Project on Spatial Representation, funded by the Leverhulme Foundation and housed, administered, and supported by the King's College Research Centre. The project was set up in the belief that substantive progress in central questions about the nature of spatial representation and its relation to self-consciousness can only be achieved by drawing on the resources of disparate areas in psychology and philosophy. A previous collection of workshop proceedings, *Spatial Representation,* marked the half-way point of the project. It brought together philosophical and psychological approaches to central problems in explaining the nature of spatial representation and its relation to grasp of the idea of an external world. This volume, which marks the end of the project, brings together philosophical and psychological approaches to explaining the relation between spatial cognition and self-consciousness. Its particular focus is on the relation between self-consciousness and the way we represent our bodies, the spatial environment, and other people. The papers collected in both volumes give, we believe, a vivid sense of how rewarding such cross-disciplinary exchange can be and how essential it is for progress in these central topics.

During the preparation of this volume, the editors have been greatly helped by many people, in particular, members and associate members of the project. Bill Brewer and John Campbell played a vital and formative role in shaping the idea of the workshop and the approach we have taken to introducing the problems raised in this volume; Roz McCarthy and Julian Pears gave much support. Long- and short-term visitors, and regular seminar attenders have also had a great influence. We would like to thank in particular Kathleen Akins, Jonathan Cole, Martin Davies, Marcel Kinsbourne, Michael Martin, John O'Keefe, Brian O'Shaughnessy, Jacques Paillard, and Christopher Peacocke.

Ulric Neisser very generously sent us a manuscript of *The Perceived Self* before it was published. It significantly influenced our approach to several issues we raise in the Introduction.

We would like to express our deep gratitude to the Leverhulme Foundation. Their funding over four years of full-time members of the project, research assistants, long- and short-term visitors, workshops, and seminars made it possible to set up a uniquely stimulating and productive interdisciplinary environment for approaching central problems in spatial cognition and self-consciousness. Together with the first volume of workshop proceedings, *Spatial Representation,* we hope that this volume gives a sense of the richness of the new avenues of research that their support made possible.

The project was initiated and housed by the King's College Research Centre, which provided the ideal framework for pursuing it. We are greatly indebted to the provost and other managers of the research center for their support. We would like, in particular, to express our appreciation for continuing commitment to the project, encouragement, and understanding of the convenor of the research center, Martin Hyland. We owe a huge debt of gratitude to Rosemarie Baines for single-handedly organizing the authors' copyediting and proof-reading of their papers, as well as for her generous help throughout the project.

A text would not have emerged without Caroline Muncey and Ann Anderson of the Medical Research Council, Applied Psychology Unit. Caroline processed and reprocessed words; Ann photocopied, distributed, and mailed almost endlessly. Together they turned anarchy into some organization.

Andrew Young, Philip Barnard, and John Campbell read the Introduction to the book at very short notice. Their comments did much to improve it, and we are grateful to them.

We are also much indebted to three anonymous reviewers for the MIT Press for very useful comments.

Finally, we express our deep thanks to our editor, Teri Mendelsohn of the MIT Press, who has seen this book through from its inception with encouragement and great forbearance, and to Alan Thwaits for his excellent copyediting.

Self-Consciousness and the Body: An Interdisciplinary Introduction

Naomi Eilan, Anthony Marcel, and José Luis Bermúdez

We think of ourselves as possessors of both physical properties, such as height and weight, and psychological properties and states, such as kindness and having just seen a tiger. This is at least the commonly held view. Descartes held that this view is false and rests on confusion. According to Descartes, our selves are purely mental entities, the bearers of purely psychological properties, and our bodies are purely physical entities, the bearers of purely physical properties. There is no one thing that is the possessor of both kinds of properties.

Although Descartes's claim is *ontological* (offering an account of what sort of things we are), it is based on plausible insights into some of the distinctive characteristics of self-consciousness. Some of these characteristics are *phenomenological*, concerning the nature of our experience of ourselves. Others are *epistemological*, concerning particular features of the ways in which we acquire knowledge about ourselves. Still others concern semantic characteristics of the first-person pronoun 'I', such as the fact that genuine uses of 'I' always pick out the person uttering it. If Descartes's dualism is wrong, then the body, contra Descartes, is arguably integral to some aspects of self consciousness and/or of the use of 'I'. The question is, In what way? This, in most general terms, is the central issue with which all the papers collected here are either directly concerned or on which they have immediate bearings.

Part of the difficulty and interest of the question lies in the fact that there are several distinct ideas and claims, bequeathed by Descartes, that get discussed under the heading of 'self-consciousness', and the relation among these ideas is complex, a complexity that feeds back into questions of the body and the self. Another, independent source of difficulty is the fact that we have many ways of using, being conscious of, and representing our own bodies. Their nature and their interrelations are very much open to debate. An account of the relationship between self-consciousness and the relations we have to our bodies must respect the complexities in each of them.

By and large philosophers have focused on the concept of self-consciousness and the complexities in explaining it inherited from Descartes, and have tended to neglect the complexities of the way we use and represent our bodies. They have also tended to ignore the wealth of psychological work on these topics. Conversely, many of the complexities in the concept of self-consciousness that inform philosophical discussion have been ignored in the rich body of psychological work on the self. In addition, within psychology itself, as within philosophy, discussions of the body and of the self have rarely made contact—most of the former being conducted within sensory physiology, neurology, and motor control, and most of the latter being conducted within clinical and social psychology (a notable exception is Neisser 1994). But, as we will try to illustrate in this Introduction, an adequate understanding of self-consciousness will profit from taking into account both philosophical and psychological work on the body and on the self.

The papers collected in this volume approach issues raised by the relation of the body and the self in very different ways and from a variety of perspectives. In this Introduction we will not try to summarize the major concerns of each paper in its own terms. This is amply done by the papers themselves. But it means that many of the fascinating issues they discuss will not be raised here. Instead, we will attempt to bring out some of the central themes that cut across individual papers, in a way that is intended to foreground interdisciplinary issues.

1   Self-Consciousness and the Body

To begin, we should have before us the rudiments of Descartes's famous argument to the conclusion that he was a purely mental entity, an argument commonly referred to as the *cogito*. Descartes found that whenever he was engaged in any conscious mental activity—thinking, feeling pains, doubting, and so forth—it was impossible for him to doubt that he was doing so—a certainty he expressed by such utterances as 'I am thinking', 'I am feeling a pain'. He then famously argued that this alone is sufficient to establish that he had substantive knowledge of the existence and nature of the self referred to in these self ascriptions, knowledge we will term 'substantive self-consciousness'. In particular, he said, this gave him knowledge of himself as an essentially mental object, an ego.

This argument is the prime source of many of the ideas and problems that, since it was published, have bedeviled philosophical approaches to self-consciousness, ideas that survive many criticisms of the structure of the argument. It contains two ideas on which we will be focusing.

The Substantive Self-Consciousness Thesis   The self is a persisting object, which is picked out when we refer to ourselves using 'I'. Self-consciousness is a matter of representing oneself as an object. (Thus stated, the thesis is neutral on the question of what kind of object, mental or physical, the self is.)

The I-as-Subject Thesis   Being a self-conscious subject of thought and experience is necessarily linked to certain ways of acquiring knowledge about one's states. When one acquires such knowledge in these ways one cannot be mistaken about who is the subject of these states.

These two ideas are both to be found in Descartes, but they are here formulated in a way that is independent of his dualism. It is in terms of these two ideas, we believe, that the papers in this collection can best be introduced, and we have structured the Introduction accordingly. In this section we briefly outline the two ideas.

The substantive self-consciousness thesis is in two parts. According to the first part, the self is an object that persists through time and that we refer to when we employ the first-person pronoun 'I'. Saying that the self is an object leaves open the possibility that it might be a purely mentally subsisting ego (as Descartes claimed it was), because something can be an object without necessarily being a physical object. But the thesis still has considerable bite, since there are constraints on what counts as an object. In this connection there are questions to be asked about the characteristics that distinguish objects, like stones, chairs, and people, from things that are not objects, like holograms, shadows, and collections of properties.

The second part of the substantive self-consciousness thesis holds that in being aware of ourselves we represent ourselves as objects. The question is what such representation involves. How exactly do general constraints on what it is to represent an object manifest themselves in representing ourselves as objects? What kind of knowledge does this require? Several of the papers in this volume address the twin challenges of specifying the sense in which the self is an object and specifying what awareness of oneself as an object requires. A central move in the history of philosophy has been to claim that, contra Descartes, representing the self as an object is only possible if the body is represented. If this is true, then the body is directly implicated in substantive self-consciousness. How papers in this volume take the body to be thus implicated is the topic discussed in section 2.

The I-as-subject thesis, in contrast, is usually illustrated by appeal to ways we have of acquiring knowledge about our mental states. Contrast hearing someone shout out in pain and actually feeling a pain oneself. In both cases one acquires knowledge that a pain is instantiated. In the first case, there is room for a further question about who the owner of the pain is, and one might go wrong in answering it. In the second case, however, many people would claim that there is no room for such further questions or for possible mistakes in answering them. If one feels a pain, then it makes no sense to wonder whether the pain is one's own. There are two different points implicit in this illustration. The first point is that the I-as-subject thesis holds only for *introspectively* acquired knowledge of one's own states. It would not apply if, for example, one was reading someone's description of one's character. In such a situation it is possible that one might ask whether the person being described is oneself, and one might be mistaken in one's answer. The second point is that introspection applies only to one's own case. The I-as-subject thesis does not apply to ways of acquiring knowledge of other people's psychological states, for example, on the basis of perception or testimony.

One question that immediately arises is whether the scope of the I-as-subject thesis should be explicitly confined to ways we have of finding out about our *psychological* states. Thus restricted, this would open up a prima facie gap between being aware of oneself as a subject and substantive self-consciousness, if the latter requires representing one's body as a physical object. Some philosophers have argued that this gap is unbridgeable: awareness of oneself as an object and awareness of oneself as a subject cannot be unified. The relation between the two theses on self-consciousness is the issue addressed in section 4.

One way of bringing together the two theses about self-consciousness is to claim that the essential distinctive features of introspection can be extended to distinctive ways we have of acquiring knowledge about our physical properties. Whether or not this can be done depends on how we understand these ways of acquiring knowledge about our physical properties. For this reason this latter issue is discussed in section 3 before turning to the relation between the two theses on self-consciousness. Many psychologists and philosophers hold that each of us has ways of using, representing, and being aware of his own body that are unique to that body. Besides proprioception, obvious examples are acting with our bodies and feeling sensations in them. Both are unique to our relation with our own bodies, in contrast to our relations with all other objects. Whether there is such a distinctiveness and how it should be explained psychologically and phenomenologically is one of the central issues discussed in section 3.

2   Substantive Self-Consciousness

The papers considered in this section all assume the substantive self-consciousness thesis, that is, that we are objects and that we are aware of ourselves as such. The problem they focus on is the role the body has to play in this awareness. Several of the papers are concerned with the relation between substantive self-consciousness and our representation of other persons and physical objects. We begin with a discussion of some of the issues they raise in the first subsection. Other papers focus on the relation between substantive self-consciousness and the representation of the spatial environment. We turn to these in the second subsection.

Representing Objects, Other Persons, and Oneself

The substantive self-consciousness thesis holds that we are objects, rather than collections of features, and that self-consciousness requires representing ourselves as such. What does this claim amount to? There are at least three questions to be addressed. First, what is it to represent an entity as an object, rather than as a collection of features? Second, what is the role of the body in providing for the grasp of a person as an object? Third, what is the role of social interaction in providing for the grasp of oneself as an object?

The first question is a direct concern of John Campbell's paper. On his account, objects are causally structured along two dimensions, a structure lacking in collections of features. First, objects are internally causally structured, in the sense that their states at any given time are, at least in part, causally dependent upon their states at earlier times. Second, a fundamental part of the causal structure of an object is that it should be capable of featuring in many different causal interactions, both at a time and over time. Campbell describes this as an object's being capable of functioning as a common cause of distinct phenomena.

The distinction between collections of features and objects lies at the heart of Andrew Meltzoff and Keith Moore's account of infants' developing grasp of the notion of a physical object, and correlatively of a person. Their general aim is strike a middle course between two positions. The first is the Piagetian view that children do not acquire the notion of an object until the relatively late stage of 18 months; the second is the reaction to this view in some recent work claiming that the core of adult concepts is in place more or less at birth. In contrast to both positions, they claim that infants progress through three distinct concepts of an object—a progression culminating in the grasp of the rudiments of the adult concept at the age of 9 months. Only then do infants achieve the beginning of an understanding of object permanence. The two more primitive concepts said to precede such understanding are called concepts of "proto-objects." What makes them more primitive is that they involve representing entities as collections of features, rather than as proper objects. Meltzoff and Moore review experiments on visual tracking of objects that, they suggest, show a development best described by the distinctions they draw between the three types of object concept. A question that arises when one compares the claims of Campbell and of Meltzoff and Moore is whether the latter would accept Campbell's account of what having the adult concept of an object requires, and if they do, what kind of experiments would be needed for testing infants' grip on the two dimensions of causal structure identified by Campbell as essential to having a grip on an entity as an object.

Campbell's account of what it is to have a grasp of an entity as an object is intended to apply to all objects, physical objects as well as persons. This raises the second question, namely of the relation between representing a person as an object and representing a person's body. On one view, what gives us our hold on persons as objects—ourselves and others—is exhausted by our understanding of persons' bodies as physical objects. This is the view implicit in the position known in the philosophical literature as "animalism," discussed by Paul Snowdon in his chapter. The animalist claim is that persons are just animals and that there are no psychological criteria for the identity of animals. According to the animalist, bodily continuity is both necessary and sufficient for the continuing existence of a person. There is no need for the sort of psychological connections over time that might be provided by, for example, memory links.

Some philosophers have used neuropsychological and psychiatric phenomena to put pressure on the idea that continuity of body provides continuity of self. In particular, split-brain patients, multiple-personality disorders, and fugue states have been put forward as instances where although there is indeed continuity of body, there is not a continuity of person, because there are argued to be two or more selves in a single body. If so, continuity of body cannot be a sufficient condition for continuity of person. Snowdon's paper explores several objections to animalism along these lines. He argues that the intuitions are not at all as clear-cut as has been assumed, and he shows how animalism might respond to the problem cases. He ends his discussion with a partial characterization of the concept of a person that goes some way toward supporting the central animalist intuitions.

If persons are just animal bodies, then having a grip on a person as an object will rely solely on a grasp of what it is for the body to be an object. Such a view is directly rejected by Campbell. He argues that consciousness of the self as an object requires an understanding of the way one's psychological properties are causally structured over the two dimensions mentioned at the beginning of this subsection. The importance of the body in giving us an understanding of ourselves as objects, on such an account, is that our understanding of the causal structure of our mental states requires an understanding of the way in which, in virtue of being embodied, we can affect and are affected by our immediate surroundings.

As Snowdon suggests, the point at issue is the nature of our concept of a person or self. One important source of information here is the acquisition of adult concepts by infants and children. In this context Snowdon makes the following claim: if, when teaching a child the concept of a person, we find out that the child believes of a person perceived at one time and place that it is the same biological animal that had been perceived somewhere else earlier, but does not treat this as sufficient for its being the same person, we will say that such a child has not yet mastered the concept of a person. A possible implication of this suggestion is that for infants and young children, grasp of physical properties will play a dominant role in their developing concept of a person.

In one sense, this claim of Snowdon's might be taken to be reinforced by Meltzoff and Moore's emphasis on the role of infants' developing grasp of the notion of a physical object in providing them with a grasp of the identity of persons over time. However, Meltzoff and Moore also argue that their work on infants' use of imitation to probe the identity of persons shows that, rather than using only spatiotemporal criteria to establish identity over time, which is what is done with physical objects, infants also use remembered behaviors when reidentifying persons. Indeed, they argue that infants are equipped from the outset with a primordial distinction between persons and other objects. This distinction is based, they suggest, on a capacity to distinguish acts from all other events, where acts are perceived as essentially goal-directed movements. Much of the work they describe is intended to demonstrate how infants' understanding of acts is progressively psychologized (via an increasingly sophisticated grasp of the notion of intention). Meltzoff and Moore treat children's developing understanding of psychological concepts as central in their developing understanding of themselves and others as persons. Such emphasis is contrary to the spirit of animalism, a thesis that denies that there is any important sense in which we are psychological entities. (In fact, further experiments are needed to test whether psychological or physical criteria of identity dominate for children at various stages, and such experiments would still leave open the question of the nature of adult concepts.)

Whatever one's views about the nature of persons and what it is to have an understanding of oneself and others as persons, an additional question is what it is that gives subjects an understanding of themselves and others as persons. The papers by Campbell, Meltzoff and Moore, and Butterworth all highlight the importance of social interaction in providing for such an understanding. This is the third question raised at start of this subsection.

Meltzoff and Moore focus on the way a child's imitation of others' actions, from very early infancy, provides the most primitive sense of, as they put it, the "like-me-ness" experienced by infants, since imitation requires appeal to an infant's sense of the identity of the felt spatial properties of its own body with the seen spatial properties of others' bodies, which relies on cross-modal spatial matching. George Butterworth's contribution also suggests that early social interaction between infants and their carers is the source of an evolving simultaneous understanding of themselves and others. He argues that the capacity for imitation of spatial movements is not sufficient to ascribe to infants an understanding of their own and others' psychological properties, and therefore is not a sufficient basis for simultaneous understanding of self and others as persons. The basis for this is to be found in the emotional aspects of such interaction. In this connection he stresses how such emotionally informed interaction reveals the extent to which infants have an understanding of their own and others' bodies as psychological entities from the earliest stages of cognition on. He cites work on the mutual coregulation of activity in mother-infant pairs, in particular, on the way in which synchronization of emotions such as pleasure in both mother and infant is linked to synchronization of movements. What makes such synchronization possible is that the cross-modal matching between felt properties of one's own body and seen properties of the other's body extends beyond purely spatial aspects of the body. Social interaction is also highlighted in Campbell's account of what gives us a grasp of ourselves as psychologically structured objects. He appeals to work by Meltzoff and Moore on infants at about 14 months who not only engage in bodily imitation but also show pleasure at being imitated and manipulate others' imitation of them. He suggests that the infant behavior reveals "a primitive echo" of subsequent understanding of the causal impact of their psychological states upon others. He argues that it is at least partly through such social interaction that the infant acquires an understanding of its own psychological causal structure.

Self and the Environment
We turn now to the relation between one's perceptual grasp of the spatial environment and one's capacity to represent oneself as an object. The central question considered here is, How must one represent oneself and the spatial environment if one is to be credited with a grasp of the distinction between them?

Once again, it is helpful to approach the issues from the perspective of debates in developmental psychology. On Piaget's account of cognitive development in infancy and early childhood, newborn infants are born into a universe of experience that is radically unlike our own, without any separation between self and the world. The infant's escape from this "profound adualism," as Butterworth calls it, is a lengthy one, and it is not until about 18 months that young children acquire a capacity to distinguish between themselves and the spatial environment. Prior to this, there is no self or world at all for the infant. Much recent work in developmental psychology has challenged Piaget's suggestion of a profound adualism at birth. Butterworth suggests in his contribution that the implications of this research support Gibson's (1979) view of the relation between perception of the environment and perception of oneself, in which the self and the environment are coperceived. On Butterworth's account, the infant's early perceptions are imbued with what he calls a "natural dualism."

A central theme in Gibson's approach to the problem of explaining the relation between perception of the self and perception of the environment (discussed further in the papers by Butterworth and Bermúdez) is a rejection of the idea that information about one's own body comes only from states and activities of the body considered in isolation from the environment. In explaining perception, he suggests, we should concentrate on the various forms of information available in the environment to be picked up by suitably sensitive perceptual systems. In contrast to the view that self-specifying information is derived only from states and activities of the body, he maintains that self-specifying, or "propriospecific," information is also available in visual information, in acoustic information, and in tactile contact with objects (a view now widely accepted, at least in research on posture and motion). For example, dynamic visual information specifies the direction and speed of a perceiver relative to the immediate environment. In this connection Gibson rejected the theoretical usefulness of the notion of a specific body sense and the usefulness of the term 'proprioception' to refer to such a sense. Proprioception, as he uses the term, is a mechanism for detecting self-specifying information that cuts across any distinction between sensory modalities. This will be returned to in section 3.

Butterworth reviews a range of data from experiments carried out in a Gibsonian framework that is relevant to the interdependence of perception of the self and perception of the environment in infants as young as 2 months. Using a distinction drawn by Neisser (1988), Butterworth describes the pickup of propriospecific information as yielding an "ecological self" (the point of origin in perception), which shares with the "interpersonal self" the property of being directly perceived, as opposed to being inferred. These are distinguished by Neisser from the notions of an "extended self" (requiring memory, anticipation, and an explicit representation of the self), a "private self" (which involves thinking of one's mental states as one's own), and a self concept (reflecting a comprehension of oneself as a member of a social community).

The papers by Thomas Baldwin and by James Russell can both be read as questioning whether a Gibsonian account of the coperception of self and environment can provide a sufficiently rich notion of self and world to generate the experience of a separateness between self and world. Baldwin suggests that to take oneself to be a subject of objective experience, understanding this to be experience as of an objective, mind-independent world, one must take the objects of one's experience to be the causes of that experience. He then argues that only the experience of agency can make available to us the idea of necessary connection, which is an essential component of the concept of causation. So the experience of agency is necessary for thinking of one's experiences as yielding information about an objective world. The negative component of his thesis is that perception of other objects can provide us only with the idea of temporal and spatial contiguity, rather than causation. The positive thesis is that the experience of agency, particularly the experience of objects as resistant to our contact with them, does provide us with an understanding of the notion of power, and hence with a basic grip on the idea of necessity that is integral to causation.

Baldwin's argument is, as he says, an argument specifically from the first-person perspective. It links the *experience* of agency with the *experience* of an objective world. In focusing on this perspective, he raises an important issue for relating psychological and philosophical work in this area, namely whether and how appeal to research on information pickup, within the Gibsonian framework, can be related to claims about the nature of experience. Consideration of this question is necessary if, for example, one wants to draw on work such as Butterworth's to characterize an infant's perceptual experiences.

An approach similar in spirit is taken in Russell's contribution. He defends a very limited version of the Piagetian view of infant development. Acknowledging the strong experimental evidence against the view that there is no self-world dualism at all in infancy, he nonetheless maintains that the experience of agency is an integral part of acquiring a detached and reflective grasp of oneself as existing within a world that is independent of one's experience of it. He holds that Gibson's theory of perception does not explain what gives one a sense of agency. He suggests that monitoring self-generated movements does this and thus is a necessary stepping stone toward distinguishing oneself from the environment. Infants must have this early on if they are to achieve any grip on themselves as separate from their environment. However, he also holds that such a mechanism is not sufficient to explain the experience of the distinction between self and environment. What is needed for this is the experience of the refractory nature of the world. By undertaking intentional acts, one learns that the world resists one's will. Yet he emphasizes not the potential for understanding causal relations that this offers but rather the way in which it underwrites a conception of the world as independent of one's actions and experience at a particular time.

If the sort of detached and reflective comprehension that both Baldwin and Russell consider necessary for having experience as of an objective world is taken to be a requirement for the experience of self-world dualism (experience of their separateness), then Gibson's account of the pickup of propriospecific and exterospecific information cannot be of much help. For there is nothing explicitly stated in Gibson's conception of perceptual information that will yield a grasp of one's experiences as being caused by a mind-independent world. Nonetheless, it might be thought that there is room for an account of the experience of self-world dualism that does not require the capacity to take a detached and reflective perspective on oneself. José Luis Bermúdez's paper moves in this direction.

Bermúdez suggests that there are ways of understanding the notion of a self-world dualism that do not require the capacity to think about oneself in the sort of detached and reflective manner discussed by Baldwin and Russell. Nonetheless, he thinks that the information given in perception at any moment is not in itself sufficient to provide a self-world dualism in experience. In particular, he links the capacity to distinguish oneself from the world with the capacity to reidentify places. This is meant in a strong sense, as involving the ability to think of oneself as having been to a given place before, and hence as requiring certain forms of memory. His paper attempts to show that subjects can be ascribed a capacity to think about themselves in this way without thereby being ascribed the capacity to reflect on themselves in a detached way.

We end this section with two comments about the connections between this debate and the subjects covered in the previous section. The first point concerns the parallel between grasp of self relative to other persons and grasp of self relative to the environment. In both cases there is a distinction between primitive and sophisticated kinds of self-consciousness. However, the concepts used here to describe these distinctions are different in the two cases. In the interpersonal case the distinctions are between representing an entity as a collection of features and as a causally structured object and between representing physical and psychological

properties. In the case of self versus environment the distinctions are between psychologically simple and complex forms of self-consciousness,
and between a less and a more detached grasp of the relation between
oneself and the environment. A question that needs addressing is whether
and how the concepts can be related.

The second point is that, although there are good grounds for appealing both to perception of the environment and to social interaction in explaining the ontogenesis of substantive self-consciousness, little work has
been done on bringing the two together. Whether or not one follows Butterworth in according them equal weight, it is clear that progress in this
area must involve combining work in the two areas and asking detailed
philosophical and psychological questions about the relationship between
these two sources of substantive self-consciousness.

3   Bodily Awareness

Many philosophers and psychologists have found compelling the idea
that we have a distinctive way of perceiving and knowing about our own
bodies. A relatively uncontroversial way of putting this point would be to
say that there is a crucial difference between the ways in which we use
and represent our bodies and the ways in which we use and represent
other physical objects. For example, it is clear that we are capable of acting with our bodies in ways in which we are not with any other bodies
or objects and capable of feeling sensations in our bodies but not in
other bodies or objects. The simple fact that we are capable of action
with, and sensation in, our bodies is sufficient to set our relations with
our bodies apart from our relations with other objects. But this raises
three important points concerning distinctiveness, which we will discuss
in this section. First, several philosophers and psychologists suppose that
we have a specific body sense that yields knowledge about our bodies
and about nothing else. (Indeed, it is interesting that the term 'proprioception' seems to reflect an intuition of a connection of body with self.)
We discuss this in the first subsection. Second, the question arises of
whether we might need to postulate certain special representations of
the body to explain action and sensation. This issue will be explored in
the next subsection. Third, one might ask whether there is a distinctive
phenomenology of the body. This issue runs through all three subsec-
tions but is separately discussed in the third subsection. Finally, in the
fourth subsection, we draw out some of the connections between these
distinctive ways of being in touch with our bodies and the substantive
self-consciousness thesis.

The Senses of 'Proprioception'

One way of making sense of the idea that we have a distinctive way of using and representing our bodies is through the suggestion that body-relative information is exclusively provided by the information channels of a body sense. Certainly there exist a range of information systems that yield information about the state and performance of the body. But this has no immediate implication for the existence of a dedicated body sense. To deal with this issue, we need to begin by listing some of the various *internal information systems* involved here:

• Information about pressure, temperature, and friction from receptors on the skin and beneath its surface
• Information about the relative state of body segments from receptors in the joints, some sensitive to static position, some to dynamic information
• Information about balance and posture from the vestibular system in the inner ear and the head/trunk dispositional system and information from pressure on any parts of the body that might be in contact with a gravity-resisting surface
• Information from skin-stretch about bodily disposition and volume
• Information from receptors in the internal organs about nutritional and other states relevant to homeostasis and well-being
• Information about effort and muscular fatigue from muscles
• Information about general fatigue from cerebral systems sensitive to blood composition

The first point to make about this (nonexhaustive) list is that these various information systems differ according to whether or not they provide information only about the body. So, for example, the systems concerned with general fatigue and with nutritional states provide information only about the body. In contrast, the vestibular system in the inner ear does not provide information just about the body; what it really provides information about is the relation between the body and the environment. Moreover, in addition to these information systems, there are those that can be employed to yield information either about the body or about the environment. The receptors in the hand sensitive to skin stretch and finger position, for example, can provide information either about the momentary shape of the hand or about the shape and texture of small objects. Similarly, receptors in the joints and muscles provide information about the spatial distribution of limbs, which can also contribute to the haptic exploration of the contours of large objects.

It is equally important to remember that these information channels are not the only way in which information about the body is acquired. For example, information about movement and relative posture of the body is also available in visual flow, to which the vestibular system is sensitive (as well as being sensitive to gravity-relative movement and posture). So, it is neither true that internal proprioceptive systems can provide information only about the body, nor is it true that information about the body comes only via the internal proprioceptive systems.

Perhaps the most important point to bear in mind here is that few of these different types of information are consciously registered, and when they do generate conscious experiences, the contents of the experience are often different from the contents of the information that generates the experience. (For example, information about the summation of joint angles may give rise to a conscious experience as of limb position). There is an important distinction to be drawn between possessing body-related information and having conscious experience of the body, where a paradigm instance of conscious experience of the body would be experiencing a bodily sensation, such as an itch or a pain. Not only is much information about posture never conscious, but also posture itself is often not conscious. Moreover, conscious experience whose source is somatic can be either about the world or about the body. An illustration of this is pressure between body surface and an object, which, depending on the focus of one's attention, can give rise to consciousness either of a sensation in a particular body part or of the object.

We propose, then, keeping distinct the following three things, which are often treated as unitary. First, there are internal *proprioceptive systems*, namely those channels of information listed above whose source is the body. Second, there is *proprioceptive information*, understood to include all the information available about the body (whether it comes from proprioceptive systems or from elsewhere). Third, there is *proprioceptive awareness*, where this is taken to be conscious experience of the body, characterized as experience of the body as from the inside. This characterization distinguishes such awareness from visual and haptic experiences of one's own body. It is also independent of whether or not the awareness is derived from proprioceptive systems, and, as noted above, such awareness should be sharply distinguished from proprioceptive information. We would like to suggest that any talk of a specific body sense will need to take into account the distinctions between these three things. Certainly, it seems wrong to suggest that there might be such a specific body sense if the existence of such a sense is taken to depend on the equivalence of systems, information, and awareness. Nonetheless, there might be other grounds for wanting to postulate the existence of such a specific body sense. Indeed, the three contributions explicitly concerned with this particular issue—those by Michael Martin, by Brian O'Shaughnessy, and by Jonathan Cole and Jacques Paillard—do not rest their case on such an equivalence but draw rather on a variety of psychological, physiological, and phenomenological considerations. A question worth bearing in mind relative to all the contributors discussed in this subsection is which accounts of the distinctiveness of proprioception, if any, might be used to yield a notion of a distinctive sense of one's body.

Representations of the Body

Psychologists and philosophers have postulated a range of different ways in which the body is represented. It is unfortunate that writers have used the terms 'body image' and 'body schema' indiscriminately to refer to quite different types of representation, often conflating them without good reason. In this section we make some distinctions that will help in addressing the issues underlying these different uses of the terms by papers in this volume.

We begin with a list of the following descriptive uses to which the terms 'body image' and 'body schema' have been put in philosophy and psychology:

• One's conscious experience of the body at a particular time
• A changing nonconscious record of the momentary relative disposition of, and space occupied by, one's body parts
• A nonconscious persisting representation of the structure and shape of one's body
• A canonical representation of what bodies in general look or feel like
• A knowledge of one's own specific appearance
• Explicit conceptualizations of the body, acquired socially or academically (e.g., that one has a liver)
• Emotional attitudes towards one's body, some of which are tacit and socially determined
• Cultural symbolizations of the body
• The neuronal vehicles for some of the contents referred to above

The first thing we need to do is to distinguish three parameters along which these different concepts of body image and schema vary. It is perfectly possible that all these different notions are genuine and useful, provided they are not conflated. First, there is variation as to the *content* of the representation. Among the different candidates here we find the long-term structural and physical properties of the body, its current posture, its physical appearance, its aesthetic qualities, and so forth. Second, there is a range of candidates for the *kind of representation or state* that bears the content. The main candidates here are conscious perceptual experiences, conscious mental images, representations underpinning available knowledge of properties of one's body, nonconscious representations used in

subpersonal computations, and neuronal projections. Third, there are differences in the *explanatory purpose* to which the particular representation
is being put. Examples of things that different conceptions of body representation have been brought in to explain are coordination of movement,
the proprioceptive awareness of posture, the felt location of sensations,
the various neuropsychological disorders of bodily awareness, the possibility of bodily imitation, one's understanding of one's body as an object,
the mechanism and phenomenology of somatic attention, and substantive
self-consciousness.

An illustration of how different representations of the body can vary
along all three of these parameters (content, kind, and explanatory purpose)
is provided by a comparison of the concepts employed by Brian O'Shaughnessy, Marcel Kinsbourne, and Shaun Gallagher. Brian O'Shaughnessy has
two explanatory aims. The first is to characterize the kind of bodily awareness that he thinks is necessary for intentional action (as opposed to nonconscious aspects of motor control). For this he invokes a short-term body
image, which is the content of whatever one experiences of the body at any
moment, an attentionally dependent awareness of egocentrically specified
postural disposition, volumetric extent, and located sensations. (In fact, he
argues that to explain current awareness of one's body, we need a distinction
between three notions of short-term body image.) His second aim is to
explain how, in the short-term body image, sensations are experienced as
located within particular body parts. For this he invokes the notion of a
long-term body image. This is a nonconscious representation of the relatively permanent structure and volumetric extent of the body. The momentary, conscious short-term body image is a product of the integration of the
long-term body image and a subset (due to attention) of all the momentary
postural and bodily information available. The persisting representation can
be the basis of certain kinds of bodily knowledge, even if there is no capacity
for sensation. Indeed, Cole and Paillard in their paper point out that deafferented patients, even when most current sensation and information about
current body position are lost, still have a sense of their body structure.

O'Shaughnessy's appeal to a long-term body image in these explanatory contexts is not threatened by rejections of appeals to a body image in
other explanatory contexts. An example of such a rejection is to be found
in Marcel Kinsbourne's paper. Kinsbourne challenges the motivation within neurology for introducing some notion of a body image, namely, to explain what is happening in the range of neuropsychological disorders in
people's experience and use of their own bodies known as *asomatognosias*.

A single example will suffice. Cases of *unilateral neglect* can involve either or both of the following two phenomena: the first is that patients ignore parts on one side of their body, and the second is that they ignore the

same side of space and of spatially extended stimuli in general. In extreme cases, particularly those when a patient is unaware of their neglect, the patient will be unaware of the existence of, or deny ownership of, limbs on the affected side of their body. One explanation of cases of unilateral neglect of the body is that it is due to damage to the relevant parts of a subpersonal neural representation of the body, located in a particular part of the brain. (This is the notion of body image with which Kinsbourne is particularly concerned.) So construed, neglect is a representational deficit. Kinsbourne argues that this appeal to a cerebral representation of the body to explain the various asomatognosias is neither convincing nor necessary. In neglect, for example, it fails to explain both the preponderance of left-side neglect and the fact that only a limited range of body-parts are neglected. If there were a single neurally unified central representation of the body, it would be natural to expect that it could be damaged in a greater variety of ways or parts. Kinsbourne offers an explanation of neglect on which it comes out instead as a deficit in attention, caused by a breakdown of the balance between the opponent processors implicated in somatic attention. What happens in cases of left neglect, he suggests, is that the processor located in the right hemisphere of the brain and directing attention to the left is damaged, and so cannot counterbalance the processor located in the left hemisphere. This diagnosis is based on an account of the mechanism of lateral spatial attention (both somatic and visual), which does not require postulating a (separate) representation of the body. In addition, Kinsbourne offers explanations of other asomatognosias that do not require appeal to a body image.

Kinsbourne's rejection of the theoretical utility of the notion of a body image is not in conflict with O'Shaughnessy's postulation of the existence of a long-term body image. Not only are these two different types of representation; they are also being employed for different explanatory purposes. O'Shaughnessy is attempting to account for the experienced location of sensations, whereas Kinsbourne is offering a functional explanation of the neural mechanics of somatic attention. Of course, one of the uses to which somatic attention can be put is attending to bodily sensations. But this does not necessarily mean that it is in virtue of attending to bodily sensations that one experiences them as located in particular body-parts. It is plausible (though disputed) that when one attends to bodily sensations one is attending to things that are already being experienced at particular bodily locations, although in the attentional background. It is thus possible to maintain that some form of body image *might* be required to explain the experienced location of sensations and yet *might not* be required to explain the mechanics of somatic attention.

Distinguishing between different contexts of explanation is not only helpful in clarifying the relation between O'Shaughnessy and Kinsbourne; it is also a project central to Shaun Gallagher's contribution to this volume. Gallagher begins by introducing a systematic distinction between the referents of the terms 'body image' and 'body schema', which are often conflated in discussions of bodily experience. For him, the body image is the usually conscious representation of several aspects of the body: the body as immediately perceived, the body as conceptually understood, and the body as an object of feelings and emotions. What is common to these is their representational nature. It is to this notion of a body image that he appeals both in characterizing momentary somatic experience and in understanding anorexia nervosa. This should be sharply distinguished from the body schema, which Gallagher describes as the way in which the body actively integrates its positions and responses in the environment. He argues that this is achieved independently of consciousness and does not involve any representation. A point worth noting here (to which we will return in the fourth subsection) is that Gallagher, in common with several psychologists, thinks that many of the ways in which we act and move are best understood at the level of the body schema, without bringing in a representational body image.

An interesting theme in Gallagher's paper is that not only is it important to distinguish between the notions of body image and body schema, it is equally important to look at the interaction between them. The operations of the body schema constrain almost all forms of conscious experience. Gallagher adduces a range of experimental evidence suggesting that changes in various aspects of bodily performance at the level of the body schema have effects not only on the way in which subjects perceive their own bodies, but also on their perception of space and external objects. More generally, he is concerned to bring out the importance that Merleau-Ponty attaches to different aspects of our embodiment in explaining the nature of perception.

Phenomenology and Spatial Content
A third way of approaching the question of what is distinctive in our knowledge and perception of our bodies is by exploring the phenomenology of the body. We can introduce the issue by considering a philosophical view originating with Wittgenstein (see Budd 1989) but propounded most forcefully by Anscombe (1962). According to this view, proprioceptive knowledge of limb position and movement is independent of bodily sensations. The suggestion is that, although we obviously do have bodily sensations, they do not themselves involve perception of posture and

movement (partly because they cannot provide sufficiently fine-grained information). Instead, a person's knowledge of posture and movement should be analyzed in terms of his immediate convictions that body-parts are positioned in a certain way or that some body-parts are moving in a certain way. These immediate convictions are presumably based on non-conscious information provided by the proprioceptive systems. This is accompanied by a revisionist view of bodily sensations, which denies that they have a felt location. Anscombe claims that we do not feel a sensation, such as an itch, at a particular bodily location. What we have instead is the conjunction of a sensation and a disposition to act towards a particular part of the body (to scratch, for example).

The claim that this view can give an exhaustive account of proprioceptively based knowledge of our bodies in general, and of sensation in particular, is rejected, implicitly or explicitly, by all the contributors to this volume. In particular, the philosophical papers on sensation (Brewer, Martin, O'Shaughnessy) hold that feeling a sensation is essentially bound up with the perceptual experience of the spatial properties of one's body. However, there are interesting divergences in how the spatial content of sensation is explained.

Bill Brewer, drawing on earlier work by O'Shaughnessy (1980), suggests that the spatial content of sensation should be analyzed as having two essential components: first, a structural representation of the body and its parts; second, an egocentric specification of the location of the sensation in the body. Egocentric specifications are, in turn, linked constitutively with dispositions to direct actions at such locations. On Brewer's account, there is nothing prima facie that distinguishes the spatial content per se of felt sensations from the spatial content of the visual perception of a located feature on an object. What is distinctive of the phenomenology of bodily sensation, in contrast to that of visual perception, is that in bodily sensation one is directly aware of a mental property of oneself (a sensation) in a physical location, whereas in vision one is not.

Michael Martin, in contrast, argues that bodily sensation has a distinctive spatial content that distinguishes the phenomenology of proprioceptive (bodily) awareness from the phenomenology of visual and haptic experiences of one's own body and other objects in external space. More specifically, he argues that an essential feature of feeling a sensation is that "any region in which it seems to one that one could now be feeling a sensation will thereby feel to one to fall within one's boundaries" (p. 271). This is his gloss on what it is to be aware of the body from the inside. What is distinctive about the spatial content of the experience is brought out by the following contrast with visual experience. In the case of visual awareness, the experienced boundaries of perceived objects fall within the experienced limits of the egocentric space within which visible objects can seem to lie. In contrast, in the case of proprioceptive awareness, the experienced boundaries of the perceived object (the felt body) are coextensive with the experienced limits of the space of somatic perception. (Cases where one's sensations are felt to be at the end of a prosthetic device or tool are not necessarily a problem for Martin's position, since, he would argue, in such cases the felt body extends to such locations). What makes such awareness a case of awareness of an object, however, is that in being aware of boundaries from the inside *as boundaries*, one is simultaneously aware of a space that extends beyond them.

One of Martin's central theses is that a sense of ownership is essential to the phenomenology of sensation and that this sense should be explained by appeal to the spatial content of sensation. That is, to feel ownership with respect to one's body, on the basis of sensation, is nothing other than to be aware of it from the inside, in the manner just sketched. This claim enables him to explain ownership without bringing in self-consciousness. We return to this issue in section 4. In that section we also consider how the deafferented patients described by Cole and Paillard put pressure on Brewer's and Martin's accounts of the spatial content of sensation.

Irrespective of its truth or tractability, Martin's account of the distinctiveness of proprioceptive awareness raises the question of what concepts are needed to describe the spatial content of perceptual awareness of the body in a way that does justice to its phenomenology. An appeal only to frames of reference used in representing objects arguably will not yield a *distinctive* phenomenology of bodily awareness. One candidate that might do so is the notion of an attentional field, appealed to by Naomi Eilan, i.e., the background ingredient in perceptual awareness in terms of which spatial targets are specified for intentional shifts of attention. This is similar to William James's description of the background to focal attention in perceptual consciousness. One suggestion might be that what is distinctive about bodily awareness is the content of the attentional field in such awareness. In visual awareness it consists of the egocentric specification of locations in space around the perceiver; in proprioceptive awareness this might consist in egocentric specification of locations on a structurally represented object (the perceiver's own body). In any case, this issue indicates the potential gain from bringing together analytic phenomenology and empirical psychology, in which there is much current research on what defines attentional targets and on the preattentive articulation of the perceptual field (see Duncan and Humphreys 1989).

Representation, Phenomenology, and Substantive Self-Consciousness
According to the substantive self-consciousness thesis, the self is a persisting object, and self-consciousness is a matter of representing oneself as such. In section 2 the substantive self-consciousness thesis was considered in the context of social interaction and perception of the environment. The central question there was, in what sense is a representation of oneself as an object implicated in social interaction and perception of the environment? A similar question, discussed in this subsection, arises with regard to the distinctive ways in which we use, represent, and are aware of our bodies. In what way, if any, do these distinctive ways of being in touch with our bodies implicate a representation of oneself as an object?

One place to look in addressing this last question is accounts of the spatial content of sensation. Martin's account is indeed intended to yield perception of the body as an object, but in a weak sense given simply by current awareness of the boundaries of the body. Brewer's account, because of its appeal to a structural description of the body, suggests that sensation involves grasp of a more robust notion of one's body as an object.

Another place to look is the various forms of representation of the body that are referred to under the label 'body image'. The more conceptualized and developed types of representation of the body, such as Gallagher's notion of a body image, arguably involve representing the body as an object. However, there may be less conceptualized ways of representing the body as an object. Clearly, the subpersonal notion of a body image discussed by Kinsbourne will not, by itself, explain awareness of oneself as an object. Campbell argues that a combination of O'Shaughnessy's long-term and short-term body images, depending on how they are used, can be employed to yield an understanding of oneself as a causally structured object at both physical and psychological levels, and much of his paper is concerned with how this works on the psychological level. Even if he is correct, it remains an open question whether the bodily representations discussed by O'Shaughnessy are the only ones that can help understand the way in which we represent ourselves as objects.

As was suggested at the beginning of section 3, one of the features distinguishing our relation to our own bodies from our relations to other physical objects is the fact that we can act directly with our bodies in ways in which we cannot with any other objects. The issue of action and bodily awareness is one that we have not been able to accord the space it deserves in this Introduction, although it is central to the papers by O'Shaughnessy and Gallagher. We can, however, make two observations. The first is that O'Shaughnessy and Gallagher seem to have very different replies to the question of whether a representation of oneself as an object is implicated in action. O'Shaughnessy suggests that both the long-term and short-term body images are required if one is to act on the world, and what he says about the way in which they are used together suggests that they might yield a sense of one's body as an object. Gallagher, in contrast, seems to suggest that an explanation of nonreflective action will not involve anything so representational. For him, action may *give rise to* an awareness of one's body as an object but certainly does not *require* any such grasp, since the body schema is nonrepresentational. Secondly, it is worth recalling that both Baldwin and Russell argue that the capacity for action is essential for distinguishing between oneself and the environment. Here too there is the suggestion of an intimate connection between action and the representation of one's body or self as an object. A question worth pursuing is how their arguments, in which action comes in as the basis for grasping the self-world distinction, relate to the arguments deployed by O'Shaughnessy and Gallagher, which turn on the nature of action and on how it should be explained.

A complete account of substantive self-consciousness will have to deal with these various issues, integrating them not only with each other but also with the issues raised by the role that representing oneself as an object has to play in social interaction and representing the environment. We turn now to another issue that such a complete account will have to deal with. This is the general question of how, if at all, the substantive self-consciousness thesis can be combined with the I-as-subject thesis.

4   I-as-Subject, Ownership, and Elusiveness of Self

Up to now we have kept apart the two central claims about self-consciousness in terms of which we have structured this Introduction. In this concluding section we develop further the I-as-subject thesis and consider a line of thought according to which it is irreconcilable with the substantive self-consciousness thesis. The reasons that there is a problem here are complex and should not be oversimplified. We will try to give a sense of how this problem is articulated in the relevant papers. Although the articulation of the problem is philosophical, a full account of the problem and its solution rest on psychological explanations of proprioceptive awareness and spatial perception.

Some preliminary setting of the scene is required. In particular, we need a more precise characterization of the I-as-subject thesis. We can appeal here to the idea developed by Shoemaker (1968) that there are ways of acquiring knowledge about one's properties that are *immune to error through misidentification relative to the first person pronoun*. What this means is that any knowledge about properties gained in these ways cannot be known to apply to an individual without one ipso facto knowing that they apply to oneself. On Shoemaker's account, such immunity to error holds only for introspectively acquired knowledge. Further, it holds for knowledge only about mental states. This has much intuitive appeal. It would strike us as peculiar if we heard someone say on the basis of introspection, 'I know that someone is thinking about this problem, but is it me?' According to the I-as-subject thesis, such immunity to error is an essential ingredient of being a self-conscious subject of thought and experience.

As we noted in section 1, this link between the I-as-subject thesis and mental states opens a prima facie gap between being aware of oneself as a subject and substantive self-consciousness if the latter involves representing one's body as physical. One way of attempting to close this gap is to argue that the kind of immunity to error discussed above can be extended from mental properties to particular ways we have of acquiring knowledge of our physical properties. Thus Evans (1982) argued that we have two ways of acquiring knowledge about our physical properties that are immune to error through misidentification relative to the first person. The first is internal proprioception, which yields knowledge such as 'My legs are crossed.' The second is visual, haptic, and auditory perception, which yields knowledge such as 'I am to the left of this tree.' The claim is that, suitably explained, these ways of acquiring knowledge of one's properties yield knowledge of one's body as a physical object. On this account, immunity to error is drawn into an account of substantive self-consciousness. This, Evans suggests, is "the most powerful antidote to a Cartesian conception of the self" (1982, 220), because what it suggests is that the subject of thought is a physically extended thing.

Brewer's paper suggests that Evans's argument cannot work. He argues that even if immunity to error applies to ways of acquiring knowledge about one's physical properties, as it does to ways of acquiring knowledge about one's psychological properties, this does not of itself ensure that there is a single bearer of both properties. However, Brewer argues, his own explanation of bodily sensation does ensure that there is a single bearer of both kinds of properties. His argument rests on what he sees as the dual structure of bodily experience. Using his account of the spatial content of sensation, briefly described in the preceding section, he suggests that what is distinctive of experiencing bodily sensations (as opposed to having visual experiences) is that what one is aware of is a psychological state as located on a part of a physical object. He concludes from this that in bodily sensation the object of awareness is simultaneously spatial and psychological. One is oneself the subject of sensations, and if sensations are spatially extended, then so too is one's self. He concludes, "The basic subject is therefore a mental-and-physical subject-object phys-ically extended in space" (p. 303).

On Brewer's account, one's sense of ownership with respect to one's body is explained by appeal to one's experience of oneself as an embodied subject. The paper most directly opposed to this claim is Martin's. On Martin's account, we should distinguish between explaining ownership of the body and explaining self-consciousness. The sense of ownership is not, for him, the product of the identity of subject and object, as it is for Brewer. Rather, it is the product of the spatial content of bodily sensa-tions. To have a sense of ownership is just to be aware of the boundaries of one's body from the inside (as described earlier). Moreover, he holds that self-consciousness is distinct from a sense of ownership. Self-consciousness requires the impossibility of failing to refer to oneself, and on his account of proprioceptive perception of the body, such perception does not have this property of guaranteed reference to oneself.

An interesting opportunity to consider the matter is provided by the two cases of extreme deafferentation presented by Jonathan Cole and Jacques Paillard. The two patients whom they describe, I. W. and G.L., have lost most proprioceptive information and touch below the collar line (I. W.) and the nose (G.L.). This was due to the destruction through de-myelinization of all the main nerves from their skin, as well as the nerves from tendons, joints, and muscles, informing them about limb position and movement. Indeed, they have lost almost all bodily sensation in those areas, retaining only a sensitivity to temperature, deep pain, and (in the case of I. W.) muscular fatigue. Those limited capacities for sensation that remain to them, though, are importantly different in spatial content from those of normal people. In the absence of vision, they are able to locate temperature and pain sensations within their body-parts (i.e., within an object-centred space). For example, G.L. can verbally describe the location of sensations on her body and can indicate their locations on a schematic diagram of the body. However, neither of them can locate sensations in egocentric space. When their eyes are shut, they cannot describe the rela-tive locations of their body parts, nor can they point to body parts or to sensations.

If, like Brewer, one analyzes the experience of bodily sensations into an egocentric component and an object-centred component, it is natural to describe the case of deafferentation by saying that what is missing is the egocentric dimension (p. 302). That the object-centred dimension persists is indicated by G.L.'s capacity to locate her remaining sensations on a schematic diagram of the body. However, it is important to note that neither G.L. nor I.W. deny ownership of their remaining sensations, and nor do they deny ownership of the limbs in which they experience the sensations to be located. The question this raises is whether their sense of ownership is normal, in which case they provide confirmation that a sense of ownership can come apart from egocentric aspects of the phenomenology of bodily sensation, or whether their sense of ownership is radically unlike that of normal people, which is Brewer's suggestion. Interestingly, denial of ownership of limbs and of felt sensations does occur in cases of left hemiplegia and hemianesthesia due to right-hemisphere stroke, especially when patients are unaware of their deficit. In these cases, reported by Bisiach and Geminiani (1991) and Marcel (1993), the patients are not otherwise clinically confused.

Let us return now to Brewer's claim that subjects are physically extended. Even if one accepts this claim and accepts that bodily sensation exemplifies it, one might still doubt the further claim he makes that in being aware of one's body when feeling a sensation, one is aware of oneself *as* a subject. Both Quassim Cassam and Naomi Eilan are concerned with the idea that there is something essentially elusive about the subject of experiences, an elusiveness that makes it impossible for any awareness of an object to constitute awareness of oneself as a subject. If this is indeed impossible, then feeling sensations in one's body cannot involve awareness of oneself as a subject.

Quassim Cassam is interested in the question of whether proprioceptive awareness, such as awareness that one's legs are crossed, falsifies Hume's claim labeled by Cassam as 'the elusiveness thesis'. This is the claim that when one is introspectively aware of one's mental states, one never comes across the subject of those mental states. All one is aware of is mental states, never their owner. The problem Cassam is concerned with is whether bodily awareness can count as introspection and thereby falsify the elusiveness thesis. Some philosophers have argued that it can, for on their account, proprioceptive awareness is a form of introspective awareness in which one becomes directly aware of oneself as one object among others. The specific version of the elusiveness thesis that Cassam is concerned with is designed to put pressure on such claims. Put in the form of an argument, it says, (1) there are certain conditions that a form of awareness must fulfill if it is to count as genuinely introspective; (2) there are certain conditions that self awareness must fulfill if it is to count as awareness of oneself as an object; (3) there is no form of awareness that fulfils both sets of conditions.

For Shoemaker (1994), immunity to error through misidentification is constitutive of introspection. The question Cassam focuses on is whether proprioceptive awareness of one's body as one object among others can be immune to error in this way, and therefore count as a form of introspection. He focuses in particular on such a strong reading of the immunity claim that, were it used to characterize proprioceptive awareness, it would rule out such awareness's counting as awareness of one's body as an object. This kind of immunity is labeled 'logical immunity' by Shoemaker. Applied to the body, it says that any body part that one is aware of proprioceptively is one's own. That is, what makes a body part one's own is that one is proprioceptively aware of it. Much of Cassam's paper examines how such a conception conflicts with what, he holds, is necessary for representing one's body as one object among others (which for many philosophers is part of what it is to represent an entity as an object). The account he develops of what is involved in representing one's body as an object is similar to Campbell's account of what this involves.

If one accepts this strong reading of the immunity claim and accepts Cassam's arguments that this is incompatible with representing one's body as an object, then proprioceptive awareness of one's body cannot count as introspective awareness. This would rule out using an extension of introspective awareness to proprioceptive awareness of physical properties as a way of reconciling the I-as-subject and the substantive self-consciousness theses. However, as Cassam notes, there are weaker notions of immunity that might be so used. But he argues that whether one should adopt them in characterizing the I-as-subject thesis must await a principled account of what it is to know oneself.

Both Brewer and Cassam are concerned with the relation between being a subject and proprioceptive awareness of one's body. Naomi Eilan, in contrast, focuses on the relation between being a subject and the spatial contents of a subject's perceptual experiences. As Cassam notes, one impetus for holding on to a version of the elusiveness thesis is the idea that, in addition to flesh and blood persons, we must recognize a metaphysical or transcendental subject, which is essentially elusive in not being an object at all. This idea is taken up by Eilan. What is right about this claim, she suggests, is that explanations of what makes perceptions yield consciousness of the environment need to appeal to the idea that such experiences are had from a point of view not explicitly represented in the experience itself. Perceptual consciousness, on this view, is at least partially constituted by such perspectivalness. However, she suggests, the explanation of the sense in which this is right for perceptual experiences involves appeal not to a metaphysical subject but rather to the idea of the subject's actual body serving as the unrepresented focal point of experiences. Eilan then develops a notion of an egocentric frame of reference that relativizes the spatial contents of experiences to the subject's body as the subject moves through space, in such a way as to give the subject an implicit grasp of herself as an object moving through that space. Finally, Eilan suggests that this notion of an egocentric frame of reference could be employed to integrate Gibson's idea that perception of the environment and perception of the self go hand in hand with work on the spatial structure of attention to yield an account of what it is for perceptions to be conscious. As noted above, on this account the subject of perceptual experiences is equated with the point of origin of such experiences, which in turn is equated with the body. There would then be no conflict between doing justice to elusiveness and treating the subject as essentially embodied.

We have structured these introductory comments around two aspects of self-consciousness. In doing so, we have raised a series of issues in various areas of psychology, philosophy of mind, epistemology, and ontology. We have only briefly discussed the question of how concerns intrinsic to each area bear on those in other areas. However, we hope to have given a sense of the interest both in pursuing these specific problems and in bringing together philosophical and psychological approaches to self-consciousness and its relation to the body.

References

Anscombe, G. E. M. 1962. "On Sensations of Position." *Analysis* 22:55–58.

Bisiach, E., and G. Geminiani. 1991. "Anosognosia Related to Hemiplegia and Hemianopia." In *Awareness of Deficit after Brain Damage*, edited by G. P. Prigatano and D. L. Schacter. Oxford: Oxford University Press.

Budd, M. 1989. *Wittgenstein's Philosophy of Psychology*. London: Routledge.

Campbell, J. 1993. "The Role of Physical Objects in Spatial Thinking." In *Spatial Representation: Problems in Philosophy and Psychology*, edited by N. Eilan, R. A. McCarthy, and M. W. Brewer. Oxford: Basil Blackwell.

Campbell, J. 1994. *Past, Space, and Self*. Cambridge: MIT Press.

Duncan, J., and G. W. Humphreys. 1989. "Visual Search and Stimulus Similarity." *Psychological Review* 96:433–458.

Evans, G. 1982. *The Varieties of Reference*. Oxford: Oxford University Press.

Gibson, J. J. 1979. *The Ecological Approach to Visual Perception*. Boston: Houghton Mifflin.

Marcel, A. J. 1993. "Slippage in the Unity of Consciousness." In *Experimental and Theoretical Studies of Consciousness*, Ciba Foundation Symposium, no. 174. Chichester: John Wiley and Sons.

Meltzoff, A. N., and M. K. Moore. In press. "Imitation, Memory, and the Representation of Persons." *Infant Behavior and Development*.

Neisser, U. 1988. "Five Kinds of Self-Knowledge." *Philosophical Psychology* 1:35–59.

Neisser, U. 1994. *The Perceived Self*. Cambridge: Cambridge University Press.

O'Shaughnessy, B. 1980. *The Will: A Dual Aspect Theory*. Cambridge: Cambridge University Press.

Shoemaker, S. 1968. "Self-Reference and Self-Awareness." *Journal of Philosophy* 65:555–567.

The Body Image and Self-Consciousness

John Campbell

1   Reference and Conceptual Role

The problem that concerns me here is the relation between, on the one hand, the way in which the reference of the first person is fixed and, on the other hand, the bases on which we make first-person judgments and the consequences we draw from them. The first person is a singular term, one used to identify a particular thing. My question is a special case of the problem of the relation between the way in which the reference of a singular term is fixed and the ways in which we go about verifying judgments using the term and drawing the implications of such judgments. This, in turn, is a special case of the problem of the relation between the ascription of a semantic value to a term and its "conceptual role": the bases on which we make judgments involving it and the consequences we draw from them.

Can we be explicit about the relation between conceptual role and the way in which the reference of the singular term is determined? There is a sense in which the bases on which a judgment is made must be "in concord" with whatever fixes reference:

Concord   The bases on which judgments using a singular term are made must yield knowledge of the object assigned as reference.

If we are given the conceptual role of the term, this puts a constraint on what we can regard as fixing its reference. If we are given the reference, this puts a constraint on what we can regard as the conceptual role of the term.

The crucial point about this epistemic condition of concord is that it can be met without the reference-determining relation itself being an epistemic relation. Russell identified the reference-fixing relation with "acquaintance," an epistemic relation that the referrer stands in to the object referred to. And many philosophers have followed him in this, though parting from him over the characterization of acquaintance. But the principle of concord can be met even if the reference-fixing relation is not acquaintance itself. It can be met in the case of the first person even though its reference is fixed by the rule that any token of the first person refers to whoever produced it.

There is more to say about the relation between reference and conceptual role. There is a need for a certain richness in the conceptual role if we are to have a term that refers to an object. Consider the possibility of subjectless reports of the sort noted by Georg Lichtenberg, such as 'There is thinking'. Here there is no reference. There is only the response to encountering the psychological state, the cry of greeting, 'Thinking!' This kind of subjectless report need not be confined to psychological states. One could also use it for laconic reports of physical condition, such as 'Drenched!' Someone speaking and thinking in this subjectless way might make reports that constitute knowledge of the properties reported. And this knowledge might all be knowledge of the very person speaking. But there would not yet be any use of a term according to the rule that any token of it refers to whoever produced it. We do not yet have the use of a term referring to an object.

There is a contrast here between the first person and the cases of 'here' and 'now'. Suppose that we have a child who has been taught to say 'Rain!' in response to rain. We wonder whether his use of this term is genuinely unstructured, or if it is to be read as elliptical for 'Rain here!' An utterance of the unstructured expression is correct just when an utterance of the structured expression is correct, so how are we to tell which the child is using? If the child is grasping the structured thought, there must be structure in his grasp of it. He must be exercising a pair of conceptual abilities: the ability to think of rain and the ability to think of it as here. If the child has these separate abilities, he ought to be able to exercise them separately. So in particular, he ought to be able to think about rain at other places: 'Rain over there', 'Rain in the valley', and so on. If he cannot do this, we should regard his utterances as unstructured. If he can do that, then this shows a grasp of 'here'. We can make a parallel point about the use of the present tense, distinguishing between significantly tensed and more primitive, unstructured talk.

Can we use this model in the case of the first person? The idea would be that what makes one's judgments of the presence of some characteristic, *F*ness, into first-person judgments, 'I am F', rather than unstructured Lichtenbergian reports of *F*ness, is understanding the possibility that other people are F, so that one also understands 'She is F', 'Bill is F', and so on. There certainly must be this structure in one's understanding of first-person judgments, but it does not seem to be enough to explain the difference between them and unstructured formulations. The difference between 'here' and the present tense, on the one hand, and the first person, on the other, is that the first person is referring to an object. Simply finding the above structure in one's understanding would be consistent with the following possibility: one's uses of '*x* is *F*' in connection with other people ascribe properties to objects, whereas one's use of the form, 'I am *F*' is actually equivalent to the unstructured '*F*ness!'

It might be said that there is no sharp difference between feature placing talk and referring talk. We can make sense of logically complex feature placing, in which a plurality of features is ascribed to a single spot. 'Leafy and green over there!' one might exclaim, pointing to the dell, or, in more sombre vein, 'Cold and dark in here!' Once one allows that logically complex features may be ascribed to a place, there is no bound on the complexity of the features that may be ascribed. Talk about a concrete thing, it may be held, is just talk about a rather large collocation of features, so there is only a difference of degree between talk about objects and feature-placing. Of course, if we try to apply this approach to the case of psychological properties of persons, there is a question about whether we can speak of all the properties as being ascribed to a single place, or if the notion of place could have only a metaphorical use here. But I will not pursue this special question about persons here, for there is a general problem with that approach to reference to concrete objects in general.

The problem with the feature-placing approach is that it does not give due weight to grasp of the causal role of a concrete object in one's ability to refer to it. We do not think of a concrete object as simply a collocation of features. This shows up in the fact that for one to be using a singular term to refer to an object, there must be a certain density and structure in the conceptual role one assigns to the term. Consider the case of an ordinary physical thing, such as a table or a tree. We take it that the condition of a thing at any one time is causally dependent upon its condition at earlier times. One of the determinants of its properties at a given time is what properties it had earlier, and this is so no matter how much it has moved around. The notion of internal causal connectedness is presupposed in our grasp of the way in which objects interact. For if we are to have any appreciation at all of the effect that one object can have upon another, in a collision, for example, we have to understand that one central determinant of the way the thing is after the collision will be the way that the very same thing was before the collision. We have to understand the dependence of objects on their earlier selves in order to grasp that their earlier selves are only partial determinants of the way they are now and that external factors may have played a role. Thus, in describing our ordinary thought, we need a distinction between the causality that is, as it were, internal to an object and has to do with its inherent tendency to keep its current properties, or for them to change in regular ways, and the causality that has to do with the relations between objects and the ways in which they act upon each other (Shoemaker 1984). There is another dimension to the ordinary notion of a physical object, and it has to do with the capacity of the object to figure as a common cause of many disparate phenomena: one and the same thing can figure in many interactions, and correlations in the upshots of these interactions may demand explanation by its having been one and the same thing that was involved in all of them. This imposes further discipline on the notion of a physical thing, over and above the fact that its later stages causally depend on its earlier stages. Without the point that one and the same thing can figure in many interactions, something might be internally causally connected and yet capable of only one type of interaction, such as being perceived. This is not how we ordinarily conceive of physical things. I want to propose that to refer to a concrete thing with one's use of a singular term, one's use of the term must display a grasp of these two dimensions of causal structure. In effect, the upshot of this requirement is that to use a term to refer to a physical object, one must grasp, as coordinate with the term, a range of predicates that can be coupled with the term. And in one's use of these predications, one must operate with the idea that the later condition of the object causally depends on its earlier condition and the idea that the object can function as a common cause of many phenomena. For one to be using a term to refer to a concrete thing, a condition of richness in the causal structure of the reasoning one can engage in when using the term is the following:

Causal Structure   To be using a term to refer to concrete object, one's reasoning using the term must display a grasp of the two dimensions of the causal structure of the thing: being internally causally connected over time and being a common cause of many phenomena.

Obviously, this condition applies to reference to concrete objects rather than to names for abstract objects, such as the numbers. I now want to look at how it applies to the case of the first person.

2   Body Image and Body Schema

Many recent discussions give central role, in one's conception of oneself, to the notion of a body schema, this being explained as, for example, "a superordinate representation at the interface between sensory and motor processes that both internally and externally specify a posture." (Bairstow 1986, Butterworth 1990). But whether this is really enough for the individual to have the conception of himself as a concrete thing depends very much on just what kind of work the representation is supposed to do.

A child without language, or an animal for that matter, can put to use a body schema, a representation of its current posture that interfaces between perception and action. A body schema could be involved in, for example, the use of vision to control and correct one's posture (Lee and Lishman 1975). But even if a body schema is implicated here, this does not establish self-consciousness. Similarly, the capacity of an infant to imitate the facial expressions of adults may show that the infant has a representation of its own face, perhaps by using the same system of spatial representation to represent its own face and that of the adult (Meltzoff 1990a; Meltzoff 1993; Meltzoff and Moore, in press). But neither use of the body schema shows that the child has a conception of itself.

The picture changes somewhat when we consider work done by Andrew Meltzoff on older children, at 14 months. These experiments still concern imitation, but what is in question is the child's recognition that it is being imitated, rather than its capacity to engage in imitation itself. These children really do seem to be displaying some rudiments of self-consciousness. In one of these experiments, the child faced two adults across a table. One of the adults imitated everything the child did; the other simply sat passively. The child looked longer at the imitating adult, smiled more often at him, and directed more test behavior at him, that is, behavior designed to test whether the adult really was imitating the child, such as sudden or unexpected movements. Of course, this might mean only that the child preferred an active adult to a passive one. So in a later experiment, two TV monitors were placed behind the infant, invisible to it but watched by the adults. One of the two screens showed a live transmission of the infant. The movements on this screen were imitated by the first adult. The second screen showed a videotape of the child from the preceding session, and this child was imitated by the second adult. Again, the result was that the child looked longer at the imitating adult, smiled more often at him, and directed more test behavior at him (Meltzoff 1990b). Here the child's use of a representation of its body seems to involve the child in grasping its own causal impact on the world around it. The child seems to be grasping that the movements of the imitating adult are controlled by its own movements.

Various distinctions have been drawn between the body schema and the body image. The body schema is the representation of one's body that mediates perception and action, that one uses in adjusting one's movements to how one sees things around one to be (Nathan 1983). The body image may be said to be more sophisticated; it is a notion of relevance to psychoanalysis (Schilder 1935, Gallagher 1986). Again, there is the notion of a representation of one's body used to locate one's bodily sensations (Melzack 1990; O'Shaughnessy, this volume). But I want to propose another way of using this terminology.

There is another distinction to be drawn. We could say that we have not just a body schema but a body image when the subject is able to recognize the way in which his own behavior causally affects others. This is not a distinction between two different types of representation. It is a distinction between ways in which a representation of one's body might be used. It might be used only in mediating one's own perceptions and actions, in which case I will speak of a body schema. Or the representation might also be used in registering the impact of one's behavior on other people, in which case I will speak of a body image.

Recognition that it is being imitated seems to require that an infant be using a body image in this sense, rather than simply a body schema, since it is registering the impact of its own movements on the adult who is imitating it. And this time it seems much more compelling that the infant must therefore be thinking of itself as an object. It is hard to resist the description of the infant as thinking, "that man is copying me," and so ascribing some grasp of the first person to the infant, even at this relatively prelinguistic stage (Meltzoff 1990b). But why should the use of the body image in Meltzoff's paradigm be thought to have any more bearing on self-consciousness than does the use of the body schema to control posture in the "moving room" experiment? That it should certainly seems compelling, but why? It seems to me that what is so compelling about it, in contrast to the use of the body schema to control posture, is that it shows some capacity to operate with a conception of oneself as a common cause. One is thinking of oneself as the common cause of the behavior of the imitating adult over a period of time. The body image enters in because through one's direct, nonobservational knowledge of one's own behavior, one has detailed knowledge of the common cause of all that other behaviour, and so one can experimentally manipulate that common cause— making sudden movements, for example, to see whether they are imitated.

I said that there are two dimensions to the causal structure of a physical thing: its functioning as a common cause and its internal causal connectedness over time. Can the use of a body image put to work the conception of oneself as internally causally connected over time? I think it can, once we make the distinction between a long-term body image and a short-term one (O'Shaughnessy 1980, Lackner 1988). The long-term body image is a settled picture of one's own physical dimensions. So this image might be changed as a result of having a skin graft or the loss of a limb or simply growing up. It describes how one is shaped and sized and hinged—what possibilities of movement are open to one. The short-term body image, in contrast, describes how one happens to be configured here and now, the particular posture one is in. One's current short-term body image, together with the long-term body image, describe all the possibilities of movement open to one. So these representations might be held to provide one with a practical grasp of one's internal causal connectedness. These representations display how one's future posture is causally dependent upon one's current posture. Of course, it is a further question how one might set up a paradigm to test for these representations in infants.

3 The Token-Reflexive Rule

So far I have been describing a range of bases on which one might make first-person judgments, all involving the use of a body image. These bases give us a conceptual role which is "in concord" with the token-reflexive rule, in the sense I explained earlier. The judgments one makes using a body image really do all give knowledge of the very thing that, using tokens of 'I', produces the judgments. And the first-person reasoning used can put to work the two dimensions of the causal structure of a thing, so that the causal-structure condition is met.

This description of conceptual role is not enough, however, to explain why the first person is governed by the rule that any token of it refers to whoever produced it. So far as this description of conceptual role goes, we could have here, rather, a demonstrative with something of the force of 'this body'. This would be a term that stands to the body image somewhat as a perceptual demonstrative like 'that tree' stands to the perception of the tree. The reference of 'I' would then be fixed as the body of which one's body image gives one information. A full description of the conceptual role of the first person ought to explain what differentiates it from such a demonstrative. One line of thought on this begins by remarking that so far we have looked only at the bases on which first-person judgments are made. But 'conceptual role' includes the consequences of the judgments. So perhaps we ought to look, in particular, at the implications for action of first-person judgments (Perry 1979). But it seems unlikely that this will help us here. The body image itself must be supposed to have some immediate role in directing action. So a demonstrative based on it, 'this body', might be expected also to have immediate connections to action. To understand what separates the conceptual role of the first person from the conceptual role of such a demonstrative, I think we have to give weight to the fact that the first person can be used in judgments about psychological states.

The role usually assigned to the body image in self-consciousness is to provide one with awareness of oneself as a physical thing, a corporeal object, rather than as something purely psychological. But the body image has a role to play in understanding one's psychological states, and not just in providing a location for one's sensations. Much of ordinary life centers around a capacity for social interaction, a capacity to react to the psychological states of other people and to recognize the impact of one's own psychological states on them. In an understanding of how one's psychological states affect other people we find the role of the body image in self-consciousness, for through use of the body image, one grasps how one is affecting other people. As I began by remarking, the notion of a concrete object is a causal notion. This notion is a notion of the kind of thing that can function as a unit in causal interaction with other objects. For example, the notion of shape is integral to how we ordinarily think of physical things: we think of them as having shapes. But an understanding of the physical significance of the notion of shape requires one to grasp how it affects the capacity of the object to interact with other things. The shape of an object will affect whether it can be stacked together with other things, rolled along, or used to smash other things. Now when we think of the causal role of psychological states, we tend to think of it as having to do with the relations among the psychological states of a single person. The fact that my gloom can have social significance, producing gloom in others or even anxiety or relief, is not thought of as being part of the causal role of gloom. But if we take seriously the analogy with the shape of a physical thing, we ought to be willing to acknowledge that the role of a psychological property in interactions between objects is part of its causal role. The fact that mental states play a causal role in interactions between people is, I will suggest, part of what makes it possible for us to think of persons as concrete objects, and reflection on the point brings out just what is special about persons and sets them apart from other concrete objects. Before turning to how one grasps one's functioning as a common cause at the psychological level, though, I want to look at how one registers one's own internal causal connectedness at the psychological level.

4   Psychological Structure over Time

How might one put to work the idea of oneself as internally causally connected over time, at the level of psychological properties? An understanding of the causal dependence of my later psychological states on my earlier psychological states shows up when I say, for example, that my grief has turned to anger. But causal dependence need not involve change of state: my later anger might causally depend on my having been angry earlier; I was angry all along.

What does it come to, though, that there is this causal dependence? Why not think simply in terms of a sequence of psychological states, without assuming anything about the causal relations between them? As a model, consider the pool of light thrown on a wall by a projector spotlight shining through heated oil, with the result that the colors on the wall move and change. Or more simply, consider someone doing hand shadows. The later stages of the pattern on the wall follow the earlier stages, but they do not causally depend upon them. So could one not think of one's own mental states in this way, as being a shifting or stable kaleidoscope, with no internal causal structure? What difference does it make if one doesn't? In the case of the pool of light, what makes it evident that we do not think of it as internally causally connected is our pattern of expectations as to what will happen in the event of an interaction between the pool of light and something else. Suppose, for example, that another pool of light, moving across the screen, crosses its path. That will change the character of the pool for the moment, but when the second spot moves on, the first pool will be exactly as it would have been anyhow. These temporary modifications to the pool of light do not affect how it will be later, and recognition of that fact constitutes our grasp of the fact that the pool is not internally causally connected over time (Salmon 1984).

If this line of thought is right, then what constitutes grasp of the fact that one's later anger causally depends on one's earlier grief is an understanding of what the impact would have been of various interactions with one's surroundings. "If only I had known!" one might say after the anger has led to catastrophe. "If only he had told me, if only I had seen her, my grief would not have turned to anger." Once one can think in this way, one is thinking of one's own psychological states as internally causally connected. Since we are forced here to think in terms of the lasting impact of interactions with the environment, it seems that an understanding of the relation between perception and memory will be central to grasping one's own internal causal connectedness. For if one has to think of the ways in which one could be enduringly affected, at the psychological level, by the things around one, then it is surely basic that what one remembers depends on what one perceived earlier.

5   The Social Dimension of Causal Role

We saw that the conception of a thing as internally causally connected gives one dimension of its causal structure. The other dimension was the idea of the thing as a common cause of various phenomena. What we have just seen is that the conception of oneself as internally causally connected can be exercised with regard to one's psychological properties. Does anything parallel hold for the idea of oneself as a common cause?

Let us return to Meltzoff's paradigm. Meltzoff himself does not remark on the role of common-cause reasoning in his paradigm. If we ask how Meltzoff sees his data as bearing on our use of psychological predicates, one part of the answer is this. He focuses on the role of imitating facial expressions in providing an understanding of other minds. His thesis is that there is an innate capacity to imitate expressions. He further remarks that there is some evidence that asking people to assume an expression leads them to have the associated emotion: making oneself look happy will lead to one's actually being happier, making oneself look grief-stricken will have the effect that one feels sad, and so on. So the hypothesis is that when the infant sees someone with a particular expression, he uses his innate capacity to imitate it, and this in turn leads to having the emotion in question, so the infant now knows what is going on in the other person (Meltzoff 1990b). Of course, this is not intended as a complete description of a mature understanding of other minds. Freud, for example, could presumably remain relatively impassive while achieving his insights. Even at the foundational level at which it operates, the model needs supplementing. There has to be some explanation of how one achieves a grasp of the causal roles of mental states—of how grief, for example, can interact with other mental states and with the circumstances to yield anger. And the model depends on, but does not explain, knowledge of one's own mental states. (This is not a complete review of Meltzoff's work on how imitation bears on understanding other minds. See also Gopnik and Meltzoff 1993; Gopnik, Slaughter, and Meltzoff, in press; and Meltzoff and Gopnik 1993.)

Much of the thrust of Meltzoff's work has been to insist on the cross-modal character of knowledge of one's own behavior and that of others. He suggests that the infant represents its own expressions in just the same way that it represents the expressions of others: it uses a cross-modal system of representation (Meltzoff 1990a, Meltzoff 1993). So the child has no problem about knowing how to match up its own expressions with those it wants to imitate. That is part of the reason why imitation is so primitive. It would, I think, be perfectly in keeping with this approach to propose that a child may use a cross-modal system of representation to represent its own expressions of mental states and the states of others. One can see the pleasure in another's face, one can tell that one is expressing pleasure oneself, and the expression of pleasure may be represented in just the same way both times. This would evidently involve the use of a body image, in the sense explained above. This proposal, which, as I say, seems in tune with Meltzoff's own position, simply finesses the need for the kind of approach to other minds he suggests.

When we looked at Meltzoff's paradigm earlier, discussing the role it gave to the body image, no place was given to the infant's grasp of mental states: we considered only its conception of its own facial configurations as the common cause of a series of facial configurations by the imitating adult. But it would be possible to view the paradigm as significant because it is the prototype of an understanding of the relation between one's own mental states and the mental states of the other person. It could happen, for example, that the subject perceives the adult as experiencing pleasure over a period and finds a common cause for all this pleasure in his own pleasure. So common-cause reasoning at the level of physical properties can be echoed at the level of psychological properties. Of course, we are considering only the very simplest type of common-cause reasoning when we look at imitation over a period. While someone else might take pleasure in my pleasure, they might also be depressed by it or be bored by it or, to look on the bright side, take steps to prolong it. And there may be no single response: one's mental state may cause a whole complex of reactions in another. Nor is there any reason why one should be confined to the reactions of one other person, rather than a social group. I am not suggesting that there is much social sophistication in the infant. What I am proposing is that Meltzoff's paradigm matters because it is prototypical for an echoing, at the level of psychological properties, of the kind of common-cause reasoning that one engages in with physical objects. And this kind of common-cause reasoning is part of the foundation for the use of 'I' as a singular term. When we have this kind of reasoning as part of the conceptual role that one associates with the first person, we have moved away from any sort of thinking that can be expressed by Lichtenbergian formulations.

As I remarked earlier, we tend to think of the causal role of psychological states in wholly individualist terms. We think of how the mental states of a single person are produced by impacts upon that person and how they interact with one another ultimately to yield actions by that person. But a fundamental aspect of the causal role of the psychological state is its role in social interactions between people. In many cases this seems to be fundamental to understanding what the psychological states are. It is scarcely believable that an understanding of what are sometimes called the 'moral emotions', for example, could be complete without some understanding of their social dimension—an understanding of how one's pride or shame, one's contempt or affection, could have an impact upon other people. Of course, this social dimension to causal roles may supervene upon the individualist dimension, in that if all the causal roles of various psychological states within individuals are given, this fixes the social dimension of their causal roles. One can acknowledge this while still holding that grasp of the social role of a psychological state is fundamental to understanding what is the psychological state, that one does not derive this grasp of social role from knowledge of an individualistically specified causal role.

Grasp of the social dimension of the causal role of one's psychological states seems to be part of possession of the conception of oneself as a concrete object; it has to do with the way in which one grasps one's own causal structure. As made apparent by Meltzoff's paradigm, which pinpoints a prototype of this grasp of one's own causal structure in recognition of imitation, there is a place for the body image in this understanding of one's own causal structure. It is through use of one's body image that one grasps just how one's psychological states are affecting other people. This seems to be a fundamental role for the body image in self-consciousness.

When one thinks of one's psychological properties as common causes of psychological reactions in other people, it is not just that one thinks of one's own psychological states as producing other instantiations of psychological properties; one thinks of them as the reactions of other people. So one is sensitive not just to the production of psychological reactions but also to the identities of the people in whom these reactions are produced. For this reason, an understanding of 'I am F' depends upon an understanding of 'He is F'. Indeed, it will also depend on understanding other people's uses of 'I'. One will have to understand that they think of themselves as concrete objects in just the same way that one thinks of oneself as a concrete object. One will need to have the idea that they use 'I' as something governed by just the same token-reflexive rule that governs one's own uses of the first person, if one is, for example, to grasp the many and complex ways in which one's emotional reactions may affect them.

This remark meshes with recent work by Meltzoff and Moore, in which the very same behavioral repertoire considered in the experiments described above turns out to be used not just in infant imitation, or recognition of imitation, but also to test the identity of the person who is interacting with the infant. Having been faced for some time with an adult making a particular type of face at it and then after a gap, finding another human in the same place, the infant will first make the same old faces, no matter what particular expression the new adult has. The hypothesis is irresistible that the infant is testing whether this is the same person as before

(Meltzoff and Moore 1994). If this is correct, then the prototypes of the conceptual skills I am describing do indeed develop together. Grasp of one's own causal structure has the same imitative capacity as its prototype but that imitative capacity is also the prototype of the ability to grasp the social significance of sameness of person, to live in the world of real people.

Acknowledgments

Thanks to Jennifer Church, Naomi Eilan, Philippa Foot, Alison Gopnik, Robert Gordon, Tony Marcel, Michael Martin, Andrew Meltzoff, and Timothy Williamson. Earlier versions were read to seminars in Cambridge and Oxford, the American Society for Philosophy and Psychology, the European Society for Philosophy and Psychology, and the meeting on Body and Self at King's College, Cambridge.

References

Bairstow, P. 1986. "Postural Control." In *Motor Skill Development in Children*, edited by H. T. A. Whiting and M. G. Wade. Dordrecht: Nijhoff.

Butterworth, George. 1990. "Self-Perception in Infancy." In *The Self in Transition*, edited by Dante Cicchetti and Marjorie Beeghly. Chicago: University of Chicago Press.

Gallagher, Shaun. 1986. "Body Image and Body Schema: A Conceptual Clarification." *Journal of Mind and Behaviour* 7:541–554.

Gopnik, Alison, and Andrew N. Meltzoff. 1993. "Minds, Bodies, and Persons: Young Children's Understanding of the Self and Others As Reflected in Imitation and 'Theory of Mind' Research." In *Self-Awareness in Animals and Humans: Developmental Perspectives.* New York: Cambridge University Press.

Gopnik, Alison, Virginia Slaughter, and Andrew Meltzoff. 1996. "Changing Your Views: How Understanding Visual Perception Can Lead to a New Theory of the Mind." In *Origins of a Theory of Mind,* edited by C. Lewis and P. Mitchell, Hillsdale, N.J.: Lawrence Erlbaum.

Lackner, James R. 1988. "Some Proprioceptive Influences on the Perceptual Representation of Body Shape and Orientation." *Brain* 111:281–297.

Lee, D. N., and J. R. Lishman. 1975. "Visual Proprioceptive Control of Stance." *Journal of Human Movement Studies* 1:87–95.

Meltzoff, Andrew. 1990a. "Towards a Developmental Cognitive Science." *Annals of the New York Academy of Sciences* 608:1–37.

Meltzoff, Andrew. 1990b. "Foundations for Developing a Concept of Self." In *The Self in Transition,* edited by Dante Cicchetti and Marjorie Beeghly. Chicago: University of Chicago Press.

Meltzoff, Andrew. 1993. "Molyneux's Babies: Cross-Modal Perception, Imitation, and the Mind of the Infant." In *Spatial Representation: Problems in Philosophy and Psychology*, edited by Naomi Eilan, Rosaleen McCarthy, and Bill Brewer. Oxford: Basil Blackwell.

Meltzoff, Andrew, and Alison Gopnik. 1993. "The Role of Imitation in Understanding Persons and Developing a Theory of Mind." In *Understanding Other Minds: Perspectives from Autism*, edited by Simon Baron-Cohen, Helen Tager-Flusberg, and Donald J. Cohen. Oxford: Oxford University Press.

Meltzoff, Andrew, and Keith Moore. 1994. "Imitation, Memory, and the Representation of Persons." *Infant Behaviour and Development* 17:83–89.

Melzack, Ronald. 1990. "Phantom Limbs and the Concept of a Neuromatrix." *Trends in Neuroscience* 13:88–92.

Nathan, P. W. 1983. "The Concepts of Body Schema." In *Centenarion de la Neurologia en Espana*, edited by the Neurology Department of the Hospital of Santa Creu and Sant Pau. Barcelona: Hospital of Santa Creu and Sant Pau.

O'Shaughnessy, Brian. 1980. *The Will*, vol. 1. Cambridge: Cambridge University Press.

Perry, John. 1979. "The Problem of the Essential Indexical." *Noûs* 13:3–21.

Salmon, Wesley C. 1984. *Scientific Explanation and the Causal Structure of the World*. Princeton: Princeton University Press.

Schilder, P. 1935. *The Image and Appearance of the Human Body*. London: Kegan, Paul, Trench, Trubner, and Co.

Shoemaker, Sydney. 1984. "Identity, Properties, and Causality." In his *Identity, Cause, and Mind*. Cambridge: Cambridge University Press.

Infants' Understanding of People and Things: From Body Imitation to Folk Psychology

Andrew N. Meltzoff and M. Keith Moore

Our interest is in the relation between the development of infants' understanding of physical objects and that of persons. We will suggest that the two are closely interwoven, so that infants' developing grasp of the nature of objects profoundly influences their idea of persons. We further suggest that newborns begin life with some grasp of people and of how people are like themselves.

Our approach to these issues is to study psychological development. Philosophers often consider abnormal patients and cultural universals as reference points in their analyses of mind. Infants have less often been considered. Nonetheless, infancy is a good place to look if one is interested in the origins of human knowledge. All adult minds were once infant minds. The nature of the infant's construal of the world and how it is revised to become the adult's conception should contribute to a fuller understanding of mind.

We suggest that accounting for infants' performance involving physical objects and persons requires that we recognize a progression through increasingly sophisticated concepts. This view stands in opposition to the idea that infants are born with adult concepts in full play (nativism) and to the idea that they start with only reflexes and have to bootstrap themselves up into anything remotely like our concepts (Piaget).

Although the idea of progression through increasingly sophisticated concepts has some intuitive appeal, the problem has always been to find the parameters to describe this development in ways that are both theoretically plausible and empirically valid. In what follows, we will first illustrate the parameters for explaining infants' progressive grip on the notion of a physical object. Then, through a consideration of imitation, we will show how there is, from the start, a special treatment of the movement of human bodies, and we will suggest parameters for describing infants' progressive grip on the concept of a person.

This essay has three major parts. First we analyze what infants understand a physical object to be. We examine the criteria infants use to maintain object identity over successive perceptual contacts. We also examine infants' understanding of human bodies as a special case of physical objects and their grasp of the idea that their own bodies are like other human bodies. In the second part we analyze infants' developing conception of persons. We examine how infants distinguish human individuals and determine their particular identity. We also examine the development of infants' understanding of humans as bearers of psychological properties. In the third part we conclude by analyzing how the developments previously described might lead to a concept of the self as an entity in a world full of others and a concept of the other possessing a subjectivity as rich as the self.

1   Early Understanding of Physical Objects

Identity

How do infants interpret an object's entering into or exiting from their field of view as it moves, as their heads turn, or as they are carried from one place to another? The adult conception of "object" does that work for us. What is the infant's conception? There is reason to suggest that the infant's conception is quite different from the adult's. Our view is that (a) infants have concepts about objects, not simply lists of actions they perform on them, (b) these concepts undergo radical change, and (c) it is not a one-step, dichotomous change but rather successive cognitive restructurings that yield a causally related series of infant conceptions. This developmental view requires a careful use of language. Because the infants' earliest conceptions of objects are not the same as adults' but only early steps toward the mature attainment, we need a new word for object when it refers to the infant's conception. In this essay we call these "proto-objects."

These proto-objects do some of the work that the concept of an object does for adults, but they do not have all the properties of the adult's objects. Our use of the notion of proto-objects relates to certain philosophical considerations as to what it means to be a physical object or thing. In particular, Campbell (1993) has recently analyzed some distinctions between feature and object and between the internal causal connectedness inherent in objects and their spatiotemporal continuity. These distinctions seem to have some empirical reality in the world of infants. For example, we will show that infants can reidentify a proto-object as the same one across two encounters without their requiring that it followed a continuous space-time path between the encounters.

Our notion of proto-objects and how they relate to the mature adult notion differs from other psychological views of the "object concept" (as it is called in the psychological literature). It differs from that of Piaget (1954), who thought that there was no concept of object that remotely resembled the adult notion during infancy (his theory focused on actions and the inseparability of objects from action), from that of Bower (1982), who thinks that young infants develop a concept of object but that only one important conceptual shift occurs (around 5 months of age), from that of Spelke (Spelke, Breinlinger, Macomber, and Jacobson 1992; Spelke and Van de Walle 1993), who thinks that infants innately hold the core adult conception of object with no significant change or overturning of this understanding, and from that of Baillargeon (1991, 1993), who attributes sophisticated knowledge about objects to young infants (like Spelke) but allows for cognitive development in certain aspects of physical reasoning to account for changes in performance.

For an adult, the flux of object appearances is organized by noting which of the many appearances are encounters with the same object. Thus an object seen at time t in place p may be identified as the same object when seen at t' in place p' by a rule for object identity. The identity referred to in this case is the object's unique or essential identity with itself and not featural sameness. No two objects, however exactly they may share the same features, are identical in this sense. Strawson (1959) calls this numerical or particular identity when it is the mature adult concept, and we call it "unique identity" when referring to the infant's less mature notion. We will argue that at different ages infants use different criteria for numerical identity, which suggests they are operating with distinct concepts of objects in development (hence the notion of proto-objects).

Three classes of events involving spatial transformations of objects seem to be significant for infants (Moore and Meltzoff 1978). Table 1 sum-

Table 1
Developmental levels in infants' understanding of unique (numerical) identity over spatial transformations of objects

Level	Age (months)	Description of level	Examples of events for which an object's unique identity is maintained
1	0–4	Identity is maintained for a steady state of the visual world.	Objects moving on a trajectory Objects staying at rest in a place
2	5–8	Identity is maintained for transformations of visible objects.	Objects in motion stopping Objects at rest starting to move
3	9–18	Identity is maintained for transformations producing occluded objects.	Objects disappearing in motion Objects disappearing at rest

marizes this typology and the corresponding developmental changes in infants' understanding from birth to 18 months of age.

In our terms, the three levels display a developmental progression from proto-object to object. The first two levels are developmental changes within the realm of proto-objects; it is only by level 3, at about 9 months of age, that a notion of an object as such is achieved.

In the first 4 months of life, infants are concerned with the identity problems associated with the steady-state structure of the visual world: objects in motion continue in motion; objects at rest stay at rest. At this level, an infant's notion of object identity is that for each perceptual encounter, an object in motion is the same one at any point on its trajectory and an object in the same place is the same object.[1] At about 5 months of age there is a shift such that infants can solve identity problems associated with changes from the steady-state structure of the visual world. At this level, they have extended their notion of objects to encompass the idea that unique identity is maintained across visible transformations of visible objects, such as an object in motion stopping, a stationary object moving, etc. At about 9 months of age there is a third developmental change, one that allows them to make sense of identity problems associated with changes from the visible to the nonvisible world, the transformations producing occluded objects such as a stationary object being covered by a moving screen or a moving object going behind a stationary screen.[2]

Moore, Borton, and Darby (1978) investigated some predictions from this developmental sequence for the transition from level 2 to level 3. They designed an experiment that distinguished three rules for object identity that infants might employ when visually tracking a moving object as it disappeared and reappeared from behind an opaque screen: featural, spatiotemporal, and permanence. Adults use the permanence rule: we believe that the object remains permanent behind the screen when it is invisible and therefore that the pre- and posthidden object are the same one (provided there is no trickery). However, more primitive construals of object disappearances and reappearances can be imagined. The experiment was designed to diagnose whether infants conceived of objects according to the permanence rule or whether they operated with only proto-objects and hence lacked this belief. Figure 1 provides a schematic diagram of the object tracking problems posed to the infants.

Young infants might possess a featural rule for object identity and treat the pre- and postocclusion objects as the same if they are featurally identical. The featural task tests this by changing the object's features while it is obscured by the screen so that it emerges with a different appearance. A spatiotemporal rule for identity treats the pre- and postocclusion objects as the same if they share the same trajectory of motion on either side of the screen.

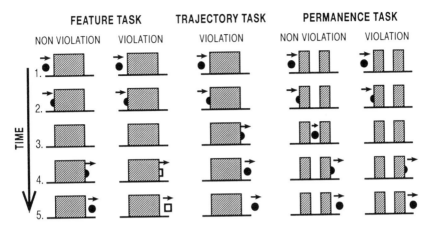

Figure 1

Schematic diagram of the object tracking tasks used to assess infants' rules for maintaining numerical identity. The diagram shows the feature, trajectory, and permanence tasks at five sequential points in time. The nonviolation condition in the trajectory task was the same as the nonviolation condition in the feature task. (Adapted from Moore, Borton, and Darby 1978.)

The trajectory of the preocclusion object specifies a unique speed, direction, and time of appearance for the postocclusion object. The trajectory task tests this rule by having the postocclusion object emerge much too soon to be on the trajectory of the preocclusion object even though their observed speeds and directions are identical. A permanence rule for identity treats the pre- and postocclusion objects as the same if an unbroken path of motion links them. The permanence task tests this rule by having the object disappear behind the first screen and emerge from the second screen still on the original trajectory but without appearing between the screens. Thus on some portion of its trajectory the object apparently did not exist.

As depicted in figure 1, the method used in the experiment was to create three object-tracking tasks (the featural, trajectory, and permanence tasks). For one condition of each task, an object disappeared and then reappeared in accord with all three identity rules; the other condition violated one of the rules. If infants showed a violation response (more disrupted tracking in the violation condition than in the nonviolation condition), this was taken as evidence that they used the identity rule in question. These tasks were presented to 5- and 9-month-old infants.

The results showed that 5-month-old infants displayed violation responses for both the feature and trajectory tasks but *not* for the permanence task. Evidently, the 5-month-olds saw no contradiction to their notions of object in the permanence-violation task. In contrast, the 9-month-olds showed violation responses in all three tasks. Moreover, the 9-month-olds showed a novel behavior pattern not exhibited by the younger infants. For example, in the permanence task they looked successively at the reappearance and disappearance edges of the first screen when it did not appear between the screens, as though expecting its reappearance from behind that screen. Their notion of object was rich enough for them to seek a resolution of the mismatch between how the world should work and how it apparently did. They seemed to believe that the object emerging from the second screen was not the original object and that the original still existed and remained at a particular invisible place in space. No such thought occurred to the 5-month-old infants.[3]

It seems that for 5-month-old infants, a moving object traces a specific trajectory, and all visible appearances of a featurally identical object on that trajectory are encounters with the "same" object. The 5-month-olds' identity rules, therefore, enable it to parse the visible transformations of moving "objects" without reference to or implications for those same "objects" when hidden. The 5-month-old employs identity rules to match present objects with internal representations of them formed in an earlier encounter, to unify successive contacts with objects over time and space under the rubric of 'same' or 'different,' and to anticipate where the next contact with them should occur. These are powerful tools to tame the flux of appearances, but they are useless when confronted with occlusion transformations that produce invisible objects. For the 5-month-old, object identity does not reduce to or imply permanence of the object. In contrast, the 9-month-olds act as though a moving object must trace an unbroken path and therefore should be sequentially visible at all exposed points along its trajectory. By this age the maintenance of an object's identity across two perceptual contacts implies continuous existence between encounters.[4]

Human Bodies as Objects

The problem of identity is one that cuts across both people and things, because whatever else people are, they are also material bodies that trace a path in space and time. From this viewpoint, people and things are fundamentally similar. In our commonsense adult psychology, however, we obviously draw a distinction between them. Do infants? If so, what characteristics distinguish people from things for infants?

It is not just that people look a certain way, for example, they have eyes. People have human bodies and perform human movement patterns. Infants too have human bodies, and they move correspondingly. This correspondence between other people and the infant eventually raises questions of the sort, "Am I one of those?" The earliest behavioral tool infants use to explore self-other correspondence is body imitation. Imitation is a two-way street: infants can copy and be copied. For infants, the possibility of having such a relation between themselves and other people makes people special and distinct from things.

In the sections that follow, we analyze infant imitation in detail. Based on recent research, we have drawn four inferences: (a) the ability to imitate is innate, (b) it is not automatic but is under intentional control, (c) it is not purely rote but reveals infants' interpretations of social encounters, and (d) it is mediated by an internal representational system. In particular, the representational system is one that does not operate on sensory specifics, but uses a modality-independent or "supramodal" code that links acts that are seen and those that are done.

The Problem of Imitation   As commonplace as imitation is, it presents a puzzle not only for developmental psychology but for philosophical analysis of the preverbal mind as well (Brewer 1993; Campbell 1994, this volume; Eilan 1993; Goldman 1992). To imitate, the infant must perceive another's acts and use this as a basis for an action plan with its own body. This translation must be accomplished without verbal instruction and despite the large differences between the other's body and its own (different size, spatial orientation, visual perspective, etc.).

All imitative acts are not of the same kind. There are key differences between manual imitation and facial imitation. In manual imitation, the child sees the adult hand movement and must generate a matching movement. One possible aid is for the child to look at its own hand and use visual guidance as a way of achieving a match between self and other. Visual guidance is, however, completely impossible in the case of facial imitation. Infants can see the adult's face but cannot see their own faces. They can feel their own faces move but have no access to the feelings of movement in the other. By what mechanism can they connect the felt but unseen movements of the self with the seen but unfelt movements of the other?

Classical psychological theories answered this question by postulating learning experiences from mirrors and manual exploration of one's own and other's faces. Mirrors made the unseen visible, rendering one's own body and that of the other into visual terms. Manual exploration rendered both self and other tangible. Facial imitation was thought to emerge at about 1 year of age (Piaget 1962).

Innate Imitation: Strong Nativism   Our research forced a revision of the conventional view of imitation and the infant's initial state. We conducted two experiments using newborn babies in a hospital setting. The oldest baby in these studies was 72 hours old. The youngest was 42 *minutes* old. The results demonstrated successful facial imitation (Meltzoff and Moore 1983, 1989). The capacity for body imitation is part of the innate endowment of human beings. If ever there was an empirical case for nativism, body imitation provides it.

What does this finding imply about the human mind? A first question is how to characterize this behavior. The spectrum ranges from reflexlike, automatic, stimulus-driven behavior on the one end to a more cognitive understanding of people on the other end. This question was addressed in several studies. Meltzoff and Moore (1977) showed that 12- to 21-day-old infants could imitate four different adult gestures: tongue protrusion, mouth opening, lip protrusion, and finger movement (figure 2). These results revealed that infants imitated with several parts of the body. Moreover, infants confused neither actions nor organs. They differentially responded to tongue protrusion with tongue protrusion and not lip protrusion; they also differentially responded to two different actions produced by the same organ (lips protruding versus lips opening). The range of gestures imitated and the specificity of the imitative acts suggested that a more generative matching mechanism than a reflexlike one is needed to account for the behavior.

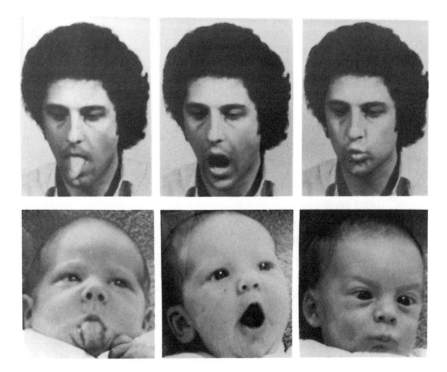

Figure 2
Young infants imitating adult facial gestures. (From Meltzoff and Moore 1977.)

A second study tested whether infants could imitate even if there was a temporal gap imposed between perception and production so that infants were disrupted from initiating the response while the adult gesture was being demonstrated. Reflexes do not jump such gaps. How do you ask an infant to watch what you are doing but delay its response until after the demonstration has ended? The technique was to put a pacifier in the infant's mouth before we showed it the gesture. The infant was thus engaged in a competing motor activity (sucking on the pacifier) during the presentation. The adult then stopped gesturing, assumed a neutral facial pose, and only then removed the pacifier. The results showed that infants were able to imitate (Meltzoff and Moore 1977), in contrast to what might be expected by the reflexive account.

The Intentional Nature of Imitation We believe that early imitation is a goal-directed, intentional activity. In one study, 6-week-old infants were shown the unusual gesture of a large tongue protrusion to the side (Meltzoff and Moore 1994). The prediction from a reflexive model is either no response, if the unusual adult gesture was not innately specified as a "triggering stimulus," or persistence in a preset motor pattern of normal tongue protrusion without revision. In fact, infants imitated and gradually corrected their imitative attempts to achieve a more faithful matching of the novel target. The initial response of most babies was not an exact copy of the adult. Instead, they made mistakes. The early attempts were to focus on the lateral components: the tongue either went into the cheek or was thrust slightly forward and then moved laterally during retraction. Strictly speaking, neither of these was shown. That infants made mistakes and then corrected them suggests that their responses are actively constructed and goal-directed.

We were also fortunate to come across an "experiment of nature," an anatomical malformation that prevented infants from fully protruding their tongues because of an attached freniculum.[5] When shown no gestures or shown the mouth-opening gesture, the imitation of such infants was indistinguishable from other babies. The interesting case is where they were shown a tongue protrusion, which, of course, they could not produce. The infants attempted to poke out the tongue and then became frustrated and cried. This suggests that even for infants there is a primitive sense in which intentions are different from consequences; in particular the intended act is distinguishable from the actual motor movements produced.

Both the correction of imitative mistakes in normal infants and the frustration of the motor-handicapped infants implies a common story. In both cases infants made repeated attempts, and their intentions were not satisfied by the initial motor performance stemming from these attempts. This suggests that infants differentiate between the representation of the target act derived from the external world and the representation of their own bodily acts. The intention is apparently to bring these two into congruence.

The Interpretive Nature of Imitation   Three sets of findings illustrated the interpretive aspect of early imitative responses.

Selectivity   In one study of 6-week-olds (Meltzoff and Moore 1994), infants were shown repetitive large mouth-opening gestures, each of a specific duration. Some infants initially responded with extremely large mouth openings, as if selecting the spatial dimension; others responded with normal-sized mouth openings of extremely long durations, as if selecting the temporal dimension. For both sets of infants, some switched entirely to the opposite dimension before finally achieving well-formed mouth openings whose duration approximated the duration of the adult's exemplars. This suggests that individual infants select different aspects of the stimulus to start with before settling on a more faithful multidimensional match.

Creativity   In the tongue-to-the-side study (Meltzoff and Moore 1994), the predominant pattern was convergence on a match to the target via successive attempts and corrections, as already described. However, some infants displayed a different interpretation of the target. They poked out their tongues and simultaneously turned their heads to the side, thus creating a new version of "tongue to the side." This head movement was not part of the stimulus, but was the infants' construction of how to get their bodies to do a novel act involving both tongue protrusion and an off-midline direction. Tongue protrusion plus head turn was not the work of a mindless reflex. It was a creative error.

Volition   The imitative response does not seem to be automatically released by the stimulus because it can jump temporal gaps, it does not burst forth fully formed, and some babies simply watch attentively and do not imitate. More compellingly, infants may choose to perform a different gesture than the one they are being shown. In particular, they may imitate a gesture they remember rather than the one they see. They demonstrate this in two ways (as will be analyzed in the next section): they imitate the gesture shown the day before when the same person returns and shows only a neutral face; when presented with two adults, they may imitate the first person's gesture when viewing the second person. Taken as a whole this pattern suggests that imitation is noncompulsory. It appears to be under voluntary control.

Supramodal Representation of Human Acts   We hypothesize that infants can represent human movement patterns they see and ones they perform using the same mental code. The perception of the adult's act is registered so that it can be directly used for executing a motor plan. There is thus something like an act space or primitive body scheme that allows the infant to unify the visual and motor/proprioceptive information into one common "supramodal" framework.

The notion of supramodality we are proposing deserves further analysis. One possibility is that the supramodal system is simply a translation device for turning visual perceptions into motor output, a perception-production transducer. There are three reasons to think that we need a more differentiated notion than this. First, the voluntary nature of the response indicates that the infant need not produce what is given to perception. The response does not pop out on the infant's seeing the act. The information gained from vision can be stored and accessed at a later time. One way of achieving this is to represent the adult's act. Thus at minimum there is an intermediary representation and not simply an automatic transduction. Second, as we have seen, the imitative acts can be corrected to achieve a more faithful match. Thus information about one's acts has to be available for comparison with the representation of the adult's act, but the representation of the visually specified act is not confused with or modified by one's own multiple motor attempts. Third, infants show special interest in being imitated themselves; they have the capacity to recognize when their facial behavior is being copied. Such recognition implies that there is a representation of their own bodies.

These three pieces of evidence go beyond the simple transducer story. They suggest a differentiation in the supramodal system such that the representation of the other's body is separate from the representation of one's own body. Although both representations use the supramodal language, they are not confused. The cognitive act is to compare these two representations, in one case to match one's own acts with the other's (imitative correction) and in the other case to detect being matched oneself (recognizing being imitated). Thus the mental code may use a supramodal "language," but the mind is not one undifferentiated supramodal whole.

One interesting consequence of this notion of supramodality is that there is a primordial connection between self and other. The actions of other humans are seen as like the acts that can be done at birth. This innate capacity has implications for understanding people, because it suggests an intrinsic relatedness between the seen bodily acts of others and the internal states of oneself (the sensing and representation of one's own movements). A second implication of young infants' possessing a representation of their own bodies is that it provides a starting point for developing objectivity about themselves. This primitive self-representation of the body may be the earliest progenitor of being able to take perspective on oneself, to treat oneself as an object of thought.

Primacy of Human Acts for Connecting Self and Other   We want to develop the notion that infants see other people in terms of *human acts* and, in imitating them, intend to match these acts. Here human acts are being thought of as an organ plus its transformation, and the goal of the act is the endstate of the transformation. A human act is neither simply a vector of movement nor an isolated body part but rather a goal-directed organ transformation.

Recall that some infants respond to the tongue protrusion to the side with a straight tongue protrusion plus a simultaneous head turn to the side. Note too that the tongue-tied infants (attached freniculum) became upset when they could not produce the full extent of the tongue protrusion shown. Both examples suggest that the adult's behavior is coded not at the level of specific movements per se but rather at the more abstract level of having an aim or goal. It is only at the level of goals that the head turn is relevant to tongue protrusion to the side. These are different as specific motor movements, but the infant's tongue protrusion ends up off the midline of the body in both cases. Although the literal movements were very different, the goals are similar.

The human act may be the earliest, most aboriginal parsing of the world into things that bear on the self and those that do not. Human acts are especially relevant to infants because they look like the way the infants feel themselves to act and because human acts are things that the infant can intend. Neither the swinging clock pendulum nor the swaying of trees bear that relation. When a human act is shown to a newborn baby, the act may provide its first "aha" experience. "Lo! Something interpretable. That (seen) event is like this (felt) event." The fact that infants can recreate the act allows them to give it special meaning. (Partly for this reason, the expressive faces of people are infants' favorite playthings and recruit more attention than other items in their world.) We thus suggest that the basic cut infants impose on the world of objects is neither self-initiated movement versus moved by a seen force (trees in the wind are not viewed as special), nor animate versus inanimate (armadillos will not be of much interest), nor even people (as adults know them) versus things. The aboriginal distinction may be something closer to *human acts versus other events*.

Infants' tendency to see behavior in terms of human acts that can be imitated has interesting implications. First, the world of physical bodies is divisible into those that perform human acts (people) and those that do not (things). Second, after one has made this division in the external world, new meanings become possible. Because human acts are seen in others and performed by the self, the infant can grasp that the other is at some level "like me": the other acts like me, and I can act like the other. The cross-modal knowledge of what it feels like to do the act seen provides a privileged access to people not afforded by things.[6]

2 Infants' Conception of Persons

Identity for Human Individuals

We have argued that there is a rich innate grounding for infants' understanding of people. This innate construal is based on human acts. Surely, however, the newborn's notion is not yet the mature, adult concept of a person with all its entailments. For example, the differentiation of people from things, the specialness of people, and even a grasp of their similarity to oneself, need not mean that there is yet any differentiation within the class of people. The adult notion obviously makes distinctions within the class. This again raises issues of identity: how does one tell one individual from another? We propose that imitation serves an identity function as regards people. Infants reenact the behavior of the adult in part to test the identity of the adult and differentiate them from other particular ones.

Consider the problem of identity as it applies to people. It is a common experience for infants to see the features of people change, sometimes quite radically, during one continuous viewing of them. For example, a mother leans down over a bassinet so that her hair falls over her brow and covers her eyes. Is the mother a series of different people as she is featurally altered? A featural analysis cannot be the sole criterion infants use for determining identity, as discussed earlier. Spatiotemporal rules concerning place and trajectory of motion must be critically important.

What action might infants take to clarify an ambiguity such as "This person does not look like Mother, but Mother was not seen to leave. Is this Mother?" We believe that infants use body-movement patterns and non-verbal gestures to clarify ambiguities about the identity of people. If infants are unsure about the identity of a person who is perceptually present, infants will be motivated to probe whether this person has the same behavioral properties as the old one seen earlier, because body actions and expressive behavioral properties are identifiers of who a person is. Body actions and distinctive interactive games are akin to nonverbal shared memories, or at least shared experiences, that can be used to probe a person's identity.

Differentiating Individuals   In a study of 6-week-old infants, we presented two different people who were featurally very different: the mother and a male stranger (Meltzoff and Moore 1992). Previous research showed that infants this young can visually discriminate their own mothers from strangers, so the fact that they were featurally different could be visually registered (Bushnell, Sai, and Mullin 1989; Field, Cohen, Garcia, and Greenberg 1984; Walton, Bower, and Bower 1992). However, we found that when these people were not clearly differentiated by spatial criteria, infants seemed confused about numerical identity.

We arranged the test so that infants saw one person perform one facial gesture and the other person perform a different gesture. For example, the mother showed the tongue-protrusion gesture and then exited. The male stranger then entered and demonstrated the mouth-opening gesture. Using this multiperson, appearance/disappearance situation, we found something quite surprising. Many infants stopped acting; stared at the new person, and then slowly and deliberately produced the previous person's gesture. Instead of the perceptual stimulus automatically triggering a matching response, the new person's gesture prompted a reenactment of the absent person's gesture. Why should the infant produce the old person's gesture and not be driven by the gesture in current view?

Further analysis revealed that the subset of infants who were reenacting the previous person's gesture were those who had not completely visually tracked the people as the switch occurred. The reactions of infants in this subset is understandable in terms of the typology outlined in table 1. These 6-week-olds faced a dilemma, because they are confined to using steady-state rules (level 1). The two adults were featurally different but interacted with the infants from the same location in space. At level 1, objects in the same place are the same object by spatiotemporal rules, hence the mere featural differences between the adults would be insufficient to establish their separate identity. The other subset of infants, who had tracked the entrances and exits of the adults, could use the different paths of motion as a spatiotemporal criterion of identity, and this, perhaps taken in conjunction with the featural difference, would have allowed them to differentiate the two adults.

This suggested a new experiment. Everything remained the same but for one factor: the degree to which spatiotemporal criteria could be applied. Once again, two people viewed at different times performed different facial gestures. The crucial change was that we ensured that the infants smoothly tracked each adult as he or she moved about in space. The adults should now be different by infants' spatiotemporal as well as featural rules. The results showed that this small change in procedure produced a large change in the results: now a significant number of infants imitated the first person's gesture and then the second person's gesture in turn, without conflict between the two (Meltzoff and Moore 1992).

The deployment of imitation to help sort out ambiguities about identity assists us in understanding this pattern of results. For those infants who did not smoothly track the adults, the identity of the person in front of them was indeterminate. They were using the first person's gestures to help resolve this ambiguity. Once the conditions were modified so that spatiotemporal and featural criteria both suggested that this was a different person, then infants imitated each person in turn with no confusion.

Reidentifying Individuals   Discussed so far was how imitation is used to distinguish individuals. We also think it is used for reidentifying an individual as being the same one over different encounters. To investigate this, we conducted a new experiment in which infants were shown a gesture by an adult on one day, and the same adult returned on successive days. Is this the same person?

In Meltzoff and Moore 1994, 6-week-old infants were assigned to one of four groups. On day 1, they saw a single adult demonstrate either mouth opening, tongue protrusion at midline, the novel gesture of tongue protrusion to the side, or a control display of no oral movement. On day 2 the same adult first sat and presented a neutral face; this assessed whether infants would remember and reenact what the adult did the day before. Then the assigned gesture was demonstrated again. Day 3 repeated the procedure from day 2.

The results showed both immediate imitation (when the gestures were shown) and imitation from memory (when the adult sat with a neutral face). The imitation from memory is noteworthy because infants were simply presented with a neutral face during this phase. The information about what to do was not in the stimulus. What differed across the groups was the infant's representation of this adult, not what the adult was actually doing. Nonetheless, the results showed that infants who had seen the adult demonstrate mouth opening 24 hours earlier were significantly more likely to look at the adult and produce mouth openings, and those who saw the adult demonstrate tongue protrusion were more likely to do that gesture. Infants were acting on their remembrance of things past.

The notion that imitation provides a functional criterion of identity helps us to understand infants' imitation of yesterday's acts. On day 1 the infant saw a person showing a tongue-protrusion gesture. Twenty-four hours later a person who looks featurally the same is encountered in the same context, but this time with a neutral face. For the 6-week-old, the most salient problem raised by this social encounter is one of the identity of the person. Is this the self-same person acting differently (no facial gesture) or a fundamentally different person who looks the same? Infants deploy imitation to help resolve this question.

A Functional Criterion for Identity: Gestural Signatures   We thus have two cases in which infants' behavior is not governed by what is presently delivered to their senses: (a) Why should infants in a multiperson situation sometimes imitate a previously seen person instead of the perceptually present person? (b) Why should infants be prompted to imitate yesterday's behavior if the current adult is displaying a neutral face? It is as if infants use imitation to ask, "Are you the one who does the ____ gesture?"

Infants are confronted with people as they come and go, appear and disappear in front of them. If infants are to make sense of such events, then some rules are needed to determine whether the person seen at time t is the same as or different from the one seen at time t'. The infant must use whatever rules for identity they have at their disposal. Interestingly, young infants can be confronted with contradictions between two identity rules. Thus in the multiperson case, the new adult was featurally different but sitting in the same spatial location. Is this person the same one, who now looks different, or is this a new person in the old location? The infant employs the person's gestural signature to tip the balance one way or the other. In the case of the person coming back after a day's break in contact, the infant sees someone who is featurally the same but who is acting differently (presenting a neutral face instead of gesturing) and for whom a spatiotemporal rule cannot be applied (because of break in contact). Our idea is that infants try to resolve uncertainties concerning a person's identity by using imitation as a gestural probe. By 6 weeks of age, distinctive human behaviors serve as *gestural signatures*, aiding the infant to differentiate individuals within the general class of people: to distinguish one individual from another and to reidentify particular individuals on subsequent encounters.

Three Criteria for Object Identity: Spatiotemporal, Featural, and Functional   At this point we need to integrate our findings from section 1 concerning identity and the new work on early imitation. We are proposing that infants use three criteria for understanding the identity of objects: spatiotemporal, featural, and functional. 'Spatiotemporal' refers to location in space and time, 'featural' refers to perceptual properties; and 'functional' refers to how an object acts or how one can act with it.[7] We are suggesting that for young infants, human behavior—in particular the type of distinctive acts we call gestural signatures—are used to identify individuals. These are the precursors of our everyday adult recognition that individual people have distinctive mannerisms, styles, and modes of behavior that can be expected from them. Even the same category of act can be so individualized that it can be used for identifying the person—my walk is not your walk. People can be recognized by their gait at a distance, although all other features are indiscernible.

From a philosophical point of view, the spatiotemporal criterion is the essence of numerical identity (Strawson 1959). From the viewpoint of psychology, the other criteria come into play and often must be used precisely because complete spatiotemporal histories are unavailable. This is especially so for the infant, who cannot move around at will, cannot ask questions, and, if young enough, may even be unable to track visually with much accuracy. Thus the featural and functional criteria are of considerable interest to developmental cognitive psychologists. Moreover, the special nature of human acts is that they allow the infant to initiate as well as to observe, which enables them to probe and test who a particular individual is. This bidirectionality makes imitation useful to the infant as a tool for addressing identity problems posed by people.

Developing Objectivity about Persons

We now wish to consider the relation between infants' notions of objects and their notions of persons. Infants have rules for determining the identity and permanence of objects they perceive. We have argued that these rules change and develop with age. People are physical bodies that exist in space and time. It follows that infants' understanding of other people change and develop as their underlying identity rules change. Looked at from this perspective, physical bodies and human bodies are understood equivalently.

This was demonstrated in a study of ours in which people were hidden behind barriers. The results showed that infants used the same rules in finding their mother hidden behind large screens as in finding a small inanimate object hidden on a table top. They made the same search errors and were essentially at the same level of understanding (level 1, 2, or 3) for both. This supports the idea that the identity and permanence rules are mental structures that apply generally to physical bodies, both people and things, regardless of the particular motor movements used in recovering the objects, etc.

We have discussed the developing identity structures as if they were used by the infant only to interpret a particular person or thing as the same or different, permanent or not. Infants also interpret the failures of these rules in different ways at different ages. For example, for 5-month-olds (level 2), when the mother leaves the room, she can be remembered, but the infant does not conceive of her as existing anywhere else. A few months later (early level 3), the mother is now conceived of as continuing to exist in a particular place or on a particular trajectory of motion, which allows for search. If the mother is not found where she is conceived of as being, the infant can for the first time confront the possibility that although she did exist, she no longer does.[8] No such thought is possible at earlier ages: there is no notion of ceasing to exist until objects can be conceived of as permanent. Before objects are permanent, infants conceive of the external world as what is present now. Nothing is hidden because there is nowhere else to be. However, this does not mean that they are solely influenced by the present. Representations constructed from previous encounters are maintained in memory, and current perceptions may be interpreted in terms of them (Meltzoff and Moore 1994). These memories create an internal realm, but before things are permanent, these memories do not refer to an enduring external world.

Toward the end of level 3, having successfully both recovered objects that disappear and reidentified objects not found where expected, the infants restructure their conception of objects. They now understand that physical bodies cannot be destroyed by simple disappearance transformations (occlusions). People and things can be lost: infants now understand that they continue to exist in a place, somewhere out of perceptual contact, but their location may be indeterminate. By about 18 months, infants have developed a notion of objects that resembles the naive adult view.

In summary, infants progressively conceive of a more objective world. The direction of development is toward construing people and things as unique entities tracing a single continuous path in space and time. This aspect of mind, which is a developmental achievement, does the work of interpreting what is not given directly by perception and of providing an enduring reality that exists in the absence of sensory input altogether.

Developing Subjectivity for Persons: Early Folk Psychology

Persons are more than enduring physical bodies that are like one's own body and move like one does. In the mature adult notion, persons also have beliefs, desires, and intentions that lie below surface behavior and can be used to predict and explain behavior. One cannot see intentions, but it is an essential part of our commonsense or folk psychology that other people have them (Dennett 1987, Fodor 1987, Goldman 1993, Searle 1983, Stich 1983). At what age do infants begin to understand people in this way?

A recent study (Meltzoff 1995) suggests that by 18 months of age children go beyond imitating the visible surface behavior of the adult. In the critical test situation, infants saw an adult who demonstrated an intention to act in a certain way. Importantly, the adult never fulfilled this intention; he tried but failed to perform the act, so the end state was never reached. The goal toward which the adult was striving therefore remained unobserved by the infant. To an adult, it was easy to read the actor's intention. The experimental question was whether infants registered this behavior in purely physical terms or whether they too read through the surface behavior to the underlying goal, which remained unseen. The subjects, who were too young to give verbal reports, revealed how they represented the event by what they chose to reenact. The infants' tendency to perform the target act was compared in several situations: after they saw the full target act demonstrated, after they saw the unsuccessful attempt to perform the act, and when it was neither shown nor attempted.

The results showed that 18-month-old infants can interpret the unsuccessful attempts of adults even when the adult does not reach the intended goal. Infants who saw either the unsuccessful attempt or the full target act produced target acts at a significantly higher rate than the controls. It was striking not only that infants could interpret the unsuccessful attempts but also that they were as likely to perform the target after seeing the adult trying as they were after seeing the actual demonstration of the target behavior itself. We interpret this pattern of data as showing, at a minimum, that 18-month-olds can infer the goal toward which a sequence of actions is aimed, even though the end state is never attained. The findings strongly suggest that infants situate people within a psychological, not purely physical, framework. In this sense, they understand people to be bearers of psychological properties.

How did the infants know that the unsuccessful act was only an attempt? They could not have decided to go beyond the literal actions of the adult on the basis of language or emotional displays, because both were strictly controlled: the actor said nothing and showed no disappointment, sadness, or frustration. The chief basis for extracting the goal was probably the fact that the adult's attempts consisted of three different but related acts. The hypothesis is that the infants used the relation between the three attempts to infer the goal of the act (which was never shown).

To underscore why the current experiment is relevant to the ontogenesis of folk psychology, it is helpful to distinguish between seeing the behaviors of another in purely physical terms versus psychological terms. The minimum case of an interpretation being psychological is interpreting human behavior in terms that go beyond a simple description of the observable movements only. A physical interpretation refers to *movements or motions*, and a psychological interpretation refers to goal-directed actions or what we call *acts*. The behavior of another person can, of course, be coded using either (or both) the psychological or physical level of description. We can say 'Sally's hand touched the cup, and the cup fell over' or 'Sally reached for the cup'. Strict behaviorists insist on the former because what is in the respondent's mind is unobservable. Our research suggests that by 18 months of age, infants are not strict behaviorists. They ascribe goals to human acts. Indeed, they infer the goal of a sequence of behaviors even when the goal was not attained. They do this in preference to literally reenacting the motions seen. Thus it appears that they code the behaviors of people in psychological terms, not purely as physical motions (Meltzoff and Gopnik 1993).

Infants' Understanding of Psychological States   The results would be nicely accounted for by postulating an innate understanding of intentions. On this account, the new findings with 18-month-olds are simply partial reflections of this innate knowledge. Taking an even stronger line, Fodor (1987) suggests that there is an innate belief-desire psychology that goes beyond the attribution of intention alone.

We favor a more developmental account. This view retains some aspects of nativism, but it differs from a full-blown innate folk psychology in two ways. First, it suggests that certain philosophical distinctions among mental states may have developmental reality. An understanding of the goals of human actions (or even simple intentions) does not demand a grasp of mental states like belief (Searle 1983); the adult's folk psychology (a belief-desire psychology) may develop from simpler beginnings. Indeed, new empirical discoveries about childrens' conception of mind suggest that a belief-desire psychology gradually emerges between 2.5 to 4 years of age (Astington and Gopnik 1991; Flavell 1988; Gopnik 1993; Harris 1989; Perner 1991; Wellman 1990, 1993). The results discussed here demonstrate that there is some primitive grasp of intended actions at an even earlier age.

An early understanding of people in psychological terms emphasizes the competence of infants, but leads to a second difference from the strong nativist view. For us, finding a surprising competence at 18 months of age does not warrant the conclusion that there is an innate grasp of intentions with a fixed nondevelopmental core. There may be significant revision in the infant's understanding of the meaning of "intention" in some or all of the following areas during early development: the locus of intentions (are they in the other's mind as mental states?), the contents of what can be understood as intentional, the equivalence between the intentions I know myself to hold and those I attribute to others, and awareness of one's own or others' intentions.

In fact, we have strong reason to suggest there are developmental shifts in the content of intentional acts that infants can understand: a progression from simple body acts, to actions on objects, to using one object as a tool to act on a second object. At the first level, infants may understand only intentions involving simple body movements, such as trying to raise one's hand or making particular facial movements. It is as yet unknown whether young infants can imitate the mere demonstration of an attempted act, rather than the whole act itself. However, even if this were the case, newborns probably would not respond to tasks involving actions on objects, the second level described above. Young infants attend to people or to things but not to the person-thing relation until the second half year of life (Campos and Stenberg 1981; Meltzoff 1988a, 1988b; Trevarthen and Hubley 1978). Thus they probably cannot give meaning to the adult's attempts to perform an action on an object, because this involves a person-thing relation. Even if intention were an ontological category available to the newborn, there could still be a developmental progression in the content of this category.

Moreover, we believe that there is development in conceptions about the locus of intention (and therefore in the meaning of intention itself). The earliest progenitor may be understanding the goals of action, which is logically separable from imputing intention to the minds of others. Even the attribution of goals requires that infants read below surface behavior. However, it does not require that they ascribe an invisible state to another's mind as the underlying cause of the behavior. Furthermore, there is room for development between having a primitive grasp of intention as an internal state and a mature folk psychology holding that if a person desires x and believes that doing y will bring about x, he will intend to do y, and that this is wholly independent of (and may be contrary to) one's own beliefs, desires, and intentions about the matter.

In summary, by 18 months of age there is a differentiation between what was actually done and the goal. Infants seem to know that every act is not a goal achieved. This indicates that they have begun to distinguish the surface behavior of people from another deeper level. They have already adopted the rudiments of a folk-psychological framework.

3   Concepts of the Self and the Other

We have explored three aspects of infant cognition—their understandings of physical objects, of human bodies, and of psychological states—in
relative independence of one another. Such independence is a fiction.
These three aspects are intertwined with each other in normal human
development. They exhibit two poles of infant knowing: the objective
and the subjective. Developing an equilibrium between these poles un-
dergirds the earliest conceptions of self, other, and persons in relation
with one another.

The objective pole of knowing is most clearly manifest in infants'
changing levels of understanding the identity and permanence of physical
objects. These changes also influence how infants objectify people and their
relations with them. A major developmental change in the first 5 months is
attaining a stable "here and now" world such that individual entities are differentiated and retain their identity as they move and change within the visual frame. Before this level of objectification, there are incomplete rules for
maintaining identity over visual transformations. Consequently, most of the
infant's energy, attention, and even acts of imitation are used in the service
of resolving basic problems of identity.

Once the world is objectified in the sense of being stable in the here
and now, and especially later after entities that are out of sight are conceived of as permanent, gestural interactions and imitation can be used
in new ways that lead to new notions of people and relations with them.
Because a particular gesture is no longer needed to differentiate or identify the individual, the issue shifts from "Who is this?" to the nature and
quality of the exchange itself. Instead of being confined by a specific imitative exchange involving one gesture, infants can now play the game of
imitation at a more general level. What matters is not the particular gesture
but the matching game, in which specific gestures are infinitely substitut-
able. Moreover, the game can be played bidirectionally, so that mother can
propose a gesture and baby can copy, or baby can propose and mother can
follow. This entails a shared understanding of a new mental (invisible, inferred) entity: the imitative game. It allows a new conception of a relationship between self and other that transcends particular acts. As these types of
relations develop with an enduring (permanent) other, the infant's understanding of social possibilities expands. Infants can seek out and initiate
interpersonal exchanges, thus bringing certain social experiences under
their own control.

The subjective pole of knowing is most clearly manifest in early imitation and its implications for developing self-other equivalences. From
birth on infants can act as they see others act, and this enables them to rec-

ognize that the other is "like me." This grasp of the other as like oneself works in two directions. On the one hand, it allows the infant to use the self as a framework for enriching its understanding of the other. Having done an action itself, the infant has subjective, experiential knowledge of that act. When the infant sees another perform an act that he knows is like his own, the infant can interpret the seen act in terms of this subjective experience. On the other hand, infants may learn about themselves through seeing the acts of others. For example, by virtue of seeing the failed attempts of others and inferring unseen goals, infants gain experience in isolating and extracting goals. This could change infants' perspectives on their own acts, so that their own goals can become objects of attention in and of themselves.

Ultimately, of course, children must bring both the subjective and objective poles into balance. The outcome of such a process is an integration of knowledge of self and other that spans both, one more like our folk-psychological conception of a person. Within such a framework the self is construed as an objective entity enduring in a world of others, and the other is ascribed a subjectivity as rich as one's own. Although the infant is innately provided with tools for interacting with and understanding people—particularly imitation and supramodal representations—the mature folk-psychological construal of a person is a developmental achievement, not an innate given.

In summary, the infant's conception of a person does not develop in isolation from the rest of their cognitive structures. On the contrary, an infant's changing concepts of physical objects interact with the development of their understanding of people. For the young infant, ambiguities about the identity of people arise because of problems in tracing their *bodies* through space and time. These ambiguities are addressed with body imitation, which permits interacting with people at a distance rather than through direct physical contact. Later in infancy their general cognitive abilities again interact with their understanding of people. The infant's developing to a level at which invisible entities are postulated may be a logical prerequisite for its understanding that people have invisible mental states that lie behind behavior. The development of an infant's notion of a person is thus not restricted to their understanding minds but involves their understanding bodies as well. For infants, these two aspects of persons are interwoven.

Acknowledgments

The order of authorship is alphabetical; the work was thoroughly collaborative. We thank Pat Kuhl and Alison Gopnik for insightful suggestions on an earlier draft. We owe an enormous debt to Naomi Eilan, Tony Marcel, José Bermúdez, Bill Brewer, and

Alison Gopnik for encouraging us to think about various philosophical issues. Naomi was a particularly generous editor; she sharpened our thinking in numerous ways. This work was funded by the National Institutes of Health (HD-22514).

Notes

1. For 3-month-olds limited to a steady-state understanding of the world, changes from steady states present a problem. They will visually follow an object as it moves, and if they temporarily lose sight of it, they will shift their eyes to anticipate where it should be on the trajectory. However, when they observe the object stop, they will simply pause to note the object at rest (the stopped object is perceptually registered), and then continue tracking out the trajectory (Bower, Broughton, and Moore 1971; Piaget 1954). This and related research leads to the inference that the moving and stopped "objects" are not interpreted as the *same one* by level 1 infants.

2. Even the 9-month-old understanding is not the final conception of object achieved (Moore, 1975, Moore and and Meltzoff 1978, Piaget 1954), but for the purposes of this discussion we no longer call it a proto-object because the 9-month-old conception entails spatiotemporal continuity.

3. The same pattern of behavior (and difference between ages) occurred in the feature task. For the 9-month-olds, the featurally different object on the same trajectory was not accepted as the original, and their looking patterns suggested that they inferred that the original must still be behind the screen. Again, the 5-month-olds do not seem to draw this inference.

4. This illustrates development within the domain of spatiotemporal rules. For the 9-month-old it is *necessary* that the object exist at all points on the trajectory for it to be the same; for the 5-month-old it is sufficient that the object be on the trajectory whenever it is seen for it to be construed as the same one. Thus both the 5- and the 9-month-olds use spatiotemporal rules, but through development, the trajectory rule is reorganized to become the permanence rule.

5. The freniculum is the thin piece of skin connecting the base of the tongue blade to the soft palate on the bottom of the mouth. In some children this skin extends to the front tip of the tongue, which prevents protrusion of the tongue.

6. The use of 'I' and 'me' in the text is not meant to imply the mature, adult notion of these terms but rather refers only to the earliest progenitors of these concepts.

7. Campbell (1993) develops a distinction between "indexical causality" and "nonindexical causality," which may be relevant here. One could think of our functional criteria for identity as being related to Campbell's indexical features.

8. Interestingly, it is at about 9 to 12 months of age, but not before, that infants burst into tears when their mothers go out of sight (e.g., Ainsworth, Blehar, Waters, and Wall 1978).

References

Ainsworth, M. D. S., M. C. Blehar, E. Waters, and S. Wall. 1978. *Patterns of Attachment.* Hillsdale, N.J.: Erlbaum.

Astington, J. W., and A. Gopnik. 1991. "Theoretical Explanations of Children's Understanding of the Mind." *British Journal of Developmental Psychology* 9:7–31.

Baillargeon, R. 1991. "Reasoning about the Height and Location of a Hidden Object in 4.5- and 6.5-Month-Old Infants." *Cognition* 38:13–42.

Baillargeon, R. 1993. "The Object Concept Revisited: New Directions in the Investigation of Infants' Physical Knowledge." In *Visual Perception and Cognition in Infancy*, edited by C. Granrud, pp. 265–315. Hillsdale, N.J.: Erlbaum.

Bower, T. G. R. 1982. *Development in Infancy* 2nd ed. San Francisco: W. H. Freeman.

Bower, T. G. R., J. Broughton, and M. K. Moore. 1971. "Development of the Object Concept as Manifested in Changes in the Tracking Behavior of Infants between 7 and 20 Weeks of Age." *Journal of Experimental Child Psychology* 11:182–193.

Brewer, B. 1993. "Introduction: Action." In *Spatial Representation: Problems in Philosophy and Psychology*, edited by N. Eilan, R. McCarthy, and B. Brewer, pp. 271–276. Cambridge, Mass.: Blackwell.

Bushnell, I. W. R., F. Sai, and J. T. Mullin. 1989. "Neonatal Recognition of the Mother's Face." *British Journal of Developmental Psychology* 7:3–15.

Campbell, J. 1993. "The Role of Physical Objects in Spatial Thinking." In *Spatial Representation: Problems in Philosophy and Psychology*, edited by N. Eilan, R. McCarthy, and B. Brewer, pp. 65–95. Cambridge, Mass.: Blackwell.

Campbell, J. 1994. *Past, Space, and Self*. Cambridge: MIT Press.

Campbell, J. (this volume). "The Body Image and Self-Consciousness." In *The Body and the Self*, edited by J. Bermúdez, A. Marcel, and N. Eilan. Cambridge: MIT Press.

Campos, J. J., and C. R. Stenberg. 1981. "Perception, Appraisal, and Emotion: The Onset of Social Referencing." In *Infant Social Cognition*, edited by M. E. Lamb and L. R. Sherrod, pp. 273–314. Hillsdale, N.J.: Erlbaum.

Dennett, D. C. 1987. *The Intentional Stance*. Cambridge: MIT Press.

Eilan, N. 1993. "Introduction: Spatial Representation in the Sensory Modalities." In *Spatial Representation: Problems in Philosophy and Psychology*, edited by N. Eilan, R. McCarthy, and B. Brewer, pp. 179–190. Cambridge, Mass.: Blackwell.

Field, T. M., D. Cohen, R. Garcia, and R. Greenberg. 1984. "Mother-Stranger Face Discrimination by the Newborn." *Infant Behavior and Development*, 7:19–25.

Flavell, J. H. 1988. "The Development of Children's Knowledge about the Mind: From Cognitive Connections to Mental Representations." In *Developing Theories of Mind*, edited by J. W. Astington, P. L. Harris, and D. R. Olson, pp. 244–267. New York: Cambridge University Press.

Fodor, J. A. 1987. *Psychosemantics: The Problem of Meaning in the Philosophy of Mind*. Cambridge: MIT Press.

Goldman, A. I. 1992. "Empathy, Mind, and Morals." *Proceedings and Addresses of the American Philosophical Association* 66:17–41.

Goldman, A. I. 1993. "The Psychology of Folk Psychology." *Behavioral and Brain Sciences* 16:15–28.

Gopnik, A. 1993. "How We Know Our Minds: The Illusion of First-Person Knowledge of Intentionality." *Behavioral and Brain Sciences* 16:1–14.

Harris, P. L. 1989. *Children and Emotion.* New York: Blackwell.

Meltzoff, A. N. 1988a. "Infant Imitation after a One-Week Delay: Long-Term Memory for Novel Acts and Multiple Stimuli." *Developmental Psychology* 24:470–476.

Meltzoff, A. N. 1988b. "Infant Imitation and Memory: Nine-Month-Olds in Immediate and Deferred Tests." *Child Development* 59:217–225.

Meltzoff, A. N. 1995. "Understanding the Intentions of Others: Re-enactment of Intended Acts by 18-Month-Old Children." *Developmental Psychology* 31: in press.

Meltzoff, A. N., and A. Gopnik. 1993. "The Role of Imitation in Understanding Persons and Developing a Theory of Mind." In *Understanding Other Minds: Perspectives from Autism*, edited by S. Baron-Cohen, H. Tager-Flusberg, and D. J. Cohen, pp. 335–366. New York: Oxford University Press.

Meltzoff, A. N., and M. K. Moore. 1977. "Imitation of Facial and Manual Gestures by Human Neonates." *Science* 198:75–78.

Meltzoff, A. N., and M. K. Moore. 1983. "Newborn Infants Imitate Adult Facial Gestures." *Child Development* 54:702–709.

Meltzoff, A. N., and M. K. Moore. 1989. "Imitation in Newborn Infants: Exploring the Range of Gestures Imitated and the Underlying Mechanisms." *Developmental Psychology* 25:954–962.

Meltzoff, A. N., and M. K. Moore. 1992. "Early Imitation within a Functional Framework: The Importance of Person Identity, Movement, and Development." *Infant Behavior and Development* 15:479–505.

Meltzoff, A. N., and M. K. Moore. 1994. "Imitation, Memory, and the Representation of Persons." *Infant Behavior and Development* 17:83–99.

Moore, M. K. 1975. "Object Permanence and Object Identity: A Stage-Developmental Model." Paper presented at the meeting of the Society for Research in Child Development, Denver, Colo., April.

Moore, M. K., R. Borton, and B. L. Darby. 1978. "Visual Tracking in Young Infants: Evidence for Object Identity or Object Permanence?" *Journal of Experimental Child Psychology* 25:183–198.

Moore, M. K., and A. N. Meltzoff. 1978. "Object Permanence, Imitation, and Language Development in Infancy: Toward a Neo-Piagetian Perspective on Communicative and Cognitive Development." In *Communicative and Cognitive Abilities—Early Behavioral Assessment*, edited by F. D. Minifie and L. L. Lloyd, pp. 151–184. Baltimore: University Park Press.

Perner, J. 1991. *Understanding the Representational Mind.* Cambridge: MIT Press.

Piaget, J. 1954. *The Construction of Reality in the Child.* New York: Basic Books.

Piaget, J. 1962. *Play, Dreams, and Imitation in Childhood.* New York: Norton.

Searle, J. R. 1983. *Intentionality: An Essay in the Philosophy of Mind.* New York: Cambridge University Press.

Spelke, E. S., K. Breinlinger, J. Macomber, and K. Jacobson. 1992. "Origins of Knowledge." *Psychological Review* 99:605–632.

Spelke, E. S., and G. Van de Walle. 1993. "Perceiving and Reasoning about Objects: Insights from Infants." In *Spatial Representation: Problems in Philosophy and Psychology*, edited by N. Eilan, R. McCarthy, and B. Brewer, pp. 132–161. Cambridge, Mass.: Blackwell.

Stich, S. P. 1983. *From Folk Psychology to Cognitive Science: The Case aagainst Belief.* Cambridge: MIT Press.

Strawson, P. F. 1959. *Individuals: An Essay in Descriptive Metaphysics.* London: Methuen.

Trevarthen, C., and P. Hubley. 1978. "Secondary Intersubjectivity: Confidence, Confiding, and Acts of Meaning in the First Year." In *Action, Gesture, and Symbol: The Emergence of Language*, edited by A. Lock, pp. 183–229. New York: Academic Press.

Walton, G. E., N. J. A. Bower, and T. G. R. Bower. 1992. "Recognition of Familiar Faces by Newborns." *Infant Behavior and Development,* 15:265–269.

Wellman, H. M. 1990. *The Child's Theory of Mind.* Cambridge: MIT Press.

Wellman, H. M. 1993. "Early Understanding of Mind: The Normal Case." In *Understanding Other Minds: Perspectives from Autism*, edited by S. Baron-Cohen, H. Tager-Flusberg, and D. J. Cohen, pp. 10–39. New York: Oxford University Press.

Persons, Animals, and Bodies

Paul F. Snowdon

The primary question to be considererd in this paper is whether a recent proposal in the debate about personal identity has a defensible conception of the relation between ourselves and our bodies. The proposal, which has acquired the title 'animalism', is, in its most concise statement, the following:

(A)   We are identical with, are one and the same thing as, certain (human) animals.

Animalism has recently been endorsed by David Wiggins, Richard Wollheim, and Michael Ayers (among others).[1] One may reasonably be skeptical about some aspects of their positions, but it is surely fair to think both that the strengths and weaknesses of the recommended way of thinking have so far not been satisfactorily articulated and, in consequence, not properly assessed by philosophy and that such an evidently commonsensical proposal should be foremost on the agenda for discussions about our identity and nature.

It is an open question what the relation is between an animal and its body. In particular, there is no consensus among philosophers over whether the animal ceases to exist at its death or should count as continuing to exist in a radically changed lifeless state. The precise commitment of animalism on our relation to our bodies is thus also open. There is no real controversy, though, over the claim that certain continuities to do with an animal's body are sufficient for the persistence of the animal. If the body of an animal remains in tact and sustains the processes we call 'life', the animal in question has survived. Animalism seems to imply that such conditions are sufficient for *our* survival. It is this particular implication about our relation to our bodies that has seemed unacceptable to some philosophers. So I will restrict my discussion to cases where life is preserved without, however, committing myself to the thesis that life is necessary for the presence of the animal.

Doubts of this sort represent one of the two major difficulties currently felt with animalism. The other and, it seems to me, dominant objection is that a person can survive without the survival of the animal, and so we are not identical with particular animals. Perhaps brain transplants represent one possible example of such survival. According to this type of objection, animalism incorporates a mistaken conception of what is *necessary* for our survival.[2] In contrast, the type of objection I wish to consider here alleges that animalism incorporates a mistaken conception of what is *sufficient* for our survival. Objections of this sort rest on two ideas. The first is that there are no significant psychological conditions that have to be satisfied for the survival of an animal. What I said above to be quite clearly enough for the survival of an animal, namely an in-tact, life-sustaining body, is silent about psychological conditions, either positive or negative. Simple life seems not to be a *psychological* state. The second idea, expressed without any precision, is that we as persons (or subjects or selves) are importantly and deeply *psychological entities*, and so the animal's survival does not entail certain psychological conditions that are necessary for the survival of the person linked with that body.

My aim is to analyze this type of objection and to explore some lines of reply.

1   Animalism and the Source of the Problem

The central claim of animalism is in some ways a curious proposition to assert. It is natural to respond to its assertion in the words of Wittgenstein: "Only whom are we informing of this? And on what occasion?"[3] Its assertion acquires point, though, in a philosophical context where it serves to exclude alternative accounts of what we are that, in the course of reflection, can seem correct. Given some supplementary assumptions, (A) excludes dualism, brain-centred theories, and Lockean and neo-Lockean analyses of our existence.

Logically, (A) is a general identity claim. It can be true without being an a priori conceptual truth, in exactly the way other quite standard general identity claims are. Think of the general and familiar identity claim that each flash of lightening is identical with an electrical discharge. The particular way in which I have picked out the range of objects concerned, namely by using the first-person plural pronoun, is not essential; other expressions with the same reference would do. Nor is it necessarily completely satisfactory. (What range of objects exactly does 'we' refer to?) There are, however, two attractions to using it. The first is that it respects the most basic assumption made when philosophers engage with these problems. The assumption is that we are objects of some type or other to which we can refer using our vocabulary of personal pronouns (and, of course, other devices) but about whose fundamental nature we are ignorant or inadequately informed. The question is, What are we? The form of (A) is thus the natural form for an answer to this basic question. The second attraction is that it avoids the need to argue for general theses about persons as a class, a task that is remarkably difficult and that, arguably, there is no obvious reason to undertake.

Does the assertion of animalism have implications? If it does, the reason is that it is advanced against the background of a partial but moderately determinate and agreed conception or theory of what sort of things animals are. The thesis claims that certain objects picked out in a certain way, namely we ourselves, are of that sort, and so it entails that the agreed part of the theory of animals applies to these objects, in fact, according to the theory, to *us*. The thesis thus has implications in virtue of this theoretical background. Of interest for the purposes of this paper are the implications generated by this background about the psychological conditions for our survival.

Animalism does not simply claim that we are animals; it also says that we are animals of a certain *human* kind. We need to ask, therefore, whether there are significant psychological conditions for the survival of such animals. The notion of a psychological condition is vague, and it is also fairly flexible, since it can relate merely to capacities. But, it seems to me, we can say two things. The first is that any justified assertion of distinctive psychological requirements for human persistence must be empirically based. Acknowledging human animals as a kind provides no vantage point for distinguishing simply by reflection the significant psychological requirements for their persistence. The second is that human animals in fact have no distinctive psychological conditions for survival. In the course of their lives they can suffer irreversible degeneration in their cognitive and sensory performances and capacities, followed by complete loss in irreversible coma. A mind seems no more necessary for the existence of a human animal than are its teeth.

Animalism, then, stands in opposition to the tradition in philosophical speculation about personal identity (that is, about *our* identity) that claims that there are a priori determinable psychological conditions for a person's survival. The opposition appears two-sided, because animalism is opposed both to the necessity of such conditions and to their supposed a priori status. We need to be careful, however, how this two-sided opposition is understood. The opposition exists because, according to the argument, human animals in fact lack psychological requirements for their persistence. There is, though, no immediate inconsistency in affirming the following three propositions: there are certain a priori determinable conditions for the survival of persons; these conditions are not a priori determinable for animals;

persons are animals. There is no immediate inconsistency because the concept under which we are considering the conditions affects what can be determined a priori, and it may be allowed that the concepts of a person and an animal are different. So the fundamental basis for the opposition is the claim about what (human) animal persistence actually involves.

We can distinguish two sorts of conditions that there has been some temptation to endorse in discussions of personal identity. One sort might be called *positive* because they express the requirement that certain psychological features be *present*. Shoemaker expresses such a positive condition in the following passage:

If 'philosophical amnesia' is taken to mean total and irretrievable loss of all memories of all kinds, then the claim that a person can survive such amnesia is far more questionable. For what we are now imagining is something close to what has been called a "brain zap"—the total destruction of all the effects of the person's past experiences, learning, reasoning, deliberation, and so on. . . . Suppose that in a terrible accident a person suffers brain damage amounting to a total brain zap, and that somehow the surgeons manage to repair the brain in such a way that its possessor is able to start again. . . . Eventually that body is the body of someone with the mental life of a mature human being. . . . It is anything but obvious that this person would be the person who had the body prior to the accident. So if total amnesia means this sort of brain zap, it is far from uncontroversial—indeed it seems just false—that it is something a person could survive.[4]

Shoemaker is asserting that for a living body to remain the body of a single person, it must retain a certain minimum stock of psychological traits, and he clearly thinks that this requirement is discernible a priori.

Other psychological conditions might be called *negative*. They require that if a body is to remain the body of a single person, certain abnormal psychological conditions must *not* develop in it. One recent expression of such a negative condition is Kathleen Wilkes's contention that the onset of multiple-personality disorder represents the emergence in a body of a new person and the (temporary) exclusion from that body of the previous person, or at least amounts, as she says, to "the fracturing of the concept of a person."[5] If this is correct, such features must *not* appear in a body if it is to remain that of a single person.

In discussions of personal identity there are frequent endorsements of such positive and negative psychological requirements for our survival.

2   Another Difficult Case

It is a mistake, though, to think of animalism as disagreeing solely with certain psychological principles emerging from the theory of personal identity (with its emphasis on diachronic requirements). It also has, or seems to have, implications that are inconsistent with certain powerful intuitions about synchronic psychological requirments for the presence of a subject.

Some of these can be displayed by considering how animalism should treat split-brain cases. There is certainly a temptation to hold that in such cases, after the corpus callosum has been severed, there are two subjects of consciousness, whereas before there had been only one. Another view holds that although this verdict is in fact not accurate as a description of actual cases, it is a description to be entertained seriously and could be true of more extreme but conceivable cases.

What does animalism say about such cases? The obvious fact is that severing the corpus callosum does not destroy the animal. It is still there. From the animalist perspective, we cannot happily suppose that the previous subject of experience has departed, which is presumably implied by the two-new-subjects view. But further, if we ask, about the animal that remains, how it successfully survives in the world more or less as successfully as before, the answer seems to be that it (he or she) can still perceive and reason and remember, etc. The animal has not been stripped of its general perceptual and cognitive capacities. In such a case the postoperative experiences are being enjoyed by the same thing that preoperatively also enjoyed them. It would not be plausible to agree, in accord with animalism, that the previous subject, the animal, is still there but no longer as the subject of the experiences, as if it were asleep or comatose, and the experiences are had by other new subjects.

Animalism, then, is committed to a single-subject view of actual split-brain cases. And it seems that similar arguments within its framework would show that it is committed to a single-subject view of any experiences within a single human animal, however disconnected the parts of the brain are, so long as the (human) animal remains. Against this stands the undoubtedly powerful intuition that the experiences of a single subject must have a significant degree of psychological unity. A concise expression of this intuition is provided by J. L. Mackie in these words: "Our ordinary concept of a person, then, is of a necessarily unitary subject of consciousness. . . . All its simultaneous experiences must be co-conscious, because it is just one subject of consciouness at any time."[6]

3   Some Responses

I have argued that the conception of the relation between a person and his or her body that animalism involves is in conflict with fairly powerful intuitions about the psychological continuities involved in the survival of a person but also with perhaps even more powerful intuitions about the necessary unity of a single subject's experiences. The general assumption underlying this style of oppostion to animalism, both in connection with the unity of consciousness and in connection with personal identity, is that reflection on what it is for there to be a single subject, or person, at a time and what it is for such items to persist yields psychological principles whose application force us to distinguish between ourselves, the subjects we are, and the animal. Are there any such true principles? I mean, Are there true principles that have this consequence?

If we are to explore the resources of animalism, there are two strategies we need to investigate. One, we might call it the piecemeal option, is to weigh up the suggested principles individually, to check how plausible and well supported they are. It might be possible to argue convincingly that there *are* no such true principles. The other, the general option, is to explore the possibility of making a case against such principles as a type of claim, to make a general case that, if sound, will imply that no such true principles exist. It might be possible to argue convincingly, that is, that there *could not be* such principles.

I will first pursue the piecemeal option, arguing that quite a lot can be said against, and nothing very substantial has been said in favor of, some of the principles that have been cited. In particular, I want to discuss Shoemaker's argument as a representative example of how such principles are supported in the theory of personal identity and then to discuss some attempts to sustain principles about the unity of consciousness. (Consideration of problems posed by cases of multiple personality I postpone for another occassion.) I will then consider whether a more general counterargument can be developed.

4   The Possibility of "Brain Zaps"

The question at issue here is whether (A) conflicts with a genuine supposed truth detectable by reflection on brain zaps. The onus in the discussion is thus on the critic of (A) to convince us that it is impossible for a person to survive a brain zap. The objection to (A) lapses if the impossibility is not established.

How plausible is the claim that a person cannot survive a brain zap? In the passage quoted in section 1 Shoemaker imagines a case in which at first a body houses a psychologically functioning person, then has its brain zapped, and then houses a psychologically functioning person whose psychology is causally unconnected to that of the earlier person. He invites us to agree that it "seems false" to think that the person there after recovery is the person there earlier, and concludes that a person cannot survive a brain zap.

Even if Shoemaker's judgment about the case he considers is sound, his general conclusion does not follow. It may be that the need to recognize the presence of a distinct person in his scenario derives from the renewed psychological functioning. Maybe without this renewed functioning, what we have is a person who has survived a zap but who is severely impaired. Admittedly, (A) is threatened by the verdict that Shoemaker accepts for his example, whether or not it is generally impossible for a person to survive a zap, but Shoemaker's general claim about zaps is not in fact supported by the example. Why, then, did Shoemaker choose that example? The explanation that most obviously suggests itself is that he assumed that unless there is (roughly) mental functioning, it *seems* that the person has not survived.

In fact, neither this general assumption nor Shoemaker's verdict from his example can be said to represent what *seems* true. If, say, my son were to suffer a zap, but remain alive and I looked after him (it is hard to describe the case without begging the question), does it not *seem* that I *am* looking after *him*, the very person for whom I earlier cherished hopes? And if a doctor were to say that he could repair the brain, that would *seem* to me absolutely wonderful. Indeed, to make to such a doctor what might be called a Shoemakerian speech explaining that this possibility is really of no interest, since it will merely result in a new and hitherto unknown person, would surely *seem* quite mad. It is, after all, along such lines that we *seem* to think about the real, and at best only marginally less extreme, vicissitudes of familiar life, with its irretrievable losses of capacity or recovery of function sustained in novel ways.

I wish, perhaps unnecessarily, to describe a related case. Suppose someone receives a massive dose of an unusual type of radiation. Within hours he has passed into a deep coma. How do we regard what comes next? The overwhelmingly natural way to think of *him* would be, as we say, to wait and see whether *he* comes round, and if *he* does, what the radiation will have done to *his* mental capacities. If the dose has zapped him, then his recovery will be long and difficult. We would think of *his* condition as the highly undesirable medical consequences of the radiation for an individual; we simply would not regard it as an unusual technique for creating new persons!

The virtually unavoidable conclusion is that Shoemaker (and others endorsing such claims) has lost touch with the reality of how such cases *seem* to us.[7] Why this typically philosophical or reflective distortion should occur is a very important question which has to be left aside.[8]

5   Split Brains

The fundamental issue raised by split-brain cases is what the warrant is for those intuitive principles about the psychological unity of subjects of experience, the application of which requires distinguishing between the subject of experience and the (human) animal. Approaching discussions of these cases with that issue firmly at the front of our minds reveals, I believe, that no convincing account of their warrant is usually offered.

In Nagel's classic paper (1979), which was among the earliest to draw philosophical attention to the deep puzzle of split brains, he argues against the thesis that split-brain patients "have one mind whose content . . . is rather peculiar and dissociated."[9] This is, I assume, a somewhat convoluted statement of the thesis that there is a single subject enjoying the experiences, which is the verdict I have already argued that (A) implies. His objection is that it conflicts with our assumptions about single minds. He says, "Roughly, we assume that a single mind has sufficiently immediate access to its conscious states so that, for elements of experience or other mental events occurring simultaneously or in close temporal proximity, the mind which is their subject can also experience the simpler *relations* between them if it attends to the matter."

Nagel has captured an assumption we make. How, though, should we regard this assumption? Nagel views it as constitutive of the concept of a single mind. But we can equally view it as a natural, prescientific assumption that new data from abnormal cases, impossible to investigate without highly sophisticated experimental techniques, requires us to modify. Its status, on this conception, is somewhat akin to that of the assumption that large metallic objects cannot fly across the Atlantic, which is false but a totally natural one for people without the falsifying technology to make.

Nagel points out that it is "difficult to conceive what it is like to *be* one of these people." But as a reason for accepting his view of the status of the unity requirement, this merely raises the question whether there *has* to be some way that it is like, conceivable by another, when there is a single subject of experience. The status of this assumption is equally hazy.

Nagel has given expression to an intuition we have, but its status remains completely undetermined by him.

Christopher Peacocke, in a more recent discussion, proposes the following principle: one person or mind cannot have two token experiences of the same type at the same time.[10] He desribes it as "undeniable." This thesis should, perhaps, not be treated as a unity requirement, since it is neutral about functional unities of the sort endorsed by Mackie and Nagel, but clearly if it is right, then whether or not the principle implies anything in relation to actual split-brain patients, it implies a two-subject account of cases easy to imagine (though more or less impossible to confidently detect) where an experimenter produces in each hemisphere of the split brain of a single human animal an occurrence of qualitatively identical experiences.

Is Peacocke's principle undeniable? The argument for it seems to rest on the assumption that if subject s has experience e at time t, then what it is like for s at t must be different from how it would have been for s if s had all the other experiences s did have at t apart from e. If we grant this assumption, then since what it will be like for s is probably the same on the assumption that s has one experience with a certain quality and on the assumption that s has two such experiences, we should never ascribe to a single subject two such simultaneous experiences. But why must different total experiences involve differences in what it is like for the subject? It seems quite possible that this link between different experiences and differences in what it is like (understood in the normal way) only holds for normal subjects. The status of Peacocke's principle seems as obscure as that of Nagel's, and at the very least, it has not earned the right to be called "indubitable."[11]

The focus of the two passages I have cited has been the *experiences* of a single subject. Other philosophers focus on the expected unities among the propositional attitudes and between them and the intentional behavior of a single subject. For example, even in simple split-brain cases there is strong pressure to attribute belief that p even when the subject sincerely denies that p. It is next suggested as a plausible principle that if s believes that p, s will not sincerely deny that p. It then becomes necessary to locate two subjects for the conflicting propositional attitudes and intentional behavior to preserve the principle. Against this style of argument it can first be suggested that it not obvious that such expected unities must be treated as constitutive principles of propositional-attitude psychology, rather than as contingent but normally true generalizations. (This is the response advanced against Nagel and Peacock above.) And second, we can point out a tension within the argument for two subjects. The proponent of the argument is prepared to attribute belief that p on the basis of certain nonverbal intentional behavior. But if this is enough for belief that p, must not the principle stating that belief contradicts sincere denial already have been abandoned as *constitutive* of belief?

Finally, the argument that was used to demonstrate the tension between (A) and the two-subject view of split-brain patients (or imagined extensions of this case) can be turned into a serious difficulty for the more-than-one-subject view. It is agreed that only one animal is being experimented on. In the experiments, what does the animal experience? Surely, in some cases, the experiment might cause it pain or distress, for example. Again, how does the animal sense its surroundings, and why does it behave as it does? It seems most plausible to say that the animal can feel pain and distress, can see certain objects, takes them to be at a certain place, and so on. But if all of these things are happening to the animal, it is the subject, *the single subject*, of the experiences and the attitudes. A more-than-one-single-subject account must answer this argument.[12] It needs to explain how the animal fits into the picture.[13]

I thus suggest that reflection on split-brain cases does not overturn (A).

6   A General Argument

My strategy so far has been piecemeal. How, though, are we to decide in the end what status the proposed principles of unity have? How are we to decide whether there really are psychological requirements for the persistance of persons? It needs to be asked what *kind* of concept fixes the subject matter of our discussion. I will assume that the concept is the one expressed in English by the term 'person'.[14] What type of concept is it?

This is, of course, a very difficult question, one that I cannot answer properly. Instead, I want to approach the issue by asking what account of the concept would be most congenial for animalism, and whether a theory approximating to such an account might be plausible. One version of such an account is that the concept of a person is akin to a natural-kind notion with human animals as the designated samples fixing its extension. Then there could not be a rational basis for accepting principles about persons that would force us to distinguish between a human and the person. To be a true principle about persons, it must be validated by the samples that fix the extension, and it cannot exclude them. This would block suggestions like those advanced by Shoemaker. The implications for the idea of a subject of experience are more debatable. But according to the model, there is a person where there is a human animal. Let us also assume, what seems to be a fundamental principle about psychological attribution, that if a psychological attribution is made true by, obtains in virtue of, the behavior and states of a certain person, then the attribution is a psychological state of that person. From these two assumptions it follows that the discernible psychological states are possessed by a single subject. There could not, then, be true principles about the psychological states of a single subject on the basis of which to distinguish the person (or subject) and the animal.

The advantages that, I have just argued, are secured for animalism by this model can, however, be secured by a less extreme account; it seems that they are secured so long as the model of the concept of a person incorporates the less extreme but unrevisable principle about persons that where there is a human animal leading a life, there is also a person leading a life. Can a case be made for this?

I will start by marking out in a rough way two classes of judgments. One class is the set of personal-identity judgments. There is no precise way to define this set, but it will include identity judgments whose expression refers to the subjects of the judgments using personal pronouns, personal proper names, and definite descriptions of the form 'the person who . . .'. For any individual i, I will call the set of judgments of this sort that i accepts 'i's personal-identity set', abbreviated to i's PIS. The second set of judgments, again I give no precise rules for recognizing them, is the class of judgments we accept about the distribution of human animals over time. Each of us has what might be called a map of the distribution of human animals over time. For any individual i, I shall call this 'i's human-animal-identity set', abbreviated as i's AIS.

The less extreme and more congenial proposal can be stated thus: if an individual is to be credited with possession of the concept of a person, then for any negative personal-identity judgment with the content 'Person 1 at place p_1 and time t_1 is not identical with person 2 at p_2 and t_2,' that the individual accepts, the correponding negative human-animal-identity judgment with the content 'Animal 1 at p_1 and t_1 is not identical with animal 2 at p_2 at t_2,' must also be accepted. I shall call this claim the PIS-AIS link.

My proposal does not rule out or create difficulties for belief in disembodied persons surviving into an afterlife or in nonhuman persons, say dolphins, angels, or robots, for it does not require as part of the concept of a person that the individual accepts a positive judgment about human-animal identity for every accepted positive judgment about personal identity.

Strong evidence in favor of the link emerges when we reflect on our attitude toward people in whose thought the link is broken. Imagine, first, a child at the stage of acquiring an understanding of what a person is. Suppose that are trying to explain to the child who a particular *person p* is. We point to the person and tell the child that this is p. We allow the child to watch p, and then we test for an understanding of 'p'. If it becomes clear that the child accepts that the human animal pointed at during the naming was at a certain place but does not accept that p was there, then, whatever brain-damaging disasters have struck p, we would take that evidence as a conclusive indication that the child had failed to understand what was being explained. Reflection on such teaching cases is particularly illuminating because they indicate what we take to be essential to an understanding of persons.

Consider next the following case. Suppose that a jury delivers the verdict that a certain person *p* did not commit crime *c* while happily agreeing when questioned that the evidence certainly established that the human animal *a*, that is, the animal whom *p* would be identical with if animalism were true, most certainly was at the scene of the crime and executed the actions constituting *c*. The jury would not be allowed to render its verdict intelligible by remarking that they had simply revised the link between personal identity and human-animal identity. This would strike people as nonsensical.

In these cases there is evidence that the PIS-AIS link is a constitutive and unrevisable component in our thought about persons. This is, of course, inconclusive, and anyone inclined to accept the existence of a priori psychological requirements of the kind ruled out by the link will look for ways to reject it. So one question is whether there is a plausible way to reject the link. Another question is whether there is evidence against the link.

There might be evidence that we allow some loosening of the link. One possible example is our attitude toward the relatives of an individual who is terminally ill and mentally malfunctioning but still alive when they speak of the person they loved as already gone, as no longer there. We do not take this way of speaking as a manifestation of a misunderstanding of the concept of a person. However, this may be because the way of speaking is grafted onto total acceptance of the link for all practical purposes (for example, when answering questions as to the whereabouts of the person in the hospital) and also as far as their own attitude toward others is concerned. How would they react to a hospital official who calmly spoke in their way? On balance, then, this example is not a counterexample to the link.

7   A Hybrid Account

Is there a plausible way to reject the link thesis? There are, obviously, many different alternatives, but a broad division into two ways seems possible. The extreme way to reject it is to deny that the inferential link has any constitutive role at all in the elucidation of the concept of a person. Insofar as people tend cognitively to respect such a link, this approach sees it as resting on the belief, in principle revisable, that certain continuities happen, in the normal case, to go along with being a human animal. This option (one version of which is the classical psychological and causal account of personal identity) requires investigation as a general characterization of the concept of a person, but here I wish to be less ambitious and to describe and comment on the less extreme option. This option is to hold that grasping the concept of a person requires respecting the inferential link but subject to a certain condition. The structure of the proposal is that so long as s does not believe the (human) animal is c, then the link must hold. Condition c might be 'is an animal sustaining a subject with "philosophical amnesia" ' or 'is an animal sustaining experiences disunified to degree d' (something requiring further specification).[15]

On this view, which might be called the hybrid account, the objections to (A) reflect attempts to articulate by some a priori method the content of c and to state its consequences. As has been seen, some intuitions indicate a diachronic psychological value for c, whereas others indicate a synchronic psychological condition. A correct account might be complex and involve both.

8   Some Difficulties

This model of the concept of a person, which fixes our subject matter, faces some problems, I wish to suggest. I am not suggesting that they are insuperable, but I believe that they represent difficulties for anyone who is sympathetic to the criticisms of animalism described in this paper and who conceives of their validity as flowing from the present conceptual model.

The first problem lies in the assumption that the concept of a person with this structure is a shared and acquired one. What plausible account is there as to how such a concept is acquired? What is there in the presumably more or less universal experience of people that would indicate to the individual acquiring the concept that it incorporates various restrictions and that the restrictions have the particular content they are supposed to have? What enables the concept acquirer to home in on the particular restrictions favored by the theorist? Any model of the concept of a person needs to be integrated with a plausible account of its acquisition, and it is not at all obvious how to do this.

Second, it is hard to see how condition c can fulfill two prima facie plausible demands on the elucidation of the central concept. These two demands are that the concept of a person marks out an important class and that it marks out a fairly precise class. The dilemma is that if c is made precise, then it threatens to be impossible to explain why the difference between animals that satisfy c and those that do not is important. An example of this dilemma would be if, following Shoemaker's intuition, it was suggested that c amounts to having undergone a brain zap. To not fall under c would then merely require the retention of a single mental state. Why, though, does that make a significant difference? Compare these cases.

Person p_1 undergoes a brain zap and then, according to the theory, a new person with a novel psychology emerges in that animal body. Person p_2 undergoes an almost total brain zap, but a single state escapes being zapped, and there then emerges in that animal body a virtually novel psychology, but not, according to the theory, a new person. What could possibly be the rationale for distinguishing these cases? To avoid this difficulty by framing c in terms of 'enough' or 'a fair amount of' psychological features, in order to confer some weight on the condition, leaves a theory that either is inherently and unacceptably vague or radically misrepresents the character of the basic concept of a person as itself vague. Again, this problem is not decisive.

Finally, it should not be forgotten—as emerged, I hope, in my earlier discussion—that there simply are no particularly salient candidates for c.

9   Conclusion

I have argued that one style of objection to the animalist account of how a person relates to his or her body assumes that there are a priori psychological principles in relation to persons that may fail to be fulfilled by intact, living human animals. Although such principles are, or can be made to appear, plausible, closer inspection reveals they are not in fact well supported. To determine their real status, we need to investigate and adjudicate between different conceptions of the concept of a person that defines our topic. It remains possible that the correct analysis of that concept will discredit such principles.

Acknowledgments

I am very grateful to Tony Marcel and Naomi Eilan for comments on this paper and to the editors for their patience in waiting for it. I am also grateful to David Mackie for comments and discussion, and to Naci Mehmet and Michael Martin for earlier discussion.

Notes

1. See Wiggins 1980, chap. 6; Wiggins 1987; Wollheim 1984, chap. 1; Ayers 1991, chap. 25. I have discussed some proposals in Snowdon 1990. An important question facing this approach is what implications it has for the conclusions about the value of personal identity urged by Derek Parfit. On this, see Cassam 1993.

2. I have discussed this objection in Snowdon 1991.

3. Wittgenstein 1963, 101e.

4. Shoemaker 1984, 87. Shoemaker's actual view is that a total loss of memory need not amount to a "brain zap," since it might occur even though other psychological traits, such as personality and taste, remain. The claim he supports is, therefore, that there

must be some degree of psychological continuity within the body for it to remain the body of a single person, but not that any memories *must* be preserved. In discussing Shoemaker I will perhaps oversimplify his view, but only because I believe my criticisms would apply to the more complex account.

5. Wilkes 1988, 131. I find interesting Wilkes's discussion, in chapter 4, of multiple personality cases, and I hope to consider it elsewhere in the detail it deserves.

6. Mackie 1976, 194.

7. There is considerable unclarity about the content and point of the concept of a brain zap. Shoemaker describes it as requiring the removal of "all the effects" of past experience. But if a shock has given me white hair, need that be removed in a brain zap? Presumably what is intended is the removal of all *psychological* effects. What does this involve? Suppose that the ability to remember requires a memory store and a retrieval mechanism. What would a zap require? Would it be enough that the retrieval mechanism were destroyed? If so, there are psychologically describable effects of past experience still present, namely a store that would yield memories if certain mechanisms were restored. I cannot see why a zap need require the excision of the store if it cannot yield memories.

8. The argument against Shoemaker is not that (A) should be regarded as correct because it fits how such cases seem to us. It is rather that one cannot object to (A), on the basis of the example that Shoemaker cites, that (A) has implications that genuinely seem wrong.

9. Nagel 1979, 160.

10. Peacocke 1983, 160.

11. My very limited purpose in this discussion of Peacocke's principle has been to raise a doubt about it. Another worry about it is that it might have rather unwanted implications when applied to normal subjects. The principle employs the notion of token experiences considered, presumebly, as identical with, or realized by, token neural events. However, given the causal grounds for locating these events and details of the neural processes, maybe even in normal cases we need to postulate distinct but qualitatively indistinguishable experiences. Peacocke (1983, 177) claims that "in the normal case, one single experience is caused by the stimulation of both nostrils." How can we possibly know this? On the assumption that he is wrong, what would endorsement of the principle force us to say about most normal cases?

12. This argument amounts to a style of argument found in Ayers 1991 and Snowdon 1990, where the target is certain theories of personal identity, but applied here to multiple-subject accounts of split-brain cases.

13. Recall the remarkably incongruous tendency by writers about to argue against single-subject accounts to describe the preliminary data using the singular term 'the patient'. Who exactly, on their approach, is "*the* patient"?

14. The situation is very complex and hard to sort out. The objections to (A) have been grounded on assumptions about the requirements for the continuity of persons (or, more accurately, for the kinds of things we are) but also on the requirements for the unity of the a subject of experience. So there are two concepts involved. It is also very obscure what the role of the term 'person' is. These complexities have to be set aside here.

15. It is not clear whether any recent writers subscribe to this idea. It fits, to some extent, the account Wilkes (1988) develops.

References

Ayers, Michael. 1991. *Locke*, vol. 2. London: Routledge.

Cassam, Quassim. 1993. "Parfit on Persons." *Aristotelian Society Proceedings* 93:17–37.

Mackie, J. L. 1976. *Problems from Locke*. Oxford: Clarendon Press.

Nagel, Thomas. 1979. "Brain Bissection and the Unity of Consciousness." In his *Mortal Questions*. Cambridge: Cambridge University Press.

Peacocke, Christopher. 1983. *Sense and Content*. Oxford: Clarendon Press.

Shoemaker, Sydney. 1984. "Personal Identity—A Materialist Account." In *Personal Identity*, by Sydney Shoemaker and Richard Swinburne. Oxford: Blackwell.

Snowdon, P. F. 1990. "Persons, Animals and Ourselves." In *The Person and the Human Mind*, edited by Christopher Gill. Oxford: Clarendon Press.

Snowdon P. F. 1991. "Personal Identity and Brain Transplants." In *Human Beings*, edited by David Cockburn. Cambridge: Cambridge University Press.

Wiggins, David. 1980. *Sameness and Substance*. Oxford: Blackwell.

Wiggins, David. 1987. "The Person as Object of Science, as Subject of Experience, and as Locus of Value." In *Persons and Personality*, edited by A. Peacocke and G. Gillett. Oxford: Blackwell.

Wilkes, Kathleen. 1988. *Real People*. Oxford: Clarendon Press.

Wittgenstein, Ludwig. 1963. *Philosophical Investigations*. Oxford: Blackwell.

Wollheim, Richard. 1984. *The Thread of Life*. Cambridge: Cambridge University Press.

An Ecological Perspective on the Origins of Self

George Butterworth

1   The Ecological Approach to Self

Ecological psychology is concerned with the relationships between organisms and their environments. The ecological approach draws our attention not only to the dynamics of the relationship between the embodied self and physical reality, as when the baby acquires self-control over posture and motor skills, but also to the infant's relationships with other people, which situate her in social reality. Perceiving the relation of the body with the physical environment may inform about the properties of the bodily self and help in mastering motor skills. By the same token, perceiving the correspondence between self and other people may inform particularly about the interpersonal aspects of self.

   This paper addresses the origins of knowledge of the embodied self in human development. I will elaborate the thesis that self-perception constitutes the foundation for self-knowledge in early human development. My evidence will be drawn almost entirely from the first three months of life, a period of the utmost importance in evaluating the contribution of early perception to the origins of knowledge of the embodied self. Some traditional tasks in the development of self, such as recognition of the self in a mirror, often taken as evidence for the acquisition of a self concept at 14 months, will not be covered here because I have dealt with them elsewhere (Butterworth 1992a, 1992b). First, however, it will be necessary to make clear some of the basic theoretical concepts in ecological psychology.

   James Gibson, whose theory of perception will be adopted here, defined the ecological level of reality as follows: "Awareness of the persisting and changing environment (perception) is concurrent with the persisting and changing self (proprioception in my extended use of the term). This includes the body and its parts and all its activities from locomotion to thought, without any distinction between the activities called 'mental' and those called 'physical'. Oneself and one's body exist along with the environment, they are co-perceived" (1987a, 418).

Gibson's (1966) theory is that information about the environment, obtained through perceptual systems, is sufficient directly to inform the perceiver about her relationship with the world. The theory stands in contrast to more prevalent "indirect" theories of perception based on sensation, where the assumption is that sensations need to be embell-ished by inference and memory. Direct perception objectively specifies the persisting and changing properties of objects. Gibson's aim is to identify, within the dynamic flux of energy available to perceptual sys-tems, those patterns of stimulation that are particularly informative about the organism's relation to the world. As Michaels and Carello (1981) point out, direct perception means that information about both objects (including the self) and events in the environment, as they relate to behavior, is preserved in the energy patterns that impinge on percep-tual systems.

Gibson (1987b) also departs from traditional theories of propriocep-tion in explaining bodily self awareness. Sherrington (1906) distinguished between proprioception and exteroception. Proprioception is feedback that is specific to the activities of one's own body, whereas exteroception concerns the perception of the outside world. As elaborated by Gibson (1987b), proprioception is a general function, rather than a special sense, and it is normally a component of all perceptual systems. Sherrington's classic model of bodily sensation assumed that proprioceptive information was given internally by a kinesthetic sense mediated by muscle and joint receptors. Gibson extended the notion of proprioception to include ex-ternal feedback arising as a normal correlate of the exploratory activity of perceptual systems. Instead of kinesthesis being considered as a special sense, proprioception becomes a general, self-specifying aspect of the in-formation-seeking functions of perceptual systems. Proprioception is a mechanism of self-sensitivity common to all perceptual systems. Aware-ness of one's own movements can be obtained through vision and audi-tion, as well as through the muscles and joints. Just as a bat may fly using echolocation to guide it, feedback from the visual environment may help the infant gain control of posture and in this sense inform about the self.

In Gibson's terminology, the pole of the perceptual system that speci-fies the self is called propriospecific, whereas that which specifies objects and events in the environment is called exterospecific. Gibson (1966) ar-gued that perceptual systems are simultaneously proprioceptive and ex-teroceptive. Thus proprioception in Gibson's theory is a general aspect of the coperception of self and environment.

Neisser (1988) distinguished five kinds of self-knowledge, and they imply rather different developmental mechanisms:

1. *The ecological self*, which is directly perceived with respect to the physical environment
2. *The interpersonal self*, also directly perceived, which depends on emotional and other species-typical forms of communication
3. *The extended self*, which is based on memory and anticipation and implies a representation of self
4. *The private self*, which reflects knowledge that our conscious experiences are exclusively our own and also depends on representation
5. *The self concept*, defined as a theory of self based on sociocultural experience

This chapter will be concerned mainly with the first and second of Neisser's types of self knowledge, i.e., the level of direct awareness of self in relation to physical and social reality. Neisser's other levels (3, 4, 5) correspond more closely with self recognition, recall, and autobiographical memory, on which I will say little here.

Neisser (1988) lists the following characteristics of the ecological self:

• The self exists objectively. Many of its characteristics are specified by objective information that allows perception both of the location of the self and of ongoing interaction with the environment.
• Much of the information is kinetic. It consists of structures that change or remain invariant over time and that are available to several perceptual systems at once.
• The ecological self is veridically perceived from infancy, but self-perception may still develop and become more adequate with increasing skill.

The distinction between the self one is directly aware of and the remembered self corresponds broadly with Edelman's (1989) distinction, in early human development, between "primary" consciousness (based on perception) and "higher-order" consciousness or reflective self-awareness). According to Edelman, primary consciousness is "the state of being mentally aware of things in the world—of having mental images in the present. . . . Higher-order consciousness includes recognition by a thinking subject of his or her own acts or affections. It embodies a model of the personal and of the past, future, and present" (1989). In essence, then, the distinction between primary and higher-order self consciousness is similar to that between consciousness of self as a (proprioceptive) product of perception and reflective self-consciousness as a product of representation memory and thought.

2   Some Implications of the Ecological Approach to the Origins of Self

The newborn baby was traditionally considered to be undifferentiated from the world in her own self-awareness. One of the fundamental reasons for the assumption of profound adualism between infant and environment is the difficulty traditional theories have in explaining how the two-dimensional surface of the retina can give rise to perception of a three-dimensional space. Piaget (1954) actually spoke of the world of the newborn as comprising two-dimensional tableaux. On his theory, vision only slowly acquires depth through sensorimotor coordination with touch and through the metric provided by the infant's own actions. Muscular kinesthesis forms a primary space against which vision is calibrated. In Piaget's theory (and other major theories, such as the Freudian account), development proceeds from total lack of differentiation, to proximal sensitivity (awareness of the kinesthetic qualities of the infant's own body) and finally to distal spatial sensitivity as the infant gradually constructs planes of depth through her own activities. By about 18 months, largely as a result of the onset of independent locomotion, the infant becomes aware of herself as a totality, contained within an encompassing space. The assumption that there can be no visual space perception at birth means that there can be no distance between the infant and the world, and hence profound adualism is a necessary theoretical consequence widely assumed to characterize early experience.

An alternative view, "natural dualism," was advocated by the Scottish philosopher Thomas Reid. Natural dualism has been defined as "an immediate knowledge by mind of an object different from any modification of its own. . . . The ego and the non-ego are thus given in an original synthesis, as conjoined in the unity of knowledge and in an original antithesis, as opposed in the contrariety of existence" (Baldwin 1901). In logic, contrariety is defined as the relationship between two contraries; in everyday use it refers to an opposition between one thing and another.

Contemporary research strongly favors natural dualism over the assumption of an initial adualism in early infant experience. Infants demonstrate at least a rudimentary differentiation between self and the physical environment, as evidenced, for example, by neonates' reaching toward a visual target (Von Hofsten 1989), and between self and the social environment, as evidenced by neonates' imitating (Meltzoff and Moore 1977). They also show previously unsuspected intersensory coordinations, e.g., between seeing and hearing (Castillo and Butterworth 1981), and between vision and touch (Meltzoff and Borton 1979), to cite just a few examples (see Butterworth 1989a for a much longer list of the visuospatial abilities of very young infants).

The lack of obvious skill in most newborn's behavior may actually give a misleading picture of the true state of motor organization, since the developmental transition from prenatal to postnatal life, with resulting

changes in gravity and body weight, may place many constraints on behavior. Real-time ultrasonic scanning of the infant before birth has given
evidence for at least fifteen different movement patterns in the fetus of 15
weeks (DeVries, Visser, and Prechtl 1984). Among the movement patterns
that can be observed are isolated arm and leg movements, movements of
the hand to the mouth, head retroflexion and antiflexion, yawning and
stretching of the arms, rotation around the sagittal or transverse axis by
means of stepping movements, and conjugate lateral eye movements (18
weeks). Movement is differentiated from an early gestational age with a
variety of postures, movement synergies, and sequences of activity. In
other words, the fetus behaves as an organized totality, and this is rather
different from what we have been led to believe from the classical descriptions of fetal and newborn behaviors as restricted to a small set of discrete
reflexes.

With video technology it is now possible to closely study behavior in
the newborn, and this too gives a rather different picture. For example,
about 15 percent of the spontaneous arm movements of the awake, alert
newborn infant result in the hand contacting the mouth. Butterworth and
Hopkins (1988) observed that the newborn, lying with the head to the
right side, opens the mouth and then moves the ipsilateral hand so that the
hand touches the mouth. The mouth "anticipates" the arrival of the hand,
which, incidentally, can find its way to the mouth by a variety of trajecto-
ries and without visual guidance. If the hand misses the mouth but lands in
the perioral region, it is then very likely to move directly to the mouth.
The action system has basic intentionality; it is not merely a mechanical
reflex. Hand and mouth function in the newborn as a well organized system, which may have benefited from practice in utero (Butterworth
1989b). Kravitz, Goldenberg, and Neyhus (1978) have described a consistent order of emergence of movements of the hand to the face in the
hours after birth, starting with movements to the mouth (167 minutes after birth), then the face (192 minutes), the head (380 minutes), the ears
(469 minutes), the nose (598 minutes), and the eyes (1491 minutes) (me-
dian values). Observations such as these suggest a particularly early onset
of tactile self-exploration and some differentiation of the parts of the face.

Martin and Clark (1982) studied the phenomenon, noted in neonate
nurseries, that babies often cry when they hear another baby crying. Calm
or crying babies, of average age of less than 30 hours, heard a tape recording of themselves or another newborn baby crying. Babies who were calm
at the start of the test cried more if they heard a tape recording of another
baby cry than if they heard themselves cry, whereas babies who were
crying at the start cried less if they heard themselves than if they heard

another baby. The baby is somehow able to recognize its own vocalizations and discriminate them from those of another baby. At least three mechanisms might allow this discrimination. (1) Babies may recognize the acoustics of their own crying. They may have previously heard themselves crying and match new instances to their memory. However, this seems unlikely, since they are so young as to have little experience of hearing their own cries. (2) They may be sensitive to the dynamics of their own vocaltract movements and recognize these patterns as self-specific. This seems possible, but it is only a partial explanation. (3) They may be sensitive to the amodal equivalence of patterning between the output of their own vocalization and the ensuing auditory feedback. That is, auditory specification of self and discrimination of their own cries from those of others may be a result of the congruence in patterning between the motor and auditory forms of proprioceptive feedback, which could be sufficient to specify the "self same" source for the sound.

Bahrick and Watson (1985) carried out an ingenious study that demonstrated that babies of 4 months perceive visual and kinesthetic feedback relating to their own limbs as emanating from the same source. Infants watched the spontaneous kicking movements of their legs on a video monitor while the legs themselves were hidden from view. Each baby was given a choice of viewing her own legs moving contingently or noncontingently on her kicking, or another infant's legs kicking noncontingently. Infants preferred to look at the live display showing their own contingent leg movements. Thus infants feel and see their leg movements as belonging together; felt and seen movements are perceived as aspects of the same bodily activity.

Stern (1985) offers a particularly interesting example of "belongingness" in a case of Siamese twins aged 3 months and 3 weeks. Twins Alice and Betty were joined on their ventral surface, from the sternum down to just below the umbilicus. Otherwise, they shared no organs, had separate nervous sytems, and almost totally separate blood supplies. Stern noticed that Alice would often suck Betty's fingers and vice versa. He compared the resistance of each twin, when sucking her own or the twin's fingers, to having the hand pulled out of her mouth. When the twin was sucking her own hand, her arm showed resistance to being pulled out but her head did not strain forward after the retreating hand. When Alice's hand was being sucked by Betty, Betty's arm showed no resistance as the hand was gently pulled from her mouth, but Betty's head did strain forward. When sucking was interrupted, the intention to maintain sucking of the infant's own hand was effected by attempting to bring the arm back to the mouth, whereas sucking the other twin's hand was maintained by moving the mouth and head. There was no confusion about which fingers belonged to whom. Stern argues that the two cases (sucking self versus sucking non-self) differ crucially in terms of the infants' volitional control of arm movement and in terms of the predictable consequences of executing the motor plan to suck. This provides sufficient invariant information for the twins to distinguish self from other.

Observations such as these suggest that there is tactile, auditory, and kinesthetic identity of the bodily self early in life. This in turn may provide evidence for the existence of some coordinating body schema or schemas that ensure that the infant behaves as an organized totality both in relation to the self and the nonself.

3   Visual Proprioception and Posture

The assumption that development begins from profound adualism ultimately rests on the assertion that the infant cannot tell the difference between sensory stimulation that is independent of her own activity and sensory feedback that is contingent on her own activity. According to Piaget (1954), there is no information in the structure of sensory stimulation to allow response-contingent feedback to be differentiated from independent sensory data. The essential problem for the baby is to differentiate a *change of place* from a *change of state* of an object, for this amounts to perceiving the difference between position changes that are reversible by a movement of the observer (change of place of a stable object) and those that are not (change of state of an object). Making this discrimination requires a distinction between observer and observed and monitoring object (or self) movement with respect to an external stable spatial framework.

Gibson (1966) coined the term 'visual proprioception' to describe the kinesthetic functions of vision. At any observation point a continuous flow of optical information accompanies movement of the observer. Whether an observer actively moves or is passively moved through a stable visual environment, there arises a systematic flow of patterned optical information at the retina. In the case of forward locomotion, the optical texture flows outward from a stationary central point, which gives the direction in which the observer is moving. Under normal conditions, where the ground and surroundings are stable, such a flow pattern can only arise when the observer is moving. Hence, within the coperception of self and environment, it is sufficient to specify the distinction between self and the world and thus to form one of the foundations for the ecological self.

Visual proprioception offers a critical test for traditional accounts, since the theory states that the optic-flow field simultaneously provides differentiated information both for the movements of the observer and for the stability of the perceived environment, with no suggestion of adualistic confusion. The first demonstration that infants use visual proprioception to monitor their posture was made by Lee and Aronson (1974). Infants who had recently learned to stand were tested inside a moving room comprising three walls and a ceiling suspended just above the ground. The infants stood facing the interior end wall of the room and the whole room, except the floor, was moved so the end wall slowly approached or receded (and the side walls moved in the periphery). Babies compensated for a nonexistent loss of balance and they swayed, staggered, or fell in a direction appropriate to compensating for visually specified instabilty. For example, when the end-wall receded, thus providing information consistent with backward instability, infants compensated and fell forward.

This rather spectacular demonstration certainly showed that babies are susceptible to visual proprioception, but it remained ambiguous with respect to the origins of the proprioceptive functions of vision. It is possible that locomotion by crawling or walking might have given visual feedback its informative function. This possibility was examined in a series of studies with younger babies by Butterworth and Hicks (1977), Butterworth and Cicchetti (1978), and Pope (reviewed in Butterworth and Pope 1983). These studies showed that babies too young to walk or crawl nevertheless monitor the stability of the standing posture, the sitting posture, and even of head control at 2 months, using visual proprioceptive feedback. Older babies lose balance in the moving room when standing or sitting. Babies as young as 2 months, when they can just balance their heads, will sway their heads in compensation for visually specified instability when they are tested in the moving room. Further evidence against the adualism of experience in newborns has been obtained by Jouen (1990). Infants were seated in a chair that could be made to move forward, inside a moving room, so vestibular and visual information for passive movement were concordant or discrepant. Forward acceleration through stationary visual space so that visual and vestibular information were congruent did not result in postural compensation, as measured by the backward pressure exerted by the infant's head on a pressure transducer. However, visual feedback specifying acceleration through visual space without vestibular information did result in postural compensation.

For good measure, we recently tested 24-hour-old chicks in a moving room and showed that they too monitor their posture with respect to the stability of the visual surround (Butterworth and Henty 1991). Thus altricial species, like human infants, and a precocial species, like the early locomoting chicks, both make use of the visual flow field in similar ways in the early control of posture. It seems very likely that visual proprioception comprises an innate feedback loop that informs the organism of its relation with the natural environment.

What are the implications for the traditional concept of adualism? The infant's involuntary compensation for the misleading optic-flow field can be thought of as an attempt to reverse a perceived *change of place* of its own body in order to maintain postural stability. By inverting the normal conditions of the ecology and inducing a *change of state* of the surround, moving-room studies reveal that the baby normally does make the distinction between a change of place and a change of state. There is no question of adualistic confusion: the young infants *invariably* perceive the visual information as signifying a change of place of their own body.

In what sense does visual proprioception imply a form of self awareness? Neisser (1988) argues that the ecological self does imply a form of unreflective consciousness but it is not what is ordinarily termed 'self-consciousness' since the ecological self is not an object of reflective thought. Nevertheless, the ecological self does amount to an irreducible, basic form of self awareness. Later in development, at about 14 months, one can observe the ability of the baby to partially overrule discrepant optic-flow patterns as it turns to see what made the room move (Butterworth and Cichetti 1978). This later behavior does seem to reflect the kind of explicit self-consciousness normally implied by the term, where the baby shows that the event is understood to have occurred outside her own agency.

Even so, the difference between self awareness and self consciousness is only a matter of degree. Adults in an unfamiliar posture can easily be unbalanced in the face of discrepant visual feedback, and they presumably have elaborated self concepts (Lee and Lishman 1975). This implies that in addition to *specification* of self through visual proprioception, there arises a form of self *knowledge* that can, at least in part, overrule what is specified visually under nonecological conditions. Normally, these different aspects of self awareness are congruent, and there is no reason to suppose that we ever grow out of relying on ecological specification of self. The developmental transition may be from optical specification of agency in the normal ecology to an autonomous self-consciousness that comprehends its own agency over the optic-flow field. Self specification remains embedded in the latter type of self knowledge.

Visual proprioception may have a particularly important part to play in the acquisition of skills in infancy. Infants gain control over the posture of the head by about 3 months, over sitting by about 8 months, and over standing toward the end of the first year. The assistance of visual proprioception may serve to stabilize involuntary postural sway. Since the ground is normally an extremely stable external referent, visual proprioception might serve to calibrate other kinesthetic systems. In developing organisms there is inherent variability introduced by growth, so a stable external referent may serve a particularly important ongoing calibrating function.

Posture, perception, and action are closely linked phenomena, with control of posture often acting as the rate-limiting factor in development. Acquiring control over head and trunk enables new skills to be acquired, such as reaching and grasping. Such skills themselves depend on establishing a "platform" of postural stability, and this has implications for the infant's developing bodily self awareness (Rochat and Bullinger 1993). The onset of independent locomotion also depends on good prior control of static postures. Each of these motor skills has a prolonged period of development, and it is not surprising that infants with visual impairments are also delayed in postural control and the onset of locomotion (Fraiberg 1977). Postural factors also enter into the social relationships between the infant and the adult, for example, as the baby moulds herself to the body of the mother in feeding (Rochat and Bullinger 1993) or as the slightly older baby offers herself to the mother, communicating her desire to be picked up (Fogel 1993). Perhaps the main implication for the origins of self is that in learning skilled, goal-directed activity, the infant can discover more about the agency of self. As Neisser puts it, "We perceive as we act and that we act; often, our own actions constitute the very characteristics of the ecological self that we are simultaneously perceiving" (1988, 40).

4   Direct Perception and the Interpersonal Self

There is no need for a hard and fast distinction between direct perception of physical and social objects. Social objects are physical objects, albeit with additional qualities. Some aspects of direct perception, such as detecting the information that specifies the elasticity or rigidity of objects, may have primary application in social perception (Walker et al. 1980). Fogel (1993) lists 14 different ways in which the dynamics of social interaction may be based on a rather small number of variant and invariant properties of perceptual information (table 1)

Evidence of interpersonal perception in infancy is especially relevant to the early origins of self. Among the most challenging research of recent years has been the demonstration of neonatal imitation. Babies just a few minutes old have been shown to imitate tongue protrusion, mouth opening, lip pursing, sequential finger movements, blinking, vocalization of vowel sounds, and emotional expressions (Maratos 1973, Meltzoff and Moore 1977, Field et al. 1982, Kugiumutzakis 1985, Reissland 1988). Imitation is not a reflex, since newborns observe the model for several seconds and

Table 1
Varieties of Perceptual Information Available to Support Social Interaction

Invariant	Information	Action
Distance displacement, expansion and contraction, increasing and decreasing intensity	1. Expansion from a point and magnification or increasing of intensity 2. Contraction toward a point and minification or diminishing of intensity 3. Maintaining constancy in size of elements or intensity	1. Approaching a partner, becoming louder, surging, crescendo, explosive 2. Avoiding, leaving or withdrawing, fading away, trailing off, becoming softer 3. Maintaining a constant distance, leveling off, framing
Lateral displacement and rotation, movement against a background	1. Deletion of background texture on one side of an object, and addition of texture on the other side 2. Shearing of texture against a constant background	1. Partner's body moves across perceptual field, hiding and revealing 2. Turning toward or away, rubbing
Elasticity and rigidity, shape and surface deformation	1. Deformation of shape 2. Deformation of surface 3. Rigidity of form	1. Changes in body posture, stance, gait 2. Changes in facial expression, dimpling, wounds, swelling, muscle contractions and flexions, changes in flow 3. Immobility, stiffness, insensitivity, impassivity
Dissolution and emergence of form	1. Dissolution of perceptual texture 2. Emergence of perceptual texture	1. Disappearance, silence pausing, leave taking, ending a topic 2. Appearance, action following pause, greeting, growth, eruption, aggregation, beginning a new topic
Color and texture	1. Changes in color 2. Changes in texture	1. Blushing, tanning, becoming pale, reddening (anger, exertion) 2. Wrinkles, creasing of skin
Frequency and regularity	1. Changes in spatial density or temporal frequency 2. Changes in regularity of time or space between events	1. Number of textural elements, beats (claps, head nods, vocal sounds), pitch of voice, synchrony in time 2. Rhythms, regularity vs. irregularity of time between beats or points, uniform vs. nonuniform distribution of spatial elements

Note: After Fogel 1993.

there is evident effort and progressive approximation to the model. Imitation in the newborn was called "participation" by Baldwin (1901), perhaps to emphasize the species recognition that it seems to imply. Such an ability certainly provides strong evidence for awareness of the similarity between the self and another person.

Newborn infants imitate the dynamics (not the statics) of the acts they observe. Vynter (1986) showed that they need to see the act in progress in order to imitate it; they will not imitate if they merely observe a static protruded tongue. Toward the end of the first year of life, however, it is sufficient for the infant to see the end state (e.g., the tongue protruded) in order to imitate it. That is, one-year-old infants can reproduce the dynamics of the movement given only the static end state. Newborn imitation also occurs only within a relatively short reaction time, whereas Meltzoff (1988) has recently shown that by 8 months babies are capable of deferred imitation over several days. By 1 year of age imitation can also take on symbolic properties; it is no longer merely literal, as in the neonate. Piaget (1962) gave the example of his daughter's attempting to imitate the modus operandi of the sliding container of a matchbox by protruding her tongue in and out, in an attempt to understand how the container could be opened to retrieve an attractive gold chain from the matchbox. In this example, tongue protrusion bears a rather metaphorical relationship to the object being imitated. Neonatal imitation is thus the first, literal level of a developing system of imitation that comes to have the capacity for deferred and symbolic responses toward the end of the first year of life.

How is neonatal imitation possible, especially when it involves parts of the body the infant cannot see, and second, why do babies imitate at all? Meltzoff and Borton (1979) illustrate a possible perceptual basis for imitation in their studies of intersensory perception in babies aged 1 month. They have shown that babies can transfer information from oral touch to vision. In their study, infants first suck a smooth or knobbly dummy without seeing it when it is inserted into their mouth. The dummy is removed, and they are then presented with two large models of the dummies on either side of the visual field. Babies prefer to look at the model dummy of the same shape and texture as the one they previously had been sucking. This demonstrates that they register a correspondence between vision and oral touch with respect to either the form or possibly the texture of the dummy. At an abstract level babies perceive the equivalence of information between vision and oral touch. This demonstration helps to explain the link between visual and motor systems in the imitation of tongue protrusion, where visual perception of the motion of another's tongue becomes equated with an action of one's own tongue.

Kuhl and Meltzoff (1982) have also shown that babies at 3 months can detect the correspondence between lip movements and speech sounds. Babies prefer to look at whichever of two videorecorded speaking faces corresponds with the sound track played between the televised displays. The face mouthing "ah ah ah" is preferred when the sound track corresponds with it, whereas the face on the other side, mouthing "ba ba ba," is preferred when that sound track is played. The implication is that imitation may assist the infant to read the lips and voice of the interloqutor and assist in communication and the earliest aspects of language acquisition.

Neonatal imitation is thus based on the mechanisms of perception. The information available to the infant about another person's actions is meaningful to the infant in terms of her own capacity for action. As to why infants imitate, Kugiumutzakis (1985) draws on evidence from neonatal preferences for voice sounds, and other aspects of their sensitivity to sound and affective tone, to infer that imitation reflects an innate motive for communication. He argues that newborns show an "innate intersubjectivity" and that they distinguish between self and others from the outset. Kugiumutzakis suggests that imitation is not a reflex act that lacks volition, since imitation is clearly selective and effortful. The variability and goal-seeking character of infants' responses suggest protointentional acts, which imply some conscious awareness of goals. He also argues that their responses are true heteroimitation, i.e., imitation of another person and not simply the cyclic repetition of stereotyped activity.

The importance of imitation for the origins of self is that consciousness of mutual human relations provides the most direct feedback about one's own personhood. MacMurray put it as follows: "Complete objectivity depends on our being objectively related, in action as well as in reflection, to that in the world which is capable of calling into play all the capacities of consciousness at once. It is only the personal aspect of the world that can do this" (1933, 134). Baldwin agreed that imitation plays a central role in the development of self-knowledge: "My sense of myself grows by my imitation of you and my sense of yourself grows in terms of myself" (1913, 185).

While the evidence on neonatal imitation supports the view that infants do recognize the correspondence between aspects their own bodily self and those of other people, this is a necessary but not a sufficient condition for an interpersonal self. Neisser (1988) defines the interpersonal self as the self engaged in immediate, unreflective social interaction with another person. He argues that the information essential for the interpersonal self comes into existence only when people are engaged in social interaction. When interpersonal behaviors become synchronized, there arises a mutuality of experience (or intersubjectivity) that is confirmed by reciprocal gestures, emotions, and expressions by the partner. The interpersonal aspect of self is brought into existence through the information created by these early forms of communication.

Evidence for very finely attuned behavior, and for the sharing of affect, between 2-month-old infants and their mothers has been obtained by Murray and Trevarthen (1985). They have studied the mutual coregulation of activity in mother-infant pairs, the fine synchrony of movements, the vocalizations and expressions of pleasure as the behaviors of partners that form an indissociable whole. Stern (1985) has described a similar process, which he calls "affect attunement," whereby the mother matches the infant's feelings with her own. If the baby is expressing joy, the mother does so too, perhaps by a different form of nonverbal expression but in a manner precisely synchronized with the infant's emotional expression.

Stern argues that through experiences such as these, the baby comes to be aware of the variants and invariants of the emotional relationship with the partner and of the organization and manifestation of each species-typical form of emotional expression. The emotions form an invariant constellation of feeling qualities experienced as belonging to the self, while interaction with others is the eliciting condition for such self-specifying experience.

Stern also speaks of "vitality effects," which are the little studied qualitative aspects of experience, or forms of feeling, that accompany vital processes of life. A vocabulary of dynamic terms such as 'fading away,' 'explosive,' 'rush' may be used to describe such vitality effects as occur in the experiences of falling asleep, the perception of sudden movements, or a rush of joy. Vitality effects are feelings, but they exist over and above the more generally recognized categorical emotions (e.g., anger, joy). Vitality effects, both from within and in social interaction with others, are an inherent aspect of the expressiveness of behavior. Stern suggests that the baby soon perceives the similarity between the dynamics of otherwise different behaviors. One example he offers is of the shared activation "contours" of the soothing behaviors of the mother expressed in both sound and actions. Stern says that perceiving the common vitality effects inherent in diverse experiences also contributes to the emergent sense of self. This occurs both through the detection of common aspects of diverse intrapersonal experiences and as a continuous aspect of the behaviours of significant others in affect attunment, that is, synchronization of interpersonal behavior that draws the baby's attention to the correspondence between self and other. As Michotte (1953) once put it, such interpersonal situations correspond to "feeling what the other is doing . . . while I remain myself. I have the impression of feeling what is happening internally in the other person" (Michotte 1953).

5   Direct Perception and the Core Sense of Self

These various pieces of evidence may now be drawn together to give an account of the origins of self in infancy. One possibility is to follow Stern (1985), who has argued that a core sense of self is given by direct perception. This core sense of self, emerging over the first six months, comprises four components:

Self-agency, the sense of the authorship of ones actions
Self-coherence, the sense of being a physical whole with boundaries
Self-affectivity, experiencing affect correlated with other experiences of self
Self-history, having the sense of enduring by noting the regularities in the flow of events

In Stern's view, the core sense of self is an experiential integration of these four invariant aspects of self-experience into a social, subjective perspective. Stern suggests that volition may be the most fundamental invariant in a core sense of self. To the extent that acquisition of skilled action is accompanied by the sense of volition, by proprioceptive feedback, and by predictable consequences, the infant gains information about the authorship of her own activity. Perceptual systems provide the means to identify the consistent aspects (invariants) of experience that eventually give rise to the remembered self. The core self is neither a cognitive construct, nor a concept of self, nor linguistic or even self knowledge. It is the foundation, in perception, action, and emotion, for the more elaborated aspects of self that are yet to be developed.

Fogel (1993) agrees that there may be a core sense of self, but he suggests that the self can never be defined independently of a context. He suggests that Stern's core sense of self is still defined insufficiently in relational terms. Fogel says that a coherent core of self-related experience might be identified at the intersection of various sources of information for the self. But he suggests that the "self is the dialogic relationship between the point of observation, the rest of the body and the perceptual flow field in which the body is immersed" (1993, 143). The roots of the dialogic self, which give the distinction between the I and the me, lie in the coperception of self and the world and the coregulation of social encounters.

In self-directed exploratory action, for example, the existential self (the I) specifies through touch an aspect of the categorical self (the me). In social interaction, the dialogic aspect of self is particularly obvious. Fogel gives an example of a baby being pulled into the seated position by the mother. In this situation, the infant perceives the self as the relationship between proprioceptive forces produced under the baby's own volition and the forces produced by the mother, to which the infant submits. As Fogel insists, the self is defined not merely by the movement of the body to the upright position but also by one's own movement in combination with other circumstances. Each time the mother and baby engage in this routine, it will be slightly different and the forces deployed will vary, until eventually the baby sits unaided. The sense of self with respect to sitting eventually excludes the contribution made by the mother, but it still remains defined relative to the surface of support. Fogel argues that this process of self-awareness is dialogic in the sense that there will always be self-specific feedback, of different kinds, as the infant makes the effort to sit. Imitation too is dialogic, because it requires self-action to be carried out in relation to another's action. The self in imitation is initially perceived in relation to the other as an aspect of "embodied cognition"; only at the end of infancy does the dialogic self become an aspect of the work of the imagination. The dialogic self exists from the outset in the inherently relational information available to perception.

In conclusion, the ecological approach to perception has revealed many unsuspected aspects of the original abilities of babies. The evidence requires us now to reconsider other aspects of early development, previously thought to be independent of perception. This work has only recently begun. There is now emerging a view of the origins of self as both a process and a product of embodied perception. This advance offers a new foundation for theories of the development of higher-order forms of self consciousness. It seems likely, however, that the ecological, embodied self will remain as the core that situates the self in the world and acts as a personal frame of reference for cognitive, linguistic, and culturally defined aspects of self.

Note

1. It might be asked why these examples of visual proprioception are not merely unconscious, reflexive responses, which need not implicate any form of conscious "self," conceived of as an organized totality of bodily experience. One reply might be that visual proprioception, prior to the onset of independent locomotion, is consistent only with a theory which postulates "natural dualism" and "primary consciousness" as the original basis of experience. While it is true that even adults are not normally conscious of the optic flow, the optic flow is meaningful and serves to provide information that serves in the postural control of the body. The body is the object of conscious awareness in the proprioceptive arena. Such "continuous flow" control processes bear little relation to reflexes as classically conceived. A second reply might be to quote A. J. Ayer, who said "If one speaks of the construction of objects out of the flux of experience, it

is indeed natural to ask who does the constructing and then it would appear that whatever self is chosen for this role must stand outside the construction; it would be paradoxical to suppose that it constructed itself" (1968, 261). Such a self might be defined as an "implicitly" represented self, rather than as an "explicitly" represented self. Within the theory of direct perception, which denies the necessity for representation as the basis for perception, the perceived self is more likely to be defined as explicit but unreflective. That is, this early stage of self is an organized aspect of perception but there is not yet the capacity for thought. The developmental transition between these levels (perception to reflection) would be both a matter of degree (as far as the continuants of bodily experience are concerned) and a matter of qualitative change as new abilities and the capacity for representation emerge.

References

Ayer, A. J. 1968. *The Origins of Pragmatism*. London: Macmillan.

Bahrick, L., and J. S. Watson. 1985. "Detection of Intermodal Proprioceptive-Visual Contingency as a Potential Basis of Self-Perception in Infancy." *Developmental Psychology* 21, no. 6: 963–973.

Baldwin, J. M. 1901. *Dictionary of Philosophy and Psychology*, vol. 1. New York and London: Macmillan and Co.

Baldwin, J. M. 1913. *Social and Ethical Intepretations in Mental Development: A Study in Social Psychology*. 5th ed. New York: MacMillan.

Butterworth, G. E. 1989a. "Events and Encounters in Infant Perception." In *Infant Development*, ed. A. Slater and G. Bremner. Hove: Lawrence Erlbaum.

Butterworth, G. E. 1989b. "On U Shaped and Other Transitions in Sensori-Motor Development." In *Transition Mechanisms in Child Development*, ed. A. de Ribaupierre. Cambridge: Cambridge University Press.

Butterworth, G. E. 1992a. "Origins of Self Perception in Infancy." *Psychological Inquiry* 3, no. 2: 103–111. See also 10 peer commentaries, pp. 112–133.

Butterworth, G. E. 1992b. "Self Perception as a Foundation for Self Knowledge." *Psychological Inquiry* 3, no. 2: 134–136.

Butterworth, G. E., and D. Cicchetti. 1978. "Visual Calibration of Posture in Normal and Motor-Retarded Down's Syndrome Infants." *Perception* 7: 513–525.

Butterworth, G. E., and C. Henty. 1991. "Origins of the Proprioceptive Function of Vision: Visual Control of Posture in One-Day-Old Domestic Chicks." *Perception* 20: 381–386.

Butterworth, G. E., and L. Hicks. 1977. "Visual Proprioception and Postural Stability in Infancy: A Developmental Study." *Perception* 6: 255–262.

Butterworth, G. E., and B. Hopkins. 1988. "Hand-Mouth Coordination in the Newborn Human Infant." *British Journal of Developmental Psychology* 6: 303–314.

Butterworth, G. E., and M. Pope. 1983. "Les origines de la proprioception visuelle chez le nourisson." In *Le developpement dans la premiere annee*, ed. S. de Schonen. Presses Universitaires de France.

Castillo, M., and G. E. Butterworth. 1981. "Neonatal Localisation of a Sound in Visual Space." *Perception* 10:331–338.

DeVries, J. I. P., G. H. A. Visser, and H. F. R. Prechtl. 1984. "Fetal Motility in the First Half of Pregnancy." In *Continuity of Neural Function from Prenatal to Postnatal Life*, ed. H. F. R. Prechtl. London: Spastics International Medical Publications.

Edelman, G. M. 1989. *The Remembered Present*. New York: Basic Books.

Field, T. M., R. Woodson, R. Greenberg, and D. Cohen. 1982. "Discrimination and Imitation of Facial Expressions in Neonates." *Science* 218:179–181.

Fogel, A. 1993. *Developing through Relationships: Origins of Communication, Self, and Culture*. Hemel Hempstead: Harvester Press.

Fraiberg, S. 1977. *Insights from the Blind*. New York: Basic Books.

Gibson, J. J. 1966. *The Senses Considered as Perceptual Systems*. Boston: Houghton-Mifflin.

Gibson, J. J. 1987b. "The Uses of Proprioception and the Detection of Propriospecific Information." In *Reasons for Realism: Selected Essays of James J. Gibson*, ed. E. Reed and R. Jones. Hillsdale, N.J.: Erlbaum.

Gibson, J. J. 1987a. "A Note on What Exists at the Ecological Level of Reality." In *Reasons for Realism: Selected Essays of James J. Gibson*, ed. E. Reed and R. Jones. Hillsdale, N.J.: Erlbaum.

Jouen, F. 1990. "Early Visual-Vestibular Interactions and Postural Development." In *Sensory-Motor Organisation and Development in Infancy and Early Childhood*, ed. H. Bloch and B. I. Bertenthal. Dordrecht: Kluwer.

Kravitz, H., D. Goldenberg, and A. Neyhus. 1978. "Tactual Exploration by Normal Infants." *Developmental Medicine and Child Neurology* 20:720–726.

Kugiumutzakis, G. 1985. "The Origin, Development, and Function of Early Infant Imitation." Ph.D. thesis, Department of Psychology, University of Uppsala, Sweden.

Kuhl, P., and A. N. Meltzoff. 1982. "The Bimodal Perception of Speech in Infancy." *Science* 218:1138–1141.

Kuhl, P., and A. N. Meltzoff. 1986. "The Intermodal Representation of Speech in Infants." *Infant Behaviour and Development* 7:361–381.

Lee, D., and E. Aronson. 1974. "Visual Proprioceptive Control of Standing in Human Infants." *Perception and Psychophysics* 15:529–532.

Lee, D., and J. R. Lishman. 1975. "Visual Proprioceptive Control of Stance." *Journal of Human Movement Studies* 1:87–95.

MacMurray, S. 1933. *Interpreting the Universe*. London: Faber.

Maratos, O. 1973. "The Origin and Development of Imitation During the First Six Months of Life." Unpublished Ph.D. thesis, University of Geneva, Switzerland.

Martin, G. B., and R. D. Clark. 1982. "Distress Crying in Neonates: Species and Peer Specificity." *Developmental Psychology* 18:3–9.

Meltzoff, A., N. 1988. "Infant Imitation and Memory: Nine-Month-Olds in Immediate and Deferred Tests." *Child Development* 59:217–225.

Meltzoff, A. and R. W. Borton. 1979. "Intermodal Matching by Human Neonates." *Nature* 282:403–404.

Meltzoff. A. N., and M. K. Moore, 1977. "Imitation of Facial and Manual Gestures by Human Neonates." *Science* 198:75–78.

Michaels, C., and C. Carello. 1981. *Direct Perception.* New York: Appleton.

Michotte, A. 1953. "The Emotional Involvement of the Spectator in the Action Represented in a Film: Toward a Theory." Translated in G. Thines, A. Costall, and G. Butterworth, eds., *Michotte's Experimental Phenomenology of Perception.* Hillsdale, N.J.: Lawrence Erlbaum, 1991.

Murray, L., and C. Trevarthen. 1985. "Emotional Regulation of Interactions between Two-Month-Olds and Their Mothers." In *Social Perception in Infants,* ed. T. M. Field and N. A. Fox. Norwood, N.J.: Ablex.

Neisser, U. 1988. "Five Kinds of Self-Knowledge." *Philosophical Psychology* 1, no. 1: 35–59.

Piaget, J. 1954. *The Construction of Reality in the Child.* New York: Basic Books.

Piaget, J. 1962. *Play Dreams and Imitation in the Child.* Norton: New York.

Reissland, N. 1988. "Neonatal Imitation in the First Hour of Life: Observations in Rural Nepal." *Developmental Psychology* 24:464–469.

Rochat, P., and A. Bullinger. 1993. "Posture and Functional Action in Infancy." In *Francophone Perspectives on Structure and Process in Mental Development,* ed. A. Vyt, H. Bloch, and M. Bornstein. Hillsdale, N.J.: Lawrence Erlbaum.

Sherrington, C. S. 1906. "On the Proprioceptive System, Especially in Its Reflex Aspect." *Brain* 29:467–482.

Stern, D. 1985. "The Interpersonal World of the Infant." New York: Basic Books.

Von Hofsten, C. 1989. "Transition Mechanisms in Sensorimotor Development." In *Transition Mechanisms in Child Development,* ed. A. de Ribaupierre. Cambridge: Cambridge University Press.

Vynter, A. 1986. "The Role of Movement in Eliciting Early Imitation." *Child Development* 57:66–71.

Walker, A., C. J. Owsley, J. Megaw-Nyce, E. J. Gibson, and E. Bahrick. 1980. "Detection of Elasticity as an Invariant Property of Objects by Young Infants." *Perception* 9:713–718.

Objectivity, Causality, and Agency

Thomas Baldwin

How does perception relate to agency? The classical pragmatist thesis is that only an agent can perceive. I will interpret this as the claim that the ability to have perceptions of an objective world depends on the ability to perform bodily actions. This is a claim that one can approach from two points of view: the third-person point of view and the first-person point of view that we have of ourselves. From the third-person point of view, the claim is that one cannot suppose a being to enjoy perceptions of an objective world without incurring a commitment to accept that the being, whatever it is, is also capable of bodily action. The shift to the first-person point of view involves the application of this hypothesis to oneself, and acceptance of this application is already implied by acceptance of the original third-person hypothesis. But I think one can also regard the first-person hypothesis as asking for a rather different kind of argument. For where the third-person hypothesis implies the existence of a necessary connection between perception and action, without any special constraints on the considerations that can be introduced to support it, the adoption of a first-person point of view is standardly associated with an epistemological perspective that introduces the constraint that one should not appeal to facts that transcend subjective appearances. Whether this is really a coherent project is, of course, much disputed, but in this context it suggests the possibility of substantiating, within an account of the contents of perception and action, the necessary connection between perception and action that the third-person hypothesis posits "from the outside." This, at any rate, is how I will interpret the first-person hypothesis, and since the arguments I advance in support of both the third-person and the first-person suppositions are not just variants of each other, I will return at the end of this paper to the question of the relationship between the two lines of argument.

1 The Pragmatist Argument

First and rather briefly, the third-person issue: can one suppose that x enjoys objective perceptions (perceptions that represent to x objective features of x's environment) without supposing that x is an agent? I think not. The mediating concept to bring out the connection here is that of belief: on the one hand, a necessary feature of perceptions is that they provide grounds for beliefs; on the other hand, beliefs dispose to action. The first point here does not require the strong claim that perceptions just are beliefs, or even presumptive beliefs; it only requires the thesis that perception could not have objective representational content unless it were part of a cognitive system in which the contents of perception were treated as prima facie believable. The reason for this is that in assigning objective content to a perception, we think of it as a representation for the subject of features of its environment, and to think of it as such is precisely to think of the role of the perception in the subject's cognitive economy. Once one abstracts from this role, one is left with the conception of perceptions as just sensory states with qualities that are correlated with features of the environment that give rise to them. But from this kind of causal correlation alone one cannot get a conception of these sensory states as representations of these features for a subject. Without an acknowledgment of their potential cognitive role, they are as nonintentional, as contentless, as the rings on a tree whose width covaries with the type of weather endured by the tree.

The second stage in this argument concerned the connection between belief and agency, and the argument here largely continues the previous point. The argument goes as follows: To think of a being as having the belief that such and such requires one to think of the being as ready to act as if such and such. Beliefs considered in abstraction from action can only be individuated causally, and, quite apart from the difficulty in understanding how this is to apply to beliefs concerning the future, this causal individuation will not provide the basis for an intentional characterization of them. This can only come through the use the subject makes of them and must ultimately rest on their role in the causation of action. This is, of course, the claim of the pragmatist theory of belief, according to which the content of a belief can be defined in terms of its role in helping to bring about actions that would satisfy the subject's desires if the belief were true.[1] But just as there was no need before to interpret perceptions as beliefs, so there is no need here to subscribe to the full pragmatist theory, which, by itself, appears to provide an account of the content of belief that is altogether too extensional. To obtain a more satisfactory account, one needs, I think, to introduce both causal considerations and an account of the conceptual structure of belief, but these matters need not concern us here. For all that is required here is the fundamental insight of the pragmatists that beliefs are essentially states whose contents enter into the explanation of actions caused by them.

2   Objects as Causes

These two points together yield the desired conclusion: that one cannot co-
herently suppose that a being has perceptions of an objective world without
supposing that the being is capable of bodily action. One can then apply this
conclusion directly to oneself, but, as I indicated above, one can also argue
for this first-person thesis in a different way. The starting point here is the
abstract conception of oneself as a subject of experience, and the question
one can then put to oneself is, What does one need to assume about oneself
to legitimate the thought that one's experiences are experiences of an objective world. This is, of course, a starting point that is at least as old as
Descartes, and there are many responses to it, including a denial that the
starting point is coherent.[2] But I will set aside doubts on this last score so
that I can concentrate on the hypothesis that to know oneself to be a subject
of objective experience, one must experience oneself as an agent.

A useful introduction to this thesis, in the kind of dialectical situation with which I am here concerned, is provided by a writer who rejects
it: Gareth Evans. In his famous paper "Things without the Mind,"[3] Evans
explores the relationship between the objectivity of experience and the
spatiality of the objects of experience by considering the situation of an
abstract subject of auditory experience ("Hero") and asking what needs
to be made available to such a subject for him to conclude legitimately
that his experience is of spatially located sounds. At one point in his discussion Evans writes as follows:

> If the hypothetical theory is to follow ours at all closely, sounds would have to be
> *occupy* space, and not merely be located in it, so that the notions of force and im-
> penetrability would somehow have to have a place, and we may well wonder
> whether we can make sense of this without providing Hero with an impenetrable
> body and allowing him to be an agent in, and manipulator of, his world. But per-
> haps this is the wrong line to pursue.[4]

Despite Evans's dismissal, it is this line that I want to pursue here. Whereas
Evans raises this option in the context of his discussion of the Kantian theme
of the relationship between objectivity and space, I want to consider the
matter in a different context. For whether or not space is a necessary feature
of objective experience, the fact that some feature of experience is experienced as located in space is certainly not sufficient for its putative objectivity,
because such sensations as pains are experienced as located within the subject's body (or, in a few abnormal cases, in its immediate proximity), yet
pains are not themselves objective features of the subject's body, items whose
existence is independent of the subject's experience of them. But if one does

not rely on the spatiality of the objects of objective experience to provide a context for a discussion of the relationship between objectivity and agency, then some other point of entry is required. As my title implies, I suggest that considerations of causality provide one. My general line of argument will be (1) that to take oneself to have objective experience, one needs to accept that the objects of experience are among its causes, and (2) that only the experience of agency makes available to us the notorious idea of a necessary connection, which is an essential component of the concept of causality. Both these points obviously need considerable elaboration and defense.

There are, I think, two ways of arguing for the first point, concerning the dependence of objectivity on causality. One is suggested by Kant's argument in the second Analogy in *The Critique of Pure Reason* (1787). Kant has already argued (in the Transcendental Deduction) that the possibility of objective experience depends upon the "unity" of consciousness, by which he seems to mean the ability of a subject to refer his experiences to himself in a coherent way as experiences of an objective world. His next move (in the Schematism) is to maintain that for us, at least, this abstract unity of consciousness takes the form of a temporally ordered stream of experience. But, Kant argues in the second Analogy, time itself cannot be perceived, so the temporal ordering of experience requires some other basis, and Kant argues that this is provided by awareness of the causal order of the objects of experience. Hence, to take oneself to have objective experience, one must take oneself to have experience of objects whose causal relationships enable one to fix the temporal order of one's experiences. Thus, for Kant, objectivity depends essentially on awareness of causality. Admittedly, he seems to think of this causality as obtaining primarily between the objects of experience, but he seems equally committed to the existence of causal relations between objects and our experiences of them, since only thus can he hope to secure his thesis that "we must derive the *subjective succession* of apprehension from the *objective succession* of appearances."[5]

This argument is plainly questionable in many ways, but one can reinforce the latter part of it, concerning the link between time and causality, with the help of Mellor's views about time.[6] Suppose we take it, as seems reasonable, that the temporal unity of consciousness that Kant has in mind is a stream of consciousness within which McTaggart's A-series temporal concepts (the indexical concepts of the past, present, and future) are applicable.[7] We can now ask, in a Kantian spirit, what makes these A-series judgments possible, and we can introduce here Mellor's plausible thesis that these indexical A-series judgments draw on the nonindexical B-series temporal ordering of events as earlier than, or simultaneous with, one another. For changes in truth values of such A-series judgments as 'It is now raining' reflect the fact that their truth conditions are determined both by the state of the world and by the nonindexical temporal context of the judgments. Thus, without seeking to reduce the A-series concepts to the B-series ones, it is plausible to suppose that the A-series temporal order depends on the B-series order. And if we ask further what determines the direction of time, the direction from earlier to later, the obvious answer is causality: causes precede their effects. So, under this reconstruction, awareness of the A-series temporal order of experience depends on awareness of the B-series context of these experiences, and this in turn depends on awareness of the causal order of these experiences and other events, which is roughly where Kant's argument ends up. Admittedly, this still leaves unexamined the first part of Kant's argument, which concerned the connection between the possibility of objective experience and the temporal unity of consciousness, but this is not the occasion to discuss this claim which, though contentious, seems to me defensible.

Instead, I want to present a different, and rather less metaphysically demanding, line of argument for the thesis that the self-ascription of objective experience depends on recognition that the objects of experience are among their causes. This argument proceeds altogether more directly, starting from the conception of objective experience as experience of objects (or events) whose existence is independent of the experience of them. Now the naive phenomenology of perception, especially vision, may tempt us to think of this as altogether unproblematic. For the naive realist builds the objectivity of experience into the conception of the content of experience itself by thinking of experience as the "transparent" or "diaphanous" awareness of objects, so that experience is conceived of as a relationship with objects that present themselves to us just as they are.[8] But a moment's reflection reveals to us that this conception really is too naive: the contents of experience just do not cohere in a way that permits us to regard them all as objective qualities of objects independent of us. Hence, the objectivity of an experience cannot in general be something that is just given unproblematically within the content of the experience itself; some further feature that implies this objectivity needs to be introduced, and the causal thesis is that recognition of the causal dependence of an experience on its object provides this feature, so that the self-ascription of objective experience requires that experience should itself furnish a basis for the recognition of this causal dependence. The idea is that since experience in fact gets its objective relational structure from its causal relationship with those objects in the world that fit its apparent content, subjects who think of themselves as subjects of objective experience must have reason to think that their experiences are caused by their objects.

My claim, therefore, is that we can make sense of the objectivity of our own experiences only in the context of a folk psychology of perception that includes the causal thesis. It is obvious that anyone who accepts that the objects of their experience have a causal role in the genesis of their experience thereby treats their experience as objective; what needs more argument is the converse claim, that belief in objectivity requires acceptance of a causal role for the objects of experience. The reason this is so is that to divorce belief in the objectivity of one's experience from the causal thesis would be to hold that one's identification of the objects of experience does not contribute to one's understanding of why one's experience is as it is. But once the objects of perception are considered not to play any explanatory role in perception itself, we are thrown back to Malebranche's occasionalism or something similar, and, as Locke observed, our reason for belief in the objectivity of experience is then radically undermined.[9] For if, as the denial of any causal role to the objects of experience implies, one supposes that one's actual experience could have been just as it was even if its apparent objects had not existed at all, one makes it quite unclear why one is entitled to hold that the content of that experience provides any reason for supposing that things are in some respects as they appear to be. We have reason to take our perceptions to be objective only where we find that their supposed objects, combined with an understanding of our sense organs and situation, yield an explanation of the content of the perception itself. No deep understanding of sensory psychology is required here: only common sense folk psychology is assumed. But we manifest our awareness of this all the time in our investigative activities, for such activities are precisely attempts to arrange our situation so that the content of experience will show us how things are, because our situation, we believe, will yield experience whose content is explained by its being veridical.

This, then, completes the second line of argument for the thesis that objectivity implies causality, that by thinking of one's experiences as objective, one is committed to thinking of their objects are their causes, or at any rate as contributing to a causal understanding of the experience. This is, in turn, just the first leg in the broader thesis I am proposing: that ascribing objectivity to one's own experience implies experience of oneself as an agent. So now I turn to the second leg, the connection between a grasp of causality and experience of agency.

3   Bodily Power

This is an old thesis with both a negative and a positive component. The negative component is that our sense experiences do not by themselves enable us to discriminate causal connections among perceived objects from bare spatiotemporal conjunctions. The positive component is that the experience of our own agency gives us a distinct idea of causal connection and enables us to see how this applies within the world. Locke provides a classic formulation of these two components:

> But yet, if we will consider it attentively, Bodies, by our Senses, do not afford us so clear and distinct an *Idea of active power*, as we have from reflection on the Operations of our Minds. . . . Neither have we from Body any *Idea* of the beginning of Motion. A Body at rest affords us no *Idea* of any *active Power* to move; and when it is set in motion it self, that Motion is rather a Passion, than an Action in it. . . . The *Idea* of the beginning of motion, we have only from reflection on what passes in our selves, where we find by Experience, that barely by willing it, . . . we can move the parts of our Bodies, which were before at rest.[10]

It is, of course, Hume who provides a classic formulation of the negative component of this line of thought. He places special emphasis on the modal implications of causal thoughts (their connections with ideas of necessity and power) and asks how the course of experience can reveal to us not only what is the case but also what has to be case, what could not be otherwise.[11] One familiar response to this argument is to appeal to our experience of the *resistance* of things, e.g., my experience now as I press against the table. For, some have said, does not this give us an experience of *impossibility* and therefore provide us with a way into the circle of modal concepts? I suspect this is what Dr. Johnson had in mind when, according to Boswell, he sought to refute Berkeley (whose views about natural causality are similar to Hume's) by reminding us of what it is like to kick a rock. Hume himself acknowledged this line of thought, writing, "It may be pretended, that the resistance which we meet with in bodies, obliging us frequently to exert our force, and call up all our power, this gives us the idea of force and power. It is this *nisus*, or strong endeavour, of which we are conscious, that is the original impression from which this idea is copied."[12] Hume rejects this proposal because it is not universally applicable and does not provide us with an a priori concept of power. These objections do not seem altogether to the point, but there is a better critical discussion of this proposal by Heidegger in a discussion of Max Scheler's presentation of a version of it.[13] Heidegger argues that the familiar tactile and kinesthetic sensations that we interpret as evidence of the resistance of things bear this interpretation, and thus the crucial modal interpretation as experience of impossibility, only because we conceptualize them from a perspective that includes the thought that they occur in the context of an attempt to effect some physical change in the world. So the experience is interpreted as experience of resistance only within a perspective that already includes the concept of causation. If this perspective is not assumed, then the experience yields no more than a peculiar type of sensation conjoined with certain bodily movements. Hence, to use experienced resistance to challenge the negative component of Locke's argument, we have already to accept something like the positive component of his argument: that our grasp of causation is founded on our experience of bodily action.

This positive component is, of course, challenged by Hume, who objects that the idea of causation cannot be founded on our experience of our own agency. According to Hume, this experience is shrouded in mystery: we understand all too little of the mechanism of action, of the way in which our thoughts give rise to movements of our bodies. Thus, so far from this experience yielding us an example from which we might gain a clear and distinct conception of causal power, we find nothing but the conjunction of acts of will with the motion of certain parts of our body: "We learn the influence of our will from experience alone. And experience only teaches us, how one event constantly follows another; without instructing us in the secret connexion, which binds them together, and renders them inseparable."[14] So the appeal to the experience of agency, which forms the positive component of Locke's account of our grasp of the idea of active power, or causation, is, according to Hume, entirely mistaken.

One part of the response to Hume must be that the account he offers of agency is not tenable. For Hume, agency is constituted by a constant conjunction of mental acts of an appropriate type (acts of will) with bodily movements, and this constant conjunction can then be interpreted, in the light of Hume's projective theory of causation, as a causal relationship. The objection to this is that physical action is not simply bodily movement caused by a purely mental act that "wills" some worldly end. For this account misconstrues the relation between acts of will and bodily movement; it is not just a conjunction worth noting for future reference (like that, say, between consumption of too much alcohol and a subsequent hangover), since the intentionality of the mental act is transmitted to the bodily movement itself. The Humean account, which treats acts of will as exclusively mental, makes it seem that I raise my arm just by engaging in an appropriate mental act and then waiting for the result of that act. But I can, in Hume's sense, "will" as hard as I like that my arm should rise without anything happening, just as I can will that the sun should shine without anything happening. To come closer to the experience of agency, therefore, we require an account in which bodily movement is integrated into the act of will itself so that in cases of successful action an act of will becomes bodily.

The kind of account that is wanted has, I think, been provided by Brian O'Shaughnessy.[15] Here I will not attempt a description of O'Shaughnessy's account. But one central point is the conception of an attempt, or a striving, which, although definitely psychological at the moment of inception, encompasses those subsequent bodily consequences that are directly under the agent's control. Thus my raising my arm is a successful attempt on my part to raise my arm; the attempt comes to "fruition" through the movement of the limb.[16] Furthermore, the experience of agency is precisely the experience of such attempts coming to fruition through the agent's control of bodily movement: the agent experiences the psychophysical unity of bodily action through experience of satisfaction of a set of conditionals connecting choice and movement. O'Shaughnessy writes,

I refer to the obtaining of a set of conditionals, which are such as to ensure the existence of a *power*. For the normal human agent can when he chooses stop the movement of his arm, . . . and he can when he chooses change the direction of its movement, . . . and he can speed up or slow or whatever. Now these properties, summed up in the concept of *the having of power or control over the limb*, are of absolutely central importance to the occurrence of a physical act of movement-making. . . . Herewith, a dialectical synthesis of the seemingly opposed bodily and psycho-physical requirements of physical action is effected.[17]

The significance of this conception of "the having of power or control over the limb" is that it implies that once one replaces the volitionist account of action that Hume invokes, his objections to the Lockean thesis about the relationship between the experience of agency and the idea of power can be set aside. For O'Shaughnessy's account of action implies that the experience of agency includes the experience of bodily powers, defined by the psychophysical dispositions that link the will to bodily movements. The experience of agency is, therefore, not one of acts of will just regularly, but mysteriously, conjoined with bodily movements; it is one of acts of will that extend themselves to those parts of the body that are under direct control of the agent.

A Humean might still object that it remains to be shown that we have reason to think that we are agents with bodily powers. Indeed, he might at this point seek to recruit O'Shaughnessy to his own side, for O'Shaughnessy shows that illusion is as possible with respect to one's own agency as with respect to ordinary perception, by describing a case in which an agent thinks he is performing a very simple arm movement that requires no effort when in fact his arm is being moved by a machine that goes into action just when the agent thinks he is starting to move his arm.[18] But recognition of this kind of possibility of error need not undermine the idea that the coherence of our experience provides us with good enough reason to hold that we are normally reliable in this respect. The thesis that it is through the experience of agency that we get a grasp of bodily power, and thus of causation, does not require infallibility with respect to our experience of agency.

Yet what remains to be clarified is the way in which the experience of bodily power enters into the constitution of objective experience. Schopenhauer provides, I think, a useful cautionary example in this respect. In some respects his account of the will anticipates that of O'Shaughnessy. Thus he writes, "Only in reflection are willing and acting different; in reality they are one. Every true, genuine, immediate act of the will is also at once and directly a manifest act of the body. My body is the *objectivity* of my will."[19] Furthermore, he endorses a version of the Lockean thesis about the idea of power or force: "Hitherto, the concept of *will* has been subsumed under the concept of *force*; I, on the other hand, do ⸤xactly the reverse, and intend every force in nature to be conceived of as will."[20] However, as this closing comment indicates, Schopenhauer goes well beyond a simple epistemological grounding of the concept of force on experience of will. He harnesses his doctrine of force as will to the Kantian conception of things-in-themselves, to draw the conclusion that will is "the innermost essence, the kernel, of every particular thing and also of the whole. It appears in every blindly acting force of nature, and also in the deliberate conduct of man, and the great difference between the two concerns only the degree of the manifestation, not the inner nature of what is manifested."[21] Exciting though this metaphysics sounds, what we need is an account that, by locating the will within experience, puts limits on it. In grounding the idea of causation on the will, we do not want to be drawn to the conclusion that all causation is willpower. For the will itself is just a causal power.

In outline, the first part of the requisite construction appears fairly straightforward. If the experience of agency is the irreducible experience of bodily power, then the way is clear for the experience of resistance to bear the obvious interpretation in terms of forces acting upon us to place limits on our bodily power. In brief, if the experience of bodily power is an experience of possibilities, the experience of resistance is the experience of impossibilities. Furthermore, since these impossibilities are experienced as arising in the context of bodily contact, the ground for these impossibilities can be (fallibly) assumed to be located outside the body. Hence the idea of external forces constraining us can be legitimated within experience. Thus, given the modal content of the experience of agency, tactile experience itself can be legitimately assigned a content in which modal concepts are used to characterize the objects of experience; in this way Hume's modal challenge can be faced down, and the objectivity of tactile experience vindicated.

An important step has, however, been omitted here in that the objectivity of tactile experience presupposes the objectivity of the proprioceptive body sense that informs us of our limb movements. For it is only because we are able to regard our proprioceptive sense as providing us with putatively objective information about our limbs that we can rely on tactile experience to extend objective content beyond the body.[22] On the basis of bodily experience one cannot form a conception of the objective physical world that only commences beyond the limits of the body: the body itself has to be included within that world, even though our experience of the body is quite unlike our experience of the rest of the world. How, then, should the objectivity of proprioception itself be handled? The question is strange because experience is always in some respect bodily, so it is not at first clear what it might be for one's own body to exist unperceived. The approach I have been following implies that the objectivity of proprioception, like that of the other senses, should rest on a causal interpretation of the relationship between proprioceptive experience and its bodily object. But if, following O'Shaughnessy, we accept the irreducible experience of bodily power as fundamental, then the availability of a causal interpretation of proprioception is implied. For the experience that some current limb movement is under the control of one's will permits one to recognize that the experience itself depends on the limb movement. In my awareness that my arm is rising *because* I have chosen to raise it, there is implied a recognition that this very awareness itself depends on the movement of my arm (and thus on my will). The experience of agency as the causal power of bodily control brings with it the objectivity of the body as a cause of this very experience.

What needs more discussion here is whether the availability of this objective information concerning limb movement does not itself depend to some extent on tactile experience to provide an objective spatial framework of the subject's body (a body image) within which the proprioceptive sense then locates the subject's limbs. This claim has been advanced by O'Shaughnessy,[23] and it poses a threat to the thesis that the objectivity of the contents of tactile experience is grounded in the objectivity of the proprioceptive body sense. In response to O'Shaughnessy, however, I want to urge that the body image has a recursive structure. At the primitive level of infancy, I suggest, the body image has a crude spatial structure given entirely by proprioception. This gives the infant a simple sense of agency and bodily power that enables it to employ its sense of touch to explore its own body and, on the basis of these explorations, enrich its body image, and thus the content of its proprioceptions, and so on. This recursive model of the successive enrichment of the body image through the sense of touch preserves the plausible part of O'Shaughnessy's thesis that the normal adult body image has a degree of spatial articulation that cannot be derived from proprioception alone, yet retains the thesis that, at the most fundamental level, proprioception does not depend on touch.

The difficult part in the story is the next: how is one to vindicate a causal understanding of the content of other modalities of sense experience (e.g., hearing and sight), and thus their objectivity? They do not include the experience of the resistance of their objects, so the ascription of causal powers to such objects, and a causal comprehension of our experience of them, cannot just follow the pattern of tactile experience. Not surprisingly, these are the senses that we think of when we think of perception as just a matter of passive receptivity. One obvious route here is to build out from the objectivity of touch via the thought that the objects of touch are usually also potential objects of sight, hearing, etc. By itself this will not give a causal understanding of the role of these objects in, say, auditory experience of the kind that tactile experience makes available. But we need not think of causes as forces that we can feel, as if we had to be able to feel sound waves striking our ears and making the inner ear vibrate in order to vindicate the objectivity of auditory experience. Instead, we can think of causes as the grounds of dispositions, so that, as long as we can attain a dispositional understanding of auditory experience that ties the experience counterfactually to the audible presence of some tangible sound source, the conclusion that the source of the sound is the cause of the experience can be fairly drawn. Admittedly, this line of thought takes it for granted that the objects of touch are also potential objects of sight, hearing, and so on. But this assumption is readily defensible: it rests on our awareness that there is just one space because of the single bodily point of origin of the spaces of the different senses. Because bodily experience locates one's sense organs within a single body space, the sense fields that open out from the different sense organs are experienced as different ways of perceiving one and the same space.

Is it right to assign this degree of priority to the sense of touch in the constitution of objectivity? Do the other senses have to build out from the conception of the objects of experience given by touch? There is certainly an intuitive inclination to judge that things are real only when we can touch them: Macbeth, confronted by the vision of a dagger, reaches forward to clutch it and, finding nothing tangible there, concludes that it is just "a dagger of the mind." But there are plenty of real visible objects that are not tangible, such as smoke, so tangibility is certainly no necessary condition of physical reality. But this is not the issue; what is in question is whether the sense of touch should have the priority that this line of thought assigns to it. Indeed, although the line of argument is primarily epistemological, it lends itself readily to a developmental interpretation and can thus be taken to support the empirical priority of bodily experience and touch in the constitution of a child's conception of the physical world. Yet once the role of counterfactual thought within nontactile experience is acknowledged, it may appear unnecessary to suppose that the other senses need to build out from a conception of objectivity that is grounded in bodily experience and the sense of touch.

The case of Ian Waterman, which Jonathan Cole has described in fascinating detail, provides a way of making this challenge especially vivid.[24] Despite lacking normal proprioception and sense of touch (though he still retains sensitivity to temperature), Ian Waterman can employ his other senses much as we do. Indeed, he relies on visual feedback to control his body. And although Waterman is confident that he is drawing on the mastery of his full perceptual capacities that he enjoyed prior to the illness at the age of 19 that deprived him of proprioception and touch,[25] it is not easy to be confident that this is an essential feature of any similar case. Could there not be someone who was struck by the same illness during early infancy and yet managed to develop abilities comparable to those that Waterman developed? Such a case would be astonishing, yet Waterman's achievements, which far exceeded the expectations of those who first treated him, are themselves astonishing and must give pause to anyone who assigns a fundamental role in the constitution of objectivity to the sense of touch and bodily experience.

I think Waterman's case and hypothetical extensions of it show that there must be an alternative to the normal, intuitively accessible route to the constitution of the objectivity of experience that passes through proprioception and the sense of touch. On this alternative route, the modal component of the causal role of objects of experience will be manifested through subjects' acceptance of counterfactuals linking the presence of objects in their environment to the condition of their sense organs and the contents of their experience. Now it is not difficult to imagine courses of experience rich enough to make explanatory hypotheses of this kind reasonable if a general framework of causal explanation can be assumed.[26] But the issues in the present context are whether this can be assumed without begging the question and whether this alternative route shows that the emphasis on agency that I have been exploring is after all in principle dispensable.

I suggest that this second conclusion does not follow, for reasons that connect with the need to confront the first issue. To suppose that agency is altogether dispensable is to revert to the model of the passive interpreter, and in support of this it may be said that the visual systems of humans and

similar organisms have evolved to include subsystems that enable visual input to be progressively interpreted as experience of a physical world that is
spatially organized from the subject's point of view without any reference
to the subject's agency. Hence, one might argue, neither from a developmental, nor from an epistemological, point of view is agency really necessary. Now I am not competent to adjudge the developmental issue here,
but the necessity for some degree of agency is strongly supported by the
famous experiment by Held and Hein in which kittens that had been rendered unable from birth to move themselves (although they were passively
carried around in circles by other kittens) were unable to develop normal
spatial vision.[27] This experiment suggests that full three-dimensional spatial experience indeed requires physical agency, the capacity to explore
space and relate visual experience to bodily experience. But Waterman-
type cases suggest the need for some caution here (especially if one imagines such a case combined with paralysis of much of the body), and I
would like to propose that a more modest degree of agency may in principle suffice, namely voluntary control of the sense organs.

Despite his lack of proprioception, Ian Waterman can turn and focus
his eyes, and indeed he relies on visual feedback to control his limb movements, but whether he or any hypothetical variant of his case could control limb movement if he were blind is doubtful. I suggest that this kind of
voluntary control of the sense organs is essential. One reason for this is that
in assigning an objective content to visual experience, the subject has to
take account of his point of view and the condition of his eyes. If these are
to some extent under voluntary control, the subject can factor them out in
interpreting his experience and identify the objects distinctively responsible for his current experience. A subject who lacks this degree of voluntary control would not be in a position to control, and thus identify, the
variables that determine visual experience, and thus he would never be
able to solve the "simultaneous equations" that experience presents. It may
be objected that this point depends on taking the interpretation of visual
input as altogether too much a matter of conscious reasoning; once it is
recognized that this interpretation is carried out primarily by subsystems
over which we have no control, it may be said, this argument for the need
for control over the sense organs is undermined. In response to this, I would
say that even though, of course, the interpretation of visual input is carried
out largely by subsystems over which we have no control, it remains to be
shown that the programming of these subsystems does not depend on
learning and feedback that assume a capacity for voluntary control. Someone with no voluntary control over his eyes would lack the ability to focus
his attention on specific regions of the visual field; hence he would lack

both the ability to visually track the path of moving objects and the ability to stabilize his visual identification of objects while his own point of view alters. Without these abilities, which have a fundamental role in the organization of the visual field, I strongly doubt whether any objective interpretation of visual experience could be sustained.

This line of thought can be reinforced by considerations that return to my earlier stress on the modal component of objective experience. By finding that some aspects of the content of visual experience, unlike its direction, are not subject to the will, a subject encounters a kind of impossibility within visual experience (a visual analogue of tactile resistance) and is thus led to think that the content concerns objects whose existence is independent of the experience and can therefore be employed to explain the experience. Yet one can only encounter this kind of impossibility within a context in which other changes are experienced as possible. If we imagine that Ian Waterman lacks voluntary control of his eyes, and thus is altogether passive in relation to the course of his visual experience, no changes in the course of his experience would be experienced as more or less possible than any other, so not only would there be insuperable problems in factoring out the contribution to the content of experience made by its objects, there would also be deeper questions as to why such a subject should imagine that his experience is experience of objects whose existence is independent of him. Nothing in the experience of such a subject would warrant the assumption that one can extract from the content of experience the materials for a causal explanation of it.

There is more to be said concerning the phenomenology of Ian Waterman's situation and other more extreme cases that might be imagined or discovered. Yet I hope that I have said enough to show that these cases do not provide decisive counterexamples to my thesis that agency helps to constitute objectivity, although they do show that one should qualify any assignment of priority to proprioception and touch. Rather than prolong direct discussion of this issue, however, I want finally to turn to the metaquestion of how this whole second line of argument for the first-person thesis that objective experience depends on the experience of agency relates to the third-person thesis that perception implies agency.

4 The Harmony Requirement

The first argument tells me that I cannot suppose myself to enjoy perceptions of an objective world without supposing myself to be an agent. Isn't this just the conclusion of the second argument? If so, wherein lies the point of that argument? Its rationale must derive from its distinctive starting point: the abstract conception of oneself as a subject of experience, wondering what kind of assumptions about oneself and one's experience warrant belief in the objectivity of experience. For from this starting point, the first line of argument, with its essential third-person perspective, is unavailable, or at any rate question-begging, as this line of argument takes it for granted that one is a subject within an objective world that includes other subjects, and that the kind of connections that apply in general among perception, belief, and agency apply in one's own case. The first argument does not aim to establish the presuppositions of rational belief in the objectivity of experience; it just concerns the connections among perception, belief, and agency, where these are conceived as states of beings whose objectivity is simply not in question. Now there is nothing wrong with this line of argument. But the second argument starts from a point of view that has bracketed such assumptions and, with correspondingly less material to draw on, seeks to draw out the presuppositions of assigning a distinctively objective content to one's own experience.

As indicated by the use of the idioms of 'legitimation', 'warrant', and 'constitution' throughout the second argument, the concern of this argument is fundamentally epistemological. The argument is not, however, primarily antiskeptical; instead its concern is transcendental: the argument seeks to show that agency is a necessary condition for the legitimate self-ascription of objective perception, and because it is of this kind, the epistemological considerations readily connect with developmental ones, as the final stages of my discussion indicate. The epistemology involved here is distinctively "internalist,"[28] for it adopts a first-person point of view from the outset and explores the lines of reasoning available to a subject of experience who seeks to explore the basis of his belief in the objectivity of his own experience. Internalist epistemology of this kind is currently out of favor, but I myself think that it is a proper part of the traditional philosophical enterprize of gaining a reflective understanding of ourselves and our place within the world. I will not attempt here to defend this claim, but in a full defense I would want to acknowledge that this kind of epistemology needs to be completed by an externalist epistemology, which confirms, from the outside, so to speak, the conception of our cognitive relation to the world that the internalist argument implies.[29] If this is right, it follows that the two arguments I have been discussing are not altogether alien to each other after all, for the first argument can be regarded as an externalist confirmation of the conclusion of the second one. On reflection, this should not seem surprising, for if one were to suppose (contrary to my argument) that the legitimation of the objectivity of one's perceptual experience did not require a conception of oneself as an agent, it would seem altogether mysterious if, in thinking of oneself from a third-person point of view as a subject of objective perceptions, one was nonetheless committed to thinking of oneself as an agent. In such a frame of mind one would seem compelled to adopt a Sartrean division of the self into one's being-for-oneself and one's being-for-others.[30] Since such an outcome can only be regarded as a reductio ad absurdum of the assumed combination of positions here, it is reasonable to require that the approaches of the first and second arguments be in harmony, and since the first argument appears hard to fault, this requirement of harmony helps to confirm at least the conclusion of the second, more contentious, line of argument.

Acknowledgments

I am grateful to Tony Marcel, Naomi Eilan, and Jim Russell for too many helpful comments on this paper.

Notes

1. This position is explored in Stalnaker 1984, chap. 1.

2. See, for example, Heidegger 1927, pt. 1, sec 43.

3. Evans 1985.

4. Evans 1985, 280.

5. Kant 1787, A193, B238.

6. See Mellor 1981.

7. See McTaggart 1927, chap. 33.

8. See Moore 1903, 37, 41.

9. See Locke 1714, secs. 20, 53.

10. Locke 1700, II.xxi.4.

11. Hume 1739, I.iii.14. In writing here of Hume's emphasis on the "modal" implications of causal thought, I employ the philosophers' concept of modality, which applies to possibility, necessity, etc., and not the psychologists' concept, which applies to the different modalities of sense, such as sight and touch.

12. Hume 1777, 67, n. 1.

13. Heidegger 1979, sec. 24.

14. Hume 1777, 66.

15. O'Shaughnessy 1980, esp. vol. 2, chaps. 11–15.

16. O'Shaughnessy 1980, 2:214.

17. O'Shaughnessy 1980, 1:119.

18. O'Shaughnessy 1980, 1:115–116.

19. Schopenhauer 1844, 101–103.

20. Schopenhauer 1844, 111.

21. Schopenhauer 1844, 110.

22. This point was urged by Naomi Eilan and Paul Snowdon in discussion.

23. O'Shaughnessy 1989, 57–58.

24. Cole 1991.

25. Cole 1991, p.123.

26. See Bennett 1966, 37; Evans 1985, 266–268.

27. Held and Hein 1963.

28. See Bonjour 1992 for a summary of the externalism/internalism debate in epistemology.

29. I have argued for this in Baldwin 1991, esp. pp. 185–186.

30. Sartre 1943, esp. pt. 3, chap. 1.

References

Baldwin, T. R. 1991. "Two Types of Naturalism." In *Proceedings of the British Academy* 80:171–199.

Bennett, J. 1966. *Kant's Analytic*. Cambridge: Cambridge University Press.

Bonjour, L. 1992. "Externalism/Internalism." In *A Companion to Epistemology*, edited by J. Dancy and E. Sosa. Oxford: Blackwell.

Cole, J. 1991. *Pride and the Daily Marathon*. London: Duckworth.

Evans, G. 1985. "Things without the Mind." In his *Collected Papers*. Oxford: Clarendon Press.

Heidegger, M. 1927. *Sein und Zeit*. Tübingen: Max Niemayer Verlag. Translated by J. Macquarrie and E. Robinson as *Being and Time*. Oxford: Blackwell, 1962.

Heidegger, M. 1979. *Prolegomena zur Geschichte des Zeitbegriffs*. Frankfurt: Vittorio Klostermann. Translated by T. Keisel as *History of the Concept of Time*. Bloomington: Indiana University Press, 1985.

Hume, D. 1739. *A Treatise of Human Nature*. Ed. L. A. Selby-Bigge. Oxford: Clarendon Press, 1888.

Hume, D. 1777. *An Enquiry Concerning Human Understanding*. Page references are to the 3rd edition edited by L. A. Selby-Bigge. Oxford: Clarendon Press, 1975.

Kant, I. 1787. *Kritik der reinen Vernunft*. Translated by N. Kemp Smith as *The Critique of Pure Reason*. London: Macmillan, 1933.

Locke, J. 1700. *An Essay Concerning Human Understanding*. Ed. P. Nidditch. Oxford: Clarendon Press, 1975.

Locke, J. 1714. "An Examination of P. Malebranche's Opinion of Seeing All Things in God." In *The Works of J. Locke*, vol. 9. London, 1801.

McTaggart, J. M. E. 1927. *The Nature of Existence*, vol. 2, edited by C. D. Broad. Cambridge: Cambridge University Press.

Mellor, D. H. 1981. *Real Time*. Cambridge: Cambridge University Press.

Moore, G. E. 1903. "The Refutation of Idealism." Page references are to the paper as reprinted in *G. E. Moore: Selected Writings*, edited by T. R. Baldwin. London: Routledge, 1993.

Held, R., and A. Hein. 1963. "Movement-Produced Stimulation in the Development of Visually Guided Behavior." *Journal of Comparative Psychology* 56:872–876.

O'Shaughnessy, B. 1980. *The Will*. Cambridge: Cambridge University Press.

O'Shaughnessy, B. 1989. "The Sense of Touch." *Australasian Journal of Philosophy* 67:37–58.

Sartre, J.-P. 1943. *L'Être et le neant*. Paris: Gallimard. Translated by H. Barnes as *Being and Nothingness*. London: Methuen, 1958.

Schopenhauer, A. 1844. *Die Welt als Wille und Vorstellung*, vol. 1. Page references are to the translation by E. Payne as *The World as Will and Representation*, vol. 1. New York: Dover, 1966.

Stalnaker, R. 1984. *Inquiry*. Cambridge: MIT Press.

At Two with Nature: Agency and the Development of Self-World Dualism

James Russell

What role does agency play in mental development? Jean Piaget (e.g., 1970) famously answered that agency is the engine of mental development. However, the past 25 years of cognitive-developmental research have given rise to a widespread dissatisfaction with that answer, mainly because we have unearthed too much innate apparatus for it to be plausible. Yet I will argue that Piaget's answer is only incorrect insofar as it is too strong. There is a case to be made, in other words, for the view that without agency there can be no mental development, or at least that adequate agency is necessary for adequate mental development. I will try to give this more modest Piagetian view a run for its money.

Like many psychologists of his and the preceding generation (notably James Mark Baldwin[1]), Piaget regarded mental development as the process of establishing a division between two kinds of reality: an objective reality grasped as independent of ourselves and a subjective reality constituted by our volitions and representational states. I will refer to this with the usual term 'self-world dualism', a mode of consciousness that one might regard as the symmetrical opposite of being-in-the-world. Self-world dualism is the basic human situation. For although most of us understand what it means to be at one with Nature, we only do so because our normal state is—as with the Woody Allen character who would stubbornly remain on rural excursions—"at *two* with Nature."

In presenting and defending a watered-down version of Piaget's developmental account of self-world dualism, I will proceed through the following stages. First, I will say why Piaget's theory is too strong and sketch the aims of the weaker version. Next, I will present the case for agency being necessary for the development of self-world dualism. My principal claim here will be that it is only by experiencing agency that a subject can experience the world as being resistant to her will, something which is necessary if any distinction is to be drawn between subjective and objective. I argue here that an essential feature of agency is a capacity for willfully determining the sequence of one's perceptual inputs. The latter two sections of this paper will concern the implications that this thesis has for infants' developing conceptions of physical objects (normally called 'object permanence') and for young children's conceptions of other minds (normally called 'theory of mind'). In the first case, the argument is that object permanence must be properly assessed in terms of the actions the infant spontaneously performs upon objects. In the second case, I argue that the central role of agency in subjectivity entails that we cannot explain development of a theory of mind solely in terms of the maturation of an innately specified processing module.

1   Weakening the Piagetian Thesis

Piaget was concerned, in part, with the preverbal roots of a dualism between the subject's experience of how things appear at particular times and her conception of a world of enduring, mind-independent objects, and consequently he studied infants' understanding of object occlusion, "object permanence." The infant's senses may tell it, for example, that all that exists within its reaching space on the carpet right now is a cushion, while, in reality, there is both a rattle and a cushion, the former occluded by the latter because of the infant's relative position in space as the viewer. In essence, Piaget argued that objective experience and our conception of ourselves as experiencers located within a mind-independent spatial world emerge as our actions become progressively more self-determined, differentiated, and integrated. He opposed nativist accounts, and in his writings on infancy in particular, he strenuously rejected nativism about spatial, causal, temporal, and object concepts, a nativism that he ascribed to Kant.

There are major difficulties with this position, quite apart from the question of what is and what is not to count as an action. Take the case of spatial concepts—the fundamental concepts for Piaget and concepts that relate intimately to object permanence. His view was that through exercising progressively greater control over what it experiences, the infant becomes able to bootstrap itself towards an allocentric, rather than purely egocentric, conception of space.[2] That is to say, by forging links between her actions and their perceptual outcomes, it develops a conception of the spatial world that is perspective-independent, environment-centred, and maplike (Piaget 1955, 198–218).

There are good reasons for dismissing the very possibility that development could happen in this way. As James Hopkins (1987, 153–154) has argued, if the primordial state of the infant mind is entirely adualistic, then no amount of activity will make the infant's experience become that of an objective spatial world: there is nothing on which to build. If there is no initial distinction between (say) hunger as having an inner source, and a looming object as having an outer source, then it is impossible to see how the development of agency could forge that distinction. In the second place, Piaget's (1955) picture of the infant as heroically "constructing" a maplike, perspective-neutral conception of space by acting on objects—as if this were something that the organism *wins through* to after a long apprenticeship—sits awkwardly beside evidence that an ability to code spatial relations allocentrically is both phylogenetically and ontogenetically early. Lynn Nadel (1990), for example, has demonstrated that 3-week-old rats are able to swim straight to a platform concealed in a pool of opaque liquid from a *novel* starting point, something they must achieve through coding the relations between the platform and landmarks in the environment. In fact, this finding is one of many that one could cite in support of O'Keefe and Nadel's (1978) hypothesis that animals possess abilities for spatial cognition that are innately specified (within the hippocampus). The fact is, nativism about allocentric coding is a good deal more plausible than constructivism, so there are both conceptual and empirical considerations ranged against the Piagetian view.

But the main point I need to make in this section is that a very wide scope for a broadly Piagetian account of self-world dualism still remains even after one has accepted that organisms' spatial awareness is (or must be) grounded in environment-centred coding. The reason is that, although this allocentric grounding may be necessary for self-world dualism, it is certainly not sufficient for it. And this is because self-world dualism is a more psychologically rich affair than the ability to code spatial relations as being independent of one's current location and activity. Rich in what sense? In human beings, at least, one can regard this dualism as requiring a primitive form of the distinction between appearance and reality insofar as it involves our distinguishing between our perspectives on the world, perspectives that can never tell more than partial truths, and the whole truth about the way things are. The world always seems to us to be a certain way, while we know that if we were differently located, it would seem otherwise, and we assume that what affords us these different perspectives is a mind-independent physical reality. It is fair to call this a 'theorylike' conception, in the sense that it is a matter of reflective understanding rather than of practical competence.

We are now in a position to see where a Piagetian account can enter this picture. It is possible to argue that agency is necessary for the development of self-world dualism, in the sense in which I have just described it, while being as nativist as one could wish about allocentric coding.

Henceforth I will refer to this weaker Piagetian position as 'piagetian' (with a small 'p'). And in general I shall take a piagetian position to be one in which a wide range of innately specified apparatus can be posited but in which one also argues for agency being necessary (though not sufficient) for developing a conception of objects and the self as distinct.

But as a way of placing the piagetian view more definitively, I need to say a little about the distinction between practical and theoretical abilities, again taking spatial abilities as the test case. As John Campbell (1993) has argued, the innate ability to construct perspective-neutral maps of the environment will not enable a creature to register the spatial connectedness of this environment (the fact that each place is related to every other) unless it can appreciate the causal significance of its own actions and perceptions in relation to places (e.g., by navigating)—an appreciation dubbed a "causally indexical" understanding by Campbell. This is not yet theoretical. But a "causally *non*indexical" understanding *is* theoretical in the sense that it is one through which the creature is able to reflect both on the causal relations between itself and objects (including its perceptions of them) and on the relations between physical objects in its environment.[3] This, then, is how the distinction can be drawn between an organism's practical abilities for interacting with objects—an organism surely does not *require* self-world dualism to find its way around—and the kind of reflective and theorylike understanding at issue in self-world dualism. The way in which the creature's location affects its experiences and its ability to reflect upon how its actions affect these is of central importance here.

Given this, piagetians claim to have a story to tell about how this theorylike conception of the organism's place in the physical world must arise, in particular about its grasp of the relations between objects and its perceptual experience of them. They argue that *our ability to change the nature of our perceptual inputs at will*—a broad definition of 'action', which includes attention shifting—is necessary for us to make the kind of appearance/reality distinction that is at the heart of self-world dualism and is at least a component of any grasp of ourselves as representers of an environment.

Just a word, before proceeding, about the intended status of what I am going to say. Piaget borrowed J. M. Baldwin's term 'genetic epistemology' to describe his enterprise, and indeed much of his work was a hybrid of developmental psychology and epistemology. Accordingly, psychologists who work within this framework tend to seek out so-called "transcendental" arguments (roughly, unless we had cognitive capacity *x*, we could not experience *y*; we do experience *y*; therefore we have *x*). As Patricia Kitcher (1990) has argued in her recent book on Kant's psychology, the line between philososophical and psychological approaches to questions about the conditions for being a subject with objective knowledge (transcendental questions) is difficult to draw.[4] As this is the kind of question I am asking here, my answers will inevitably have a rather ambiguous status.

2   What Agency Gives Us

In this section I will argue for the view that self-world dualism can only develop in agents. What are the relevant features of agency here?

In the first place, there are certain kinds of mental operation that are deeply implicated in agency, and in the second, there are modes of experience and knowledge that are only available to agents when they are behaving *as* agents. I will be concerned almost entirely with the first topic and mention one aspect of the second only in passing. Under the first heading, 'mental operations', I will discuss two integral components of agency, which I will call '*action monitoring*' and '*reversibility*'.

First, action monitoring. There are two main ways in which changes in my perceptual inputs can be brought about. There are changes originating in the world for which I am not responsible (e.g., a cat walks across my path), and there are changes for which I am responsible, insofar as they originate in my body (e.g., as my head moves to the left, a sleeping cat shifts to the right of my visual field). An organism needs to be able to register the difference between these two kinds of changes.

For illustrative purposes, I will describe the simplest and most famous case of action monitoring, that studied by von Holst and Mittelstaedt (1950, translated in Gallistel 1980). Fruit flies produce a so-called "opto-kinetic reaction," which means that they turn in the direction of world movements. A moment's reflection tells us that if the fly had no mechanism for distinguishing between changes in the visual flow caused by its own movements and changes caused by movements in the world, it would be paralysed every time it produced the optokinetic reaction. If, for example, the world moves to the fly's left, the fly's head moves to the left, but this leftward movement will cause the world to (apparently) move to the right, and so this in turn should cause a rightward movement, which in turn. . . . In other words, if every apparent movement of the world were taken as a real movement, the creature would be as paralysed as Buridan's ass.

What is required, therefore, is a mechanism that can record the fact that the insect has launched a movement and then use this information so as to treat the resulting visual changes as signaling an apparent change rather than a real change. The mechanism that von Holst and Mittelstaedt proposed is called *efference copying*. A copy is made of the initial turn-commanding signal. For example, if the signal was '+3' (+ meaning egocentric right, with '3' being a unit of extent), then the efference copy would also be '+3'. The phenomenal outcome of this action will be a so-called "reafferent" signal of '−3', i.e., the world appears to move to the left. These positive and negative values cancel, and so the animal's nervous system records the fact that there has been self-movement but no world-movement. Had there been no efference copy and just the afferent signal of '−3', then it would have recorded the fact that the world had *really* moved to the left.

The mechanisms of action monitoring obviously become more complex in more complex organisms, and our understanding of them becomes predictably fuzzier. Indeed, we might want to abandon the assumption that a process as simple as efference copying can tell the whole story about how action monitoring works in higher-level cognition. But enough has been said to make two points. First, what we see here is a very primitive mechanism for distinguishing real from apparent changes in sensory input (it is an appearance/reality distinction, remember, with which the piagetian thesis is primarily concerned). Action monitoring is an integral feature of information processing in agents, and this in turn is integral to our making at least a primitive distinction between how the world appears and how it is in fact.

The second point is about what is intended by the term 'monitoring' in 'action monitoring'. The point is both a caveat and a passing reference to the kind of question, mentioned at the start of this section, about the mode of knowledge and experience uniquely available to agents when acting as agents. The caveat is that 'monitoring' does not imply the presence of some inner eye, a spectator in the 'Cartesian theater' (Dennett 1991), watching the launch and course of a movement. As I hope was clear from my description of primitive efference copying, this is a "subpersonal" mechanism with no higher-level homunculus.[5] Indeed, the same can be said at the personal level, insofar as talk about a homunculus overseer inspires exactly the *wrong* account of agency, as we experience it. And this point brings me to the passing reference to a special mode of knowledge and experience available only to agents that I promised earlier. It is that if a subject has to observe or monitor herself to find out what she is doing, she is *not* acting intentionally: we know the nature of our intended actions nonobservationally. Personal level, inner-eye action monitoring cannot exist alongside true agency (see O'Shaughnessy 1980, 31–32).

But there is obviously more to acting intentionally than monitoring bodily movements and attention shifts. Indeed, we can imagine a creature whose action-monitoring mechanisms are in good order but that never acts willfully because all of its actions are called forth by stimuli in the external world. What needs to be added to the picture is the fact that a true agent—as opposed to a mere reactor—determines what she does and when: an agent is in control of her behavior.[6] This is a somewhat self-evident, if not actually tautologous, statement about agency, but my aim in making it is to draw attention to a single fact about self-determined actions: that the order in which they are produced can be *reversed*. Because actions alter perceptual inputs, this ensures that there is a class of our *experiences* that is self-determined (and reversible) rather than world-determined (and irreversible)—a distinction owing to Kant, though he did not draw it to make a point about agency.[7] I will now explain what this means.

The sequential ordering of actions can be independent of the ordering of events in the world: I can look at *a*, *b*, then *c* and then *c*, *b*, and *a*. This means that, because actions determine perceptual inputs, the flow of the resulting percepts is independent of the flow of events in the world. For when we witness an occurrence, the flow of events is in one direction, and it happens once: *a* happens, then *b*, then *c*, and this is the end of the story. The order in which events unfold is thus world-determined and is as *irreversible* as action-generated perceptual sequences are *reversible*. For example, if I am stationary and a cat walks across my path, I have no choice but to see the animal on, say, my left before seeing it on my right. And if I want the event to occur again, I have to wait on the cat. Similarly, when somebody comes into my office, I have no choice but to see him open the door before he sits down. The order of perceptions is irreversible, and its possible repetition is something over which I have no power. However, if I am looking at a motor car or leafing through a book, I am free to experience portions of the objects in any order I wish: rear wheels then grill, index then preface, or vice versa. In this case there is relative freedom to determine what we experience at a given time and in the order we choose, while in the former case we are constrained to experience something and its features in a particular order. Moreover, agents are also free to determine *which* objects are members of the array to be ordered in experience. I can, for example, ensure that the eraser on my desk is not part of the array visible to me by moving my body to the right, occluding the eraser behind the coffee mug.

I should add in passing that my use of the term 'reversible' here is in fact a synecdoche for the various respects in which perceptual inputs may be self-determined. Other characteristics of self-determined perceptual sequences are that simple sequences can be combined into more complex ones and that detours and short-cuts en route to a location can be made. Nothing would be gained by listing them.[8] Conversely, 'irreversible' is supposed to apply here to *any* kind of perceptual sequence over which we have no power. The term 'reversibility', as many readers know, also plays a central role in Piaget's theory, where it was taken to be the central distinguishing feature of "intelligence," as opposed to "perception." But again, nothing would be gained by listing the similarities and differences between my usage and Piaget's.

The (rather paradoxical) moral I wish to draw here is this: the reversibility of self-generated perceptual sequences can reveal to us how the scope of our experience is *constrained*. It is difficult to imagine how a conception of the irreversible, world-dependent nature of some modes of experience could arise if we never experienced the reversible, action-dependent nature of others. Moreover, the freer we are to determine the nature and order of our inputs (and the less our behavior is called out by stimuli and the less our attention is captured rather than directed), the *more possibilities for resistance to our will* we encounter. The more we can do, that is, the wider the variety of ways in which our will can be resisted and its experiential outcomes limited. The freer we are to alter our perceptual inputs, the more we learn of the *refractory* nature of the world and, correlatively, the richer the conception we gain of ourselves as determiners of our immediate mental life. This refractoriness, therefore, sets limits on what our agency can achieve in determining our experiences, thereby engendering a conception in us of something as setting these limits, as causing them to be set. (The word 'refractory' is borrowed from J. M. Baldwin [1906], who used it in much the same way as I am using it, to describe how objectivity in the child's experience emerges partly as a function of the world's resisting the child's will [see Russell 1978, part 1.2, for a summary of his theory].)

Clearly, not *all* kinds of actions are reversible—many kinds of actions cannot be performed backwards—but this only serves to highlight the special status of actions that *are* reversible and points up the intimate relationship between reversible bodily movements and attention shifts. Attention shifts are always reversible for the mature thinker. For the class of reversible actions contains all those actions that change the subject's perspective on the environment, where we take these perspective changes to encompass everything from moving around in the world, to changing visual fixations, to shifting auditory attention. Recall that at the end of the first section I said that the piagetian interprets 'action' in a very broad sense to refer to the changing of perceptual inputs at will and that this includes attention shifts.

Also recall that I earlier described the achievement of self-world dualism in terms of an appearance/reality distinction, which in this context is a distinction between how the world appears to us from instant to instant and our conception of a mind-independent reality that is the condition of these changes of appearance. On the present view, it is the experience of reversibility, the experience of changing our inputs by changing our physical or mental (attentional) relation to objects, that affords us such changes of appearance, while the manifest constraints on how appearances can be altered (e.g., by moving round an object) show us that limits are set on how one appearance can follow from another. And recall that this experience of changing our inputs is not only a matter of changing *how* things are perceived; it is also a matter of changing *what* we perceive as we change perspective. It is in this latter sense that the notion of refractoriness—resistance of the world to our will—has the clearest application, simply because the term 'will' has such a clear application when we are dealing with *what* is experienced. A baby desperately desiring the nipple and turning to its left when the nipple is on its right is a potent example of the experience of refractoriness.

Arguing from reversibility is not the only route to the thesis of refractoriness. So I will describe another route to it to round out my account. David Hamlyn (1990, 105–106) and Thomas Baldwin (1995), for example, have both argued that experiencing the resistance of substantial objects to the willed movements of our *bodies* (when we touch things, lie on them, push against them, and so forth) is necessary if we are to regard objects as mind-independent. Baldwin (1995) begins his argument from a position different from the one used here. Rather than arguing from a form of experience that agency affords us, he starts with the thought that if we are to view ourselves as perceivers of an objective world, then we must regard objects as the *causes* of our experiences. This in turn requires us to acknowledge the *modal* nature of causality (i.e., that causes *necessarily* precede events, while it is *possible* that events could have unfolded differently). He then argues that if we adopt a view of volition in which voluntary action is taken to be the exercise of a bodily power, we can explain how this modal conception can arise: when substantial objects impede the exercise of our will, we experience the *impossibility* of certain bodily attempts, we encounter "forces acting upon us to place limits on our bodily power" (Baldwin 1995, 116).[9]

According to my position, by contrast, felt resistance is not necessary for the modal conception to emerge. That is to say, out of *non*physical interaction between one's body and the world (such as moving the eyes in relation to scenes, or moving the body in relation to objects) refractoriness will emerge—I argue—from the tension between how and what things *must* appear to us and how and what things *may* appear to us. This said, the similarities between our two views are far more notable than their differences: they are both arguments for objectivity from refractoriness via agency. Indeed, toward the end of his paper Baldwin leaves the door open for a thesis not unlike mine in which "it is by finding that the content of visual experience, *unlike its direction*, is not subject to the will that such a subject encounters a kind of impossibility within visual experience (a visual analogue of tactile resistance), and is thus led to the thought that the content concerns objects whose existence is independent of the experience and can therefore be employed to explain the experience" (Baldwin 1995, 121; my italics).

If either of these arguments from refractoriness establishes that knowing oneself to be the subject of objective experience requires experiencing oneself as an agent, then the link between agency and self-world dualism is more or less complete. However, the implications that this thesis has for objectivity (to be considered developmentally in section 3) are much clearer than its implications for subjectivity (to be considered developmentally in section 4). Accordingly, before ending this section, I will say a few words about how refractoriness theses bear on the question of self-awareness. 'Self-awareness' implies a capacity richer than the capacity to regard oneself as a subject of objective experiences. It implies an ability to regard oneself as not merely existing *in relation* to objects. It implies a *reflective* orientation to one's subjective experiences and the possibility of entertaining first-person thoughts about them, as well as about one's intentions.

Accounts of self-awareness that place agency at the center of the picture suggest that an essential component here is a primary awareness of oneself as a being that wills (which we are to take as encompassing everything from self-determination of one's experiences, to instinctual striving, to having rational goals). But even Schopenhauer—the philosopher, above all others, who took a volitional view of the self—did not believe that willing is *all* there is to selfhood. He accepted that the self both wills and apprehends (believes, knows, perceives, etc.), saying that the self's willing and the self's knowing "flow together into the consciousness of one I," which he pronounced to be "the miracle par excellence" (Schopenhauer 1844, 243). As Janaway (1989) has recently commented, this "miracle" is at least a truth about and condition for selfhood, in the sense that without the coreference of the 'I' in 'I will' and 'I perceive', there is no possibility of either action or knowledge. The subject is conscious of herself as a being that strives to alter the world (and her experiences of it, one should add) and at the same time as a knower. "This," Janaway writes, "is because the point of acting is to change something about the world that *I* perceive, or about *my* relation to it, while the capacity to perceive essentially informs, through beliefs and desires, the way I actively modify myself in response to what is perceived" (1989, 89). If willing is indeed necessarily present in self-awareness, as Janaway suggests, then an adequate conceptualization of one's mental states will depend on adequate experience of oneself as an agent—to which I will return in section 4.

3   Object Occlusion and Object Permanence

In this section I will discuss what piagetian views about the role of agency in cognition imply about how object permanence should be assessed and about how it develops. The second topic cannot be addressed without regard to the first.

What counts as evidence for prelinguistic children knowing that objects continue to exist when they are completely occluded from view? A piagetian must take a very strong and distinctive line on how this question should be answered, and if this line cannot be sustained, the theory loses much of its force. That is to say, if you think that an infant's awareness of the division between itself and the physical world is determined in part by its agency, you will tend also to think that its knowledge of the mind-independent existence of objects should be assessed in terms of what it *does*.

Piaget's (1955) own research showed—and it has been massively confirmed since—that there is a long period in development during which infants will not retrieve completely occluded objects *although they have the motor capacity to do so*. For example, a baby of 6 months can lift an inverted polystyrene cup, but if it sees a trinket that it strongly desires being hidden under such a cup, it does nothing. There is no sign of frustration, and the infant acts as if the trinket has ceased to exist. Why? Piaget's answer was that this is a manifestation of *egocentrism*, which broadly means a fusing of one's current experience with reality, a failure to grasp how the appearance of the world is relative to one's perspective on it, an incomplete self-world dualism, in fact. A perspective-relative conception is supposed to be achieved through the experience of willfully changing one's perspectives.

I will mention only in passing Piaget's actual account of how egocentrism was supposed to be overcome. The only explanatory tools that he allowed himself were the "circular reactions" of J. M. Baldwin (1906), movements that can be repeated at will, unlike reflexive movements evoked by stimuli. As the infant grows older, circular reactions become progressively directed toward having effects in the physical environment (unlike, say, thumb sucking) and become more integrated. For instance, means-end behavior is described as an example of the 'coordination of secondary circular reactions', with 'secondary' roughly meaning having an environment-centered effect rather than a bodily-centered effect. Furthermore, the significance for development of what I am calling 'the experience of refractoriness' is represented within Piaget's theory of learning, which proposes an interplay between the child's attempts to *assimilate* new data to preexisting action schemes and the *accommodations* she has to make to adjust the mental contours of the old scheme, where the greater the novelty, the greater the degree of accommodation required. As James McClelland has indicated, there is a strong parallel between Piaget's principle of accommodation and the connectionist back-propagation algorithm, insofar as both are founded on the principle "Adjust the parameters of the mind in proportion to the extent to which their adjustment can produce a reduction in the discrepancy between expected and observed events" (McClelland 1989, 20). If there were no experiences of refractoriness, there would no need for accommodation. (Some of the earliest connectionist simulations were of Piagetian tasks [e.g., Papert 1963].)

However, piagetians need not be committed to Piaget's theory of learning, and as we saw in the first section, they can avail themselves of nativist accounts of spatial coding. That said, my view about why younger infants fail to search for occluded objects is entirely at one with Piaget's. The assumption is that the baby fails to search because, given its inadequate grasp of how its visual experience depends on its actions, the question of whether something that has ceased to be perceptible can be rendered perceptible again through action *cannot arise*. It is *not* that the baby "believes"— insofar as very young infants believe anything—that the object has ceased to exist; rather, any conception of an unexperienced but existing object is beyond its grasp.

There is, however, a natural and plausible objection to this inference from lack of searching to lack of knowledge. It is entirely possible that very young infants are able to mentally represent the continuing existence of presently unperceived objects while being unable to organize, for whatever reason, a successful search. Given this, many contemporary developmental psychologists would argue that the information available to infants about object permanence can best be detected by experimental techniques that do not require action. That is, we need to find out how infants *react* to different kinds of physical events. The reaction typically studied is that of surprise (strictly, recovery of interest), the rationale being that if an infant witnesses an anomalous event, an event that *violates the principle of object permanence*, and shows surprise at this, then we can infer that it was coding the event *as* anomalous and therefore had expectations about permanence.

The most discussed study in this area, and the one that speaks to the existence of such early knowledge most strongly, was carried out by Renée Baillargeon (1987).[10] Baillargeon showed that infants between 3.5 and 4.5 months of age are surprised (the index being *dishabituation*— recovery of looking toward the display) when a screen, swinging like a

drawbridge toward and away from the infant *fails to be impeded* by a
wooden block that has been temporarily rendered invisible by the screen
on its backward journey. This age is about 4 months before infants search
for completely occluded objects and about *14* months before they attain
Piaget's criterion for possession of the concept of an object, namely, searching after invisible displacements of an object.

Still, piagetians can place this finding within their theoretical framework by drawing the following distinction. On the one hand, there is the
maintenance of a representation of an object that happens to be currently
occluded, a representation that drives reactive behavior (such as dishabituation) and, on the other, there is the conception of a physical datum as
distinct from and external to the self. I refer to the first as 'representation
permanence' and to the second as 'externality' (see Russell, in press, for a
defence of this distinction).

Let us consider first what representation permanence amounts to.
It would surely be a badly designed nervous system that routinely ex-
tinguished representations of objects at the instant that they ceased to be
visible (and it is difficult to imagine how such extinguishings would be
achieved within the constant flux of the perceptual input). Baillargeon's
experiment is an elegant demonstration that such representations are indeed maintained, but the demonstration does not inform us about how
the very young infant conceives of the relation between itself and the
wooden block. Studying the situations in which such infants retrieve objects does, however, tell us something about this, because a subject who
searches for an occluded object is manifesting a degree of knowledge
about where she is located in relation to the occluder and the object. Surprise at nonresistance can occur, however, without any knowledge of how
one is spatially related to the occluder and the object.

The piagetian position, then, is that search is an appropriate diagnos-
tic criterion for self-world dualism because there is a conceptual linkage
between what one knows about one's spatial relation to an object and
what one is inclined to do, given certain desires. Consider an infant of, say,
6 months of age who wants its occluded toy back. If it knows the relation
between itself and the occluder, the relation between the toy and the occluder, and the relation between the toy and itself, and if it is able motor-
wise to remove the occluder, then why does it not search? There would
seem to be a contradiction between saying that the infant knows where a
still-existing object is and saying that the infant does not know how to act
on that knowledge.

Note that the contradiction just described is present only if we take
'knows where the still-existing object is' to mean 'knows where the still-
existing object is *in relation to me*'. My point is that if it can truly be said of

somebody that she knows where something is and that she knows where that location is in relation to her present location, then it must also be true that she knows how to act to gain sight of that thing. And note also that I am not discussing here the development of knowledge that an object may continue to exist when its location is unknown (e.g., a departed parent or a lost toy). I think that it is fair to regard this as a more sophisticated and later-developing form of externality. Perhaps it requires what Piaget (1955) called 'mental representation'—the ability to evoke conscious representations of absent objects—whose arrival he timed at about 18 months, *after* the development of searching for currently occluded objects was complete.

But the fundamental distinction here is that between representation permanence and externality, since maintaining a representation of a currently invisible object beyond the instant at which it was rendered invisible implies no grasp of the relation between itself and the object on the infant's part. This is not to deny that the 'representation' in 'representation permanence' has content, because it is possible for there to be a representation with a particular content and with certain causal liasons to output (hence the surprise reaction) without this representation being that of something external to the self, of something that is the cause of one's actual or possible perceptual experiences.[11] Such a representation may even fall short of being 'causally indexical' (p. 130 above).

Recall that what we are concerned with here is the development of a subject's reflective, theorylike grasp of its place in the physical world. Studying the conditions under which a subject will search for an occluded object will inform us about this development because an integral feature of this theorylike understanding is a reflective awareness of the implications that arrays of objects have for what can be experienced, avoided, and reached for (see Campbell 1993, 88). Infants of around 8 months who search for completely occluded objects for the first time may not yet be manifesting this understanding in a reflective from; indeed, Piaget insisted that they were not.[12] But they are taking strides along the royal road to this reflective understanding if there is any truth in what I argued in the second section.

Finally, I want to consider in this section an objection to my distinction between representation permanence and externality. Despite the broad sympathy, noted above, that workers in connectionism have with Piaget's account of sensorimotor development, an objection arises out of current attempts to model object permanence in neural networks.[13] The objection is, in effect, that there is no deep mystery about why infants are surprised by anomolous occlusion events at 4 months of age but do not search until they are twice as old. The situation for the 4-month-old is that its representation of the occluded object is strong enough to drive a surprise reaction but too weak to drive a search. The research program for connectionist modeling of object permanence then becomes that of modelling the kind of information that strengthens the representation sufficiently to drive a search.

The reply is that it only makes sense to regard the developmental progression in this way if we treat search as a *reaction to events*. But search is not a reaction to events (and, so far as we know, there is no period of "reactive search"): it is action taken on the basis of knowledge of where something is in relation to us. It is not even strictly correct to treat it as means-end behavior, because a means may be *arbitrarily* related to an end. To thus talk of representations "driving" or "causing" search is to use a misleading metaphor that assimilates acting to reacting.[14] Search is only intelligible when it is regarded as an action carried out from knowledge of how the world is configured in relation to us: representations do not cause it.

4 Self-World Dualism and a Conception of Other Minds

Having looked at the world half of self-world dualism, I now turn to the self. I will argue that because experiencing oneself as an agent is necessary for being a subject of objective experience, a conception of mentality (a "theory of mind" as it is now called in developmental psychology) will depend upon the experience of agency. That is to say, for the child to develop a conception of mind sufficient for her to explain and predict the behavior of other people, she must have experienced first-person agency. (Note that I am assuming the identity of the self in 'self-world' and 'self-other'.) As we will see, this way of arguing means that we cannot dismiss the view that the rudiments of a representational theory of mind are innate, though piagetians do not hold that such a theory *has* to be innate.[15] But even were we to succeed in establishing that an innate representational "theory" exists, we would not thereby have succeeded in explaining how we come to have our conception of mentality, given that it depends on the experience of agency.

Whereas nativism about spatial and object concepts is based on foundational arguments from philosophers such as Kant and on a wealth of empirical evidence, nativism about mental knowledge is based on Platonic arguments about concept acquisition of the kind fielded by J. A. Fodor (1975, 1987), as well as on rather controversial evidence from developmental psychology and from the study of abnormal populations (Russell 1992).[16] Fodor's argument is essentially that no organism can learn mental-state predicates such as 'think' and 'intend' without having the prior capacity to represent the extension of these predicates in an innate "language of thought." Within developmental psychology, Leslie (1987), among others (e.g., Premack, 1990), has proposed that a theory of mind in which an innate, modular device matures in the second year of life, thereby enabling the child to compute relations between a subject, her propositional attitudes, and her propositional contents. According to Leslie, this can be first seen in the child's comprehension of pretence in other people, where another's deviant treatment of an object is coded by the child as her purposefully representing that object as being other than it is (e.g., a mother's pretending that a banana is a telephone receiver, in Leslie's example). PRE-TEND is taken to be a symbol in the language of thought (Leslie 1988).

Let us accept, for the sake of argument, that this view is correct, that human beings do indeed possess an innate apparatus for computing propositional contents and—in Fodor's (1987) metaphor—for placing these contents into different propositional-attitude "boxes"—belief boxes, pretend boxes, and the like. Now imagine a system that is able to perform all these operations. It observes somebody picking something up and codes this as an intentional act; observes somebody being startled and codes this as nonintentional; observes somebody putting a banana to her head and talking into it and records this as a case of pretence; observes somebody leaving his house, turning on his heels to go back indoors, and reemerging with an umbrella and computes the propositional contents of his belief and desire attitudes. In short, this mentalizing system is a prodigious parser of mental categories. However, it has no capacity for monitoring and reversing its actions, and so it is not an agent in the present sense.

Predictably, the piagetian will say that this system has no conception of other minds, despite its skills at parsing mental categories. The first reason for saying so emerges naturally from what has gone before. The refractoriness thesis (whether expressed in the form of reversibility or felt resistance) seeks to establish that experiencing oneself as an agent is necessary for knowing oneself to be the subject of objective experience—is necessary, in other words, for subjectivity. As the system in our thought experiment is not an agent, it cannot, on this view, possess subjectivity, and if it does not possess subjectivity, then it makes little sense to say that it is a mind. So we have the paradoxical state of affairs that a nonmental entity is parsing mental episodes. What's wrong with this? Cannot minds be known purely "from the outside," as it were? A negative answer to this question emerges with two further considerations.

The piagetian will say (a) that a conception of other minds depends on a conception of others as agents, and (b) that conceiving of others as agents is possible only if one can experience oneself as an agent. A proper defence of both of these claims would take a long time, but they can be defended briefly. With regard to (a), to ascribe mentality to others means conceiving of them as *rational*, and this requires us in turn to see them as "capable of assessing positions, of following out reasons, and possibly of being critical. All these things presuppose our not being merely passive in relation to putative objects of knowledge" (Hamlyn 1990, 148). With regard to (b), agency is grounded in first-person experience unmediated by observation of oneself: we cannot gain a conception of what an agent is by watching how we and others behave—a view that bears a more than accidental resemblance to the denial that our knowledge of what we are doing could be gained by self-observation (see section 2). Something of this is captured by Thomas Nagel when he speaks of "a clash between the view of action from the inside and *any* view of it from the outside. Any external view of an act as something that happens . . . seems to omit the doing of it" (Nagel 1979, 198–199).

The basic idea here is that agency is something that can only be known "from the inside," as it were. So the system in our thought experiment must be achieving its feat (*if* such a feat can be achieved at all) by coding (what J. B. Watson called) "colorless movements," not by coding the actions of agents. It will have no conception of agency, on this view, because this conception depends on *the experience* of trying to achieve goals and of being in control of one's body and thus—a point I have labored—of one's immediate mental life. It is an experience no less than, say, pain is an experience. (See O'Shaughnessy 1980, chap. 11, on the parallels between our knowledge of our own trying and of sensory experiences like pain.) A creature that never felt pain could accurately code pain behavior, but its conception of pain would be empty. The parsings of agency by our imagined system would be similarly empty.

Moreover, it is questionable whether this imagined system could ever entertain first-person thoughts. Because it is not an agent, it possesses only an apprehending self and not a willing self. It is the point, as it were, at which informational input terminates. But if the position sketched at the end of section 2 is correct—if, as Janaway (1989) argues, selfhood requires the 'I' in 'I will' and 'I perceive/believe/know/etc.' to corefer—then the system will be incapable of entertaining first-person thoughts even if it, per impossibile, developed subjectivity.

There is a natural objection to this claim that knowledge of others' agency is grounded in first-person experience. Some might say that this view is Cartesian, insisting that there are tried and trusted arguments against the Cartesian view that knowledge of our own mental states is immediate, incorrigible knowledge that can be projected to others by analogy. Wittgenstein (1953, §243 onwards) has shown us, the objector might say, that because the meaning of a term is grounded in public corrigibility, if one is the sole arbiter of whether a mental-state predicate has been correctly ascribed to oneself, then no predicate has been meaningfully ascribed in fact. The following argument from Strawson might also, perhaps, be recruited: If one can succeed in picking oneself out as the argument of a mental-state predicate, then one must already be in a position to pick others out as an argument for that predicate. "One can ascribe states of consciousness to oneself only if one can ascribe them to others" (Strawson 1959, 100).

But an anti-Cartesian objection is beside the point here. The child will obviously come to apply agency predicates, among other kinds of predicates, when she acquires language, but seeing other as agents, *appreciating that some observations of others are observations of their agency*,[17] is not a matter of ascribing to others a predicate one first ascribes to oneself. Indeed, calling agency an 'experience' is tantamount to denying that it consists in the ascription of predicates to oneself. When a baby of 4 months extricates its rattle from the rungs of its cot, it is experiencing agency, not ascribing predicates.

To bring the discussion round to empirical issues in development, we can see that the piagetian view is well placed to describe the role of social interaction in the development of selfhood. For, in clear contrast to the nativist, the piagetian is in a position to acknowledge that self-awareness will emerge, in part, through social interaction, though in equally clear contrast to writers like Mead (1934) and Vygotsky (1962), the piagetian would *deny* that this process is one of social transmission or internalization.

Consider the executive demands that social interaction makes on the subject. Compared to inanimate objects, other people "go off like guns on the stage of [the child's] panorama of experience," to use J. M. Baldwin's evocative phrase (1906, 49). Although social psychologists and students of early communication (e.g., Bruner 1975) have tended to stress the rule-boundedness of early social interaction, here it is its *un*predictablity that must be noted. In order for them to deal successfully with other people, young children must be prodigious decision makers: they must constantly be on social guard to select new but appropriate behaviors in the light of what the other has done. As was the case for interactions with physical objects, there must be instigation, inhibition, planning, and monitoring of behavior, but the most crucial in social life is the ability to improvize. To illustrate, in their model of the "executive systems" Norman and Shallice (1986) distinguished between routine-action "scripts" (with triggering and inhibiting relations between their subcomponents) and the "Supervisory Attentional System," the executive overseer that takes control in novel situations.[18] In social interaction there is constant novelty, in the sense that new things—if not new *kinds* of things—are constantly being done, and so the supervisory system is, loosely speaking, in constant use.

What does this imply about the developing conception of other minds? From the first-person perspective, the experience of piloting itself through the relatively uncertain waters of social interaction will provide the infant with the experience of being in charge of itself. The more novelty *required*, the more one's experience becomes that of the supervisor of one's behavior and immediate mental life. From a first-person perspective, in terms of the executive demands of social interaction, the other is refractory, is uncontrollable and unpredictable—to return to this (J. M.) Baldwinian theme. As I have argued, the first-person perspective is primary, but it also makes sense to talk of self- and other-awareness as being constructed in social interaction. The more autonomous—the more *self-determined*—the subject, the more successful the process of ego development.

This account makes a very clear prediction about what the consequences would be of early impairments in agency. We can assume that one form that these impairments might take is that the "executive system"—meaning roughly the system responsible for inhibiting, monitoring, and regulating behavior and for the instigation and transformation of strategies—will be dysfunctional, and that early executive dysfunctions will lead to impaired self-awareness and thus to an impaired conception of other minds. In the syndrome of autism there are indeed such co-occurences of executive dysfunctions (e.g., Hughes and Russell 1993; Hughes, Russell, and Robbins 1994; Ozonoff, in press; Ozonoff, Pennington, and Rogers 1991; Russell, Mauthner, Sharpe, and Tidswell 1991) and very well-documented difficulties in predicting and explaining behavior mentalistically (see the papers in Baron-Cohen, Tager-Flusberg, and Cohen 1993). This is highly consistent with the piagetian view.

By contrast, nativists about mental knowledge have tried to explain autism in terms of the delay or deviance in the maturation of the "theory of mind module" or TOMM (Leslie and Thaiss 1992), but in doing so, they have difficulty in explaining why "mentalizing" impairments should coexist with executive impairments. There have, however, been attempts. Christopher Frith (1992), for one, argues that performing executive tasks relies heavily on action monitoring, and this requires the adequate functioning of a TOMM-like system whose core is a mechanism for representing one's own mental states. Consequently, he refers to the neurological impairment that he takes to underlie the mentalizing difficulties within autism and schizophrenia as ones of "metarepresentation," after Leslie (1987).

At this point the debate between the nativist and the piagetian must obviously be decided empirically. The piagetian would predict, for example, that administering executive tasks such as attention shifting (Atkinson, Hood, Wattam-Bell, and Braddick 1992) in order to screen infants at risk of acquiring autism (with relatives suffering from autism, autismlike disorders or schizophrenia) should successfully identify which of these at-risk infants will acquire the disorder. So, despite its derivation from an essentially philosophical position, the piagetian thesis has a clear empirical cash value.

Acknowledgments

In writing this chapter I received invaluable advice from the editors and also benefitted from the comments of the following people, to whom thanks are due: Chris Frith, Susan Goodrich, Suzanne Hala, Paul Harris, Jane Heal, Jennifer Hornsby, and Paul Noordhoff. For an extended treatment of the themes covered here, see my *Agency: Its Role in Mental Development* (in press).

Notes

1. James Mark Baldwin was an American philosopher-psychologist who produced his influential work around the turn of the century, most notably his three-volume *Thought and Things*. See Russell 1978 for an extensive discussion of Baldwin and a comparison of his theory with Piaget's.

2. To code spatial locations and relations allocentrically is to code them without regard to one's point of view ("egocentric" coding). Some relations are allocentric per se, such as place *b* lying *between* place *a* and place *c*. An "allocentric representation" is a rather theoretically loaded term (Brewer and Pears 1993). However, in experiments with animals and human infants, the term 'allocentric coding' simply means coding in terms of the relation between two points without regard to where the subject is positioned.

3. Causally indexical representations are those made purely in terms of the implications for the subject's own movements, "within reach," for example. A causally nonindexical representation is reflective, in contrast to the indexical variety, in the sense that its character is not entirely determined by the implications that it has for what the organism can do.

4. In her book *Kant's Transcendental Psychology*, Patricia Kitcher attempts to reinstate Kant's psychological doctrines, taking the term 'transcendental psychology' to mean "the psychology of the thinking, or better, the knowing self" (1990, 22). She treats this as being roughly equivalent to the analysis of cognitive tasks. This is not empirical psychology. But, as Kitcher points out, much of what we call psychology involves the conceptual analysis of tasks rather than experimentation, Newell and Simon's (1972) work on problem solving for example.

5. The term 'subpersonal' is a term coined by Daniel Dennett, originally in chapter 4 of his *Content and Consciousness*. The personal level is the level on which we talk about acts, intentions, beliefs, thoughts, reasons, feelings, and the like (some call this the 'folk-

psychological level'), while the subpersonal level, as Dennett puts it elsewhere, is the "behind-the-scenes *machinery* that governs speech dispositions, motor subroutines, information storage and retrieval, and the like" (Dennett 1978, 216; my italics).

6. The obvious distinction to be drawn at this point might appear to be one between reactions (or responses) and actions (see Dickinson and Balleine 1993), where we take actions to be goal-directed behaviors, movements made *for the sake of* a goal. However, I do not wish to make a strong commitment to the goal-directedness of self-determined actions. What I mean by being 'self-determined' involves more than goal-directedness. Moreover, self-determined actions may be aimless.

There is a distinction to be made between what Brewer (1993) calls the "mere capacity" to get things done and the genuine ability for basic bodily action that involves control over one's body, the "ability to direct the will's extension into the body" (1993, 308). Goal-directed actions, may be the former without being the latter.

7. Kant drew this distinction in an (apparently unsuccessful) attempt to establish that world-generated causal sequences possess a form of "necessity." But this does not make it irrelevant to our concern with agency.

8. Piaget (1955, chap. 2) attempted to explain the relation between an objective conception of space and the forms of activity necessary for this conception in terms of mathematical group theory. Reversibility (or "inversion") is one of the four properties of the relation between operations and elements in a mathematical group.

9. Hume argued that such a position is untenable because in acting voluntarily, we are only experiencing the conjunction of occurrences of willing with bodily movments. Following O'Shaughnessy, Baldwin adopts a non-Humean account of action couched in terms of "the having of power or control over the limb": action is not a causal conjunction between a mental and a physical event but an act of will "coming to fruition." See pages 112–116 of Baldwin's chapter in this volume.

10. The work of Elizabeth Spelke (e.g., 1991) and her coworkers should be mentioned in this context. They have performed a number of dishabituation studies showing that infants have expectations about some principles of naive physics (e.g., inertia).

11. Chrisley (1993) has argued that infants' representations of objects prior to attaining full object permanence (on Piaget's criteria) have "nonconceptual content" (Crane 1992). He has also equated the attainment of conceptual content with meeting Evans's (1982) generality constraint, as have I (Russell 1988). However, there is a good deal of debate over how the line between nonconceptual and conceptual content should be drawn, on which question, see the chapter by José Bermúdez in this volume.

12. In fact, in light of subsequent failures to search (after visible and invisible displacements of the object), Piaget regarded search at 8 months as being little more than an instrumental procedure. Equivalent to a reflective understanding of object permanence was what Piaget called 'mental representation', which was supposed to be attained at around 18 months of age.

13. This view was put to me by Kim Plunkett, and a version of it can be found in Munakata, McClelland, Johnson, and Siegler 1994.

14. I do not think that David Hamlyn is putting it too strongly when he writes, in a commentary on the view that representations cause behavior, "it could be said that an appeal to representations at this point is something of a fraud: the appeal is made simply

to provide an otherwise missing connection between the central processes and behavior." (1990, 128–129).

15. Broadly empiricist theories of the development of a theory of mind are those in which the developing child is regarded as being in a position similar to that of a scientist testing hypotheses against the behavioral data (e.g., Gopnik and Wellman 1992). I have argued against such views in Russell 1993.

16. Some theorists (see papers in Baron-Cohen et al. 1993) argue that the fact that people with autism are specifically handicapped on tests supposed to measure "mentalizing" ability suggests that they lack the "theory-of-mind module."

17. I am grateful to Jennifer Hornsby for suggesting this way of putting it.

18. 'Executive systems' is a rather loose term used to refer to the mental functions carried out by the prefrontal cortices. These center on the control of behavior via inhibition, monitoring, planning, and selection of strategies. Some theorists, such as Shallice, stress the importance of control in nonroutine circumstances while others (e.g., Goldman-Rakic 1987) stress the control of behavior by models held in working memory.

References

Atkinson, J., B. Hood, J. Wattam-Bell, and O. J. Braddick. 1992. "Changes in Infants' Ability to Switch Attention in the First Three Months of Life." *Perception* 21:643–653.

Baillargeon, R. 1987. "Object Permanence in 3.5- and 4.5-Month-Olds." *Developmental Psychology* 23:655–664.

Baldwin, J. M. 1906. *Thought and Things*, 3 vols. London: Swann and Sonnenschein.

Baron-Cohen, S., H. Tager-Flusberg, and D. Cohen, eds. 1993. *Understanding Other Minds*. Oxford: Oxford University Press.

Brewer, B. 1993. "The Integration of Spatial Vision and Action." In *Spatial Representation: Problems in Philosophy and Psychology*, ed. N. Eilan, R. McCarthy, and B. Brewer. Oxford: Blackwell.

Brewer, B., and J. Pears. 1993. "Introduction: Frames of Reference." In *Spatial Representation: Problems in Philosophy and Psychology*, ed. N. Eilan, R. McCarthy, and B. Brewer. Oxford: Blackwell.

Bruner, J. S. 1975. "The Ontogenesis of Speech Acts." *Journal of Child Language* 2:1–19.

Campbell, J. 1993. "The Role of Physical Objects in Spatial Thinking." In *Spatial Representation: Problems in Philosophy and Psychology*, ed. N. Eilan, R. McCarthy, and B. Brewer. Oxford: Blackwell.

Chrisley, R. L. 1993. "Connectionism, Cognitive Maps, and the Development of Objectivity." *Artificial Intelligence Review* 7:329–354.

Crane, T. 1992. "The Non-conceptual Content of Experience. In *The Contents of Experience*, ed. T. Crane Cambridge: Cambridge University Press.

Dennett, D. C. 1978. "Why You Can't Make a Computer That Feels Pain." In his *Brainstorms*. Hassocks, U.K.: Harvester Press.

Dennett, D. C. 1991. *Consciousness Explained*. Harmondsworth, U.K.: Penguin Books.

Dickinson, A. J., and B. Balleine. 1993. "Actions and Responses." In *Spatial Representation: Problems in Philosophy and Psychology*, ed. N. Eilan, R. McCarthy, and B. Brewer. Oxford: Blackwell.

Evans, G. 1982. *The Varieties of Reference*. Oxford: Oxford University Press.

Fodor, J. A. 1975. *The Language of Thought*. New York: Crowell.

Fodor, J. A. 1987. *Psychosemantics*. Cambridge: MIT Press.

Frith, C. D. 1992. *The Cognitive Neuropsychology of Schizophrenia*. Hove, U.K.: Lawrence Erlbaum.

Gallistel, C. R. 1980. *The Organization of Action: A New Synthesis*. Hillsdale, N.J.: Lawrence Erlbaum.

Goldman-Rakic, P. S. 1987. "Circuitry of Primate Prefrontal Contex and Regulation of Behavior by Representational Memory." In *Handbook of Physiology: The Nervous System*, ed. F. Plum. New York: Oxford University Press.

Gopnik, A., and H. M. Wellman. 1992. "Why the Child's Theory of Mind Really *Is* a Theory." *Mind and Language* 7:145–171.

Hamlyn, D. W. 1990. *In and Out of the Black Box*. Oxford: Basil Blackwell.

Hopkins, J. 1987. "Synthesis in the Imagination." In *Philosophical Perspectives on Developmental Psychology*, ed. J. Russell. Oxford: Basil Blackwell.

Hughes, C., and J. Russell. 1993. "Autistic Children's Difficulty with Mental Disengagement from an Object: Its Implications for Theories of Autism." *Developmental Psychology* 29:498–510.

Hughes, C., J. Russell, and T. W. Robbins. 1994. "Evidence for Executive Dysfunction in Autism." *Neuropsychologia* 21:643–653.

Janaway, C. 1989. *Self and World in Schopenhauer's Philosophy*. Oxford: Clarendon Press.

Kitcher, P. 1990. *Kant's Transcendental Psychology*. Oxford: Oxford University Press.

Leslie, A. M. 1987. "Pretence and Representation: The Orgins of 'Theory of Mind'." *Psychological Review* 94:412–426.

Leslie, A. M. 1988. "Some Implications of Pretense for Mechanisms Underlying the Child's Theory of Mind." In *Developing Theories of Mind*, ed. J. Astington, P. L. Harris, and D. R. Olson. Cambridge: Cambridge University Press.

Leslie, A. M., and L. Thaiss. 1992. "Domain Specificity in Conceptual Development: Neuropsychological Evidence from Autism." *Cognition*, 43:225–251.

McClelland, J. 1989. "Parallel Distributed Processing: Implications for Cognition and Development." In *Parallel Distributed Processing*, ed. R. Morris. Oxford: Clarendon Press.

Mead, G. H. 1934. *Mind, Self, and Society*. Chicago: University of Chicago Press.

Munakata, Y., J. L. McClelland, M. H. Johnson, and R. S. Siegler. 1994. "Now You See It, Now You Don't: A Gradualist Framework for Understanding Infant's Successes and Failures in Object Permanence Tasks." Department of Psychology, Carnegie Mellon University, technical report PDP.CNS.94.2, May 1994.

Nadel, L. 1990 "Varieties of Spatial Cognition." In *The Development and Neural Basis of Higher Cognitive Functions*, ed. A. Daimond. New York: New York Academy of Sciences.

Nagel, T. 1979. "Subjective and Objective." In his *Mortal Questions*. Cambridge: Cambridge University Press.

Newell, A., and H. Simon. 1972. *Human Problem Solving*. Englewood Cliffs, N.J.: Prentice-Hall.

Norman, D. A., and T. Shallice. 1986. "Attention to Action: Willed and Automatic Control of Behavior." In *Consciousness and Self-Regulation*, vol. 4, ed. R. J. Davidson, G. E. Schwartz, and D. Shapiro. New York: Plenum.

O'Keefe, J., and L. Nadel. 1978. *The Hippocampus as a Cognitive Map*. Oxford: Clarendon Press.

O'Shaughnessy, B. 1980. *The Will*, vol. 1. Cambridge: Cambridge University Press.

Ozonoff, S. In press. "Executive Functions in Autism." In *Learning and Cognition in Autism*. ed. E. Schopler and G. B. Mesibov. New York: Plenum Press.

Ozonoff, S., B. Pennington, and S. Rogers. 1991. "Executive Function Deficits in High-Functioning Autistic Children: Relationship to Theory of Mind." *Journal of Child Psychology and Psychiatry* 32:1081–1105.

Papert, S. 1963. "Intelligence chez l'enfant et chez le robot." In *La filiation des structures*, ed. L. Apostel, J. Grize, S. Papert, and J. Piaget, Etudes d'epistemologie genetique, no. 22.

Piaget, J. 1955. *The Child's Construction of Reality*. London: Routledge and Kegan Paul.

Piaget, J. 1970. "Piaget's Theory." In *Carmichael's Manual of Child Psychology*, vol. 1, ed. P. Mussen. New York: John Wiley.

Premack, D. 1990. "The Infant's Theory of Self-Propelled Objects." *Cognition* 36:1–16.

Russell, J. 1978. *The Acquisition of Knowledge*. London: Macmillan Press.

Russell, J. 1988. "Cognisance and Cognitive Science. Part 1: The Generality Constraint." *Philosophical Psychology* 1:235–258.

Russell, J. 1992. "The Theory-Theory: So Good They Named It Twice?" *Cognitive Development* 7:485–519.

Russell, J. 1993. "On Leaving Your Children Wrapped in Thought." *Behavioral and Brain Sciences* 16:76–77.

Russell, J. In press. *Agency: Its Role in Mental Development*. Hove, U.K.: Lawrence Erlbaum.

Russell, J., N. Mauthner, S. Sharpe, and T. Tidswell. 1991. "The 'Windows Task' as a Measure of Strategic Deception in Preschoolers and Autistic Subjects." *British Journal of Developmental Psychology* 9:331–349.

Spelke, E. 1991. "Physical Knowledge in Infancy: Reflections on Piaget's Theory." In *The Epigenesis of Mind: Essays on Biology and Cognition*, ed. S. Carey and R. Gelman. Hillsdale, N.J.: Lawrence Erlbaum.

Schopenhauer, A. 1844. *Die Welt als Wille und Vorstellung*, vol. 1. Page references to *The World as Will and Representation*, vol. 1, trans. E. Payne. New York: Dover Press, 1966.

Strawson, P. F. 1959. *Individuals: An Essay in Descriptive Metaphysics*. Oxford: Oxford University Press.

von Holst, E., and H. Mittelstaedt. "Das Reafferenzprinzip: Wechselwirkung zwischen Zentralnervensystem und Peripherie." Translation by R. D. Martin published in *The Behavioral Physiology of Animals and Man: Selected Papers of E. von Holst*, vol. 1. Coral Gables: University of Miami Press, 1973.

Vygotsky, L. S. 1962. *Thought and Language*. Cambridge: MIT Press.

Wittgenstein, L. 1953. *Philosophical Investigations*. Oxford: Basil Blackwell.

Ecological Perception and the Notion of a Nonconceptual Point of View

José Luis Bermúdez

There are many distinct layers of self-consciousness. Obvious examples are the capacity to think of one's body as one's own; to recognize oneself as the bearer of mental states; to master the grammar of the first-person pronoun; to view oneself an one object in the world among others, or as one person in the world among others; to have memories about one's past self; to construct autobiographical narratives; to formulate long-term plans and ambitions. Whichever one of these one is considering, however, it is tempting to think of it as somehow parasitic on a more primitive and already-existing form of self-awareness. So, for example, it seems intuitively hard to imagine that one could formulate long-term plans without having some sort of autobiographical narrative at one's disposal or, indeed, that one could formulate such an autobiographical narrative without having a stock of memories about one's past self. If this is so, however, and if a regress is to be avoided, then it seems plausible to suppose that all these layers must eventually be grounded in a form of self-awareness primitive enough not to depend on a more basic self-awareness.

One of the attractions of the Gibsonian concept of ecological perception is that it seems to provide us with a basic level of self-awareness that could serve as a core for such comprehensive accounts of the phenomenon (or phenomena) of self-consciousness. On the ecological understanding of perception, a form of sensitivity to self-specifying information is built into the very structure of perception from the earliest stages of infancy in such a way that, as Gibson famously put it, all perception involves coperception of the self and the environment. In this paper I propose to explore the implications of this suggestion. I will argue that by starting with ecological perception and seeing how it needs to be built up, we can reach an understanding of the features that a basic form of self-awareness must incorporate.

1   The Ecological View of Perception

For many psychologists and philosophers the five senses are directed "out-
wards"—they are exteroceptive or exterosensitive, designed to inform us
about objects and events in the world. They can, of course, be turned on
oneself, as, for example, when one looks at oneself through a mirror, but
doing this provides a distinct sort of information about oneself, information
that objectifies the body, failing to do justice to the sense in which the subject of perception is also the object of perception. This objectifying form of
perceiving oneself is often contrasted with the form of self-perception from
within, gained through what has been termed a 'body sense'. Receptors in
the skin, muscles, tendons, and joints, operating in conjunction with the
vestibular system, yield proprioceptive information about bodily position
and movement that is crucial in orienting and acting within the world. This
has led to a firm distinction in both operation and function, with the five
exteroceptive senses deemed to provide information about the external
world, while the proprioceptive system provides information about the self,
in particular about bodily posture and movement.

It is instructive to view the Gibsonian theory of ecological perception as challenging precisely such a strict distinction between proprioceptive and exteroceptive senses (see also Neisser 1988, 1991). Gibson claims
that the five ostensibly outward-directed senses provide both exteroceptive
and proprioceptive information, rejecting the traditional division of labor
between the five exteroceptive senses and proprioceptive body sense.

A deep theoretical muddle is connected with proprioception. . . . In my view,
proprioception can be understood as egoreception, as sensitivity to the self, not as
one special channel of sensations or as several of them. I maintain that all the perceptual systems are propriosensitive as well as exterosensitive, for they all provide
information in their various ways about the observer's activities. . . . Information
that is specific to the self is picked up as such, no matter what sensory nerve is delivering impulses to the brain. (Gibson 1979, 115)

Although propriospecific and exterospecific information are distinct types
of information, they are simultaneously available to each sense, rather than
each being the province of a distinct sensory system.

Perhaps the most basic form of propriospecific information arises
through the structure imposed upon the visual array by the perceiver's body.
As Gibson stresses, every animal has a field of view which is bounded by its
body, and the particular way in which each animal's body blocks out aspects
of its environment is unique to that animal. "Ask yourself what it is you see
hiding the surroundings as you look out upon the world—not darkness,
surely, not air, not nothing, but the ego" (Gibson 1979, 112). In this limited

but important sense the self is actually present in visual perception, as the frame of the field of view, as what surrounds and gives it structure.

More sophisticated forms of visual proprioception exist because the perceiving subject moves through the world. The mass of constantly changing visual information generated by the subject's motion poses an immense challenge to the perceptual systems. How can the visual experiences generated by motion be decoded so that subjects perceive that they are moving through the world? How can one simultaneously experience oneself as moving and the world as stationary? Gibson's notion of *visual kinesthesis* is his answer to this traditional problem. Every movement made by the subject generates a systematic pattern of flow in the visual field. The surfaces in the optical array change in structure, and in their relation to the self-specifying invariants. There are some striking experiments displaying the importance which this type of optical flow has in the determination of posture. In so-called "moving-room" experiments, subjects are placed on the solid floors of rooms whose walls are independently moveable (Lishman and Lee 1973, Lee and Aronson 1975). Young children in this situation will sway and lose their balance if the walls are moved in either direction on the sagittal plane, because the optical flow yields the information that the subjects are moving.

The third relevant form of self-specifying information available in the environment is encapsulated in the Gibsonian notion of *affordances*: "At any given moment the environment affords a host of possibilities: I could grasp that object, sit on that chair, walk through that door. These are examples of *affordances*: relations of possibility between actors and environments. It is affordances that animals most need to see: here is prey that I might eat, a predator who might possibly eat me, a tree I might climb to escape him" (Neisser 1991, 201). The claim here is that the perception of affordances is relativized to the perceiving subject, so that, for example, in looking at a window one perceives not just an aperture but an aperture that presents the possibility of one's looking through it. The ecological suggestion is that the perception of affordances is partly a mode of self-perception. Furthermore, it is such constitutively. The whole notion of an affordance rests on relating environmental information to one's own possibilities for action and reaction.

2   Ecological Perception and the Notion of Point of View

Ecological self-perception falls a long way short of fully-fledged self-consciousness. There is a crucial difference between having information about oneself as part of one's ecological experience and being fully self-conscious,

where fully fledged self-consciousness is taken to involve the capacity to entertain 'I' thoughts or to maintain some form of detached perspective on
oneself. Neither of these two sophisticated capacities is required for ecological self-perception to take place. What the ecological approach might more
plausibly be argued to provide is a way of understanding the notion of a point
of view on the world. The most developed account of this notion has been
offered by Strawson in his discussion of Kant's Transcendental Deduction in
The Bounds of Sense, where he suggests it as a necessary but not sufficient
strand in a complete account of self-consciousness. I will consider his position in some detail because it sets the framework for this paper.

Strawson argues that possession of a point of view rests on the possibility of a subject's experiences being such "as to determine a distinction
between the subjective route of his experiences and the objective world
through which it is a route" (Strawson 1966, 104). That a subject's experiences contain such a distinction over time is what yields the subject's point
of view on the world:

A series of experiences satisfying the Kantian provision has a certain double aspect. On the one hand it cumulatively builds up a picture of the world in which
objects and happenings (with their particular characteristics) are presented as possessing an objective order, an order which is logically independent of any particular experiential route through the world. On the other hand it possesses its own
order as a series of experiences of objects. If we thought of such a series of experiences as continuously articulated in a series of detailed judgements, then, taking
their order and content together, those judgements would be such as to yield, on
the one hand, a (potential) description of an objective world and on the other the
chart of the course of a single subjective experience of that world. (Strawson 1966,
105–106)

Strawson's conception of a point of view is intended to draw together two
distinct (sets of) conceptual capacities: the capacity for the self-ascription
of experiences and the capacity to grasp the objectivity of the world. Why
do they need to be brought together?

Strawson is considering the question, What conditions have to be fulfilled for experience to be possible? He approaches it through the hypothesis that there might be an experience whose objects were sense data, "red,
round patches, brown oblongs, flashes, whistles, tickling sensations, smells"
(1966, 99). This would not count as anything recognizable as experience,
he maintains, because it would not permit any distinction to be drawn between a subject's experiences and the objects of which they are experiences. In such a case, the *esse* of the putative "objects of experience" would
be their *percipi*. There would be no distinction between the order of experiences and the order of the objects of experience, and this, according to

Strawson, effectively means that we cannot talk either about objects of experience or about a subject of experience, and hence we cannot talk about experience at all.

The general idea is that no creature can count as a subject of experience unless it is capable of drawing certain very basic distinctions. What is important about a point of view, as Strawson conceives it, is that experience which reflects a temporally extended point of view on the world will ipso facto permit those basic distinctions to be drawn, and this is so because experience reflecting a point of view has the double aspect outlined in the passage quoted earlier. Experience reflecting a point of view just is experience that permits the right sort of distinctions to be drawn between a subject's experiences and the objects of which they are experiences.

Suppose we grant that such a purely sense-datum "experience" is impossible. And suppose we also grant that experience with the sort of double aspect that he describes qualifies as genuine experience by making available the sorts of distinctions that could not be drawn in a purely sense-datum experience. This still leaves open an important question. Are the capacity to ascribe experiences to oneself and the capacity to grasp the objectivity of the world necessary conditions of any possible experience that has the dual structure impossible in a putative sense-datum experience?

One reason for thinking that these conceptual capacities might not be necessary conditions is provided by research on object representation in infancy. Much recent work in developmental psychology strongly suggests that very young infants are capable of primitive forms of object representation which involve, for example, the capacity to perceive object unity and to employ certain basic principles of physical reasoning, such as the principle that objects move on single connected paths (Spelke 1990, Spelke and Van de Walle 1993). Such a level of object representation does not demand a conceptual grasp of causality or of the connectedness of space, and hence does not involve possessing the sort of comprehension of the objectivity of the world built into Strawson's notion of a point of view. Nor, of course, does it involve having a theoretical grip on objects and the principles of naive physics.

It would be rash to suggest that these experiments alone provide evidence that the infants have anything like a point of view, but they at least suggest the need to formulate the basic distinction at the heart of the notion of a point of view in such a way that it does not come out as a matter of definition that the infants cannot have experience that reflects a point of view. Just as there are ways of representing objects that do not require mastery of the relevant concepts, might there not be ways in which a creature's experience might incorporate the basic distinction at the heart of the notion of a point of view without a conceptual grasp of the distinction? In this paper I would like to suggest that there are indeed such ways. Before going any further, however, I need a way of understanding that basic distinction that at least leaves this possibility open.

If we formulate the central distinction as one between subjective experience and what that subjective experience is experience of, we capture what seems to be the crucial feature missing in the hypothesized purely sense datum experience, without immediately demanding any relevant conceptual capacities on the part of the subject. Using this as the central notion, we can reformulate the original characterization: having a temporally extended point of view on the world involves taking a particular route through space-time in such a way that one's perception of the world is informed by an awareness that one is taking such a route, where such an awareness requires being able to distinguish over time between subjective experience and what it is experience of.

The matter can be further clarified by adverting to the concept of a *nonsolipsistic consciousness*, which Strawson introduces in *Individuals*. There he refers to "the consciousness of a being who has a use for the distinction between himself and his states on the one hand, and something not himself or a state of himself, of which he has experience, on the other" (1959, 69). We can see the notion of a point of view as fleshing out what experience must be like for any creature that is to count as nonsolipsistic in this sense. Putting it like this brings out why one might expect the notion of a point of view to play a foundational role in a comprehensive account of self-consciousness. The thought would be that being a nonsolipsistic consciousness is the most basic form of self-awareness, and since the notion of a point of view is put forward to capture what experience must be like to support such a nonsolipsistic consciousness, it would seem that here, if anywhere, we have the sort of primitive form of self-awareness that would anchor an account of self-consciousness as a whole.

Because this new formulation is trying to sidestep any demand for sophisticated concept mastery, we can term it the *nonconceptual point of view*. The notion of the nonconceptual at work here can be elucidated with reference to current work on representational content. It has been suggested by various writers on the philosophy of content that it is theoretically legitimate to refer to mental states that represent the world but do not require the bearer of those mental states to possess the concepts required to give a correct specification of the way in which they represent the world (Cussins 1990, Peacocke 1992). The most plausible candidates for such states are perceptual states and subpersonal computational states. For present purposes only the former is relevant. The notion of nonconceptual content as applied to perceptual states is a reaction to the idea dominating much philosophy of perception that all perceptual experience is structured by the concepts possessed by the perceiver. Now, as formulated, the notion of nonconceptual content is neutral on the question of whether the bearer of the appropriate states possesses any concepts at all, because it is nonconceptual in virtue of the fact that the bearer is not required to possess the concepts involved in specifying it. So a point of view will be nonconceptual just in case a creature can be ascribed such a point of view without it being ipso facto necessary to ascribe to it mastery of the concepts required to specify the way in which its experience reflects a point of view. Nonetheless, it is important to distinguish between a conception of *autonomous* nonconceptual content, which does not require that a creature to which it is attributed possess any concepts at all, and a conception of nonconceptual content, which denies that a creature possessing no concepts at all can be in contentful states (Peacocke 1992, 90; Bermúdez 1994). I am interested in the former.

Of course, the possibility of formulating the notion of a point of view so that no relevant conceptual requirements are built into it does not mean that it is possible to have a point of view in the absence of those concepts. It is not ruled out by definition any longer, but there might be other reasons to rule it out. Nonetheless, on this weaker formulation of the notion of a nonconceptual point of view it seems promising to elucidate it through the idea of ecological self-perception. No special argument is needed to show that it is possible to have a nonconceptual point of view, it might be suggested, because such a nonconceptual point of view is built into the very structure of perception. The propriospecific information involved in all exteroception seems to be information about the spatiotemporal route that one is taking through the world, as is particularly apparent in visual kinesthesis. One has, it might seem, a continuous awareness of oneself taking a particular route through the world that does not require the exercise of any conceptual abilities, in virtue of having a constant flow of information about oneself qua physical object moving through the world. On this view, ecological coperception of self and environment is all that is needed for experience with a nonconceptual point of view.

Before evaluating this possibility, it is worth being more explicit about why a point of view has been described as temporally extended. The reason is that a creature whose experience takes place completely within a continuous present (i.e., who lacks any sense of past or future) will not be capable of drawing the fundamental nonsolipsistic distinction between its experience and what it is experience of. We can bring this out by reflecting that being able to make this distinction rests on an awareness that what is being experienced exists independently of any particular experience of it. Such a grasp of independent existence itself involves an understanding that what is being experienced at the moment either has existed in the past, or will exist in the future, that what is being experienced at the present moment has an existence transcending the present moment. By definition, however, a creature which experiences only a continuous present cannot have any such understanding.

The important question, therefore, seems to be, What form must experience take if it is to incorporate an awareness that what is being experienced does not exist only when it is being experienced? Alternatively put, what must the temporal form of any such experience be? Clearly, such an awareness would be incorporated in the experience of any creature that had a grasp of the basic temporal concepts of past, present, and future, but we are looking for something at a more primitive level. What I would suggest is that certain basic recognitional capacities offer the right sort of escape from the continuous present without demanding conceptual mastery. Consider the act of recognizing a particular object. Because such an act involves drawing a connection between one's current experience of an object and a previous experience of it, it brings with it an awareness that what is being experienced has an existence transcending the present moment.

But it is important to specify what it is that the recognitional capacities are being exercised on. A creature could recognize an experience as one that it has previously experienced without any grasp of the distinction between experience and what it is experience of. Clearly, the recognitional capacities must be exercised on something extraneous to the experiences themselves. But what? Physical objects are an obvious candidate, and any creature that could recognize physical objects would have experience that involved drawing the right sort of distinctions. However, one might wonder whether the distinctions could be drawn at a level of experience that does not involve objects. The answer one gives here depends upon one's ontological position on the issue of whether there are "things" that can be reidentified and recognized but are not physical objects. Many philosophers would deny this (including Strawson 1959, chap. 1). The debate is too tortuous to go into here, and I merely state my position without attempting to defend it. There are indeed "things" that can be reidentified and recognized and are neither physical objects nor require experience of physical objects for their recognition. These "things" are places, which can be recognized in terms of distinctive features holding at those places even by a creature that has no grasp on the notion of a physical object (Campbell 1993).

If this is right, we seem in a position to argue that any creature being ascribed a point of view must be capable of exercising the basic capacity to recognize places. If a creature can recognize a particular place, we have a nonsolipsistic consciousness, because we have an object of experience that is grasped as existing independently of a particular experience of it. By the same token, in the absence of such a recognitional capacity (and assuming that there is no grasp of basic temporal concepts nor a capacity to recognize physical objects), it does not seem appropriate to speak of a point of view in the sense under discussion. This yields a strong sense in which a point of view is temporally extended. It is temporally extended not just in that it must extend over time but also in that it must involve the use of memory and recognition to register the passing of time.

It is useful at this point to make a distinction between two types of memory. There are, on the one hand, instances of memory in which past experiences influence present experience, but without any sense on the part of the subject of having had the relevant past experiences, and, on the other, instances in which past experiences not only influence present experience but also the subject is in some sense aware of having had those past experiences. In the former case what licenses talk of memory is the fact that a subject (or an animal, or even a plant) can respond differentially to a stimulus as a function of prior exposure to that stimulus or to similar stimuli. This is not to deny that such memory can be extremely complex. Quite the contrary, such memory seems to be central to the acquisition of any skill, even the most developed. The differential response does not have to be simple or repetitive. Nonetheless, we can draw a contrast between memory at this level and the various forms of memory that do involve an awareness of having had the relevant past experiences, as, for example, when a memory image comes into one's mind or one successfully recalls what one did the previous day. Clearly, there are many levels of such memory (which I shall term 'conscious memory'), of which autobiographical memory is probably the most sophisticated. One thing that these forms of conscious memory all have in common, however, is that previous experience is consciously registered, rather than unconsciously influencing present experience. The distinction is a crude one, precisely because the term 'conscious memory' is so hazy, but it will be sharpened up below.

It follows from our discussion of the notion of a point of view that the place recognition it requires must involve some conscious registration of having been there. Reflect on the case of a creature, perhaps a swallow, that is perfectly capable of performing complicated feats of navigation that involve finding its way back to its nest or back to the warmer climes where it spends the winter but nonetheless does not in any sense consciously recognize the places that it repeatedly encounters. This is not a case, I think, in which one would want to claim that the creature has the appropriate awareness of the route that it is taking through space-time, although it is sensitive to certain facts about that route, because those facts clearly determine behavior (facts, for example, about how to get from one place to another and then back to where it started from).Yet if the creature is credited with exactly the same behavior, only this time accompanied by some form of conscious recognition of the relevant places, the situation seems fundamentally different. Insofar as it recognizes a place, it is aware of having been there before, and insofar as it recognizes having been at a place before, it has the beginning of an awareness of movement through space over time. It is emerging from a continuous present and moving toward possession of a temporally extended point of view.

This enables us to evaluate the suggestion that an ecological analysis of perception shows that a temporally extended point of view is built into the structure of perception. Does ecological self-perception involve anything like conscious memory? If it does, then we will be in a stronger position to claim that the two notions are very intimately connected (although, as stressed above, conscious place recognition is a necessary rather than sufficient condition of possessing a temporally extended point of view).

On the ecological view, perception is fundamentally a process of extracting and abstracting invariants from the flowing optical array. Organisms perceive an environment that has both persisting surfaces and changing surfaces, and the interplay between them allows the organism to pick up the sort of information that specifies, for example, visual kinesthesis. The key to how that information is picked up is the idea of direct perception. The mistake made by existing theories of perception, according to Gibson, is construing the process of perception in terms of a hierarchical processing of sensory inputs, with various cognitive processes employed to organize and categorize sensations. A crucial element of this serial processing is bringing memories to bear on present experience. Gibson rejects this.Accepting that present experience is partly a function of past experience, he firmly denies that this sensitivity to past experience is generated by processing memories and sensations together. His alternative account rests on the idea that the senses, as perceptual systems, become more sensitive over time to particular forms of information as a function of prior exposure.Although Gibson was rather polemical about what he termed 'the muddle of memory', it would seem that his account involves the first notion of memory discussed above, namely a differential response to stimuli as a function of past experience. Gibson's position seems to be that conscious recognition is not implicated in ecological perception, although it might or might not develop out of such ecological perception. It is perfectly possible for a creature to have experience at the ecological level without any conscious recognitional capacities at all. If, then, the exercise of a capacity for conscious place recognition is a necessary condition of having experience that involves a temporally extended point of view, it seems that the dual structure of experience involved in the ecological coperception of self and environment must be significantly enriched before yielding a point of view.

Of course, this does not mean that we should abandon the basic idea of ecological perception; rather, it means that the materials offered by Gibson's own account need to be supplemented if they are to be employed in the theoretical project under discussion, and it is perfectly possible that Gibson's concepts of information pick-up and direct resonance to information in the ambient environment will have a crucial role to play in such an extension of the basic way in which ecological perception is sensitive to past experience (as they are, for example, in the account of perception and memory developed in Neisser 1976). The point is that, as it stands, the Gibsonian account cannot do all the work it was earlier suggested it might be able to do. The suggestion was that the Gibsonian account of ecological perception could show how something like a nonconceptual point of view is reflected in the very structure of perception. It now seems, however, that this will not be achieved until the appropriate capacity for conscious place recognition is added to the ecological coperception of self and environment. In the next section I will further discuss the constraints that this imposes upon the notion of a point of view.

3   Awareness of Action and Points of View

The discussion in the previous section stressed the importance of place recognition in yielding a sense of objects of experience existing independently of their being experienced. But surely, it might be argued, place recognition involves more than this. A creature recognizing a particular place is aware not only that that place has existed in the past but also that it itself has been there before. How, it might be asked, could it have the former without the latter, since the capacity for place recognition seems to rely on both a sense of the transtemporal identity of places and a sense of the transtemporal identity of the self.

This intuition has been emphatically endorsed by Christopher Peacocke, who makes the stronger claim that any genuine attribution to a creature of a capacity for place recognition (which he terms place reidentification) entails that the creature have mastery of the first-person concept. I have taken the liberty of schematizing the rather condensed discussion within which this claim emerges (1992, 90–92):

1. The attribution of genuine spatial representational content to a creature is justified only if that creature is capable of identifying places over time.
2. Identifying places over time involves reidentifying places.
3. Reidentifying places requires the capacity to identify one's current location with a location previously encountered.
4. Reidentifying places in this way involves building up an integrated representation of the environment over time.
5. Neither (3) nor (4) would be possible unless the subject possessed at least a primitive form of the first-person concept.

Peacocke's reason for maintaining (3) and (4) is that the existence of navigational abilities—however sophisticated, systematic, or structured—is not sufficient to compel the ascription of states with genuine spatial content. Simply being able to find one's way from one place to another is not enough. What is needed is some form of grasp of having been there before, and Peacocke places a strong requirement on any such grasp. The possibility of reidentifying places, he argues, requires the capacity to entertain thoughts or protothoughts of the form 'I have been to this place before', and such thoughts could not be entertained by a creature lacking the first-person concept. The capacity for such thoughts goes hand in hand, for Peacocke, with the capacity to engage in spatial reasoning, where this "requires the subject to be able to integrate the representational contents of his successive perceptions into an integrated representation of the world around him, both near and far, past and present" (1992, 91). The thought seems to be that reidentifying places in the appropriate manner involves representing those places as existing unperceived within a spatial framework also constructed so that it is independent of any particular perception. The construction of this spatial framework implicates a rudimentary form of first-person thought, because it involves the subject's not only representing its own location within the framework but also grasping that the location can change over time. It involves "the subject's appreciating that the scene currently presented in his perception is something to which his own spatial relations can vary over time" (1992, 90).

This poses a serious threat to my argument. My account of what it is to possess a temporally extended point of view on the world has, as a necessary condition, the capacity for conscious place recognition. If Peacocke's argument is sound, then any creature possessing this capacity will possess a primitive form of the first-person concept, and this creates serious difficulties for the suggestion that an account of the notion of a point of view can be given at the nonconceptual level. Evidently, if experience reflecting a point of view involves possessing a form of the first-person concept, albeit a primitive one, then it cannot count as a form of autonomous nonconceptual content in the sense discussed earlier, because any creature with such experience will have to possess at least some concepts. But a stronger conclusion also follows: that such experience cannot be a form of nonconceptual content at all. This is so because the key distinction that the notion of a point of view is intended to capture is that between subjective experience and what it is experience of, and the concept of the first person will be involved in specifying how this distinction is manifest within the experience of any particular creature. Indeed, precisely this constraint characterizes the notion of a point of view: that it can be specified only in the first person.

One way of resisting this conclusion would be to deny the strong conditions that Peacocke places upon the capacity for place reidentification. In particular, one might query the suggestion that place reidentification is only available to creatures who have the capacity to construct suitably integrated representations of their environment and to engage in spatial reasoning in a way that necessarily involves grasp of the first-person pronoun. This could be done, for example, by appealing to the notion of causally indexical comprehension developed by John Campbell (1993). Grasping a causally indexical notion is just grasping its implications for one's own actions. Examples of such causally indexical notions are that something is too heavy for me to lift, or that something else is within reach. As he points out, grasp of causally indexical notions may be linked with a reflective understanding of one's own capacities and of the relevant properties of the object. But, on the other hand, it need not be so linked: it makes sense to ascribe to creatures a grasp of such causally indexical notions without ascribing to them any grasp of notions that are not causally indexical (even though those noncausally indexical notions might be essential to characterize the causally indexical notions) because the significance of such notions is exhausted by their implications for perception and action. And as such, causally indexical mental states qualify as states with nonconceptual content.

In this context, then, one might attempt to defend the idea of a nonconceptual point of view by suggesting that the spatial abilities involved are causally indexical. Such an objection would maintain that we need not place the theoretical weight that Peacocke does on disengaged reflective and reasoning abilities. Rather, we should be looking at the way in which a creature interacts with its surroundings, because this will be how it manifests its grasp of the spatial properties of its environment (of the connectedness of places, for example). On such a view, a creature could possess an integrated representation of its environment in the absence of any capacity to reflect upon its interactions with its environment. If this line is pursued, then it seems to provide a way in which we can retain the idea of place reidentification without accepting Peacocke's claim that it implicates possession of a primitive form of the first-person concept—precisely because it denies Peacocke's central claim, that any creature capable of place reidentification must be capable of explicitly representing itself and its location in its surroundings.

The trouble with this suggestion, however, is that there is a strong tension between the idea of causally indexical content and my earlier insistence on the importance of conscious recognitional abilities. The idea of an awareness that is exhausted in its implications for perception and action does not mesh well with the account I have been developing of the essential features of experience reflecting a point of view. On the causally indexical conception of place reidentification, we ascribe to a creature a grasp of the spatial properties of its environment because its behavior is suitably complex and the relevant connections between perception and action seem to hold. It would seem, however, that appropriately complex behavior could exist at the primitive level of nonconscious memory and skill acquisition. On the causal indexicality account, the ability to track places and perform complicated feats of navigation of the sort regularly carried out by homing pigeons and migrating swallows would be good grounds for ascribing the relevant grasp of the spatial properties of the environment, but it does not implicate the sort of recognitional sense of the transtemporal identity of places that has been argued to be a crucial element in the notion of a point of view.

There seems, then, to be the following challenge for the idea of a nonconceptual point of view as developed in the first part of this paper. To keep the connection with conscious experience of the transtemporal identity of places that, I have argued, is required to distinguish a genuine point of view from the sort of capacity to distinguish proprioceptive and exteroceptive invariants evidenced in ecological perception, we need to reject the causally indexical account of place reidentification. In doing this we move toward understanding the representation of places in a way that is explicit and (relatively) disengaged, rather than exhausted in its implications for action. The question is whether this can be done without moving the notion of a point of view out of the realm of nonconceptual content altogether, as Peacocke does.

It would seem that the only way out here would be to resist Peacocke's suggestion that a primitive form of the first-person concept is involved in the type of spatial reasoning involved in place reidentification and recognition. Could there not be a way of representing the self that does not count as fully conceptual but nonetheless enables the subject to engage in basic reasoning about places? Toward the end of this paper I will suggest that this is indeed a possible direction. Before doing so, however, it is important to make clear that there are theoretical reasons driving such a move that are independent of the attractiveness of the notion of a nonconceptual point of view.

An initial worry that one might have with implicating the first-person concept in spatial reasoning is that doing so seems to link spatial reasoning with unwarrantedly sophisticated conceptual abilities. Matters can be focused here by asking whether a creature's mastery of the first-person concept involves the capacity to ascribe to itself psychological predicates. If mastery of the first-person concept does involve such a capacity, then one seems committed to the idea that spatial reasoning is available only to creatures capable of conceiving of other subjects of thought and experience, for the following reason. Suppose we take the ability to generalize as the mark of a genuine concept user, in the way suggested by Gareth Evans's Generality Constraint, so that it is a condition upon a creature's being credited with the thought a is F, and hence of possessing the concepts of a and F, that it be capable of thinking a is G for any property G of which it has a conception, and of thinking b is F for any object b of which it has a conception (Evans 1982, 100–105). Now if a creature's conceptual repertoire contains psychological predicates, it will have to be capable of generalizing them in the appropriate manner, and for obvious reasons, such generalization can only take place over other psychological subjects. So, on the assumption that mastery of the first-person concept requires the capacity to generalize psychological predicates, spatial reasoning is available only to subjects who have a relatively sophisticated grasp of folk psychology.

Nobody (I think) would want to maintain this. So a position like Peacocke's clearly requires a form of the first-person concept that does not implicate the capacity for the self-ascription of psychological predicates, and indeed, he stresses that it is supposed to be primitive. We could think of it as involving only the capacity to apply certain very basic temporal, spatial, and relational predicates, and hence as requiring only a very limited conceptual repertoire. Certainly, this would completely avoid the difficulty raised in the previous paragraph. One might, however, have doubts about such a proposal. One very general worry here would concern the ontogeny of self-consciousness. The proposed primitive form of the first-person concept is clearly intended to be ontogenetically primitive. That is, it will be the key to understanding an early, if not the earliest, form of self-conscious thought. But in employing such a concept, a creature would be thinking of itself only as a subject of spatial, relational, and temporal properties. It would be thinking of itself just as a physical object. The ontogenetic story to be told here would then be one in which the higher forms of self-consciousness emerge from such a restricted but nonetheless detached mode of presentation of the self. And the worry that one might have would be that this gets the ontogenetic order the wrong way round: the capacity to think of oneself as a physical object (thought in which one features as one object among others) does not emerge until relatively late in the developmental process.

A satisfactory development of this line of argument awaits a satisfactory account of the ontogenesis of self-conscious thought. But someone tempted by it might find additional support in reflecting on Gareth Evans's account of how first-person thought meets the Generality Constraint. According to Evans, the Generality Constraint can only be properly met (and hence one can only speak of genuine mastery of the first-person concept) when the subject is capable of conceiving of himself in an impersonal manner as an element of the objective order (1982, chap. 7, particularly pp. 208–210). Clearly, this involves an even more detached perspective on the self than that discussed in the previous paragraph, and one may well baulk at making this a condition on the capacity for genuine place reidentification. Of course, a defender of Peacocke's position does not have to accept Evans's account of how the Generality Constraint is met for first-person thought, but if he does not accept it, it is incumbent on him either to give an alternative account or to explain why it is not applicable at the putatively primitive level under discussion.

What this brings out, I think, is a significant tension in Peacocke's suggestion that a primitive form of the first-person concept is involved in basic spatial reasoning. It seems inappropriate to claim that the constraints and conditions operative in the case of fully fledged first-person thought are operative in this primitive case. But on the other hand, there is a danger of stripping away so many of the trappings of fully fledged first-person thought that it is no longer clear what the force is of claiming that we are dealing with a form of the first-person concept at all. The bottom line of Peacocke's position seems to be that the self has to be explicitly represented for genuine spatial reasoning to take place. It is, to my mind at least, a moot point whether this forces us to conclude that a conceptual grasp of the self has to be present. And certainly the matter will remain undecided until we have a clearer account of spatial reasoning. In the remainder of this paper I would like to make some preliminary moves toward the suggestion that the self can be explicitly grasped in a manner that is not conceptual.

As a first step in this direction, we need suitable criteria for determining, first, whether something is being explicitly represented and, second, whether such an explicit representation is conceptual. A preliminary suggestion on the first issue would be that a creature can only be described as explicitly representing something when, in explaining that creature's behavior, we need to go beyond stimulus-response (S-R) psychology. The sort of explicit representation relevant here comes into play when S-R explanations cease to be applicable. Of course, appeal to mental representations is crucial to S-R psychology (see, for example, the discussion of the associative-cybernetic model in Dickinson and Balleine 1993), but the type of mental representations I am interested in are those that feature in (proto)intentional accounts of behavior. Clearly, this is not a sufficient condition, but it at least gives us something to work with (compare Peacocke 1983, chap. 3). On the second issue, that of what qualifies a mental representation as conceptual, I propose that we stick to some form of the Generality Constraint, as discussed earlier. On this criterion, a representation counts as conceptual if it can be combined with any other representations the subject possesses.

Prima facie, it seems that the first of these criteria could be satisfied without the second being satisfied, that is, that we might need to appeal to an explicit representation in a protointentional account of behavior, even though that representation does not support the appropriate form of generalization. If this were the case for the first person, then we would have an explicit but nonconceptual grasp of the self. In the remainder of this paper I would like to discuss a set of experiments carried out by Watson and Ramey (1987) on 3-month-old infants that seem to offer an example of just such a way of grasping the self.

The experiments examine the responses of young infants only 3-months-old to the movements of a mobile suspended above their cribs. The mobile could move in two different ways. In the first, a control situation, it could be rotated electrically by the experimenter (in this case the infant's mother). In the second, the experimental situation, it was set up with a pillow sensitive to pressure in such a way that it would move when the infant moved its head. For a further control group, the mobile was set up not to move at all. The experimental apparatus was set up in the homes of the 48 infants involved, and the infants were exposed to it for 10 minutes a day over 14 consecutive days. The number of pillow activations in each 10-minute period were counted to see if it increased over the 14 days of exposure. Significant increase was found in the experimental group but not in either of the control groups.

The most common way of explaining these experiments is as a form of instrumental conditioning. All that is shown is the gradual development of S-R links between head movements and the movements of the display, so that whenever the infant sees the display, it moves its head. The S-R links develop because the infants enjoy watching the display move. Such an explanation of their behavior need not appeal to any explicit mental representations at all. In this respect the explanation suggests that the experimental behavior is to be explained at the same level as the ecological behavior discussed in the previous section. I do not want to claim that this interpretation is incorrect. What I would like to do, though, is give one reason for thinking that it might not tell the whole story and, on the basis of this, sketch out an alternative interpretation. This alternative interpretation involves attributing to the experimental infants an explicit representation of the self that is nonetheless not conceptual.

The mothers of the experimental infants almost universally reported that their children took great interest and pleasure in the movement of the display. They smiled, cooed, and laughed a lot, fixating intensely on the mobile, with this behavior developing after only a few days' exposure to the apparatus. In contrast, those infants in the first control group, for whom the mobile moved according to a regular pattern, rather than in response to the infants' own movements, showed considerably less interest in the mobile. If, as the S-R account suggests, what drives the reinforcement process is the pleasure taken in watching the mobile move, then it fails to account for the discrepancy between the degrees of pleasure shown by the experimental infants and the first set of control infants. Its prediction would presumably be that both sets of infants should display substantially similar behavior, because they both watch the mobile move and watching the mobile move is an interesting and pleasurable experience—just as for rats, eating food pellets is an interesting and pleasurable experience even when the food pellets arrive without the rat having had to press any levers. But this, of course, is not what happens. The experimental infants are far more interested and amused than the control infants. Why? It is very tempting to suggest that what they take pleasure in is the fact that they have made the mobile move. The source of their pleasure is a power to affect the world that they are discovering in themselves, a capacity to bring about changes in the world. They repeat the action both to confirm the discovery and for the sheer pleasure of it.

By claiming that the infants are taking pleasure in their own agency I am, ipso facto, claiming that they are aware of what they are doing, and therefore aware that they are acting on things that are distinct from them. It seems to follow that they appreciate in a conscious manner the distinction between their own intentions or acts of will and the movements of objects in the world. And this seems to involve just an explicit representation of the self. If this line of interpretation is accepted, the first criterion is satisfied. But what about the second? Does this implicate a grasp of self that satisfies the Generality Constraint?

One reason for thinking that it might do would be the thought that the infants' grasp of their causal agency could be generalized via a grasp of the causal properties of other objects, the idea being that what they are discerning in their own case is a special case of ordinary causal interactions in the world. But even if the infants were capable of grasping causal relations between physical objects, this would still not count as an appropriate generalization of their own agency, for two reasons. The first is that the infant's power to affect the world is importantly different from the causal impact of one physical object upon another. We talk about agency in the one case and not in the other precisely because the first case has an intentional dimension lacking in the other. So we do not have a generalization of the predicate. The second reason is that we do not have a generalization of the subject either, because the appropriate generalization would have to be one across psychological subjects rather than across physical objects. The Generality Constraint would only be satisfied here if the infants were capable both of generalizing the special sense of agency involved and (relatedly) of grasping the existence of other agents. And it is surely implausible to attribute such sophisticated cognitive abilities to infants at this stage of development.

Now the interpretation I have offered of the infants' behavior may well be resisted, but it will not be resisted because it is in principle impossible. The S-R interpretation could perhaps deal with the apparently recalcitrant features of the behavior, but this would not affect my main point, which is that the coherence (and indeed plausibility) of the interpretation I have put forward suggests that there might be a way of representing the self that is explicit but not conceptual. And if this point is accepted, we have taken the first step to meeting the challenge discussed earlier in this section: the challenge of explaining how the self might be represented in spatial reasoning without it being necessary to ascribe to the subject a grasp of the first-person concept.

Of course, it is one thing to show that the self can be represented in a manner that is explicit but nonconceptual and quite another to show how such a representation can feature in spatial reasoning so as to support the sort of protothoughts that, if Peacocke's argument is accepted, are implicated in conscious place recognition. The second of these tasks has clearly not been done. Considerable work is required here but, by way of conclusion, I offer some brief remarks on the sort of role that this explicit but nonconceptual representation of the self could play in spatial reasoning.

Remember that on Peacocke's account a crucial element of spatial reasoning is "the subject's appreciating that the scene currently presented in his perception is something to which his own spatial relations can vary over time" (1992, 90). This is one of the vital respects in which first-person thought enters the picture. There are various different ways in which one can flesh this idea out, depending on how one construes the subject's grasp that he can enter into varying spatial relations to a particular scene. One plausible idea, though, would be that fully grasping this is conditional on realizing that one can intentionally act in a perceptually presented scene— by realizing, for example, that if one decides to return to it from *here*, one can do so by passing through *these* intermediate places, or that if there is something *there* that one wants, one should take *this* route to obtain it. In this sense, appreciating that the scene currently presented in perception is something to which one's spatial relations can vary over time depends on appreciating how these varying spatial relations afford different possibilities for action. Of course, there is a crucial difference between being able to react in varying ways to one's environment and grasping that there are different possibilities for action open to one. The latter is what I am stressing here, and what is interesting about it is that it seems to implicate the subject's representing himself as an agent. What the subject grasps, on this account, is the close connection between his own intentions and the spatial configuration of the environement. Here, I would tentatively suggest, is where we will find the connection between the primitive nonconceptual mode of representing the self as an agent and the first-person component in spatial reasoning.

4   Conclusion

If this is right, we are considerably closer to an understanding of the notion of a nonconceptual point of view, originally put forward as a way of capturing the minimal requirement on self-conscious thought that it support the right sort of distinction betwen experience and what it is experience of. We started with the basic coperception of self and environment described in Gibson's ecological account of the structure of perception and built it up by arguing that creatures to which it is legitimate to ascribe a point of view should be capable of conscious place recognition and of representing themselves in an explicit manner. In the final section, following Peacocke, I discussed the connection between these two demands and

suggested, *pace* Peacocke, that they could both be accepted without it being necessary to move beyond the nonconceptual level.

Acknowledgments

I have been greatly helped by comments from Bill Brewer, my coeditors, and an anonymous referee.

References

Bermúdez, José Luis. 1994. "Peacocke's Argument against the Autonomy of Nonconceptual Representational Content." *Mind and Language* 9:402–418.

Campbell, J. 1993. "The Role of Physical Objects in Spatial Thinking." In *Spatial Representation: Problems in Philosophy and Psychology,* edited by N. Eilan, R. A. McCarthy,
and M. W. Brewer. Oxford: Basil Blackwell.

Cussins, Adrian. 1990. "The Connectionist Construction of Concepts." In *The Philosophy
of Artificial Intelligence,* edited by Margaret A. Boden. Oxford: Oxford University Press.

Dickinson, Anthony, and Balleine, Bernard. 1993. "Actions and Responses: The Dual
Psychology of Behaviour." In *Spatial Representation: Problems in Philosophy and Psychology,* edited by N. Eilan, R. A. McCarthy, and M. W. Brewer. Oxford: Basil Blackwell.

Evans, Gareth. 1982. *The Varieties of Reference.* Oxford: Oxford University Press.

Gibson, J. J. 1979. *The Ecological Approach to Visual Perception.* Boston: Houghton,
Mifflin.

Lee, D. N., and Aronson, E. 1974. "Visual Proprioceptive Control of Standing in Human Infants." *Perception and Psychophysics* 15:529–532.

Lishman, J. R., and Lee, D. N. 1973. "The Autonomy of Visual Kinaesthetics." *Perception*
2:287–294.

Neisser, Ulric. 1976. *Cognition and Reality.* New York: W. H. Freeman.

Neisser, Ulric. 1991. "Two Perceptually Given Aspects of the Self and Their Development." *Developmental Review* 11:197–209.

Peacocke, Christopher. 1983. *Sense and Content.* Oxford: Oxford University Press.

Peacocke, Christopher. 1992. *A Study of Concepts.* Cambridge: MIT Press.

Spelke, E. S. 1990. "Principles of Object Perception." *Cognitive Science* 14:29–56.

Spelke, E. S., and Van de Walle, G. 1993. "Perceiving and Reasoning about Objects: Insights from Infants." In *Spatial Representation: Problems in Philosophy and Psychology,*
edited by N. Eilan, R. A. McCarthy, and M. W. Brewer. Oxford: Basil Blackwell.

Strawson, P. F. 1959. *Individuals.* London: Methuen.

Strawson, P. F. 1966. *The Bounds of Sense.* London: Methuen.

Watson, John S., and Ramey, Craig T. 1987. "Reactions to Response-Contingent Stimulation in Early Infancy." In *Cognitive Development in Infancy,* edited by J. Oates and S.
Sheldon. Hillsdale, N.J.: Lawrence Erlbaum Associates.

Proprioception and the Body Image

Brian O'Shaughnessy

1 Is Proprioception a True Perceiving?

At first blush the phenomenon of proprioception[1] looks like a bona fide example of perception. And yet it is natural to entertain doubts on the matter. For one thing proprioception is attentively recessive in a high degree, it takes a back seat in consciousness almost all of the time. Might it perhaps be that we are misdescribing as a perceiving or noticing what is in fact no more than an immediate knowledge of limb presence and posture, caused let us say by either cerebral events or postural sensations produced by limb posture? Why posit an intervening event of perception? May it not be functionally otiose? In addition, if perceiving is the same thing as noticing, and noticing invariably makes demands upon the attention, surely bodily perception ought to intrude in some distracting fashion in our daily practical dealings with the objects in the immediate environment. However, this is not our experience. Catching a ball, we do not find our limbs attentively getting in the way. On the contrary, in fact! The body does not appear to consciousness as a rival object of awareness as we actively engage with our surroundings. Why not abandon the theory of a body-directed attending, and substitute in its place an account in which we postulate an immediate knowledge of limb presence and posture which is generated by psychocerebral phenomena regularly associated with such states of affairs?

I am convinced this would be a mistake. To help explain why, I will begin this examination of proprioception by considering an atypical example of the species. Namely, the case in which we involve some of our perceptual attention away from its natural visual and auditory objects, and actively turn it instead in an immediate mode onto some body part like an arm. This is an atypical example of proprioception, partly because of its purely inquisitive character, but above all because it draws its object out of its natural obscurity into the full light of awareness. Yet I doubt whether it differs much from the everyday recessive examples in other significant respects. In any case, it is surely an example of perception. Thus, it is an experience, of the type attending, whose content is caused nondeviantly by its object, and it can form the basis of an inference to the existence of its object. Above all, it is no kind of cognitive attitude, nor tendency to entertain a cognitive attitude; even though, as befits perception, it causally sustains one. It is not a case of knowing, nor of believing, suspecting, or any such, since one could in principle have this experience when one knows irrefutably that the bodily facts are other than they seem in the experience. In short, we have here an attentive experience in which a small sector of physical reality appears one way, which is to be sharply distinguished from cognitive attitudes of all kinds, even though it naturally sustains such. In a word, a perceiving.

Is it a new or sixth sense, to be added to the famous five? The concepts involved here are perhaps too vague to admit of a precise answer, and I will not really pursue this issue. I will instead ask another more precise question, namely whether we have reason to distinguish this self-conscious variety of proprioception, and indeed proprioception itself, from the mode of perception closest to it in character, the sense of touch. It will I think on investigation emerge that they differ in a number of highly significant respects, and that as a result neither mode of perception can be subsumed under the heading of the other. In any case let us at this point make a few comparisons between these two bodily-related types of perceiving. But first, what are we to count as an exercise of the sense of touch? There can be no doubt that this sense encompasses extremely heterogeneous phenomena, ranging from instantaneous point contact to active tactile exploration in which, as it seems to me, one's own bodily movements play a mediating role of a causal and maybe also attentive type. Nevertheless, common to all these cases is a property of great relevance to the question under consideration; namely, in absolutely every instance of tactile perception an awareness of one's body *stands between one and awareness of the tactile object.* And so the sense of touch must depend upon proprioception, as not vice versa. Therefore whether or not proprioception is *absolutely* immediate, it must be immediate in ways not open to tactile perception. This differentia carries the implication that neither mode of perception can be a subvariety of the other.

Here we have one major difference between proprioception and touch. A second major difference between them lies in the character of their perceptual objects. One glaringly obvious difference consists in the *scope* of the objects open to them: whereas touch ranges far and wide without restriction, proprioception is more or less of necessity confined to the body of the perceiver (nontrivially, surely). But another important difference lies in the type of the properties, and in particular the type of the *spatial properties*, open to these modes of perception. Thus, through the sense of touch we discover surface properties like roughness and smoothness, shape properties like sphericity and cubicality, and in general a broad array of fully determinate spatial properties. It is surely of some import that not all of these are accessible to proprioceptive discovery. For example, roughness and smoothness are not. And determinacy of shape seems to be discernable only in some rather eccentric cases of proprioception. For example, I can see no reason why we we should not across time proprioceptively discover highly determinate shape properties of (say) hand movements, such as the property of moving along a rectangular path. But there seems no prospect of proprioceptively discovering, either instantaneously or across time, that a particular limb is a cylinder or sphere or cone, or suchlike. Whether or not the latter differences in the type of spatial object given to the two kinds of perception constitutes a major difference between them, the mediacy/immediacy difference undoubtedly does. This difference is fundamental, and if anything can prove that these two modes of perceiving are different senses rather than the two subvarieties of one sense, it surely ought to. However, since the very same variety of sensation is put to use in these perceivings, and since no secondary quality is essential to either of these types of perception, it begins to look as if the concept of a perceptual sense is vague and therefore as if we ought not to press the issue any further. Perhaps we should settle for the following more exact claim concerning these two closely related varieties of perception; namely, that the sense of touch and proprioception are radically dissimilar on a number of fundamental counts, and neither can be reduced to the other—and leave the matter at that. When we reflect that they each in different ways depend inextricably upon the existence of the other, this guarded conclusion seems all the more judicious.

2   Proprioception and the Attention

Proprioceptive Attending in Physical Instrumental Action

So much for the question whether proprioception, and in particular the highly self-conscious variety of the species I have chosen to study, is to count as an example of perception and as the exercise of a new or sixth sense. I now want to take a look at more typical cases of proprioception. After all, introspective proprioception (as we might call the above) is the exception rather than the rule. Even self-concerned bodily acts, such as occur when a cat washes behind its neck, are cases in which the attention passes beyond the active limb and focusses on a distinct object (which in

this case happens to be part of its own body). Thus, the mode of proprioception involved here cannot be what I am calling 'introspective proprioception'. What is special about this latter variety of proprioception is
merely that the limb is the *focal point* of the attention: it is the focal point of
an immediate proprioceptive attending. While this looks like a form of introspection, in that we involute the attention away from its outer mediated
objects and turn it immediately onto something in oneself, it is so
markedly dissimilar even from attending to a sensation that I think it
should be acknowledged that the title 'introspective proprioception' is a
little misleading. Its value lies in the emphasis that it places on the somewhat unnatural involution of the attention that occurs in such cases.

Then what is it that occurs in most animals most of the time in the
way of body awareness? Is it something other than proprioception? If it
lacks this interioristic convoluted character, might it not be something different? I can see no reason for saying so. In any case, I now intend to consider examples of proprioception which happen to abound in normal
animal life, phenomena that are practical rather than merely inquisitive in
function: I propose at this point to examine the part played by proprioceptive attention in physical instrumental action. More exactly, the variety of
proprioceptive awareness that occurs when we are engaged in intentionally manipulating instruments, like a car or tennis racquet. In short, when
we are in the midst of the most *familiar* and *typifying* of deeds.

A difficulty arises at once. I have already had occasion to mention the
problem in section 1. It is a problem posed by the fact that we have at any
instant only so much attention to go around and no more. If perception
consists in items coming to the attention, and if proprioception is a variety
of perception, proprioception must one assumes make demands upon the
attention. But if attention needs in part to be absorbed in proprioception
of the acting limb, it rather looks as if when we engage in intentional manipulative action the phenomenon of proprioception ought to be a dis-
cordant and distracting item, competing for our attention with both the
act itself and (say) visual perception. Yet this is not our experience. When
we play a stroke in tennis we are not conscious of a conflict within the attention, we do not experience the limb as competing for our attention
with the ball (whose path occupies so much of our attention), nor with
the playing of the stroke (which does the same). Ours is not the experience, say, of a novice juggler. What is the explanation of this state of affairs?
Given the somewhat impoverished content of introspective proprioception, one might begin to question whether proprioception actually occurs
at all in such instrumental cases! Might it not be that it simply drops out of
the picture, and that the attention is directed wholly onto (say) the path of

the ball and racquet, to the exclusion of the body itself? For are not these latter phenomena our prime concern?

The first thing we need to do here is reaffirm a very simple principle first formulated by Elizabeth Anscombe. Namely, that acts can be intentional under multiple descriptions, some instrumental and some basic. Thus a particular act can be intentional under both 'unlocking a door' and 'turning a key', and we bring this out by saying things like 'I decided to unlock the door by turning the key'. Then it seems plain that in cases like this we can add 'I decided to unlock the door by turning the key by swiveling the hand that grasped the key'. Here both ends and means are chosen and hence are intentional, and the means in this present example are chosen right down to the basic bodily means of swiveling a hand. The next thing to be said is that swiveling is in general a proprioceptively detectable phenomenon: if someone swivels my left hand unexpectedly, I will usually be immediately and proprioceptively aware of the existence and type of that movement. Finally, we should add that most intentional acts are known to their owner under the headings under which they are intentional. The conclusion in such a case as the above is that the act will be known to its owner under the heading 'swiveling a hand'. Then since one can scarcely know one has swiveled a hand without knowing one's hand has swiveled, and since one must surely discover this last proprioceptively, we are forced to conclude that in a case of this kind—where an act is intentional under both instrumental and basic-act descriptions *and* where the latter is a spatially determinate description, like 'swivel'—one must have been proprioceptively aware of a determinate bodily movement and therefore also of body positions across time. Despite the fact that the attention may be focused ahead of the actively intervening limb, despite the natural epistemological recessiveness of limb movements in such cases, when an instrumental act is intentional under a description that mentions spatially determinate bodily means, then proprioceptive awareness of the bodily phenomenon is a necessary condition of the deed. If playing a sudden-snap forehand volley is intentional not merely under 'hitting the ball to the corner' and 'playing a forehand volley' and 'swinging the racqet' but also under 'moving my right hand forward thuswise', then proprioception of arm position is a necessary condition of such a deed. Even though one's attention is focused primarily on the path of the ball, and doubtless also though to a much lesser extent on the path followed by the racquet, some small measure of attention must be left over for the movement of the arm. Short-term memory and knowledge are, I suggest, a good test of what occupied the attention at a particular instant in time. Since, immediately after playing such a tennis stroke, one will surely have some sort of short-term memory and knowledge of one's own arm movement, and in fact would usually be prepared to place bets on the matter if challenged, we may reasonably conclude that arm movement was proprioceptively perceived at the time. Indeed, we may also conclude that such proprioception was a necessary condition of the act in question.[2]

Here we have a familiar series of situations—tennis, driving a car, opening a door, and the like—where proprioception is a necessary condition of the intentional instrumental manipulative deed. Nonetheless, other examples of intentional manipulation of the environment exist in which the role of proprioception is more problematic. These are the cases in which the natural epistemological and attentive recessiveness of the bodily means increases to such an extent that they become invisible to the agent. Special activities like knacks (whistling) and skills (darts) are examples. But despite the relevance of these phenomena to the problem under discussion, which is the existence, content, and role of proprioceptive attending in the course of physical acts of manipulation, I will for the moment set these cases to one side. My reason for doing so is that I wish to pursue the question of proprioceptive content in the familiar kinds of instrumental situations that we have just been examining; that is, where the instrumental action is intentional both under an instrumental description *and* a determinate basic bodily description like 'moving my arm forewards', *and* is at the same time such that the attention moves outward to a focal point that lies beyond the bodily means. In a word, in the typical active intervention of mind in physical nature. It seems to me that the attentive situation needs to be better understood than we have thus far managed.

I have already commented on the puzzling nature of these cases. The puzzle is that even though the bodily movement engages one's attention, it seems in no way to constitute a distraction as one focuses the attention onto the environment. Now it is true that the quantity of attention utilized by proprioception is mostly rather small, but it must be emphasized that the resolution of the puzzle is not to be found in such quantitative considerations. The following remarks will make that clear. Consider once again the example of hitting the tennis ball. It is important to note that there are different ways of performing such an action, and that in some of these situations perception does indeed constitute a distraction. Leave aside the issue of proprioception, and consider for a moment the relation between playing the stroke and looking at the ball, since that exemplifies the problem of focus and recessiveness in a very clear manner. These latter two acts can take different forms, in some of which looking is undoubtedly a distraction. Whether it distracts depends above all on *the content* of that looking. If the content is studying the ball's color, plainly it will. If it is studying the ball's path, very likely it will not. If it is studying that path to see if it is parabaloid in character, very likely it will once again constitute a distraction. And so it is clear that for perception not to distract, but to enhance and enable performance, the object-content must be of a special and indeed unique kind: it must be the path of the ball qua (say) object-of-a-volley. Whatever exactly this content consists in, it must one assumes include direction, speed, relation to the space available for that type of shot, and so on. This content cannot be acquired merely additively, but must somehow be realized naturally and synthetically and through the intentional headings under which one acts. Then once the attendant perceptual activity acquires this requisite character, it ceases to be in competition for attention with the stroke. The activities of looking and volleying are two, are distinct existents, and each occupies so much of the limited space of one's attention, and yet if the contents of these two activities are of the required kind, they cease to be in competition for the attention. Though attention is divided, it is not the scene of a tug of war, provided the behavior of the agent is suitably integrated in character. Such looking as we have described is, one assumes, functionally subordinated to the playing of the stroke: it appears in a hierachy, whose presence is manifested in the interdigitated content of the two enterprises. My surmise is that proprioception takes its place even lower down in this hierachy, and in such a way as likewise to constitute no sort of distraction. Here, too, internal object or content must play a decisive role.

A new difficulty appears at this point. It concerns the nature of the proprioception involved in this case (and others). Thus, a genuine *activity* of looking at the tennis ball takes place as one engages in this instrumental action, but does a parallel and second *activity* of proprioceptive attending join it? On the face of it, one would say no. While one is openly conscious of engaging in an activity of looking, one seems not to be embarked on a project of proprioception. Such an answer poses a problem for the theory that the resolution of the problem of distraction lies in the harmonious content of a sequence of hierachically related activities. But in any case, the answer runs into difficulties of its own. If I am engaged in playing the violin, what goes on in my feet and legs is of lesser interest to me than what goes on in my fingers and arms, is known and remembered less by me, and presumably therefore is proprioceptively perceived less. Now nothing but an intention and act-desire with an indexically given present-tense time content set me in active motion, and this deed was copresent with and surely essentially dependent on an enhanced attentive awareness of certain body parts. Accordingly, the increased proprioception must owe its existence to that same intention and act-desire. Then if we bear in mind that the intention was to use an arm of which one was aware to stroke a ball one can see, it is difficult to avoid the conclusion that an active process of proprioception was generated along with the act of stroking the ball. In that case, three simultaneous and internally linked activities—looking, proprioceptive perceiving, and stroking—must have been ushered into being by a single decision to act. The internal content of these three activities establishes a hierachy which is such that harmony rather than dissension reigns within the attention. Within this hierachy, proprioception will normally play a role that is at once recessive and harmonious. This squares with our experience.

Proprioceptive Attending and the Whole Body

I have so far discussed problems arising about the reality, and the perceptual content of proprioception in two sorts of cases: introspective proprioception, in which limb presence and posture are the focus of immediate active interest, and intentional manipulative instrumental action, where they are not. Before I leave the question of proprioceptive content, I should like to say a little about one's perception of the body *as a whole*, not in the atypical case of introspective proprioception, but such as occurs for most of our waking (and perhaps sleeping) lives. In the light of some of the observations just made concerning the proprioception that occurs in instrumental action, I think I should at this point disavow a theory I have endorsed in several places in print (O'Shaughnessy 1980, vol. 1, chap. 7).

The theory in question recommended itself to me for the following kinds of reasons. Struck by the extraordinary recessiveness of proprioceptive perception, and above all by the fact that whenever we need to intentionally move a limb we are able to do so immediately and without further ado, it seemed to me that at any particular moment we must be aware of the presence and position of every sensuously differentiable point on the body outside. If I feel a slight tickle on my chin, I can at once scratch it; if I see a missile near my head, I will duck automatically; and so on. These facts made it seem as if in some nearly subliminal way the entire body outside was continually perceived in all its detail, even though consciousness seems not to *record* the multifarious detailed items such a perception would involve, and despite the fact that such a theory implies the absence in proprioception of the familiar and important phenomenon of *attentive selectivity*. This latter implication certainly troubled me, since perception of its very nature seems to be a phenomenon in which the attention culls what it needs, and discards what it does not, out of a much richer given set of data. But I could see no alternative at the time I endorsed these views. However, the theory now strikes me as both unparsimonious and ill sorted with certain facts. Those facts are that when I attend self-consciously to a limb or intentionally use one body part to the exclusion of the rest, that excluded remainder tends inevitably to recede in my awareness. The limb stands out on a "ground" or background of the body as a whole, which is perceived also to be sure, but perceived less differentially and vividly than the limb in question. Unless we are to embrace the improbable idea that *two* qualitatively different kinds of perception go on simultaneously all the time, one vastly complex and nearly subliminal, the other selective and accessible to memory centers, there seems no alternative but to abandon the doctrine of comprehensive detailed proprioception. Accordingly, a more parsimonious theory suggests itself, namely that we all of the time perceive the body as a whole, recessively and with a limited measure of differentiation of detail, and that particular bodily sensations and/or intentional bodily actions automatically usher into being a perceptual awareness of the body point or part sensuously or actively singled out, an awareness that takes place on the "ground" of the body as a whole. Since every differentiable point or part on the body outside is capable of playing such a role and since we are continually aware of the body as a whole, it is easy to misconstrue the latter property as identical with the property of being actually, albeit nearly subliminally, perceived.

3   The Short-Term Body Image

The Distinction Between Short-Term and Long-Term Body Image
I want to say something at this point about the distinction between what I called the 'short-term' and 'long-term' body image (O'Shaughnessy 1980, vol. 1, chap 7). When most people speak of the body image, they have something in mind that approximates more closely to what I called the 'long-term body image' than to what I described as the 'short-term body image'. Nevertheless, a case exists for singling out several different items and giving them these various titles. Indeed, I will argue that the expression 'short-term body image' might with justice be applied to three diverse phenomena. But for the moment, let me briefly try to justify the prime distinction, that between long-term body image and short-term body image.

When I postulated the existence of a long-term body image, I was entertaining a particular hypothesis; namely, that there exists a perceptual sense of 'How at instant t_1 one seems to oneself to be disposed in spatial respects R in space'[3] which is such that what it singles out is to be causally explained by the joint operation of *two* causally potent factors. The first of these factors is something present and phenomenal that is causally sensitive

to, and probably causally explained by, the spatial properties singled out in
the perceptual experience; for example, postural or kinesthetic sensations,
but maybe instead or in addition neurological phenomena. The second
causal factor is something that is singled out by a very different and quite
special sense of 'How at instant t_1 one seems to oneself to be disposed in
spatial respects R_a in space'.[4] A rough example of this kind of causal
explanatory claim would be this: 'At instant t_1 one seems to be aware of a
flexed arm *because* in general (and in fact over a period of decades) one
takes oneself to be a being endowed with an arm which can adopt postures like flexed, straight, etc.; and *because* of the operation of postural sensations, etc., at t_1'(the sense of 'takes oneself to be' being something quite
other than that of 'imagines oneself to be' or 'has the cognitive attitude
that one is' or 'perceptually experiences oneself as'). The hypothesis is that
if in general one took oneself to be (say) octopus-shaped instead, then despite having a human shape and despite the presence of posture-caused
phenomena like sensations of posture, one could not have the experience
of seeming to be in the presence of a flexed (very roughly) arm-shaped
thing. The supposition is that *something* (let us call it 'I', a long-term body
image) *whose content encompasses arm-shape* functions as a necessary but insufficient condition of these experiences of shape and posture. That is, that
one continuously carries within one's mind/brain certain (probably) mental "luggage" that one's mind/brain brings to bear upon the data of the
moment (which is in fact probably sensational and possibly also neurological in character), whose nature is such that the causal conjunction of these
several factors results in a proprioceptive perception whose spatial content
in part repeats and is in any case tightly constrained by that psychocerebral
"luggage" (I). Just what kind of a thing this item I is supposed to be, and
whether anything answers to it in reality, remain to be considered. And so
does the validity of the above very complex hypothesis. But for the moment I want to take a look at what the item I is supposed to explain,
namely what I have called the 'short-term body image'.

Three Different Kinds of Short-Term Body Image

It turns out that more than one thing might naturally qualify for this title.
Three phenomena can be distinguished, which I shall call (α), (β), and (γ).
The first (α) is *the content of the proprioception* of the body at any moment.
This is something that mutates from instant to instant, and not just because
body posture continually changes but also because attentive focus shifts,
whether because of the odd passing bodily sensation or else in accord with
the intentional bodily occupations of the moment. Thus you could have
the same bodily spatial state on two occasions t_1 and t_2, but because you

were physically active in one way at t_1 and either physically inactive or active in some other way at t_2, different proprioceptive experiences would almost certainly occur at t_1 and t_2. Here we have one reality, the proprioceptively *perceived* of the moment (α), which it is natural to describe as a 'body image'. However, another equally significant reality is the proprioceptively *perceptible* of the moment, which I shall call (β). For any given bodily spatial state of affair of the moment, this latter (β) will, one presumes, be a fixed content. We would arrive at the value of that content by distributing the attention all over the body, while the body remains in one given posture, and synthesizing the multiple findings in a single spatial image. This single spatial image (β) is what is available for perception, or as we say what is perceptible, given a determinate spatial posture.

Now (α) and (β) have certain common features. Thus whatever in (α) happens to stand out upon the ground of the body as a whole, for example the spatial properties of the bowing arm of a violinist, is certain to find itself in (β), or the perceptible variety of 'body image at that instant'. But another important common property between (α) and (β) consists in the *very kind* of those common contents. Crudely expressed one might say that they are alike in a quite peculiar impoverishment of detail/parts. This commonality owes its existence to a special feature of all proprioception, namely the fact that particular limbs and bodies as a whole come to proprioceptive awareness otherwise than via the mediation of their parts, which is to say that the perceptibility of parts is not the *epistemological foundation* of that of wholes (in contradistinction to sight).[5] In any event, whatever the exact description of this latter special feature may be, it seems to me evident that (α)- and (β)-type body images will be alike in lacking the presence of the full complement of tactilely differentiable parts of the body outside. Then this property of (α) and (β) suggests the need for a third sense of 'short-term body image', for it brings to our notice a third reality which is (like (α) and (β)) causally determined by the conjunction of long-term body image and postural sensations, etc. (and ultimately therefore by posture itself). This is what one might perhaps call the *potentially perceptible* of the moment.

This third reality (γ) is arrived at in the following manner: we merely take the content of the (β) image of the moment and augment it with all the points and parts that *might in principle* come to consciousness were a highly localized tactile sensation to take up residence at that point. This image fills in all the lacunae of (α) and (β) and is in this sense an image of a continuity. Now whereas the (α)-type body-image was the content of a particular perception, the (β)-type was not, and it goes without saying that the (γ)-type likewise is not, irrespective of whether the entire body outside was clad in a hairshirt or whatever. Despite their unrealizability in experience, the (β) and (γ) images are, I think, genuine fixed realities which correspond to any determinate posture.

The Constitutive Raw Material of Body Images

A problem arises as to the "metal" in which these images are cast. We know that (α) is the content of a special variety of perception, proprioception, and that (β) and (γ) are constructs out of such, but precisely what sort of thing goes to constitute (α)? At the very least, (α) contains what can be brought by the subject under concepts, and expressed in his language: for example, 'My right hand rested on my right knee, and my right arm was straight'. But this fact tends to conceal the problem. Thus when we say 'straight', how exactly are we using this term? Are we merely opposing it to 'crooked', or do we literally mean that the arm is as rulers and Roman roads are? Neither answer strikes me as altogether satisfactory. The first because the same problem must break out over 'crooked'; the second because it seems to go beyond what we strictly perceive and in any case assumes a synthesis of points that it is hard to credit. The content seems somehow to be "subconceptual," as one might say, not ineffable but forged out of something other than the concepts enshrined in our language. After all, the proprioceptions of nonrational animals may not differ from those of rational animals in the dramatic way that the visual perceptions cannot help doing. Does speaking a language help one to run? It certainly helps one to look for next Saturday's theater tickets. The content of proprioception seems best expressed in a practical medium rather than in conceptual terms: for example, in the act of raising one's arm to catch a ball, though it is, I think, unclear, just what this tells us about the actual character of proprioceptive content. Finally, the content of (γ)-type images is, I believe, best and concretely given by a physical model of one's body surface. And what this means is, not that one might in principle perceive such a thing, but that for any given body posture all of the acts of pointing to all of the sensuously differentiable perceptible points on one's body surface would in the end delineate such a surface. Since this content includes (α) content, it seems fair to describe it as putting on dispay the sum total of what might in principle at any instant be perceived.

Whatever the answer to these questions concerning content, the justification for speaking of these three kinds of body image (α), (β), and (γ), which is to say the evidence for believing that they stand for realities, is twofold. In the first place it is conceptual: each sense of 'body image' can be precisely expressed as a bona fide concept. Thus the (α) image is of *the perceived* at any instant, the (β) image is of *the perceptible* at any instant, and the (γ) image is of *the potentially perceptible* at any instant. The second justification is available only for (β) and (γ) images, and consists in the fact that for any given posture one and only one (β) and (γ) value exists—a property that doubtless follows simply enough from the first justification. While only one of these three phenomena can be accounted an event, let alone an experience, they are phenomenal realities nonetheless. Their cause lies in body posture, together with whatever mind-impinging phenomena body posture regularly causes, whether it be postural sensations or neurological events, taken in conjunction with the presence of something else which I have called 'the long-term body image' (about which I speak in a moment). Posture and long-term image causally determine the (β) and (γ) image at any instant, while posture and long-term image, together with attention distribution, jointly determine the (α) image of the instant. Since what is perceived depends upon what is perceptible, the (β) image of the moment must encompass the (α) image, and since they each depend on what is potentially perceptible, the (γ) image must encompass both.

4 The Long-Term Body Image

A Conceptual Preamble

None of the three phenomena that I have labeled 'short-term body image' seem to be what most people who speak of "the body image" have in mind. While this latter notion is in my view for the most part an unformed or vague or malformed concept, I think it likely nonetheless that people are conscious here of something that is a fourth reality, to be set alongside the other three. However, this claim needs to be hedged in somewhat, because of an *ambiguity* in the use of 'body image'. Thus there exists on the one hand a *mentalistic* concept of 'body image', which is exemplified in such comments as 'Anorexics often have a distorted body image'; but there exists in addition what is probably a less overtly mentalistic concept, which we find at work in assertions like 'Infants already possess a body image' and 'Amputation has no instantaneous effect on one's body image'. I see no prospect of unifying these two usages, for the simple reason that they are in my opinion concerned with different entities. Then when I speak of a 'long-term body image', it is the second less overtly mentalistic phenomenon that I have in mind. I am convinced that something real exists here, to which it is natural to append the label 'body image' or 'long-term body image'. A large part of the philosophical problem of the body image consists in putting together a proper concept of this entity, and in setting out what kind of considerations would constitute an adequate justification for the usage in question. It should not be thought that the *mere expression* 'body image' carries us through to that destination; indeed, one might say that it is itself so far little more than an image or verbal picture, and in any case the existence of ambiguity disposes of that suggestion without further ado. Now when I remark that the concept is for the most part unformed or vague or malformed in people's minds, I mean *either* that they have not engaged in the work of fashioning a concept *or* that they assume that the mere expression is self-explanatory *or* that they have not even noticed the existence of an ambiguity. And yet I think it is often enough the case that people are aware of this elemental phenomenon. We find ourselves in the curious situation where not merely does awareness precede the delineation of an individuating concept, but in addition an improperly differentiated double awareness precedes both. In any case, I wish to emphasize that my concern in the ensuing discussion is with the particular something that those who have resort to the *less overtly mentalistic usage* have in all probability actually noticed.

The Peculiarities in Our Concept of Long-Term Body Image

Why do we believe that there exists something which it is natural to describe as 'a long-term body image'? And why do we believe that this something is endowed with a spatial content (let us call it C) matching the body outside? Well, what preliminary data makes us posit this something? The first thing probably is that C is common to all examples of the three varieties of short-term image (to all i's, as we called them) over an extended period m like decades. And yet the mere existence of this common property of countless proprioceptive experiences cannot on its own constitute reason for believing in a distinct image of the body (in any natural sense of 'image'). Doubtless the regularity is of significance and requires explanation, and doubtless it even demands a causal explanation in terms of something endowed with value C; but this still falls far short of what needs to be the case if we are to posit an item of the kind of the long-term body image. After all, the above complex causal property will surely be realized by the body itself. Thus we are assuming that all of the short-term images (the i's) are veridical perceptions of the body shape, and we know that the value C is common to all instantiations of the body shape, so the regularity in question must be realized and caused by something with value C (to wit, the body). Clearly, there is more to the concept of body image than the obtaining of this regularity amongst one's proprioceptive experiences, or the inherence of value C in something which explains the regularity. What we are looking for *at the very least* is something with value C, set in the mind/brain, intervening causally between the body itself and the regularity amongst the short-term images (the i's), and explaining this latter regularity.

It takes us an important step nearer to grasping what goes into our actual concept of long-term body image, to understand just how the latter specifications fall short of the necessary requirements. They do so in an interesing way. A visual example helps to bring out how. Suppose that a person is confronted with a dense array of colored points set out on a page, and that this array harbours the clearly visible outline in red points of a beetle of type *x*; assume that he is confronted by a succession of such pictures, in each of which an *x*-type red beetle appears, only differently postured each time; and suppose that this person identifies the red *x* beetle each time. He might do so in *two very different ways*. He might, for example, know each highly distinctive profile as 'a particular profile of the *x* beetle': a piecemeal collection of individual cognitions—not unlike that possessed by "airplane spotters" in Britain in 1940. But he might instead know exactly what the *x* beetle looks like, just as we all know exactly what the human hand looks like, and so come to recognize those beetles in innumerable postures and from a variety of angles as a result of this comprehensive knowledge of a particular visual appearance. Now this latter example of knowledge intervenes in the viewer's mind between the beetle itself and the event of its visual recognition, and does so again and again in the course of many recognitions, and thus explains the common presence of a spatial content (call it C') in an extended sequence of visual experiences. Bearing this in mind, one might with some justification say of the viewer that he harbors a 'long-term image of beetle shape' (with content C') in a sense that seems at first blush to closely parallel that invoked when we speak of a 'long-term body image'. However, in actual fact the two senses differ quite fundamentally.

Note a few of the characteristics of this visual case. A perceiver is presented with a scattered and complex perceptible array, out of which his mind culls a particular shape; and then another such array, out of which he culls another shape; and so on. It so happens that the culled shapes have a common content, of which the viewer was but need not have been apprised, and it also so happens that the knowledge in question helps him to single out the particular shapes. Thus in each particular perception he imposes one interpretation out of possible others upon a spatially complex datum that has a spatial character of its own, arriving thereby at a particular visual experience. And he might have accomplished this *either* through knowing merely that specific beetle posture *or* through knowing of a structure C' that is common to the entire set of displayed postures. The above are some of the main features of the imagined visual situation. Then the respects in which that visual situation is a flawed model for proprioception highlight the peculiarities of the proprioceptive long-term body image. Several features of the visual situation find no analogue in the proprioceptive situation. In particular:

1. The nature of the sensation or secondary quality mediating the perception of the material object is not as such of any *specific material object*, nor as such of any specific *type* or *shape* of material object, nor indeed as such of *material objects* at all. (By contrast, proprioceptive sensations are as such of one's unique, determinately shaped, human body; more, they come to consciousness as situated in relation to the outside/surface of such a given shape.)

2. The parts of the immediate perceptual datum (here, the visual field) can be differentiated, individuated, and ordered without in any way employing the perceived material object as an individuating framework. Thus I can individuate a point in my visual field either as 'red and at midpoint in my visual field, i.e., 0° right/left, 0° up/down', or else as 'red and directly out in front of my head'. (By contrast, we individuate proprioceptive sensations, and indeed bodily sensations generally, by positioning them in relation to the outside/surface of the material object that they make perceptible.)

3. Many points are perceived or perceptible that fall a perceptible distance away from the perceived material object, e.g., all the other visible points on the page may be blue. (By contrast, we do not feel sensations outside our own body.)

4. One might have noticed the visual array in question without singling out any particular shape. (By contrast, we inevitably experience bodily sensations as determinately set in an entity with a given shape, viz. one's own body.)

Etc.

Clearly, if there exists something with value C mediating the causal transactions between the body and the perceptual images or i's, that something or "image" must have a radically dissimilar function from the function of the visual image with the value of a beetle shape (C') in determining particular visual perceptions of beetle postures. While the latter was the imposition of a spatial structure upon something that already had a spatial structure that could be expressed in any number of structuring systems, the former seems to be not so much the imposition of a (secondary) structure upon something already (primarily) structured, as the acquisition of a structured matrix for what otherwise would lack structure and being. This bodily image seems to be not so much something that is perceptually discerned in its object, as something that manages to be at once veridically instantiated in its perceived object *and yet* imposed from within by us. Just what this image is, is yet to be established, but for the moment I note this fundamental property.

The peculiarities of the proprioceptive situation that determine this divergence in function between the visual image (of a beetle) and the the long-term image (of a body), stem above all from the vitally important property 2 (above). Here we encounter a unique situation in perception, and a very strange one at that: namely, the *revealed* (material object) constitutes the very system of ordering/individuation/differentiation of the *revealer* (bodily sensations). This property is a direct corollary of the radical immediacy of proprioceptive perception: the fact that proprioceptive sensations do not attentively mediate the perception of the object they help to make perceptible; for if they did, they would have an ordering system that was independent of their object.

The Origin of the Concept of a Long-Term Body Image

Then how did we come by this unusual concept of a long-term body image? I think it begins in the following way. It arises out of the fact that the very existence and general veridicality of proprioception *stand in need of explanation*. There is a puzzle as to how such a phenomenon as proprioception can so much as exist, which will soon become apparent. Thus since bodily sensation is a necessary condition of almost all proprioception, bodily sensation must help to cause proprioception and must help to explain its veridicality. Now the bulk of the content of proprioception is the spatial state of the body. But how can bodily sensation help to generate that spatial content? And how can it help to explain the veridicality of that content?

One theory is that bodily sensation occupies much of the body outside when proprioception occurs, that this entire complex of sensation maps reliably onto the body outside, and that awareness of these sensations and their spatial properties is *epistemologically prior* to awareness of the body and its space. In short, bodily sensation makes possible and explains proprioceptive spatial content by bringing to awareness its own shape, which in turn represents that of the body. This theory would fill in the lacuna between efficacious bodily sensations and proprioception, and also explain how proprioception is possible. However, the theory faces overwhelming difficulties. Thus sensations always require a principle or framework of differentiation, and even in the case of sight it is the body that satisfies this need through providing directional differentia, while it is certainly the body that provides the framework in the case of bodily sensations. It follows that the spatial properties of bodily sensations cannot be the epistemological foundation of the spatial content of proprioception. In any case, relative to what would these epistemologically prior sensations acquire a place in space for their owner? If we say relative to the body, we are thinking in a circle, while if we say relative to nothing, how can spatial differences be given to the perceiver? The conclusion must be that a sensation-representationalist theory of proprioception is false, and that bodily sensations come *in the first place* to awareness with a body-space as the required framework of location, differentiation, and individuation.

It is at this point that the aforementioned puzzle concerning proprioception appears. *Whence* the spatial content of proprioception if not via that of postural/bodily sensations? Whence that content, particularly if bodily sensation is the *means* through which we experience such a content? This is the puzzle, and it requires a drastic solution. The only way out of this difficulty is to posit a massive contribution on our part to the formation of the proprioceptive experience—something which ought in principle to be possible, if we bear in mind that in proprioception we continually perceive the one and the same object. It seems that we ourselves must bring the spatial content to the proprioceptive experience, and do so upon receiving the stimulus of sensation. More exactly, remembering that sensations mutate as posture alters, we must bring all of the space that we encounter in proprioception—minus the differentia of posture. It is, I think, *in this way* that we come by the theory of the long-term body image. Once we recognize the untenability of sensation representationalism in proprioception, it seems unavoidable.

Filling in the Concept of the Long-Term Image
We arrive via this route at the concept of a something (which we call I) permanently ensconced in the mind/brain, already endowed with a relatively rich spatial content, and playing a significant part in the determination of the spatial content of proprioception. And upon this foundation we build up in stages a richer conception of that something (*I*). As already noted in Section 3, the proper delineation of *I* begins with our entertaining a double hypothesis, the first part of which takes the following form. We first of all hypothesize that there exists an entity *I* in the mind/brain which is endowed with the following properties *at least*:

1. It is natural to say of it that, in a very special sense that needs spelling out, it is of 'how at time *t* one seems to oneself to be disposed in spatial respects R_a in space' (where R_a as a general rule tends to coincide with the stable surface properties of one's body).
2. The content of R_a transcends *particular postures*: for example, while the content includes arm and leg shapes, it excludes such posture values as being crooked or straightened.
3. The entity *I* transcends one's *states of consciousness and states of esthesia*, indeed one's *psychological states* generally. That is, a man will retain this image, he will in the special sense seem to himself thus shaped (etc.) when comatose or stunned, and were it (improbably) to be the case that some drastic brain event switched off all sensation (and proprioception) while waking consciousness continued unabated. More, it would survive an attack of madness in which he seemed to himself to be an octopus.
4. The contents of this entity (*I*) tend to change very slowly, generally paralleling changes in actual body size and shape: the image may be presumed to change its dimensions during the time of our life when we are growing, and to change its shape during adolescence or maybe somewhat during pregnancy and very likely over the decade in which we became hugely fat.

So much for the first hypothesis. The second hypothesis, which is explanatory in type, is that the something (*I*) answering to the above characterization, when it is conjoined with certain phenomena of the moment which probably include the sensational and/or cerebral effects of posture, helps causally to explain the short-term body images of the moment, and in particular the first proprioceptive-perceptual variety of short-term image. That is, *I* helps to cause short-term image i_x at instant t_x. Now if something answers this dual specification, if something actually has the above constitutive and causal properties, such a something will be what we are calling 'the long-term body image'; while if nothing does, the concept and usage fizzle out.

Let me now expand the characterization of the hypothesized long-term image. Since, apart from content, its properties are almost entirely causal, and since these causal properties almost certainly pertain to origins, I will begin with an account of its *origin properties*.

The hypothesis is that *I* is largely innately determined, but exhibits a malleability at the hands of protracted coordinated experience. More specifically, it seems on the one hand unlikely that natural developmental alterations, such as growing or the changes of adolescence, are going to find themselves represented in the body image *solely* as a result of coordinated motor-perceptual experience; and even more unlikely that the representations of the presence and shape of one's limbs (e.g., fingers) can be *largely* the product of experience. It is on the other hand simultaneously hypothesized that experience, and therefore one's own personal experiential history, leave their mark on the image of the present moment. The supposition is that—especially in the case of novel and, most of all, unnatural shapes, such as a newly acquired hump, which could not have been genetically anticipated—sustained coordinated experience can enable their incorporation in the image. This malleability at the hands of experience might be thought to have functional, and therefore also selective, value for the individual in facilitating veridical proprioceptions and therefore accurate intentional manipulations of the environment. In sum, I have hypothesized three kinds of origin properties: changeless-innate (e.g., fingers), developmental-innate (e.g., growing), and experience-acquired (e.g., hump, corpulence). To these I add what might be described as *conditions of persistence*: for example, the property of transcending postural change, indeed body shape of the moment, together with psychological states generally, including states of consciousness and esthesia. To learn that *I* is such as to be unaffected by sudden changes of body shape or states of esthesia, is to learn something about its conditions of origin.

The richness of the origins of *I* attests to its links with genetics and personal history. By contrast, the *effect-property* of *I*—there seems to be only one—is surely indicative of *natural function*. The conjectured effect of I is (as I have already noted) that it causes the short-term body image i_x of the moment t_x, when assisted by two kinds of contemporaneous phenomena. The first of these agencies is the standard effect of present posture, notably postural/kinesthetic sensations and maybe also certain cerebral effects; while the second may well be short-term memory of recent movement, bearing in mind the effect upon proprioception of protracted immobility. That is, the explanatory half of the double hypothesis is that *I*, together with certain contemporaneous effects of present and immediately past posture, causes the proprioception of the moment. The upshot of these several causal hypotheses is that I proves to be a natural device whereby the changeless innate, the developmentally innate, and a certain past history wherein the contingencies of development find recognition, are brought to bear upon the data of the present and immediate past, in generating the proprioception of the moment. Perhaps the most noteworthy feature of this causal hypothesis is, that the present body shape is simply bypassed in this causal transaction, and that present posture is merely associatively operative.

The Type and Ontological Status of the Long-Term Body Image
But what *kind of thing* is the long-term body image? And is it a *psychological phenomenon*? A preliminary note of caution before attempting to come to grips with these two questions. In speaking of the long-term body image, I remarked earlier that it is (in a special sense yet to be spelled out) 'how at a certain time one seems to oneself to be in spatial respects R_a''. Then it has at this point to be admitted that the latter sentence is somewhat misleading. Whatever variety of "seeming" it is that we are talking of, it can be none of the familiar psychological "seemings": it is not a perceptual experience of a certain shape, nor an imagining-of or imagining-that one is possessed of a certain shape; indeed, it is not any kind of experience at all. And neither is it a cognitive attitude with such a content, whether we are thinking of a belief, an expectation, an inclination or tendency to believe, and so on. And in fact we ought to abandon any attempt to fit the long-term body image into any such familiar psychological boxes. It is not just that it is wrong. By importing the element of psychological self-reference, with its overtones of self-consciousness, such an approach suffers in addition from the basic failing of construing the body image in far too *elevated* terms. In reality, we are dealing here with something extremely primitive. There can be no doubt that in the less overtly mentalistic sense of 'body image' that is my present concern, the body image is present in animals of all kinds and levels of compexity in precisely the sense it is present in rational self-conscious adult humans. In my opinion, we simply ought not to

assume that it is or that it is not psychological in status. Let us for the moment agree that it is cerebral *at the very least*. And let us note in passing that there is, as I observed earlier, another phenomenon worthy of the title 'long-term body image', which unquestionably is psychological in status and is in all probability a type of *imagining*.

What can we say in a positive vein about the type and status of the less overtly mentalistic body image? It is ringed in with causal properties, some of which are surely of definitional import. These ought to provide a lead on the two questions above. Thus I hypothesized the long-term body image as something at least cerebral, with relatively fixed content C, mostly innately determined—whether developmentally in advance (e.g., breasts) or so to say timelessly (e.g., fingers), but malleable in ways by protracted coordinated experience and having the unique and vitally important function of being such as to cause i_x when assisted by the postural/kinesthetic sensations of the moment (and possibly also by short-term memory of just-passed short-term images). It is plain that the latter functional causal power is absolutely central to its nature, and it seems to me probable that malleability at the hands of protracted coordinated experience is of near central importance. Then it is noteworthy that the long-term image is thus defined in terms of causal properties which link it above all to *psychological* items, such as proprioceptive experiences and bodily sensations. This at least suggests the likelihood of its being a dispositional property cast in psychological terms, and presumably therefore of being psychological in status. It may be that I is a disposition to harbor i_x's at the instigation of the postural/kinesthetic sensations Σs_x. More exactly, I define I (with content C) as a differential causal element in the genesis of i_x's that manage to realize C-content. It is not just that I and Σs_x cause i_x (with a content matching the posture P_x of the moment): I is hypothesized as responsible for the realization of C-ness in the latter i_x, which has a content matching P_x. These considerations lead me to assume that I is psychological in status.

5   Is the Long-Term Body Image an A Priori Postulate?

The justification for positing a long-term body image (I as I call it) begins with the fact that a common content C exists in all short-term body images (the i's as I call them) over an extended period. This justification is immeasurably strengthened by the consideration that, while the content of proprioception is spatial and while postural (etc.) sensations cause proprioception, postural sensations cannot be *the original bearer* of spatial content in proprioception. Accordingly, I hypothesized the existence of an I with spatial content C, transcending posture and psychological states of all kinds, which joins with the postural/kinesthetic sensations Σs_x of the moment t_x, and maybe also with short-term memory of the immediate past $i_{x-\varepsilon}$, to cause the i_x of the moment. This hypothesis is an empirical explanatory hypothesis, and presumably therefore cannot possibly be construed as a priori necessary. However, once we assume that certain vastly familiar features of the animal condition obtain, the theory of a long-term body image is forced upon one with something resembling necessity. At the very least, possession of a long-term body image is a deeply embedded element in animal existence as we know it. The demonstration of this claim is the aim of the ensuing discussion.

Since the hypothesis of an I is an empirical explanatory hypothesis, alternative hypotheses ought to be able to be entertained. I propose at this point to advance such an alternative, and then to draw out the implications of that hypothesis with a view to establishing the above claim concerning the centrality of I to animal life. The following possibility comes to mind. Let us suppose it were the case that all points on the body outside cast a versimilitudinous literal image in the brain, thanks to the mediation of neurological events of one kind or another, an image which constantly mutated as the body shifted and moved. Suppose also that the content of this 3D image (which we shall call I_{3D}) automatically determined immediate bodily perceptual "seemings" which are cast in the spatially impoverished respects typical of proprioception generally. And let us assume that this is all the immediate body perception that there is. Now if this was how matters stood, we would I think have no grounds for postulating a long-term body image: its explanatory rationale would have been removed. And much else would vanish along with the long-term image. For example, a natural conservatism in relation to one's own bodily being would be supplanted by a permanent readiness for "revolutionary change." Thus were it to be the case that one's body suddenly rebelled against the constraints of nature and adoped an octopus shape, then all one's immediate bodily perceptual "seemings" would instantaneously acquire an octopoid character: one would not, so to say, recognize oneself from the inside! And the past would drop out altogether as a causal determinant of present bodily perceptual content. And so too would innate or genetic determining factors. Spatial content would be constantly renewed, instant by instant, in this wholly ahistorical account. Everything causally relevant would be at once literally physically superficial and in the "here and now."

Certain difficulties begin to appear for this theory. The ahistorical character, the possibility of sudden octopoid body "seemings", are disconcerting to say the least; but not, I think, essentially unintelligible. The first real problem arises when we ask the question: How necessary is it, in the supposed generation of body "seemings" by the literal image I_{3D}, that it act in conjunction with the bodily sensations of the moment Σs_x?

One's first thought is that it can hardly be a necessity. After all, the posture of the moment P_x is presumed to have the cerebral effect I_{3D}, so the informational basis necessary for a veridical perception of P_x must be installed within the perceiving organism, and quite independently of the existence of sensation Σs_x. Why should not an anaesthetic perception of the body exist? Well, I can see no reason why it should not. But where does that conclusion get us? The trouble with this suggestion is that it considers the phenomenon of perception from too general or abstract a point of view. It is not just *perception* of a limb that we are hoping to realize in the absence of a long-term image: after all, we can see the limb already! Nor is it merely *immediate knowledge* of limb presence and posture: there seems to be nothing especially problematic in supposing that the posture of the moment P_x might generate an immediate anaesthetic knowledge of P_x. It is the *short-term body image*, the i_x of the moment, that we wish to realize without I and possibly also without Σs_x. And what *is* i_x? It is not merely perception of a limb (for we can see it already), nor knowledge (since sight breeds knowledge), nor even the immediate perception of a limb with a content that matches the normal impoverished spatial content of proprioception. A new sense might arise that managed to match the latter specification but failed nonetheless to be the kind of phenomenon I am trying to generate in the absence of the long-term body image *I*. I am specifically interested in the production of the particular perceptual phenomenon *i*. That is, an event endowed with the latter property of being at once a perceiving *and* immediate *and* with a spatial content matching that of normal proprioception—*and* in addition being endowed with the further vitally important property of giving to the bodily will its *immediate bodily object*. (For this is the natural function of proprioception).

We know that proprioception has this vital property. Then might I_{3D} manage to cause a *proprioception* of the limb? Might I_{3D} manage to lead to the instantiation of the above vitally important property via this particular route? Perhaps; perhaps not. But if it is to do so, it cannot but make use of the proprioceptive sensations of the moment Σs_x. This is because proprioception is an immediate mode of feeling one's limbs to be present and disposed in a certain way, and it is as trivially impossible to immediately feel the presence of a limb in the complete absence of feeling as it is to have visual experience in the complete absence of visual secondary qualities and/or visual sensations. Accordingly, we must abandon the idea of engendering short-term body images (*i*'s) purely at the hands of I_{3D} and in the complete absence of bodily sensation. This is not to deny that I_{3D} might, without the assistance of bodily sensation of any kind, manage to produce an immediate perception of limbs that had the requisite kind of spatial content *and* the vitally important property of giving to the bodily will its immediate bodily object. It simply affirms that such an unprecedented variety of perceiving would not be a form of proprioception, which is as essentially a "feeling so" as is sight a "looking so" and hearing a "sounding so." Whether or not this unusual possibility is in principle realizable somewhere somehow, it seems at the very least a great remove from the animal condition as it is realized terrestially. For this reason, I have chosen to confine my discussion to the proprioceptive mode of realizing the property of giving to the bodily will its immediate bodily object. But if we do thus opt for the proprioceptive mode, we have no choice but to assign a perceptual role to Σs_x.

The question remains: Might I_{3D} (rather than I), acting in conjunction with Σs_x, manage to conjure up a truly proprioceptive "feeling it so," namely i_x? Here another difficulty stands in the way. It is that of managing simultaneously to involve Σs_x essentially in the perceptual transaction and to discover a function that will confirm that involvement. Now we have earlier seen that Σs_x does not spatially represent the body to its owner, so that all representational functions must, one assumes, be held by I_{3D}. Then what informational function is left for Σs_x? None? But can Σs_x succeed in discharging its necessary function of ensuring that the body "feel thuswise," and at the same time pass informational function completely over to I_{3D}? It seems to me that it cannot. Wherever there exists a perceptual relation, wherever the attention can truly land upon a distinct existent, latent knowledge is instantiated in the situation. How can Σs_x ensure a "feeling so" and shed all cognitive import? For the attention to pass "feelingly" via sensation to a limb, surely the "feel" Σs_x must relate to that limb in a manner which accords with a regularity of some kind, and therefore through a relation bearing cognitive import. These considerations force me to the conclusion that if a properly proprioceptive "feeling it so," if a true i_x, is to be caused by I_{3D}, then Σs_x will have to be of cognitive significance, and thus capable of *interpretation*. More, since representationalism is false of proprioception and the content of proprioception is spatial, Σs_x will have to admit of a *nonprojective spatial* interpretation. That is, Σs_x will be thus interpreted by something present in the mind/brain. This latter item must be such that, acting in conjunction with Σs_x, it will automatically interpretationally generate i_x. And this is in effect to say that the something in question must be very close in character to the long-term body image (rather than to I_{3D}).

Thus, once we opt for a truly proprioceptive "feeling" perception of the body, such as would manage to give to the bodily will its immediate body object; and once we recognize the falsity of sensation representationalism in proprioception; then we are more or less compelled to posit a long-term body image. I conclude, that the long-term body image is as deeply embedded in animal existence as proprioception. To be sure, it is no kind of a priori necessity; however, once we introduce into the scene such fundamentals of the animal condition as proprioception and the bodily will, it is strictly unavoidable.

Appendix

Here is a diagrammatic representation of the possible origins of the proprioceptive experience i_x of the present moment t_x. I rejected the ahistorical accounts given in figure 1. But I recognized the possibility—maybe only in different life-systems—of the ahistorical account of the origins of i_x given in figure 2. Ultimately, however, I have opted for the near necessity of the historical theory presented in figure 3.

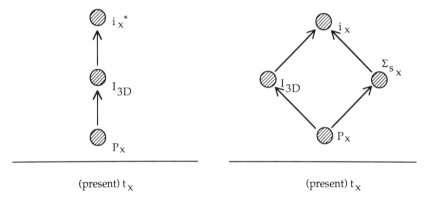

(present) t_x (present) t_x

Figure 1
Rejected ahistorical theories.

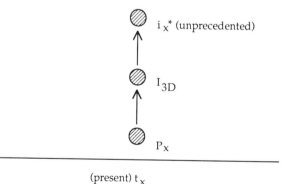

(present) t_x

Figure 2
Possible ahistorical theory.

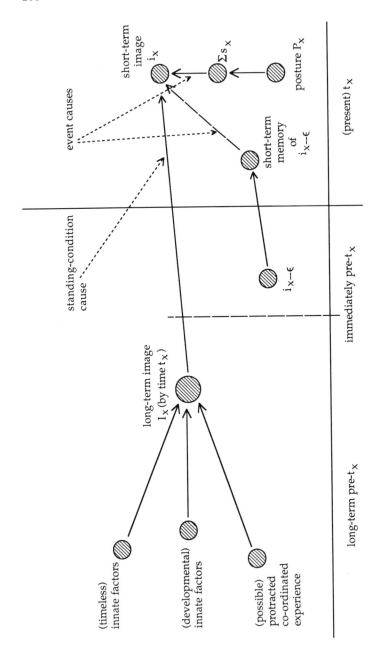

Notes

1. The term 'proprioception' has many uses. I employ it initially to stand for our awareness of our own limbs and body—vaguely conceived. It rapidly turns out that there exists an attentively immediate intuitional awareness uniquely of these material objects, in short a distinctive sub-variety of perception. Thereafter I precisely employ the term to stand for *this specific mode of perception*. Therefore it is not to be described as 'a kind of information', if that means the possession of cognitive attitudes. And it is to be sharply distinguished from the attentive awareness of bodily feelings like fatigue, whose objects are psychological and near-incorrigibly given.

2. Not everyone is of the same mind on this important issue. Thus in *Human Motor Behaviour*, we discover the following comment by M. T. Turvey et. al.: "What must be understood is that in the course of performing *any* activity, the *perceptual information available* is of these three kinds. In order to *guide any activity* you need to be able to pick up on the properties of the environment, you need to have *some appreciation of where your limbs are with respect to each other*, and you need to know where you are with respect to the layout of the environment" (1982, 276; my italics). Meanwhile in *Spatial Representation* Bill Brewer (introducing his own discussion of visually guided motor acts) remarks that the short-term body image i_x of the moment "is not essential for Brewer's simple reaching and grasping, on the Bernsteinian account he develops," and he states that "little to no knowledge of current bodily configuration is required for this kind of task" (1982, 274).

What perplexes me is that Turvey explicitly takes himself to be giving expression to the 'Bernstein Perspective'. How can Bill Brewer's account simultaneously be "Bernsteinian"? In any case, how are we to understand Turvey's "some appreciation of where your limbs are with respect to each other"? I can only assume that he means some knowledge of *some* of the internal spatial properties of one's limbs. What else? And his claim that "in order to guide *any* activity" one needs such knowledge is in complete agreement with the position I have been urging (above). I will briefly repeat the reasons that support this view. Thus, we know that acts fall under multiple descriptions, under some of which they are intentional, and it is evident that intentional action necessitates beliefs whose content matches these intentional headings. Accordingly, one thing that seems to be at issue with Bill Brewer is whether simple acts like visually guided reachings are sometimes (often? mostly?) *not* intentional under *any* description that makes *some* mention of the internal spatial properties of the limbs. I do not mean under beautifully precise exhaustive descriptions. I merely mean under descriptions making mention of *some* internal spatial properties. Then surely they are thus intentional. When I reach for a cup of tea, do I not intend to move my hand *out* from my body? And *in this direction* out (very roughly demarcated)? And some *relatively short* way out? Is not this familiar act intentional under at least *some* of these spatial descriptions? Would not one be grossly surprised by *some* hand movements (e.g., by a zig-zag)? And would not such surprise indicate a loss of *control* over the act? But control implies a match of intention and actuality. The characterization offered by Bill Brewer of everyday acts of simple reaching imports a cognitive hiatus that is simply not present: a hiatus that is in fact encountered in more extreme examples of the species. Thus the normal acts of reaching are scarcely on a par with (say) sudden high-speed duckings from what shows as a mere blur in one's visual field! These latter wild unpremeditated lurchings are acts in which one's expectations of spatial path are minimal, and the act is intentional under 'avoiding something that I glimpsed nearby' but under precious few other spatial headings! One more or less "finds" oneself at a point in space at the end of these convulsive deeds! That, precisely, does not happen in the case of "simple reaching and grasping."

Then if we can agree that everyday reaching necessitates some knowledge concerning "where your limbs are with respect to each other," which, as Turvey points out, is to be acquired through perception, the question arises as to the mode of perception through which this is accomplished. It has to be either proprioceptive, visual, or a combination of both. While Brewer seems to think that both postural knowledge *and* short-term image are inessential to these familiar acts, I will consider whether sight alone might meet one's cognitive needs in such cases. Suppose I am playing tennis, coordinating sight and physical action with skill, and my right arm of a sudden becomes completely anesthetic, indeed suddenly does not seem present at all! Would not this have *some* detrimental effect on my serve? It may perhaps be that in some imaginable realm it would fail to do so, but on the tennis courts I have bestrode, I have little doubt that most of us would botch the shot! Then if *some* esthesia is a necessary condition of the normal stroke, why so? It can scarcely be that one needs *intellectual reassurance* that the limb still exists! Then in the first place what reason can there be for refusing the hypothesis that proprioception meets the binding need for *an immediate concrete seeming-presence* (which sight cannot provide)? And can proprioception occur without spatial content, and thus without *short-term image*? Second, what reason can there be for refusing the hypothesis that feeling plays some part in informing us of *the whereabouts* of the active limb? Or are we to believe that reaching for (say) a cup of tea depends upon an "appreciation of where your limbs are with respect to each other" that is *wholly visual* in origin? It is one thing to suppose that sight is here to a degree an informant concerning body configuration, it is quite another to confer upon it the role of sole informant. Is reaching for a visible cup of tea so unutterably different from reaching into one's pocket for one's handkerchief? As remarked above, Brewer describes the former familiar cases along lines that better fit exceptional cases like a high-speed ducking that is triggered by sudden visual stimulus. In the light of these considerations I conclude that simple acts like reaching require *a measure of proprioceptive awareness*, a proprioceptive perception whose content is what I (later) call a 'short-term body image' or 'i'. Indeed, the few apparent exceptions (such as inhaling) depend on an already established present proprioceptive setting. I suspect that Bernstein's valuable findings are of less philosophical import than Brewer supposes. Personally, I would surmise that the well-worn philosophical concept of 'under a description' (of *intentional aspect*) already captures much of what is philosophically interesting in these findings. While philosophers ought not to be insensible of scientific achievement, it is desireable at the same time that they have some faith in their own methods and discoveries. Out of the frying pan (of factual ignorance), into the fire (of scientism)!

3. R can either be ostensively explained, say as the sort of thing you now spatially perceive with regard to your limbs, or discursively and less precisely explained as including posture and motion, but not three-dimensional shape, etc.

4. R_a at the very least is more comprehensive than R, and probably coincides with the spatial properties of one's body outside (minus minutiae).

5. This is a contentious claim, demonstrated elsewhere, but not really required for the point under consideration.

References

Brewer, Bill. 1993. "Introduction: Action." In *Spatial Representation,* ed. Naomi Eilan, Rosaleen McCarthy, and Bill Brewer. Oxford: Blackwell.

O'Shaughnessy, Brian. 1980. *The Will*, 2 vols. Cambridge: Cambridge University Press.

Turvey, M. T., et al. 1982. "The Bernstein Perspective, III." In *Human Motor Behaviour,* ed. J. A. Scott Kelso. Hillsdale, N.J.: Lawrence Erlbaum.

Awareness of One's Own Body: An Attentional Theory of Its Nature, Development, and Brain Basis

Marcel Kinsbourne

I am body entirely and nothing beside.

Nietzsche, Thus Spake Zarathustra

This discussion addresses a person's awareness of the disposition of his body parts and his belief that they are his own, and makes suggestions about their brain basis. In what way and under what circumstances are we normally aware of these facts about ourselves, and what can neuropsychological analysis contribute to our understanding of the mechanisms involved? Specifically, is there a localized neuronal representation dedicated to bringing the body into awareness, separate from the cerebral representation of somatosensory input in the sensory strip? Or does awareness of the body derive from selective attention to somatosensory input from the various body parts, without need for the ad hoc construct of a separate "body scheme"? If the latter is the case, how are shifts in attention to body parts organized? What reciprocal relationships might exist between attending to body parts and awareness of the self (self-consciousness)? How does awareness of the self develop?

1 Impairments of Bodily Awareness

Critchley (1950a) listed diverse organically determined anomalies in people's experience of their own bodies. Among these are neuropsychological impairments of bodily awareness labeled asomatognosias. These deficits comprise the inability to specify parts of one's own body by naming them or indicating them when named (autotopagnosia) (Pick 1908) and the unawareness that a body part is one's own (some cases of neglect) or that its function is impaired (anosognosia). Bonnier (1905) argued that what is lost in these disorders is the spatial representation of body parts whose sensation is preserved. Such a representation would be distinct from the mapping that constitutes the first cortical relay in the somatosensory cortex. There certainly are multiple somatosensory maps in the cortex (e.g., Mori et al. 1991) but they are not hierarchically organized. Also, critical findings in neuropsychology are not captured by this still prevalent concept of an egocentric body image represented as such in the brain (e.g., Vallar et al. 1993). I first discuss the disparity between the number and distribution of syndromes of partial asomatognosia that this formulation predicts, on the one hand, and the much smaller number documented, on the other. In this discussion I assume that only those syndromes that have been discovered to date exist. The future may falsify this assumption, but if it does, it will probably do so only to a minor extent, since the search for asomatognosias has been on for the best part of a century.

Among syndromes construed as partial impairments of the body image, a puzzling imbalance obtains. There is a prominent, even bizarre, but nonetheless well recognized syndrome of left neglect of the body that primarily implicates the left hand and arm. The patients ignore and often even disown these left body parts, and some deny any abnormality of their body. Have they suffered damage to the corresponding sections of their centrally represented body image? A far less striking but comparable deficit that involves the right side of the body also occurs. But reports of instances in which other parts of the presumed body image (face, neck, abdomen) are selectively ignored or disowned are conspicuously absent. If, as is generally supposed, the body image is specifically represented somewhere in the cerebrum and if left personal neglect is due to a lesion that inactivated the corresponding part of that representation, why are there no lesions that compromise other parts of the body image than those located at the extremes of the body's lateral axis? The cell assemblies that represent other parts of the body image could hardly be immune to naturally occurring damage. Why are there no other focal or partial asomatognosias? For that matter, why is anosognosia for dysfunction of a body part so disproportionately prominent for hemiplegia, and for left hemiplegia at that (Cutting 1978)? This disparity may imply that our neuropsychological theory of the body image is wrong. Specifically, there may not be any central representation dedicated to body image. I here revisit the concept of the body image and find reason to amend it so as to arrive at a different conceptual framework. To establish a foundation for this argument, I first discuss normal body awareness.

2   When Does One Attend to the Relative Disposition of One's Body Parts?

The locomotor system's specialization for movement and for posture (which is often preparation for movement) is primarily adapted toward exploring the environment and either acting upon a particular target or withdrawing from it. Toward these ends, detailed awareness of the position of the body is generally not needed and generally not available. Instead, unconscious machinery is invoked. This automatized system was called the body scheme by Head and Holmes (1911–1912). (For the distinction between body image and body scheme, see Gallagher 1986.) 'Schema' in this sense, rather than in the conscious sense as used by Bonnier (1905), is not implicated in asomatognosias, which are conceptualized as domain-specific disorders of bodily awareness.

In their mechanical detail, skilled movements are automatic and generally not under attentional scrutiny. Differences in the configuration and rate of displacement of body parts are experienced not as such but rather in terms of what is being explored or manipulated. These specifics of movement are used to infer properties about the environment—the size, shape, texture, and distance of a thing—and this is what is represented and available to awareness. A person only infrequently attends to the position of his body. As for the intention to move a body part, this is generally so quickly followed by the movement that the intention is not registered in awareness. The intention to move incorporates an image of the part to be moved as it reaches the target location. If the individual hesitates, then the lingering intention may convey the limb into awareness. When no objects are being acted upon or when the exploration of the environment goes awry, then attention may focus on the body parts themselves (as when any skilled-movement sequence fails, attention shifts to the level of individual moving parts). This type of bodily awareness is referred to the 'short-term body image' by O'Shaughnessy (this volume). Correspondingly, loss of bodily sensation primarily becomes apparent in terms of disordered movement and disordered posture, and we more frequently become aware of the body parts that customarily participate in action plans. Impaired awareness of body parts does not give rise to anything patients complain about. It usually only comes to notice on direct questioning.

Awareness of body parts during action can be likened to the marginal awareness of information in the peripheral visual field during focal attention. To contemplate the specific shape and disposition of one's body parts calls for focusing attention, which can be implemented only sequentially, one body part at a time. (The maximal extent of a body part that can simultaneously be the focus of attention remains to be determined.) Failing that, only some very general information is immediately available. But even in the absence of detailed information about body parts, one feels that one's body is complete. It appears that the body feels complete if no specific signals in awareness indicate that it is not, and such signals can only enter awareness if attention is focused on the representation of the body part in question. Hence the patient does not complain that body parts that are "neglected" are missing (see below). The body feels as it always felt. Correspondingly, since all movement is differential (i.e., selected from a set of alternative possible movements), it may be that when one moves, one has background awareness of alternative movement possibilities. But the exact nature of the set of alternatives is *not* in awareness, and if the set is depleted, this would not be experienced as a loss, and therefore would not be complained of.

3   How Does One Focus Attention on a Body Part?

The control of visual and bodily attention have in common that they are both subject to lateral bias when dysfunctional. Syndromes of unilateral neglect have been documented in both modalities, and with comparable left-sided preponderance. In experimental animals with appropriately placed unilateral brain resections, "circling" can be elicited by either visual or tactile ipsilesional stimulation. Attention is drawn ipsilaterally toward the lesion, and locomotion in that direction follows the anticipatory orientation (Kinsbourne 1974). If when the animal turns, the stimulus array still extends in the direction of turning, further turning, that is, circling, results.

Ample evidence indicates that visual orienting, at least along the lateral plane, is under the control of opponent processors and is directed along the vector resultant of their interaction (Kinsbourne 1974, 1994). I now suggest that somatosensory attention is also directed along the vector resultant of directionally organized opposing processors. An attentional shift to a unilateral body part requires an increase in the activation of the contralateral processor and reciprocally decreased activation of the ipsilateral processor. Attending to a unilateral body part might be a two-stage process: the segmental level of attending is established by an axial shift; then the lateral opposing interaction is calibrated so as to reach its target. If the processor on the right, which ordinarily directs attention leftward, is inactivated, this disinhibits the left processor so as to generate a rightward bias, attention being withdrawn from the left and overinvested in the right, as has so often been described in the visual-neglect syndrome (Kinsbourne 1994). A similar lesion on the left has the converse effect, though this is usually much less striking.

This proposed mechanism implies that the play of attention across body parts relies on some implicit knowledge of their structural articulation (perhaps hardwired into the somatosensory cortex). This I conclude from the fact that a neglect patient's ability to attend to a neglected body part does not appear to be modified by its location in egocentric space at that particular time. For instance, I have observed that if the patient's left forearm is placed across his chest, this does not result in lessened neglect of the hand and intensified neglect of the elbow, which is now the leftmost located body part. The implicit knowledge of the articulation of the body parts corresponds to the long-term body image, in the sense of O'Shaughnessy (this volume). In interesting contrast, within a body part, specifically the hand, there is a lateral gradient of response to double simultaneous touch, the direction of which depends on whether the hand is positioned palm up or palm down (Mattingley and Bradshaw 1994). The fact that both hands are so affected vividly demonstrates the somatosensory gradient of attention (Moscovitch and Behrmann 1994).

4   Why Are There No Local Autotopagnosias?

Somatosensory input from each side of the body is projected to the contralateral cortex. The cortical relay neurons are not the substrate of a body image in the sense of being essential to awareness of the existence of the body parts they represent. When a somatosensory map is lesioned, the individual feels a local numbness. He loses sensory acuity, but he remains aware of the existence of the body part itself. An extreme case is "conscious hemisomatognosia," in which the patient feels as though one side of his body has been amputated and that, unlike neglect, can equally involve either side of the body and is attributed to subcortical, not cortical, injury (Frederiks 1985). It has therefore been supposed that a representation (image) of the body is housed separately in the brain, distinct from the purely contralateral somatosensory maps. The findings of Semmes, Weinstein, Ghent, and Teuber (1963) implicate the left hemisphere as the site of such a map. Neuropsychologists believe that they are assessing the integrity of this map of the body when they ask patients to name body parts, indicate named body parts, or indicate body parts on a sketch of the body. Partial or complete destruction of this body image allegedly gives rise to partial or complete "autotopagnosia" (Nielsen 1938, Roth 1949, Critchley 1955).

As mentioned above, if a representation of the body image were hardwired into one hemisphere, or elsewhere in the brain for that matter, it would be expected to have suffered damage in its several parts in diverse patients, to the point that the anatomical correspondence between any body part and its representation in the body image should by now have been documented in cumulative case reports. But nothing of the kind has occurred. Local autotopagnosias have proven surprisingly hard to come by. Indeed, the literature presents local autotopagnosic syndromes only for left-sided body parts, in neglect of the person (see Critchley 1950b). The only bilateral partial autotopagnosias is finger agnosia. In this condition, which is due to left posterior parietal injury, the patient cannot name his finger or point to named fingers. But Gerstmann 1924 notwithstanding, finger agnosia is not a localized autotopagnosia. The difficulty that the finger agnosic experiences in naming her fingers or recognizing them when named is a consequence of a more general disability in discriminating on the basis of relative position, as are the other three elements of the Gerstmann syndrome (see Kinsbourne and Warrington 1962).

5   Is There a General Autotopagnosia?

Neither the inability to name body parts nor the inability to point to named body parts, Pick's operational criteria for autotopagnosia, are unequivocal evidence of a selective disorder of the body image. DeRenzi and Scotti observed that if disordered pointing to named body parts extends also to objects external to the body, this reflects a "general inability to analyze a whole into its component parts" (1970, 202). The patient may have a visuospatial agnosia. The visuospatial agnosic cannot use peripheral visual cues to help him direct his gaze. He is aware of only one object at a time, even if they overlap, and thus is lost in space. The patients described by Pick (e.g., 1922) mislocate body parts not only on their own body surfaces but elsewhere. Such a patient may reach across the table or under the chair for his eye or ear. He clearly suffers not from a static disruption or distortion of the body image but from an inability to shift attention flexibly among parts of the body. The fact that his search ranges beyond the confines of the body shows that the patient is unable to use somatosensory cues from body parts as targets toward which to orient, or at least as landmarks to constrain his search.

Some aphasics find it disproportionately difficult to name body parts (Goodglass et al. 1966, Assal and Buttet 1973, Dennis 1976, Semenza and Goodglass 1985, Goodglass and Budin 1988). This is to be construed as a semantic deficit, or "word category aphasia" (Yamadori and Albert 1973) rather than an autotopagnosia. That dementia also complicates the interpretation of apparent autotopagnosia was stressed by Poeck and Orgass (1971). However, Ogden (1985) reported a patient whose apparently selective difficulty in finding parts of the body was paralleled by an inability to describe their spatial relationships in words. Ogden believes that the patient is unable to form a mental image of his own body.

6   Opposing-Processor Imbalance and Impaired Body Awareness

The static view of how the body is centrally represented, which leads one to expect that partial autotopagnosias should occur, is paralleled by the mistaken assumption that the parietal cortex represents "external space" in some static manner, for which reason some right-parietally lesioned patients cannot represent the left side of space. It is not so much that neglect patients cannot represent left-sided spatial extent per se as that they cannot use sensory or remembered information to represent the left sides of things, wherever the things might be located (evidence is reviewed in Kinsbourne 1987). An analogous situation obtains for body sensation. The brain activates a representation of whatever part of the body the individual orients to when and only when she orients to it. While she retains knowledge of the fact that there is a left side to her body, the patient with somatosensory neglect cannot use sensory information to represent the left extreme of the body.

If attending to body parts is under opponent processor control, as suggested above, a complete set of partial autotopagnosic syndromes would not be expected to occur. There can be no focal impairment in body awareness (just as there can be no "island of neglect" in a visual field). Impairments are most apparent at the extremes of the lateral axis. But which parts should be considered more lateral in the body? To judge from neuropsychological evidence, the hand and feet appear to be at the lateral extreme of the conceptual bodily field (or long-term body image). This is indicated by unilateral bodily neglect, which regularly implicates the hand most of all, the elbow (and foot) less, and more axial structures, like the left shoulder and left face, far less and only in the more severe cases (Bisiach 1991). It is as if the body were conceptualized in the "anatomical position": back straight, with arms outstretched to either side and legs straight and wide apart. That would make the hand and the foot the most lateral body parts. It is true that as the hand is most subject to neglect in the upper extremity, so the foot is most often neglected within the lower limbs. But why is neglect of the hand so much more striking than neglect of the foot?

Again I use as a model the visual control of lateral attention. It has become clear that the preponderance of neglect of the left is a consequence of a normally present bias of attention to the right (summarized by Kinsbourne 1987). The reason why the most severe neglect affects the left hand may be that the right hand is a particularly efficient attractor of attention. Whereas ownership of the left hand is denied in left personal neglect, ownership of the left foot is more typically conceded, though the fact that it is paralyzed is often denied (possibly a milder manifestation of the same malfunction). The representations of the two feet may not be in such pronounced potential imbalance as those of the hands in the neglect patient. The shoulders, sides of the back, and hips, which are bilaterally innervated, so often work in concert (rather than reciprocally) that there is little tendency even for a damaged unilateral processor to be overwhelmed by an intact one on the other side. It would follow that the paired body parts will prove to be subject to neglect in proportion to the extent to which the intact individual is normally selectively aware of these body parts.

7   What Explains the Indifference and Denial Syndromes?

A patient may disregard a gross deficit such as hemiplegia on account of a general tendency to minimize problems, as occurs in some cases of frontal-lobe disease. But a selective denial of hemiplegia has to be otherwise explained. In such a case, ownership of the limb is acknowledged, and therefore the representation of the limb must be preserved. I suggest that what is lost in this case is the cerebral substrate of the intention to move the limb. If one cannot conceive of intending to move a limb, one cannot become aware that one would have difficulty in doing so. The sensory loss that so often coexists with denial of hemiplegia may render the intention more difficult to form, or it may exert some other effect.

When a limb is completely disowned, representing it kinesthetically and representing intentions for moving it have presumably been precluded by the cerebral damage. The limb, both in terms of experience and of agency, has lost its place in the patient's direct awareness. Visual information about the limb evidently does not suffice to generate the feeling of limb ownership. Therefore, its presence in plain sight and its visible attachment to the rest of the body poses a logical problem to the patient, though it by no means counteracts his proprioceptive nonexperience of the limb. The rationalizations with which patients disown the affected limb can be highly idiosyncratic (your hand, a nurse's, a monkey's, a snake) but usually exhibit negative valence: (cold, dead, alien). Conspicuously, the patients seem eager to evade any conversation that addresses the paradox that the limb they claim they have moved has not been seen to move, or that the limb they claim is not theirs is continuous with their body. The patients' ill-concealed aversion is to an analysis that could threaten their attempt at holding at bay a conflict between their knowledge and their experience, one that threatens an existential crisis.

In certain congenital and infantile hemiplegias the affected limb is not explicitly denied but is disused out of proportion to the severity of the motor deficit, except in bimanual activities. It would be of interest to find out whether vestibular stimulation is effective in temporarily shifting attention to such a limb, as it is in neglect (Bisiach, Rusconi, and Vallar 1991; Rode et al. 1991). If the central cell assemblies that react to signals from the limb are weakened, vestibular stimulation could activate them and return such a limb to full awareness. If they are so completely eliminated that neither deliberate nor automatic use of the limb is possible, vestibular stimulation may or may not be effective. (Both types of outcome have been documented in neglect.)

8 To What Does One Attend When One Attends to the Body?

It is not clear that attending to a body part brings proprioceptive sensations into consciousness. Subjectively, the experience when attending is more akin to a local touch, perhaps self-generated by means of a slight muscular contraction (see Humphrey 1992 for discussion of the relationship between body sensations and movements).

Whether, in order to attend to a body part, one has to be aware of its actual position (as derived from the short-term body image) is unclear. The perceived position of the body is the result of interacting information of kinesthetic, tactile, and visual origin. Schilder (1935) points out that the awareness of body position is synesthetic. It requires an act of deliberate analysis to identify the modality through which information about the position of the body is being acquired at any moment. Because visual and tactile representations can become conscious in their own right, attention can be selectively focused upon their individual contributions to the awareness of body parts. In contrast, kinesthetic contributions are unconscious and cannot be deliberately deconfounded. In the absence of the other indicators of bodily position, touch can serve. In the weightless condition (zero gravity) a touch to the flat of the heels gives the feeling of being upright; a touch to the top of the head, of being inverted (Lackner and DeZio 1984).

As already discussed, in the extreme pathological case in which a body part is disavowed, there is a clear conflict between vision, which continues to register the continuity between the implicated part and the rest of the body, and proprioception, which no longer represents the part in awareness. In cases of phantom limbs there is a similar conflict, but in the reverse direction. 'Phantom limb' refers to an experience not infrequently reported by amputees. The patient with a phantom continues to experience the limb, and even to incorporate it into the movements of his body (Straus 1970). For instance, when a man with an amputated leg stumbled, he felt himself extend his missing phantom leg, as it were, to save him from falling. The state of preparedness to move will normally not persist long enough to be included in awareness (in order to join the dominant focus of awareness, a representation has to endure for longer than a minimal period of time, as discussed by Kinsbourne, in press), because the movement itself rapidly supervenes and supplants the intention. When the limb has been amputated or did not develop, it cannot move, and the persisting intention unmatched by the expected movement feedback, conveys the limb into awareness (indeed, into excessive, unwanted awareness: the phantom limb is continually in consciousness, whereas normal limbs fade into the background). But that this cannot be the only explanation of the continual obtrusiveness of a phantom is demonstrated by the existence of a phantom breast, a situation in which movement is not an issue.

Kinesthetic dominance in the perception of a body part is illustrated in normal people who experience an illusory stretching of particular muscle groups when vibration is applied to the overlying skin under isometric conditions. The examples that follow derive from Lackner's systematic application of a method that induces in the subject the illusion that his limb has moved (e.g., Lackner and DeZio 1984). If a limb muscle is vibrated so as to stimulate the muscle spindle receptors, there follows a reflex muscle contraction, known as the "tonic vibration reflex" (Eklund and Hagbarth 1966). If the vibrated limb is precluded from moving, then the subject experiences a movement in the same direction as would result were the vibrated muscle stretched (Goodwin, McCloskey, and Matthews 1972). It follows that commands to the musculature are monitored, and their expected consequences are compared with the actually resulting patterns of proprioceptive activity and body motion. This effect is most pronounced in darkness, but though attenuated, it still occurs in the presence of disconfirming visual feedback.

Vibration was applied by a hand-held electromagnetic physiotherapy vibrator, 120 pulses per second, for three minutes per trial, to the skin overlying selected muscles of blindfolded subjects. Three postures were studied:

• The subject touches his nose with his index finger. The biceps muscle is vibrated. The arm appears to extend, and the finger and nose also feel longer. The triceps muscle is vibrated. The body parts seem to shorten. Individuals vary. For some, the nose is pushed back into the head. For some, the index finger passes through the nose. For some, the head is extends backward.
• The subject touches the top of his head with his palm or finger tip. With biceps vibration, the head seems to extend upward to a point. With triceps vibration, the finger feels as though it has penetrated the skull, or as if the head is pushed into the trunk.
• The subject stands with arms akimbo, hands pressed to the waist. With biceps vibration, his waist seems to balloon. With triceps vibration, there is the feeling of a narrowed (wasp) waist.

Even positions that violate the laws of physics, in that two body parts occupy the same location, are reported. The experienced position of a phantom limb may also coincide with another body part. One learns that the sense of joint position counts for little. The changes in the apparent lengths of muscles are not effectively counteracted by signals from the joints to the effect that the implied joint displacement has not occurred. If a veridical representation (image) of the body exists in the brain, this evidently does not preclude people from readily experiencing their bodies in physically improbable or even impossible ways. This type of observation is more readily accommodated by the view that the representations of separate body parts are separately referred to their spatial locations and then related to each other than that an articulated image of the body is adjusted on an ongoing basis to reflect changing sensory input.

Static (as distinct from moving) visual stimuli have little effect on body sensation. When people see themselves in distorting mirrors, the visual alteration does not induce a corresponding change in felt body shape or position. But can a change in how a body part feels change how it looks? Apparently so, as evidenced by numerous accounts of neglect patients perceiving their left upper limb as swollen or otherwise distorted (Schilder 1935, Critchley 1950b, Weinstein and Kahn 1955). If there is no visually stable framework, vision follows kinesthesis in normal subjects. If vibration is applied to a limb in the dark, a source of light attached to the pointed index finger appears to move according to the felt movement of the limb (Lackner and DeZio 1984).

The dominance of proprioception in the control of normal perception of bodily shape and position sets personal neglect apart from largely visually based extrapersonal neglect, and these two types of neglect are indeed often dissociated (Bisiach et al. 1986). Opposing processors that control lateral visual and somatosensory attending are presumably separately localized in the brain.

9   A Body Scheme Acquisition Device?

Like the syntactic competencies of the "language-acquisition device," the computations that enable fluent postural change become increasingly available as the nervous system matures, and this is largely how motor milestones are attained. In a classic experiment, Held and Hein (1963) reared kittens in darkness, except for three hours each day, during which they were yoked together in such a manner that one ("active") kitten could move, whereas the other ("passive") one are was pulled along with it but could not independently initiate locomotion. In this way, both animals obtained the same visual experience, but only one could practice visually guided behavior. When the passive kitten, up to that point deprived of visuomotor experience, was unyoked from its actively moving partner, it staggered and lacked age-appropriate motility. Less stressed but actually more telling was the corollary finding that although kittens were maintained in this yoked arrangement for up to six weeks, the resulting gap in visually guided behavior was found to be completely closed at a 48-hour retest. This shows that the emergence of locomotion depends rather little on practice and very much on neural maturation. Within at most two days, kittens caught up on six weeks of deprived experience. Rather than learn movements one at a time, we seem to calibrate our motor-control systems to prevailing circumstances, including terrestrial gravity. This computation is quickly done (and quickly adjusted in other than the usual one-gravity circumstances). The long time that it takes for motor development to be completed is due not to the need for protracted practice but to the slow emergence of ever more differentiated neural motor-control mechanisms.

Activities of the types described above suggest preprogrammed responding to situations involving a body scheme, and this could be dramatized by saying that there is a device for acquiring a body scheme. The body image may also emerge at an early stage.

10   A Body-Image-Acquisition Device

Applied to the classical question of the ontogeny of awareness of one's own body and its noncontinuity with external objects, the attentional approach suggests a new formulation. The developing child may first acquire a sense of self when it becomes able selectively to attend, in however ill differentiated a fashion, to its individual body parts in the somatosensory modality. It would then become acquainted with the internal causal consistency of their positions and displacements relative to its own volitions. The assumption that the visual channel soon reveals to the infant which body parts are its own (Neisser 1978) may be mistaken. Logically, the visual channel should soon betray which (body) parts are always present and one's own and which (external) objects are present only sometimes (Neisser 1978). But the mechanisms for accomplishing this during development (Gibson 1969, Bower 1974) may follow rather than precede somatosensory attending. Poeck and Orgass (1964a, 1964b) found that blind children developed knowledge of their body at about the same age as sighted children.

The top-down nature of an infant's earliest knowledge of its body is indicated by the observation that children with amelia, where the limbs never begin to develop, sometimes report phantom limbs (Weinstein and Sersen 1961, Poeck 1964). If these claims can be sustained, there must be a cerebral representation of topographically differentiated proprioceptive input that develops regardless of whether any input from the part in question ever reaches the brain. It may be relevant that phantoms, which involve exaggerated rather than reduced attention to a body part, are, in contrast to neglected limbs, more common on the right side of the body (Shukla, Saku, Tripathi, and Gupta 1982). Whether such a purely centrally established representation is stable in the absence of sensory input is a separate question. Poeck's data show that phantoms are less frequent and more often transitory in the very young. Such findings are quite consistent with other "disuse effects" that have been documented in the developing nervous system, for instance in amblyopia. But if an amelic infant really can have a phantom limb, that indicates that cerebral somatosensory representations can become established independently of feedback from the periphery.

It is possibly relevant that amelia is usually bilateral. This means that there is no rivalry for attention by the representation of an intact contralateral limb, and this favors the genesis of a phantom, according to the attentional model.

11   The Self as Emerging from Background Body Sensation

The amelia findings teach us that simply attending to the representation of a body part (without any possibility of seeing it or feeling it touched or knowing where it is) suffices to identify a body part as existing and being (conceptually) one's own. The ability to attend to (i.e., activate) one's own representations of the parts of one's body may be an essential precursor of the acquisition of the concept of the self ("self-consciousness"). Also, if one can attend to a body part via bodily sensation, one will not make the mistake of misidentifying it as another's (Evans 1982), a mistake that could occur if one were to use the visual modality only.

The focus of attention, the figure, is experienced as arising in or emerging from a ground. In the case of the body, the ground is the familiar feeling that one's body exists as a backdrop to whatever one is thinking, experiencing, or doing, though its various parts are not being monitored. This ever present background may be the basis for constructing the continuity of the experiencing self.

The background "buzz" of somatosensory input may indicate his body to the child. It would be in line with principles of cognitive development (Vigotsky 1962, Gibson 1969) if a decontextualized construct of a self as "mental" and distinct from the body were a later emerging abstraction. (Analogous would be the relationship between purposive movement, which is present early on, and internalized thought, feasible only later when the child has acquired the inhibitory capacity that enables him to dissociate central activity from its realization in differential movements.) Underlying the person's feeling of ownership of the body would be the ownership of the rest of the body by each body part, specifically, whichever body part happens to be the focus of attention at the time. The body part at the focus of attention "owns" its background of body sensation. The construct of the self is abstracted from this origin in sensation. Thus the self has no specific location but rather is coextensive with the field of bodily sensations. It must have called for a very refined sensibility on the part of Zarathustra to have been able to see through the abstraction of a self having a body to the self's origin in being a body, and to realize that, stripped of elaborations, "I am body entirely and nothing beside."

I liken an attended body part to an attended object in the visual field, and its background (the somatosensory field) to the background visual field. The somatosensory field does not present the rest of the body in detail as an articulated object. The undifferentiated nature of the background to focused somatosensory attention might explain why the patient who neglects a limb nonetheless does not feel incomplete (in his body or himself). The background sensation is not experienced as different from before the injury. The neglect patient's inability to attend to the implicated limb means that he cannot conceive of attending to it. So there is no way in which any abnormality with respect to the neglected limb can come to the patient's attention by the somatosensory route.

12   Body Sensation, Episodic Memory, and the Self

Any act of episodic (autobiographical) remembering must include a representation of the self in the context of the remembered event (Kihlstrom 1993). If the individual is engrossed in what is happening, there will be no spare attention available to represent the self as part of the scene. But the background of body sensation may nonetheless anchor the event to the individual's autobiography. Background awareness of one's body (its feeling, its potential for action) puts the stamp of personal experience on the scene. Conversely, one may imagine a scene and know that it has not been previously experienced because the background of bodily sensation is missing from the image. In infancy, this awareness of the body, as a salient source of immediately available sensation, may be more obtrusive than in the adult, as currently (concretely) experienced percepts are thought generally to capture the infant's attention (e.g., Gibson 1969, Kinsbourne 1993). If so, recollection of an early event might depend on a regression to this early concrete stage in body awareness. This might explain infantile amnesia.

13 How Are Body Parts Represented?

How is the predetermined representation of body parts structured? Perhaps a body part's relative prominence is determined by the extent to which one would normally use it in action under focused attention. As we have seen, phantoms exhibit distortion in favor of an emphasis on moving parts, such as the hand and wrist experienced as direction attached to shoulder and missing forearm and upper arm. An interesting parallel is to be found in the apparent systematic distortions in the body image of congenitally blind children. Kinsbourne and Lempert (1980) observed how such children represented the body in plasticine; moving parts (arms and neck) as well as the ears, were exaggerated in size relative to the trunk. Moving parts are also prominent in phantoms, which leads to distortion in the virtual anatomy of the phantom limb in favor of its most motorically differentiated components.

Roughly speaking, the representation of body parts is carved at the body's joints. Joints permit differential movement of the articulated parts. Multiply jointed body parts (fingers, hands, forearms) appear to be more discretely represented than larger but unjointed parts (abdomen, back, buttocks), and this is consistent with the view that body representation is primarily referenced to action. So, attending to a body part might have little to do with its moment-to-moment egocentric position.

The representations of discretely moving parts appear to depend least on sensory input, since they can be enhanced by selective attention alone. When a pathological bias in the control of attention leaves them unrepresented, however, the patient is most apt to deny ownership of these moving parts, regardless of sensory input and however plausible ownership might seem on other grounds. Indeed, sensory stimulation, if experienced, is referred to the other side of the body (allesthesia). Yet while the attentional imbalance is temporarily corrected by use of vestibular stimulation, even a severely neglected limb is experienced in the normal manner (Bisiach, Rusconi, and Vallar 1991). Manipulating unilateral central activation corrects what appeals to reason and to manifest visual reality cannot.

14 Conclusions

The attentional shifts that focus awareness on individual body parts are organized along axial and lateral (and perhaps saggital) coordinates as they play across the sensorimotor cortex. Disordered bodily perception results either from spatial disorganization of attentional shifts or from their extreme lateral bias. The mental operations that result in the conscious awareness of the body are guided by a person's knowledge about the relationships between his body parts, not by a separate fixed egocentric representation of the body. As with any familiar articulated dynamic structure, specifics of articulation between body parts can on occasion be brought into awareness by activating the corresponding areas of the sensorimotor cortex. The sensation of the body derives from a virtual rather than a hardwired set of representations.

If one cannot activate a representation by selective attending, it will not contribute its content to focal awareness. If the representation is in a weakened state, it will not participate in the control of automatic activities either. As long as one can focus somatosensory attention on a body part (even if it be an invisible and intangible phantom body part or it is completely numb), one feels that it is one's own. If one cannot focus somatosensory attention on it, one may even disown it (as in neglect) even though it is visibly, palpably, and logically part of one's body. As soon as the infant becomes able to focus attention on its body parts and their internally causally coherent behavior, it is equipped to develop a sense of self. This it will acquire not by bringing into play a homuncular representation of its body but as an expression of the coordination of information about its several body parts that is represented primarily in the somatosensory modalities.

References

Assal, G., and J. Buttet. 1973. "Troubles du schema corporel lors des atteintes hemispheriques gauches." *Praxis* 62:172–179.

Bisiach, E. 1991. "Understanding Consciousness: Clues from Unilateral Neglect and Related Disorders." In *The Neuropsychology of Consciousness*, edited by A. D. Milner and M. D. Ruff. London: Academic Press.

Bisiach, E., M. L. Rusconi, and G. Vallar. 1991. "Remission of Somatoparaphrenic Delusion through Vestibular Stimulation." *Neuropsychologia* 29:1029–1031.

Bisiach, E., P. Vallar, D. Perani, C. Papagno, and A. Berti. 1986. "Unawareness of Disease following Lesions of the Right Hemisphere: Anosognosia for Hemiplegia and Anosognosia for Hemianopia." *Neuropsychologia* 24:471–482.

Bonnier, P. 1905. "L'aschematie." *Revue neurologique* 13:604–609.

Bower, T. G. R. 1974. *Human Development.* San Francisco: Freeman.

Critchley, M. 1950a. "The Body Image in Neurology." *Lancet* 335–340.

Critchley, M. 1950b. *The Parietal Lobes.* London: Arnold.

Critchley, M. 1955. "Personification of Paralyzed Limbs in Hemiplegics." *British Medical Journal* 30:284.

Cutting, J. 1978. "A Study of Anosognosia." *Journal of Neurology, Neurosurgery, and Psychiatry* 41:548–555.

Dennis, M. 1976. "Dissociated Naming and Locating of Body Parts after Left Anterior Temporal Lobe Resection: An Experimental Case Study." *Brain and Language* 3:147–163.

De Renzi, E., and G. Scotti. 1970. "Autotopagnosia: Fiction or Reality?" *Archives of Neurology* 23:221–227.

Eklund, G., and K. E. Hagbarth. 1966. "Normal Variability of Tonic Vibration Reflexes in Man." *Experimental Neurology* 16:80–92.

Evans, G. 1982. *Varieties of Reference.* Oxford: Clarendon Press.

Frederiks, J. A. M. 1985. "Disorders of the Body Schema." In *Clinical Neuropsychology*, edited by J. A. M. Frederiks, Handbook of Clinical Neurology, rev. series no. 1 (old series no. 45). Amsterdam: Elsevier.

Gallagher, S. 1986. "Body Image and Body Schema: A Conceptual Clarification." *Journal of Mind and Behavior* 7:541–554.

Gerstmann, J. 1924. "Fingeragnosie: Eine Umschriebene Störung der Orientierung am eigenen Körper." *Wiener klinische Wochenschrift* 37:1010–1012.

Gibson, E. J. 1969. *Principles of Perceptual Learning and Development.* New York: Appleton-Century-Crofts.

Goodglass, H., and C. Budin. 1988. "Category and Modality Dissociation in Word Comprehension and Concurrent Phonological Dyslexia." *Neuropsychologia* 26:67–78.

Goodglass, H., B. Klein, P. Carey, and K. J. Jones. 1966. "Specific Semantic Word Categories in Aphasia." *Cortex* 2:74–89.

Goodwin, G., D. I. McCloskey, and P. B. C. Matthews. 1972. "The Contribution of Muscle Afferents to Kinesthesia Shown by Vibration-Induced Illusions of Movement and by the Effects of Paralysing Joint Afferents." *Brain* 95:705–748.

Head, H., and G. Holmes. 1911–1912. "Sensory Disturbances from Cerebral Lesions." *Brain* 34:102–254.

Held, R., and A. Hein. 1963. "Movement-Produced Stimulation in the Development of Visually Guided Behavior." *Journal of Comparative and Physiological Psychology* 56:872–876.

Humphrey, N. 1992. *A History of the Mind.* London: Chatto and Windus.

Kihlstrom, J. F. 1993. "The Psychological Unconscious and the Self." In *Experimental and Theoretical Studies of Consciousness*, Ciba Foundation Symposium, no. 174. London: John Wiley and Sons.

Kinsbourne, M. 1974. "Lateral Interactions in the Brain." In *Hemispheric Disconnection and Cerebral Function*, edited by M. Kinsbourne and W. L. Smith. Springfield, Ill.: Thomas.

Kinsbourne, M. 1987. "Mechanisms of Unilateral Neglect." In *Neurophysiological and Neuropsychological Aspects of Spatial Neglect*, edited by M. Jeannerod. Amsterdam: Elsevier.

Kinsbourne, M. 1993. "Development of Attention and Metacognition." In *Handbook of Neuropsychology*, vol. 7, edited by I. Rapin and S. Segalowitz. Amsterdam: Elsevier Biomedical.

Kinsbourne, M. 1994. "Orientational Bias Model of Unilateral Neglect: Evidence from Attentional Gradients within Hemispace." In *Unilateral Neglect, Clinical and Experimental Studies*, edited by I. H. Robertson and J. C. Marshall. New York: Lawrence Erlbaum.

Kinsbourne, M. 1996. "What Qualifies a Representation for a Role in Consciousness?" In *Scientific Approaches to the Study of Consciousness*, edited by J. D. Cohen and J. W. Schooler, 25th Carnegie Symposium on Cognition. Hillsdale, N.J.: Erlbaum.

Kinsbourne, M., and H. Lempert. 1980. "Human Figure Representation by Blind Children." *Journal of General Psychology* 102:33–37.

Kinsbourne, M., and E. K. Warrington. 1962. "A Study of Finger Agnosia." *Brain* 85:47–66.

Lackner, J. R., and P. DeZio. 1984. "Some Efferent and Somatosensory Influences on Body Orientation and Oculomotor Control." In *Sensory Experience, Adaptation, and Perception*, edited by L. Spillman and B. R. Wooten. Hillsdale, N.J.: Erlbaum.

Mattingley, J. B., and J. L. Bradshaw. 1994. "Can Tactile Neglect Occur at an Intralimb Level? Vibrotactile Reaction Times in Patients with Right Hemisphere Damage." *Behavioral Neurology* 7:67–77.

Moscovitch, M., and M. Behrmann. 1994. "Coding of Spatial Information in the Somatosensory System: Evidence from Patients with Neglect Following Parietal Lobe Damage." *Journal of Cognitive Neuroscience:* 6:151–155.

Mori, A., N. Hanashima, Y. Tsuboi, H. Hiraba, N. Goto, and R. Sumino. 1991. "Fifth Somatosensory Cortex (SV) Representation of the Whole-Body Surface in the Medial Bank of the Anterior Suprasylvan Sulcus of the Cat." *Neuroscience Research* 11:198–208.

Neisser, U. 1978. *Cognition and Reality: Principles and Implications of Cognitive Psychology.* San Francisco: W. H. Freeman and Co.

Nielsen, J. M. 1938. "Disturbances of the Body Scheme: Their Physiological Mechanism." *Bulletin of the Los Angeles Neurological Society* 3:127–135.

Ogden, J. 1985. "Autotopagnosia." *Brain* 108:1009–1022.

Pick, A. 1908. "Über Storungen der Orientierung am eigenen Korper." *Arbeiten aus der Psychiatrischen Klinik in Prag* (Berlin), vol. 1.

Pick, A. 1922. "Störung der Orientierung am eigenen Körper." *Psychologische Forschungen* 1:303.

Poeck, K. 1964. "Phantoms following Amputation in Early Childhood and in Congenital Absence of Limbs." *Cortex* 1:269–275.

Poeck, K., and B. Orgass. 1964a. "Die Entwicklung des Körperschemas bei Kindern im Alter von 4–10 Jahren." *Neuropsychologia* 2:109–130.

Poeck, K., and B. Orgass. 1964b. "Untersuchungen über das Körperschema bei blinden Kindern." *Neuropsychologia* 2:131–143.

Poeck, K., and B. Orgass. 1971. "The Concept of the Body Schema: A Critical Review and Some Experimental Results." *Cortex* 7:254–277.

Rode, G., N. Charles, M. T. Perenin, A. Vighetto, M. Trillet, and G. Aimond. 1991. "Partial Remission of Hemiplegic and Somatoparaphrenia through Vestibular Stimulation in a Case of Unilateral Neglect." *Cortex* 28:203–208.

Roth, M. 1949. "Disorders of the Body Image Caused by Lesions of the Right Parietal Lobe." *Brain* 72:89–111.

Schilder, P. 1935. *Image and Appearance of the Human Body*. New York: International Universities Press.

Semenza, C., and H. Goodglass. 1985. "Localization of Body Parts in Brain Injured Subjects." *Neuropsychologia* 23:161–175.

Semmes, J., S. Weinstein, L. Ghent, and H.-L. Teuber 1963. "Correlates of Impaired Orientation in Personal and Extrapersonal Space." *Brain* 86:747–772.

Shukla, G. D., S. C. Saku, R. P. Tripathi, and D. K. Gupta. 1982. "Phantom Limb: A Phenomenological Study." *British Journal of Psychiatry* 141:54–58.

Straus, E. 1970. "The Phantom Limb." In *Aisthesis and Aesthetics*, edited by E. Straus and D. Griffiths. Pittsburgh: Duquesne University Press.

Vallar, G., G. Antonucci, C. Guariglia, and L. Pizzamiglio. 1993. "Deficits of Position Sense, Unilateral Neglect, and Optokinetic Stimulation." *Neuropsychologia* 31:1191–1210.

Vigotsky, L. S. 1962. *Thought and Language*. Cambridge: MIT Press.

Weinstein, E. A., and R. L. Kahn. 1955. *Denial of Illness*. Springfield, Ill.: Thomas.

Weinstein, S., and E. A. Sersen. 1961. "Phantoms in Cases of Congenital Absence of Limbs." *Neurology* 11:905–911.

Yamadori, A., and M. L. Albert. 1973. "Word Category Aphasia." *Cortex* 9:83–89.

Body Schema and Intentionality

Shaun Gallagher

The explicit and nearly universal rejection of Cartesian dualism in the cognitive sciences is for good reason. Strategies for avoiding mind-body dualism include reducing mental events to brain processes and replacing intentional explanations with neurophysiological accounts. Quite often these approaches also involve reducing the *body* to the brain. In some cases one type of reductionism, mind to brain, assumes another type, body to brain. In the neurosciences, for instance, it is difficult to find any acknowledgment or explanation of the role played by the body as a whole in the cognitive operations of the brain. The body is reduced to its representation in the somatosensory cortex or is considered important only to the extent that it provides the raw sensory input required for cognitive computations. In other cases, the body is first reduced to the mind, which in turn is reduced to the brain. This approach is more apparent in psychology. The body is first treated as an intentional object, an image, a mental representation, and then reduced to neural computations. Functionalism, of course, is a major strategy that refuses to attribute an essential role in cognition to the human body.

There are important exceptions to this theoretical denial of the body. Some cognitive psychologists (Piaget 1971, Neisser 1987, Medin and Wattenmaker 1987) have indicated that the body plays an irreducible role in cognition. Neisser suggests that cognitive schemata often begin their development as meaningful structures at the level of our bodily movements through space, in an interaction between an organism and its environment. In a similar fashion, Johnson maintains that "propositional content is possible only by virtue of a complex web of nonpropositional schematic structures that emerge from our bodily experience" (1987, 5). In some cases, however, the frequent exclusion of the body from considerations about perception and cognition forms the basis of a critique of cognitive science, especially in those authors influenced by phenomenology (e.g., Dreyfus 1972).

I want to suggest that both psychological and phenomenological studies raise important issues about bodily experience, and that these issues need to be taken into account in the scientific explanation of cognition. This suggestion will take shape through an exploration of the question, What constraints are placed *by* one's own body on perception in general, and on the conscious experience *of* one's own body in particular? I will address this question using a phenomenological model of intentionality expanded to include what I call "prenoetic" factors, among which I list the body schema. This task involves thinking of the human body on both sides of the intentional relation. On one side, the body can be the object or content of intentional consciousness. I perceive (remember, imagine, conceptualize, study, love, hate) my own body as an intentional object. In psychological studies, this is usually termed the *body image*, a mental construct or representation, or a set of beliefs about the body. The body image can include at least three aspects:

• The subject's *perceptual* experience of his body
• The subject's *conceptual* understanding of the body in general (including mythical and/or scientific knowledge)
• The subject's *emotional* attitude toward her own body

These distinctions have recently been clarified in the literature (see, for example, Cash and Brown 1987, Gardner and Moncrieff 1988, Powers et al. 1987).

Less well explicated, however, is the role of the body as it functions on the other side of the intentional relation, that is, as it functions to make perception possible and to constrain intentional consciousness in various ways. Here I refer to the body's nonconscious appropriation of habitual postures and movements, its incorporation of various significant parts of the environment into its own experiential organization. Head (1920, 1926) called this nonconscious postural model, which actively monitors body posture and movement, the *body schema*.[1]

The body schema, I will argue, is neither reducible to neurological functioning nor equivalent to the body image, i.e., an intentional object of consciousness. Neurological accounts of the human body, which are usually called upon in this context, do not adequately capture the schematic operations in which the body acquires a specific organization or style in its relations with a particular physical and social environment. Body posture, for example, is not equivalent to objective or represented position in objective space; rather, it involves a preintentional spatiality that is never fully represented in consciousness or conceptualized by objective measurement. Still, if the operations of the body schema cannot be reduced to either physiology or phenomenology, it does not seem possible to work backward from intentional contents to physiological performances, or forward from physiological performances to intentional contents, without crossing the path of the body schema and finding at least indirect evidence of its operations, operations that are neither strictly mental (intentional) nor strictly physical phenomena, although their effects reach across this distinction.

1   Body Image and Body Schema: A Clarification of Some Common Confusions

In psychological studies the concepts and terms 'body image' and 'body schema' are often confused, and this leads to methodological and conceptual confusions, as well as numerous inconsistencies in experimental results. This situation has motivated various questions about the validity of the body-image construct (Cash and Brown 1987, Gallagher 1986a, Shontz 1974).[2] The confusions can be traced back to the historical start of the psychological discussion. Henry Head, for example, defines the body schema as a postural model of the body that actively modifies "the impressions produced by incoming sensory impulses in such a way that the final sensations of position or of locality rise into consciousness charged with a relation to something that has gone before" (1920, 606). The notion that the body schema rises into consciousness introduces an immediate confusion. Although Head goes on to deny that the body schema itself is a conscious image, Schilder (1935), who claims to be in agreement with Head, equates the postural model of the body with the conscious sensation of position. He equates the body schema, as defined by Head, with the image or representation of "our own body which we form in our mind" (Schilder 1935, 11). He calls this mental representation both a 'body image' and a 'body schema'.

Terminological and conceptual confusions persist in the more recent literature. Fisher, for example, provides the following influential definition of the body image: "Body image can be considered synonymous with such terms as 'body concept' and 'body scheme'. Broadly speaking, the term pertains to how the individual perceives his own body. It does not imply that the individual's concept of his body is represented by a conscious image. . . . Body image . . . represents the manner in which a person has learned to organize and integrate his body experiences" (1972, 113). In many of his studies Fisher uses terms like 'body schema', 'body image', 'body concept', 'body perception', and 'body image schema' interchangeably. Most of his studies, however, focus on the subject's perception of his own body in experimental situations where the subject is

either explicitly asked about his own body or indirectly tested about attitudes towards his own body (Fisher 1978, Fisher and Cleveland 1958). In
this regard Fisher is not alone. The majority of psychological studies in
this area concern the body image defined as a mental representation (see,
for example, Adame 1991, Gardner and Moncrieff 1988). Some studies refer to the body schema as a postural image that functions outside of consciousness (Kolb 1959); others classify the body schema as one aspect of
the body image (Clark 1984, Toombs 1988), or vice versa (Cumming
1988). There are also studies that equate the body image or schema with
body position in objective space (Gibson 1966) or with a cortical representation (Straus 1970) or with an abstract cognition (Tiemersma 1982).
In effect, the schema or image of the body is alternatively represented as a
physiological functioning; a conscious model or mental representation; an
unconscious image; a manner of organizing bodily experiences; an artificially induced reflection; a collection of thoughts, feelings, and memories;
a set of objectively defined physical positions; a neurophysiological body
map located in the brain; and high-level conceptual knowledge concerning the essence of the body.

Those who criticize the lack of a clear conceptual understanding of
these various notions sometimes go on to develop valuable suggestions
about testing procedures and conceptual distinctions (Garner and
Garfinkel 1981, Shontz 1974). Such clarifications, however, are limited to
considerations about the body image as a mental representation, an intentional object with perceptual, conceptual, and emotive or affective dimensions. In contrast, I have attempted to resolve some of the confusions by
proposing a systematic distinction between body image and body schema
(Gallagher 1986a).

There are at least three distinguishing characteristics that define the
difference between body schema and body image:

• The *body image* has an intentional status; that is, it is either a conscious representation of the body or a set of beliefs about the body. Although the perceptual, conceptual, and emotional aspects of the body image are not always actually present to
consciousness, they are nonetheless maintained as a set of beliefs or attitudes, and
in this sense are intentional. In contrast to the intentional (and sometimes conscious) nature of the body image, a *body schema* involves an extraintentional operation carried out prior to or outside of intentional awareness. Although it has an
effect on conscious experience, it may be best to characterize it, as Head did, as a
subconscious system, produced by various neurological processes, that plays an active role in monitoring and governing posture and movement.
• In the body image, the body is experienced as an owned body, one that belongs to the experiencing subject. In contrast, the body schema functions in a

subpersonal, unowned, anonymous way. In part, this distinction involves the issue of control. I can consciously decide to raise my hand, for example, and then
do so with my perceptual attention focused on this action. In this case, control
over this movement is achieved by means of a perceptual experience of the
body, that is, by means of the body image. This act is intentional both in the
sense that it is a conscious action and in the sense that it is a willed action. Even
in intentional bodily motion, however, certain postural adjustments of the body
that serve to maintain balance are not under conscious control. Various muscle
groups make automatic schematic adjustments that I remain unaware of, and in
this sense do not control.

• The body image often involves an abstract, partial, or articulated representation
of the body insofar as conscious awareness typically attends to only one part or
area of the body at a time. The body schema, on the other hand, functions in a
holistic way. A slight change in posture, for example, involves a global adjustment
across a large number of muscle systems. This can also be seen in the fact that various proprioceptive inputs coming from different parts of the body do not function in an isolated manner but "add together in modulating postural control"
(Roll and Roll 1988, 161).

The body image is not always intentionally present, that is, one is not
always conscious of one's own body as an intentional object. This efface-
ment of the body is possible because in normal circumstances a particular
body schema functions in a way that makes movement and posture close
to automatic and in no need of conscious control. "We all know that in
normal conscious states our awareness of bodily sensation is limited—
pushed aside by the fact that our attention is locked upon some social or
situational issue. It is almost as if (as in the learning of a task) the functions
of the body are on automatic pilot and do not usually have to be attended
to consciously" (Crook 1987, 390–391). The distinction between paying
conscious *attention* to the body and being marginally *aware* of the body is
important. Sometimes we do attend specifically to some aspect or part of
the body. Most of the time, however, our attention is directed away from
the body and toward the environment or some project we are undertaking. In cases where our attention is not directed toward the body, we may
remain consciously aware of it. Some theorists argue that this is a constant
awareness that accompanies all cognitive activity (e.g., James 1890, Quinton 1975). Such awareness may vary by degree among individuals—some
more aware, others, at times, not at all aware of their bodies. In any case, attention to or awarensss of the body is part of what I mean by the body
image. Whatever the degree of body consciousness, however, the body
schema continues to function in a nonconscious way, maintaining balance
and enabling movement. Yet by defining the body schema in terms of its
prenoetic function, I do not mean to rule out the possibility that the body

image and body schema can work (or fail to work) together in a comple-
mentary fashion.

In contrast to the results discussed in many studies on body image
concerned with the estimation of body size, the issue of conscious objective measurement does not pertain to the body schema. Rather, the body
schema, operating in a tacitly lived (nonobjective) space, automatically
takes measure of its environment and allows a subject who is immersed in
conversation, for instance, to walk beneath the low hung tree branch without bumping her head, or enables her to maneuver around objects in her
path without having to think about what she is doing. On the other hand,
in studies of size estimation of the body image, the size of one's own body
is consistently overestimated relative to other objects (Shontz 1969, Gardner et al. 1989). If we needed to depend solely on the body image to get
around—something that does occur in rare instances—our movements
would be inexact and awkward. Just consider, for example, the prospect of
having to *think through* every step of walking across a room. In this sense,
an account of body image is not equivalent to an account of body schema
and does not fully represent the way in which the body functions in human experience. In general, the focus on body image in psychological
studies ignores the prenoetic role played by the body schema.

Some of the methods and experimental situations employed in psychological studies of body perception actually produce an accessory or
artificial body image by calling the subject's attention to her own body in
circumstances that otherwise would not entail a consciousness of body.
Ruggieri et al., for example, points out that when a subject "focuses on his
body, different components or images of body parts, of which the subject
himself usually is unconscious, can emerge" (1983, 800). Precisely because
the body schema operates in a holistic, unified way, whereas in the body
image the body appears with certain parts emphasized or singled out, the
body image is not a veridical representation of the body schema.

In this paper I want to suggest two things. First, a critical examination
of the phenomenological concept of intentionality, and its development
from Husserl to Merleau-Ponty, can help to clarify the distinction between
body image and body schema. Second, by focusing on the performances of
the body schema, we can deepen our understanding of how the body contributes to the determination of intentional consciousness and, in particular, of the perception of the body, that is, the body image. To view the
prenoetic performances of the body schema as continually and persistently
constraining intentionality is consistent with, and may contribute to, some
already noted approaches taken in cognitive psychology (Neisser 1987)

and semantic theory (Johnson 1987). A theory of intentionality that recognizes the effects of the prenoetic functioning of the body schema can help to clarify both the role played by the body in the organization of mental life and the implications that this holds for cognitive science.

2 Intentionality and the Prenoetic Body: Husserl and Merleau-Ponty

In the attempt to explain cognition, philosophers and scientists have appropriated various psychological or phenomenological models of intentionality. Despite explicit attempts to move away from Cartesian dualism, however, these models of intentionality fail to provide an adequate account of the role of the body in cognitive acts and intentional states. This can be seen most clearly in Husserl's analysis of intentionality.

Despite his explicit critique of Descartes, Husserl's starting point remains Cartesian. His method of phenomenological reduction is inspired by Descartes's methodical doubt. By employing this kind of methodology, Husserl attempts to isolate consciousness and explore its intentional structure. A simplified version of Husserl's theory of perceptual intentionality is represented by the following diagram:

Noetic act ——— Noema ——➤ [Intended object]
(perception)

The "noema," the sense or meaning of the perceived object, is that by which the intentional relation to an object is set up; the brackets, representing the phenomenological reduction, signify that the reality or nonreality of the perceived object is not at issue. Through the use of his reduction, Husserl "suspends" or "brackets" the question of the reality of the intended object and, by doing so, confines himself to a purely descriptive account of intentionality. This limitation means that naturalistic, causal explanation is excluded from his account; intentional analysis is confined to a description of what presents itself to transcendental consciousness.

In Husserl's model of intentionality, the role played by the body is subject to this same methodological exclusion. The body makes its appearance as an appearance only, as an intentional object, as the body image. As a result of the phenomenological reduction, analysis is limited to a description of the body as it is presented and represented in consciousness. The body can be described in its noematic appearance, but all theories about how the body might operate as a prenoetic constraint on perceptual consciousness are suspended. Thus, while Husserl acknowledges the possibility of developing a special science of the body that he calls 'somatology', he suggests that it can be based only on "the direct *somatic perception* that every empirical investigator can effect of his own body" and on interpretations of the perception of other human bodies (1980, 7). This would be a science of the body image, but it would have nothing to say about the body schema. In this regard, Husserl's approach shares the same focus as the majority of psychological studies of body perception.

The focus on body image, to the exclusion of the body schema, is due to the limitations of Husserl's model of intentionality. Intentionality appears ex nihilo, a pure spontaneity that begins at the noetic act of consciousness and moves in the direction of the noema. Everything of importance happens in full phenomenological view, "out in front" of the noetic act. Husserl ignores the "from whence" of the act. What happens backstage, toward the rear of intentionality? Are there not factors that have an effect on us, that operate in a way that is "behind our back" and yet efficaciously anterior with respect to our experience? This question motivates Merleau-Ponty's critique of Husserl. For Merleau-Ponty, the body cannot be reduced to consciousness of the body. There is, he contends, a truth to be found in naturalism that is lost in a purely transcendental approach (Merleau-Ponty 1963). To capture this truth, he develops an expanded model of intentionality that includes a role for the prenoetic functions of the body schema.

Although Merleau-Ponty does not make an explicit terminological distinction between 'body image' and 'body schema', in contrast to the psychological literature I have cited, he is conceptually more careful and consistent. His carefulness, is completely obscured, however, in the English translation of his *Phenomenologie de la perception* (*Phenomenology of Perception*), where *schema corporel* is rendered as 'body image'. Although he does note the ambiguity involved in these concepts, his own discussion is consistently unambiguous. When he introduces the term *schema corporel* (1962, 98), his first reference is to Head's concept of a postural model, and he clearly means schema and not image. He characterizes it as the anterior condition of possibility for perception, a dynamic form, a "being-in-the-world." Furthermore, although he is careful not to confuse body schema and body image on the conceptual, analytical level, he nonetheless argues that on the existential or behavioral level, there is a continuous development between them, that they are elements of one system, and that on the level of our ordinary lived experience, there is an "indistinction" between these elements (Merleau-Ponty 1964, 135). If in certain texts he suggests that the body schema involves a "global awareness" or a "tacit understanding," he also denies that this is a "positional consciousness, a representation, *Vor-stellung*."

Rather, he contends that the body schema might best be expressed as a set of laws rather than as a set of images (1962, 99–101, 104; 1964, 133).

In Husserl's transcendental analysis, the body is reduced to a perceived object and appears to have no role in the production of perceptual experience. Merleau-Ponty sets out to show that the body itself is doing the perceiving, and that the operations of the body schema provide specific conditions that constrain perceptual consciousness. Meaningful perceptual structures originate in certain prenoetic performances of the body. The body operates according to a "latent knowledge" it has of the world, a knowledge anterior to cognitive experience. The body and the natural world work together to deliver to consciousness an already formed meaning: "There is a logic of the world to which my body in its entirety conforms, and through which things of intersensory significance become possible for us. . . . To have a body is to possess a universal setting, a schema of all types of perceptual unfolding" (Merleau-Ponty 1962, 326).

The prenoetic role of the body schema is impenetrable to phenomenological reflection and must be worked out conceptually with the help of the empirical sciences. Yet Merleau-Ponty steers a course that avoids reductions of either the phenomenological or the empirical variety. Empirical theories that would reduce cognitive experience to physiological activity are no better at understanding the body as a perceiving subject than the phenomenological analysis that would reduce the body to noematic content.

Using Merleau-Ponty's model of embodied intentionality, we can develop an account of how the body, prior to or outside of cognitive experience, helps to constitute the meaning that comes to consciousness. This can be worked out in terms of bodily systems that operate on a subpersonal, automatic level. For example, internal autonomic adjustments play a role in the perceiver's ability to attend to or concentrate on particular intentional objects without the distraction caused by changing environmental conditions. In dealing with temperature fluctuations, for example, the body at first operates outside of intentionality. It interprets environmental changes and regulates its own functions (metabolism, blood pressure, respiratory volume, adrenalin levels, etc.), so when the subject eventually becomes aware that she is too cold or too hot, the intentional meaning of that feeling will have already been conditioned by the body's prenoetic performance. Similar performances of the body can be described in cases involving stress, pain, hunger, fatigue, lability, and so forth (Gallagher 1986b). Body schemas operate in a similar way.

In the case of eyestrain, for example, the body begins to make automatic postural and motor adjustments prior to the subject's becoming aware of the oncoming headache. Absorbed in the act of reading, for instance, the subject is not explicitly conscious of the body's adjustments, which may include squinting and moving closer to the text. The body performs these functions, coping with the demands made on it in this environment, without the subject's reflective awareness. Yet such prenoetic adjustments will determine intentional content in important ways. In the case of eyestrain, body-schema adjustments may motivate the subject first to fix on the environment or the text as problematic: the lighting seems too dim; the book becomes difficult or boring (Buytendijk 1974). Postural adjustments may allow the subject to continue reading by keeping her attention directed away from her body. In the end, however, the inadequacy of such adjustments force her to become aware of her bodily discomfort and the developing headache.

Evidence of the prenoetic functioning of the body schema can also be found within the intentional realm itself, specifically, within various kinds of perceptual noemata. To see, for example, is not only to *see something*, as Husserl's principle of intentionality would indicate, but also to *see from somewhere*, that is, under conditions defined by the position and postural situation of the perceiving body. In the normal situation, to see is also to see with binocular vision, that is, to see something under conditions defined by certain physical possibilities of the body and its sense organs. The visual-noematic field appears as spread out in a continuous, although variable, horizon or visual distribution. Within this setting, and always relative to the perceiving body, somethings appear closer than others; somethings are to the right, others to the left; some are in front, others to the rear. Things appear in a spatial gestalt organized in terms of foreground and background. The world appears only partially and in egocentric perspective; things show themselves only one profile at a time. All of these features are built into noematic meaning in the form of perceptual presuppositions and horizons. Such conditions placed on perception by the body and the various postures that it takes, help us to organize the perceptual world in a meaningful way.

These conditions are both constraining and enabling factors produced in the ecological interaction between body and environment, or as Merleau-Ponty puts it, produced in a logic shared by the body and the world. What Gibson calls "affordances" (1979, 127 ff.), for example, or what Neisser explains as "the possibility of actions that we have not actually undertaken" (1987, 12) are defined as such for intentional consciousness only on the basis of possibilities projected by the body schema. The floor affords walking, the chair affords sitting, and so forth, only in conjunction with the possibilities of particular postural models. All such features afforded by the environment, and evidenced in the implicit structure of noematic meaning, are predicated on the prenoetic functioning of the body schema.[3]

As prenoetic, the postural and motor adjustments of the body schema always remain "behind the scene," *a tergo*. When I perceive, I do not perceive my body making the schematic adjustments that both enable and shape perceiving. They do not appear as explicit parts of the perceptual meaning, although implicitly they help to structure such meaning. For this reason, body posture is not reducible to objective position. The body projects a pragmatic spatial sense that does not correspond precisely to objective spatial measurements. Body schemata enable us to find our way in space; to walk without bumping into things; to run without tripping and falling; to locate targets; to perceive depth, distance, and direction; to throw and to catch a ball with accuracy. Such things happen despite and independently of the discrepancy between the conscious size estimation of one's own body and the size estimation of other objects (Shontz 1969). In other words, the body image does not normally interfere with the performance of the body schema.[4]

3 Body Schema and Physiology

The prenoetic operations of the body schema are not reducible to physiological function. Even if various physiological events are necessary conditions, the body *actively organizes* its sense experience, the incoming stimuli, in relation to pragmatic concerns (Merleau-Ponty 1962). How the body reacts to a particular environment, even if automatic, is not a matter of simple mechanics or reflex. Pragmatic circumstances and intentional activities call forth appropriate movements and determine whether physiological events are integrated into, for example, a thermal experience rather than a tactile experience. Thus physiological processes are not passively produced by incoming stimuli. Rather, the body *meets* stimulation and organizes it within the framework of its own pragmatic schemata. An excitation, "when it strikes a sensory organ which is not 'attuned' to it," does not reach perceptual consciousness (Merleau-Ponty 1962, 75). Although the attuning process remains nonconscious, the intentional interests of the subject, in part, define that attunement. Even if more stimuli than consciousness requires are recorded on the physiological level, only those values relevant to the intentional project are elicited and translated to the level of consciousness (see Marcel 1983). To the extent to which the body schema plays a role in producing, prenoetically, the postural balance for an intentional behavior or the adjustment of sense organs for a perceptual act, it is always selective among what is physiologically possible.

My body is capable, physiologically, of many different movements. But in any particular context I produce a specific movement. When, for example, in the context of a game I jump to catch a ball, that action cannot be fully explained by the physiological activity of my body. The pragmatic concern of playing the game motivates the action, while the physical environment, the effects of all my practice (or lack thereof), and even the rules of the game as they are habitually expressed in the practiced movements of my body may define how I jump to make the catch. Without a certain amount of selectivity, built up by practice and the cultivation of habitual movements, the body might move in any one of multiple ways since, the possibilities allowed by physiology are much greater than the particular movements necessary to catch the ball in the proper way. Thus the body schema is much more selectively attuned to its environment than what physiology will allow. To explain this selectivity, or what Rosenbaum et al. (1993) call "soft constraints," one needs more than physiology.

Constructivists speak of feedforward mechanisms in this context (see, e.g., Weimer 1979). It is often pointed out that sensory impulses from the retina "can influence—but not specify—activity in the visual cortex. On the average, as much as 80 percent of what we 'see' may be a tacit construction 'fed forward' from the superior colliculus, the hypothalamus, the reticular formation, and the visual cortex itself" (Mahoney 1991, 101). Maturana and Varela (1987) generalize this feedforward model to apply to all other aspects of the central nervous system. Rather than viewing these feedforward or selective mechanisms as reducible to neurophysiological processes accomplished by a brain in a vat, we need to consider the brain as consisting of specialized parts of a holistic system. Feedforward mechanisms can only be the result of interactive mechanisms found in relations between the brain, as one important part of the body, and the body as a whole, within a specific environment. Neuroscientists have demonstrated that neural paths and cortical connections develop and are constantly transformed on the basis of sensory and motor experiences (Shatz 1992, Kandel and Hawkins 1992). At the same time, developmental psychologists point out that sensory experiences, for example, the localization of a particular sound or visual object, depend on postural adjustments (Neisser 1976). It is also clear that the organization and functioning of the brain depend on certain "adjustment reactions" that take place throughout the body (Gellhorn 1943, Mason 1961). Precisely because the brain in its neurophysiological performance does not originate, but at best can only mediate the various performances of body schemata and the individual's linguistic, cultural, historical, and personal experience, what is fed forward to define the body's perceptual attunement can neither be reduced to physiology nor inflated to conscious control.

Studies of phantom-limb phenomena offer further evidence for this claim. Physiological factors do not explain why in certain instances the phantom retains the position and feel that the real arm had when it was injured (Merleau-Ponty 1962). Yet the phantom limb is not simply a conscious memory or belief, since the severance of afferent nerves sometimes abolishes phantom pain and, in a few rare cases, the phantom itself (Browder and Gallagher 1948). The phantom remains part of the body schema, part of the practical attunement of the body to its environment, part of a capability that the amputee acts upon when he tries to walk across the room only to find, in falling, that his leg is not really there. In this case there is a phantom part of the body schema that has no equivalent phantom part in the conscious body image. The advantage provided by a body schema, that one does not think about appropriate limbs before one walks, may be a disadvantage for some amputees. A body schema is to walking what a cognitive schema is to thinking. Like a cognitive schema, a body schema is corrigible: with rehabituation and without severing the afferent nerves, the phantom can disappear from the schema. Prosthetic devices also provide evidence that a body schema cannot be mere physiology or mere consciousness in that a prosthetic device may be incorporated into a schema, just as a carpenter might incorporate a hammer, although these instruments are not necessarily reflected in the body image.

4 Recent Psychological Studies and Implications for Cognitive Science

I have been exploring the idea that the various performances of the body, and specifically those that can be expressed as performances of the body schema(ta), place constraints on intentional consciousness. Although one can find evidence for these constraints manifested in intentional experience, following Merleau-Ponty, I have argued that such performances are prenoetic. They cannot be completely captured by the intentional model. Neither can they be reduced to physiological or neurophysiological functions.

Beyond the phenomenological studies of Merleau-Ponty, one can find, in recent psychological studies, evidence to support the view that the prenoetic performance of the body schema has an effect on intentionality. These studies indicate that changes in various aspects of body schemata have an effect on the way subjects perceive their own bodies, that is, changes in body schemata lead to changes in body images. More generally, changes in body schemata also affect spatial perception and the perception of objects. Consider the following conclusions drawn from a variety of studies.

• Changes in, or differences from normal, posture, motility, physical ability and other aspects associated with the body schema, imposed by abnormality, disease, or

illness (for example, obesity, rheumatoid arthritis, multiple sclerosis), or by temporary physical changes (like pregnancy) have an effect on perceptual, cognitive,
and/or emotive aspects of body image. For example, degeneration of bodily functions and changes in motility lead to decreases in the senses both of body integrity
and of strong body boundaries (Gardner et al. 1988, Halligan and Reznikoff 1985,
Keltikangas-Jarvinen 1987, Powers et al. 1987).

• Exercise, dance, and some other practices that affect motility and the postural
schema have an effect on the emotive evaluation of one's own body image (Adame
et al. 1991, Dasch 1978, Davis and Cowles 1991, Skrinar et al. 1986). In these
studies, subjects who through exercise improve in neuromuscular coordination,
strength, and endurance, or experience increased coordination, balance, agility, and
improved posture, gain a perception of body competence and achieve a higher degree of satisfaction with their own bodies. Thus changes in body schema associated
with exercise alter the way that subjects emotionally relate to and perceive their
bodies.

• Changes in muscular tone involve adjustments to the body schema. In cases of
increased muscular tone, interpreted as a sign of a higher degree of preparedness to
action or readiness for external response, body-perception scores decrease, corresponding to a low awareness of one's own body. A decrease in muscular tone is
correlated with an increase in body-perception scores (Ruggieri et al. 1983; Sabatini, Ruggieri, and Milizia 1984). Thus changes in muscular schemata correlate
with changes in the subject's bodily awareness and perceptual awareness of the environment. These studies also suggest that unconscious adjustments of the body
schema allow the subject to direct attention to external rather than internal stimuli. More generally, to the extent that the body schema makes its prenoetic adapta-
tions to the environment and remains in the perceptual background, cognitive
attention can be focused elsewhere in any variety of intentions.

• Retardation in the development of the body schema caused, for example, by an
absence of early crawling experience has a negative effect on the development of
spatial perception. Studies by Joseph Campos and his colleagues have demonstrated
that crawling and locomotor experience in infants have an effect on the perception
and evaluation of spatial heights (Campos, Bertenthal, and Kermoian 1992). Self-
produced locomotion also plays a role in the development of visual attention to
changes in the environment (Bertenthal and Campos 1990) and strategies for perceptually searching for objects (Kermoian and Campos 1988). Crawling experience
and locomotion facilitate the development of the body schema. The longer the
subjects have been moving in these ways and the more developed their body
schema, the better their spatial perception. In broader terms, "the process of crawling provides a state of eye-hand coordination, vestibular processing, improvement
of balance and equilibrium, spatial awareness, tactile input, kinesthetic awareness,
and social maturation" (McEwan, Dihoff, and Brosvic 1991, 75).

• Experimental alterations of the postural schema (for example, by asymmetrical
body tension induced by experimental tilting of the body) lead to perceptual shifts
in external vertical and horizontal planes (Bauermeister 1964, Wapner and Werner
1965). Like the studies by Campos and his colleagues (cited above) these studies
show that changes in the body schema result in changes in external space perception. Merleau-Ponty refers to related studies of spatial perception, in situations
where the apparent external vertical is tilted, to argue that perceptual orientation

is not made on the basis of a consciousness of my body as a thing in objective space. Rather, visual perception is reoriented in terms of a body schema, a set of motor equivalencies that allow the body to reorder perception according to "a system of possible actions" (1962, 248–250).

• Several studies indicate that proprioceptive adjustments of the body schema help to resolve perceptual conflicts. Adaptation in the realm of visual experience involves changes in proprioceptive information. For example, perceptually adaptating to 180-degree rotation of the retinal image is facilitated by "changes in the position sense for various parts of the body" (Harris 1965, 419). In experiments in which visual information comes in conflict with proprioceptive input, for example, where an object is viewed through a reducing lens while in tactile contact with the body, adjustments take place in the interpretation of proprioception so that the body schema accommodates vision (Rock and Harris 1967). Studies such as these lead Shontz to conclude that "body schemata themselves are not fixed photographs of bodily structure but are active, changing processes" (1969, 162).

• It is well known that vision contributes to a proprioceptive sense of posture and balance (e.g., Jouen 1988), but it is also the case that posture and balance contribute in a reciprocal fashion to how we visually perceive the surrounding environment. Experimental studies indicate that there is a "close linkage between eye posture or movements and the spatial organization of the whole-body posture" (Roll and Roll 1988, 159). Thus vibration of extraocular eye muscles result in body sways and shifts in balance. But also, vibration-induced proprioceptive patterns that change the posture of the whole body are interpreted as changes in the perceived environment. Under experimental conditions where the subject is limited to monocular vision of a small luminous target in darkness, "a directional shift of the visual target was elicited by vibration applied to neck muscles . . . and, more surprisingly, to ankle postural muscles," that is, a change in the posture of the head or whole body induced by vibrations is "interpreted by the stationary subject in darkness as if it were an upward displacement of the target" (Roll and Roll 1988, 162). It follows that alterations in proprioceptive information, information closely connected to the organization of the body schema, lead to changes in visual perception.

In all of these cases, changes or distortions introduced at the level of the body schema result in changes or distortions in intentional consciousness. But this simply reflects the general rule. In all cases, prenoetic performances of the body schema influence intentionality. They operate as constraining and enabling factors that limit and define the possibilities of intentional consciousness.

I have argued that intentional experiences, specifically spatial perception and perception of one's own body, are affected by the body schema(ta) in ways not reducible to either neurophysiological occurrences or consciously controlled representations. The body schema is neither the cortical representation discussed by neuroscientists nor the body image discussed by psychologists and phenomenologists. Rather, the body schema reflects a practical attunement of the body to its environment. Its development in the various social practices that lead to habitual dispositions—think here of jumping to catch the ball within the context of a game—involves it in relations to physical and social environments that, on the one hand, fall short of intentionality, that is, remain prenoetic, and, on the other, transcend neurophysiology.

What implications do these considerations hold for the cognitive sciences? If the body as a whole, and body schemata in particular, significantly affect cognitive functions, then neither the privileging of physiology over intentionality, or vice versa, nor the development of a discourse that strictly correlates physiological functions with intentional meanings will be adequate as a complete model of cognitive behavior. If one reduces the performances of the body schema to neurophysiology or inflates them to an intentional body image, certain aspects of embodiment that place important constraints on cognitive life are overlooked. To the extent that some cognitive scientists persist in approaches that refuse to recognize the complications introduced by the various roles of the human body in cognition, they run the risk of creating abstract and disembodied paradigms.

Acknowledgments

Research for this paper was supported by a Faculty Research Fellowship at Canisius College. Max Latona, supported by a Hearst Foundation grant, provided valuable research assistance for this project. I benefited greatly from comments made by participants at the Workshop on the Perception of Objects and Subjects, King's College Research Centre, Cambridge, and especially from recommendations made by the editors of this volume.

Notes

1. Although I sometimes use the singular 'body schema' in the following, I do not mean to rule out the possibility of there being more than one schema. Head (1920) discriminated between a postural schema and a surface schema. One could also conceive of a plurality of individual schemata corresponding to a plurality of specialized movements and postures.

2. Terminological confusions and conceptual difficulties related to the lack of clear operational definitions of 'body image' are noted in many studies. See Clark 1984; Cumming 1988; Fisher and Cleveland 1958; Garner and Garfinkel 1981; Kolb 1959; Schontz 1969; Straus 1967, 1970.

3. Here I am looking at only one side of the body-environment relation. I do not mean to deny that the environment plays an important part in defining the operations of the body schema (see Gallagher 1986c). It is well established, for example, that perceptual experience affects the performance of the body schema (Gibson 1979, Neisser 1976).

4. This does not mean that the body image cannot affect the body schema. For example, in cases of learning dance or athletic movements, focusing attention on specific

body parts can alter the established postural schema. See Gallagher 1986a for other examples.

References

Adame, D. D., S. A. Radell, T. C. Johnson, and S. P. Cole. 1991. "Physical Fitness, Body Image, and Locus of Control in College Women Dancers and Nondancers." *Perceptual and Motor Skills* 72:91–95.

Bauermeister, M. 1964. "The Effect of Body Tilt on Apparent Verticality, Apparent Body Position and Their Relation." *Journal of Experimental Psychology* 67:142–147.

Bertenthal, B. I., and J. J. Campos. 1990. "A Systems Approach to the Organizing Effects of Self-Produced Locomotion during Infancy." *Advances in Infancy Research* 6: 1–60.

Browder, J., and J. P. Gallagher. 1948. "Dorsal Cordotomy for Painful Phantom Limbs." *Annals of Surgery* 128:456–469.

Buytendijk, F. J. J. 1974. *Prolegomena to an Anthropological Physiology.* Translated by A. I. Orr. Pittsburgh: Duquesne University Press.

Campos, J. J., B. I. Bertenthal, and R. Kermoian. 1992. "Early Experience and Emotional Development: The Emergence of Wariness of Heights." *Psychological Science* 3: 61–64.

Cash, T. F., and T. A. Brown. 1987. "Body Image in Anorexia Nervosa and Bulimia Nervosa: A Review of the Literature." *Behavior Modification* 11:487–521.

Clark, D. F. 1984. "Body Image and Motor Skills in Normal and Subnormal Subjects." *International Journal of Rehab. Research* 7:207–208.

Crook, J. 1987. "The Nature of Conscious Awareness." In *Mindwaves: Thoughts on Intelligence, Identity, and Consciousness*, edited by C. Blakemore and S. Greenfield. Oxford: Basil Blackwell.

Cumming, W. J. K. 1988. "The Neurobiology of the Body Schema." *British Journal of Psychiatry* 153, suppl. 2:7–11.

Dasch, C. S. 1978. "Relation of Dance Skills to Body Cathexis and Locus of Control Orientation." *Perceptual and Motor Skills* 46:465–466.

Davis, C., and M. Cowles. 1991. "Body Image and Exercise: A Study of Relationships and Comparisons between Physically Active Men and Women." *Sex Roles* 25:33–44.

Dreyfus, Hubert. 1972. *What Computers Can't Do: A Critique of Artificial Reason.* New York: Harper and Row.

Fisher, Seymour. 1972. "Body Image." In *International Encyclopedia of the Social Sciences*, vol. 2, edited by D. Sills. New York: Collier-Macmillan.

Fisher, Seymour. 1978. "Body Experience before and after Surgery." *Perceptual and Motor Skills* 46:699–702.

Fisher, Seymour, and S. E. Cleveland. 1958. *Body Image and Personality.* Princeton: D. van Nostrand.

Gallagher, Shaun. 1986a. "Body Image and Body Schema: A Conceptual Clarification." *Journal of Mind and Behavior* 7:541–554.

Gallagher, Shaun. 1986b. "Hyletic Experience and the Lived Body." *Husserl Studies* 3:131–166.

Gallagher, Shaun. 1986c. "Lived Body and Environment." *Research in Phenomenology* 16:139–170.

Gardner, R. M., R. Martinez, T. Espinoza, and V. Gallegos. 1988. "Distortion of Body Image in the Obese: A Sensory Phenomena (sic)." *Psychological Medicine* 18:633–641.

Gardner, R. M., and C. Moncrieff. 1988. "Body Image Distortion in Anorexics as a Non-sensory Phenomenon: A Signal Detection Approach." *Journal of Clinical Psychology* 44:101–107.

Gardner, R. M., J. A. Morrell, D. N. Watson, S. L. Sandoval. 1989. "Subjective Equality and Just Noticeable Differences in Body-Size Judgments by Obese Persons." *Perceptual and Motor Skills* 69:595–604.

Garner, D. M., and P. E. Garfinkel. 1981. "Body Image in Anorexia Nervosa: Measurement, Theory, and Clinical Implications." *International Journal of Psychiatry in Medicine* 11:263–284.

Gellhorn, Ernst. 1943. *Autonomic Regulations: Their Significance for Physiology, Psychology, and Neuropsychiatry*. New York: Interscience Publications.

Gibson, J. J. 1966. *The Senses Considered as Perceptual Systems*. Boston: Houghton-Mifflin.

Gibson, J. J. 1979. *The Ecological Approach to Visual Perception*. Boston: Houghton-Mifflin.

Halligan, F. R., and M. Reznikoff. 1985. "Personality Factors and Change with Multiple Sclerosis." *Journal of Consulting and Clinical Psychology* 53:547–548.

Harris, C. S. 1965. "Perceptual Adaptation to Inverted, Reversed, and Displaced Vision." *Psychological Review* 72:419–444.

Head, Henry. 1920. *Studies in Neurology*, vol 2. London: Oxford University Press.

Head, Henry. 1926. *Aphasia and Kindred Disorders of Speech*, vol 1. Cambridge: Cambridge University Press.

Husserl, Edmund. 1980. *Phenomenology and the Foundations of the Sciences*. Translated by T. E. Klein and W. E. Pohl. *Collected Works*. Hague: Nijhoff.

James, William. 1890. *The Principles of Psychology*. New York: Dover, 1950.

Johnson, Mark. 1987. *The Body in the Mind: The Bodily Basis of Meaning, Imagination, and Reason*. Chicago: University of Chicago Press.

Jouen, F. 1988. "Visual-Proprioceptive Control of Posture in Newborn Infants." In *Posture and Gait: Development, Adaptation, and Modulation*, edited by G. Amblard, A. Berthoz, and F. Clarac. Amsterdam: Excerpta Medica.

Kandel, E. R., and R. D. Hawkins. 1992. "The Biological Basis of Learning and Individuality." *Scientific American* (U.K.) 267, no. 3: 53–60.

Keltikangas-Jarvinen, L. 1987. "Body-Image Disturbances Ensuing from Juvenile Rheumatoid Arthritis." *Perceptual and Motor Skills* 64:984.

Kermoian, R., and J. J. Campos. 1988. "Locomotor Experience: A Facilitator of Spatial Cognitive Development." *Child Development* 59: 908–917.

Kolb, L. C. 1959. "The Body Image in Schizophrenic Reaction." In *Schizophrenia: An Integrated Aproach*, edited by A. Auerbach. New York: Ronald Press.

Mahoney, M. J. 1991. *Human Change Processes: The Scientific Foundations of Psychotherapy.* New York: Basic Books.

Marcel, Anthony J. 1983. "Conscious and Unconscious Perception: An Approach to the Relations between Phenomenal Experience and Perceptual Processes." *Cognitive Psychology* 15:238–300.

Mason, Ronald. E. 1961. *Internal Perception and Bodily Functioning.* New York: International Universities Press.

Maturana, H. R., and F. G. Varela. 1987. *The Tree of Knowledge: The Biological Roots of Human Understanding.* Boston: Shambhala.

McEwan, M. H., R. E. Dihoff, and G. M. Brosvic. 1991. "Early Infant Crawling Experience is Reflected in Later Motor Skill Development." *Perceptual and Motor Skills* 72:75–79.

Medin, D. L., and W. D. Wattenmaker. 1987. "Category Cohesiveness, Theories, and Cognitive Archeology." In Neisser 1987.

Merleau-Ponty, Maurice. 1962. *Phenomenology of Perception.* Translated by Colin Smith. London: Routledge and Kegan Paul.

Merleau-Ponty, Maurice. 1963. *The Structure of Behavior.* Translated by A. L. Fisher. Boston: Beacon Press.

Merleau-Ponty, Maurice. 1964. *The Primacy of Perception.* Translated by W. Cobb. Evanston: Northwestern University Press.

Neisser, Ulric. 1976. *Cognition and Reality: Principles and Implications of Cognitive Psychology.* New York: W. H. Freeman.

Neisser, Ulric, ed. 1987. *Concepts and Conceptual Development: Ecological and Intellectual Factors in Categorization.* Cambridge: Cambridge University Press.

Piaget, Jean. 1971. *Biology and Knowledge: An Essay on the Relations between Organic Regulations and Cognitive Processes.* Chicago: University of Chicago Press.

Powers, P. S., R. G. Schulman, A. A. Gleghorn, and M. E. Prange. 1987. "Perceptual and Cognitive Abnormalities in Bulimia." *American Journal of Psychiatry* 144:1456–1460.

Quinton, A. 1975. "The Soul." In *Personal Identity*, edited by J. Perry. Berkeley: University of California Press.

Rock, I., and C. S. Harris. 1967. "Vision and Touch." *Scientific American* 216, no. 5: 96–104.

Roll, J.-P., and R. Roll. 1988. "From Eye to Foot: A Proprioceptive Chain Involved in Postural Control." In *Posture and Gait: Development, Adaptation, and Modulation*, edited by G. Amblard, A. Berthoz, and F. Clarac. Amsterdam: Excerpta Medica.

Rosenbaum, D. A., J. Vaughan, M. J. Jorgensen, H. J. Barns, and E. Stewart. 1993. "Plans for Object Manipulation." In *Attention and Performance XIV: Synergies in Experimental Psychology, Artificial Intelligence, and Cognitive Neuroscience*, edited by D. E. Meyer and S. Kornblum. Cambridge: MIT Press.

Ruggieri, V., M. Milizia, N. Sabatini, and M. T. Tosi. 1983. "Body Perception in Relation to Muscular Tone at Rest and Tactile Sensitivity to Tickle." *Perceptual and Motor Skills* 56:799–806.

Sabatini, N., V. Ruggieri, and M. Milizia. 1984. "Barrier and Penetration Scores in Relation to Some Objective and Subjective Somesthetic Measures." *Perceptual and Motor Skills* 59:195–202.

Shatz, Carla J. 1992. "The Developing Brain." *Scientific American* (U.K.) 267, no. 3: 35–41.

Schilder, Paul. 1935. *The Image and Appearance of the Human Body*. London: Kegan, Paul, Trench, Trubner, and Co.

Skrinar, G. S., B. A. Bullen, J. M. Cheek, J. W. McArthur, and L. K. Vaughan. 1986. "Effects of Endurance Training on Body-Consciousness in Women." *Perceptual and Motor Skills* 62:483–490.

Shontz, F. C. 1969. *Perceptual and Cognitive Aspects of Body Experience*. New York: Academic Press.

Shontz, F. C. 1974. "Body Image and Its Disorders." *International Journal of Psychiatry in Medicine* 5:461–472.

Straus, Erwin. 1967. "On Anosognosia." In *Phenomenology of Will and Action*, edited by E. Straus and D. Griffith. Pittsburgh: Duquesne University Press.

Straus, Erwin. 1970. "The Phantom Limb." In *Aisthesis and Aesthetics*, edited by E. Straus and D. Griffith. Pittsburgh: Duquesne University Press.

Tiemersma, D. 1982. "Body-Image and Body-Schema in the Existential Phenomenology of Merleau-Ponty." *Journal of the British Society of Phenomenology* 13:246–255.

Toombs, S. K. 1988. "Illness and the Paradigm of Lived Body." *Theoretical Medicine* 9:201–226.

Wapner, S., and H. Werner. 1965. "An Experimental Approach to Body Perception from the Organismic Developmental Point of View." In *The Body Percept*, edited by S. Wapner and H. Werner. New York: Random House.

Weimer, W. B. 1979. "A Conceptual Framework for Cognitive Psychology: Motor Theories of the Mind." In *Perceiving, Acting, and Knowing*, edited by R. Shaw and J. Bransford. Hillsdale, N.J.: Erlbaum.

Living without Touch and Peripheral Information about Body Position and Movement: Studies with Deafferented Subjects

Jonathan Cole and Jacques Paillard

Today, as ever, we talk of only five senses: vision, hearing, touch, taste, and smell. This despite the fact that possibly the most crucial of all our senses, position and movement sense or proprioception, was first described nearly 200 years ago. It is so deep within us and so integral to our independence and movement through the world that it has for the most part remained hidden from our personal and collective consciousness.

One reason for this may be that it was impossible to imagine being without it. While the blind and the deaf have been with us, and hence have shown us the consequences of their loss, individuals who have lost the senses of joint position and touch have not been recorded. Recently, however, several such subjects have emerged. This paper will consider some of the scientific work that has been performed with two of these subjects.

In a neurological context, the interest of such patients is that they allow, for the first time, investigation of the mechanism of movement without peripheral feedback in humans. They also allow some reflections on the sense of one's own body and the sense of self in the absence of these important sensory feedback modalities, which, as will be seen, have profound effects on movement and its automaticity.

1   Touch, Proprioception, and the Peripheral Nervous System

That part of the nervous system that lies outside the brain and spinal cord, the peripheral nervous system, may be divided anatomically and functionally into several parts. Those nerves that transmit impulses from the peripheral organs to the spinal cord and brain, the sensory nerves, are conventionally divided into myelinated and unmyelinated nerve fibres. Myelinated nerve fibres are larger and conduct their impulses faster, in part because of their cross-sectional diameter but mainly because of the electrical properties of their myelinated sheath, which acts as an insulator. These large myelinated sensory nerve fibres are divided further into those that originate with receptors in skin and those with receptors in muscle, the latter called muscle spindles and Golgi tendon organs, which are sensitive to stretch. Smaller myelinated fibres convey impulses that are interpreted as muscle fatigue, tiredness, and some forms of pain and warmth. Unmyelinated nerve fibres convey impulses concerned with pain and cold temperature.

The distributions of the receptors that underlie these sensations and of the nerve fibres that conduct the somatosensory information are not uniform throughout the body. The cutaneous organs are found more frequently in the hand, where they respond to touch and stretch of the skin, while there are far fewer receptors over the back and buttocks. Muscle spindles are found most frequently in those muscles where fine control of movement is important. Perhaps surprisingly, half the spindles in our body are found in the neck muscles, where exquisite control of head position is important for stabilization of the eyes and inner-ear balance organs in space (a fact whose importance will become more obvious later).

The senses of joint position and of movement were first described by Charles Bell in 1833. He talked of the consciousness of muscular exertion as being a sixth sense: "The muscles are from habit so directed with so much precision that we do not know how we stand. . . . If we attempt to walk on a narrow ledge we become subject to apprehension. . . . The actions of the muscles are magnified and demonstrative" (Bell 1979 [1833]). In his original description Bell considered these peripheral organs to occupy a middle ground between the afferent information that reaches consciousness and that which does not. At various times muscular information might be part of one or both of these perceptual sets, which have been described as the unconscious motor schema and the conscious body image (see below).

Phillips (1985) was well aware of the difficulty of talking of a muscular sense of which we are sometimes not aware. He suggested instead that one should talk of the perceptions of movement and of position rather than of the sense of joint position, or proprioception. His definition divorces the impulses originating in given peripheral receptors from a given perception. For example, the muscles concerned with facial expression do not have muscle spindles, and yet there is exquisite sensitivity, mostly at the body-schema level, of position and movement. This information probably arises from peripheral organs sensitive to stretch in the skin. In the hand, information about movement and position of the fingers probably arises from muscle spindles and joint and tendon organs and, most important, from stretch receptors in the skin itself. Muscle spindles and Golgi tendon organs may be more important in joint-position and movement perceptions at the larger, more proximal joints, like the shoulder and hip.

The term 'proprioception' has come to be used, among British physiologists, for those sensory signals that arise from the moving parts of the
body, including the head segment and the vestibular apparatus of the inner
ear. The visual sense, in contrast, is generally considered as being mainly
devoted to exteroception, i.e., to the collection of information about features of the environment in the extrapersonal space. It is possible, however,
to talk of visual proprioception as providing visual information about our
own body position and movement (see Gibson 1979). The questions of
how far visual proprioception may supplement the lack of proprioceptive
information arising from the muscles and skin in deafferented patients and
how these different sources of peripheral information have different attentional requirements at a conscious level are two of the major themes of this
paper.

2   The Physiological Loss in I.W. and G.L.

There have been a number of reports of patients with severe purely sensory, peripheral neuropathies in the last twenty or so years. They were
first described in the United States and may have been associated with
excess vitamin B_6, or Pyridoxine. These were written up originally by
Sterman et al. (1980). Other patients have since been discovered with
similar syndromes (e.g., Sanes et al. 1985). The origin of their neuropathy remains still largely unknown, though it is likely that they suffered
destruction of their nerves by their own antibodies raised to external infections and cross-reacting to their own nervous tissue. The patients to
be discussed here fall into this group. I.W. suffered from a viral diarrhoea
and/or infectious mononucleosis, while G.L. had an acute attack of a viral infection. Four years previously she had a classic Guillain-Barre syndrome, a postinfectious neuropathy with severe motor weakness, from
which she made a complete recovery.

As a result of these infections both I.W. and G.L. lost sensations of
touch and muscular proprioception, I.W. from the collarline down, G.L.
from a level at about the mouth. Neither patient is able to perceive touch
or movement from below that level. I.W. has apparently normal position
sense in the neck, while G.L. has no afferent information from her neck
muscles or from the lower part of her mouth and face. Both patients, however, have preserved vestibular information about position and movement
of their head in the gravitational field.

Perceptual tests on these patients have been backed up by clinical neurophysiological ones showing a complete absence of large myelinated sensory nerve function. Nerve-conduction studies show no sensory potentials,

and no reflex activity has been elicited. In contrast, nerve-conduction studies of motor fibres and EMG in both subjects is normal. In G.L.'s case, a biopsy from a small sensory nerve in the leg confirmed the complete loss of large myelinated fibres.

Their neuropathies have been extraordinarily selective and complete. All large myelinated sensory nerve function from below their levels has been removed as a consequence of the neuropathy, though motor nerve function and small myelinated and unmyelinated nerve function is apparently intact.

3 Case Histories

I.W. was a successful butcher when at the age of 19 he suffered a flulike illness. He became increasingly weak and at one stage fell in the street and was thought to be drunk. On admission to the hospital he had slurred speech and was unable to feel anything in the mouth, as well as having no touch or positional information from his body. He remembers lying on the bed but being unable to feel it—a floating feeling, which was extremely frightening.

When he tried to move an arm or his trunk, he had absolutely no control over where the moving part ended up, though he had the ability to produce the movement. The facial numbness and problems with chewing disappeared over a few weeks. As the weeks passed, it became evident that little recovery was likely, and he was discharged from the hospital three months later.

He had little understanding as to what had gone wrong but had at least realized that if he was to move with any degree of control, he would need intense mental concentration and constant visual vigilance. After 2 months he had just about managed to sit and was beginning to learn to feed himself.

He spent 5 months at home being cared for by his mother and determined not to admit defeat. He did not allow himself to be seen in this condition, nor did he sit in a wheelchair. He subsequently destroyed all photographs from this time. He taught himself to dress and to feed himself. He preferred a cold meal that he fed to himself to a hot one that someone else would feed him. Then he was admitted to a rehabilitation hospital, where he stayed for the next 18 months.

It was an enormously supportive environment, though it was largely through his own efforts that he stood after a year and began to walk several months after that. He enrolled in the local college and took O (ordinary) level exams successfully (despite severe problems in writing, he neither asked for, nor was given, any extra time to perform the exam) and then took a job in the civil service. He spent the next fifteen years or so working as a clerk in a job alongside able-bodied people, telling of his bad back rather than having to explain a problem he still did not really understand. After his discharge from Odstock, the rehabilitation hospital, he was not seen by a doctor for about twelve years, during which time he had been promoted at work and married.

The time course and consequences of G.L.'s illness were slightly different. She suffered her neuropathy around seventeen years ago. It affected a higher level, however, since it began at the level of the mouth, extending over the cervical-supplied back of her head. To this day she has no reliable touch or proprioceptive sensation in the tongue or mouth itself and no unconscious ability to control her neck muscles. There were several important consequences of the fact that her neuropathy began at a higher level than I.W.'s. Speaking and chewing were almost impossible, and for several months she existed solely on pureed food. Then she became so exasperated by this that she began to experiment in eating. She learned to push food to one side of the mouth, chew a certain number of times, and then push the food to the back of her mouth and swallow it automatically. Facial expression was severely limited because of the absence of proprioception from the lower face. She refused to look in a mirror for two years after the illness. For a similar time, she had to remember to concentrate to keep her mouth from opening.

She, like I.W., began her own rehabilitation. She was married with a young child and rapidly realized that her main priority was to keep the house together and bring up her son. She decided not to make any concentrated effort at walking but rather settled for a full life from a wheelchair. While I.W. was spending most of his waking life learning to stand and walk, G.L. was immersed in the problems of bringing up a child, doing the housework, and cooking.

Few, if any, of their movements are recognizably normal. Though they show many similarities in movement, the surprising level of walking ability acquired by I.W. compared with the severe impairment in standing and walking observed in G.L. raises an important problem. Psychological problems and differences in their motivational drives are probably not sufficient to explain these striking differences.

The fact that I.W. has intact neck-muscle afferentation, whereas G.L. has not, is most likely the main source of proprioceptive information that allows I.W. to locate his own insentient body with respect to his head segment. This in turn allows him to organize his body balance with respect to the inertial platform of a head oriented with respect to the gravity force field by means of the vestibular apparatus of the inner ear, and with respect to the stabilized visual field by means of the ocular system. G.L. is devoid of any proprioceptive information about the head-trunk body linkage and therefore is unable to maintain the erect posture of her body that may be necessary for her to achieve, like I.W., an efficient strategy of walking. With her eyes closed, G.L. rotates and bends her head to the right, something of which she is unaware. Likewise with her eyes shut, she is unaware of slow passive rotation of her head. She may lose the location of her head in the same way that she and I.W. lose location of their body segments.

I.W. also has a sense of fatigue in his muscles, whereas G.L. may not, which suggests that I.W. has retained activity in a class of small nerve-fiber sensory afferents in which G.L. has not.

4   Strategies for Everyday Movement

Several factors in these subjects' recovered movement are accessible to scientific investigation to varying degrees. The requirement for visual monitoring of movement is relatively easy to test. On the other hand, these patients' requirement for mental concentration and their dependence on motor programs learned before the onset of their neuropathies are far more difficult to quantify.

Constant visual vigilance is required for any purposeful movement. Both I.W. and G.L. report that they sleep with the light on. I.W. claims that he has to wake up to think about turning over during the night, whereas G.L. reports that she turns spontaneously and changes position while sleeping. She does need light in the room, however, to visually control the actual position of her body in the bed when awakening. Preserved small sensory fibers signaling the lack of blood skin irrigation, which results from prolonged maintained position, may trigger reflex changes of body position in G.L. during sleep, while they apparently awaken I.W.

When one talks with the patients, it soon becomes apparent that this visual feedback can only be used with concentration and intellectual effort. When I.W. first sat up in bed, he was so overwhelmed by this achievement that he stopped thinking about sitting and immediately collapsed. Once he had learned to walk, if he sneezed, and thus disrupted his mental concentration, he would fall over. The limits to how much he can do in a day he describes as having to do with his own mental concentration, rather than the amount of physical effort required.

As well as having temporal limits during a day or a week, I.W. and G.L. also have limits in their focus of concentration. Both I.W. and G.L. use an egg as an example. Having learned the amount of force required for their handgrip to pick up eggs without breaking them (a very challenging task indeed for both of them!), they can hold them in their hands as long as their attention is not directed toward another task. However, they are sure that if distracted, say during standing for I.W., the concentration required would mean they could no longer think about the eggs and the eggs would be crushed.

We are also forced to use examples rather than measurements to describe their dependence on previously learned movements for the success of motor rehabilitation.

Although both patients claim that they cannot rely on motor automatisms for action and that they have to concentrate on each purposeful movement they want to make, I.W., for instance, is sure, as far as his autonomic locomotion is concerned, that he was greatly helped in rehabilitation by his previously learned movements. In contrast, G.L. stresses the difficulty she encountered in elaborating new strategies for grasping and transporting objects on the basis of visual cues, steering her wheelchair on the basis of thermal cues derived from the cold metallic part of the chair, and even relearning a correct articulation of speech on the basis of her voice sounds.

The more general question of whether or not such patients are able to access a previously learned repertoire of motor habits in the absence of peripheral feedback in order to improve their mobility after the neuropathy is not known and is obviously difficult to investigate. In this connection, how far they would be able to acquire and automatize new motor skills would be worth studying. I.W., for instance, refused to learn to swim, something he had not done before the neuropathy. This, he says, is partly because it would be a completely novel movement but partly because he is inherently unsafe in water, being unable to feel the bottom and unable to see his limbs in order to coordinate movement. He may not have a large enough focus of concentration to move all four limbs together in a coordinated fashion without constant visual feedback. He did, however, pass his driving tests after the neuropathy, with a hand control for braking and acceleration and an automatic gearbox. Driving is one of the most relaxing tasks for I.W. It may not be coincidental that this is the task in which he most closely resembles the nondisabled people.

The distinction between motor activities that are stimulus driven and those that are memory driven (the reactive/projective distinction of Goldberg 1985) is probably apposite here. Stimulus-driven activities generally use ready-to-work motor programs and therefore presuppose the existence of some kind of repertoire of motor habits, motor command programs that can be released and executed automatically. In contrast, memory-driven activities concern goal-directed movements structured on the basis of a representation of the expected sensory consequences of the planned action once performed. It presupposes the existence of a repertoire of kinesthetic engrams characteristic of the goal to be achieved.

Hence the revival in contemporary studies in motor control of James's old concept of a goal image, which prompts the question of its neural representation. William James stressed the distinction between motor or efferent programs directly (reflexly or automatically) triggered by the stimulus and voluntary actions indirectly driven by way of kinesthetic traces associated with previous movements.

The impairments observed in our deafferented patients raise the basic question of how far reafferent information of proprioceptive origin is necessary to update these traces and/or to steer voluntary action toward its prescribed goal by comparing the desired state represented by these traces and the actual state of our motor apparatus. They also raise the problem of how far proprioceptive information of visual origin may supplement and replace missing proprioceptive information of muscular origin in remapping a repertoire of kinesthetic traces, to restore voluntary control, onto an intact efferent system of motor commands.

To return to James's schema, the apparent persistent absence of stimulus-driven automatisms, often stressed as a motor characteristic of our patients, is at the heart of an unresolved question. Differences between the two subjects in their ability to move deafferented parts, e.g., limbs and body, lead to the conclusion that I.W. may have been far more able to construct motor images. This may have been because, having a stable head and neck posture that G.L. lacks, he was more able to focus his attention on motor planning.

5   Perceptual Frames of Reference

Spatial frameworks are incorporated in our perceptual and motor experiences. The general distinction between a body-centered egocentric frame of reference and a visual exocentric frame of reference is generally accepted (see Paillard 1987). Lacking information about position and movement from their bodies, deafferented subjects should have an impaired egocentric system of reference. Reaching and pointing tasks have been used to test their performance.

Within the calibration process involved in the location of targets in space, several different frames of reference may be distinguished. Visual inputs are coded in a retinal frame, whereas the direction of gaze is egocentrically coded in the body frame, as are most of our motor commands. The object frame is the local space occupied by the object, with its internal geometric relations. The stabilized visual background with its structures and landmarks constitutes a world frame, with respect to which relative positions of the body and of objects might be evaluated.

The relative contribution of these different frames to overall performance may vary according to circumstances. For instance in a normally illuminated structured visual background, the object frame, which may be a target goal for a reaching movement, may give both the visual cues that allow the preshaping of the grip posture to accord with the characteristics of the object and the proprioceptive location cues (derived from the gaze direction of the head and referred to in the egocentric body frame) that allow the directional transport of the hand toward the target. Moreover, a final position adjustment may intervene on the basis of an evaluation of the residual distance between the target and the moving hand in an exocentric system of reference.

Suppressing the structured visual background in a pointing task (for instance by using a luminous target in darkness and by preventing vision of the moving hand) forces the subject to use egocentric cues to perform the task because none are available in the exocentric frame of the visual field. The performance of the deafferented subject (G.L.) is greatly impaired in this experimental condition, whereas that of control subjects is not, which suggests that the latter are normally able to steer their motor activity in either the egocentric or exocentric frame, according to the task requirements, whereas the deafferented patient has a clearly deficient egocentric system. When a world frame is available, however, the patient is as accurate as control subjects in her pointing performance, which suggests that she is able to visually guide her actions in an exocentric frame (Blouin et al. 1993).

Interestingly, when vision of the hand is precluded, preshaping the grip posture to the size and shape of target objects (object frame), which one still finds in control subjects, is absent in deafferented patients. This suggests either that the visual stimulus alone cannot trigger such learned automatisms or that such kinds of learned grip postures are no longer available in these patients. Similar results were described for patients with central deafferentation subsequent to a parietal lesion (Jeannerod et al. 1984). Grip posture may therefore be affected by either central or peripheral deafferentation.

6   The Body-Schema Problem

The divide between body schema and body image is discussed by Shaun Gallagher in this volume. In spite of the clear distinction between the two made by Head and Holmes (1911–1912), confusion persists. Though these concepts may not always have a clean interface between them (some postural adjustments considered at the schema level can be perceived if concentrated on, for instance), they are very useful models.

Paillard (1980) proposed a similar distinction in extending to somesthesia the functional dichotomy he introduced in the study of visual function between "where" and "what" problems. He suggested that the location of body parts in a body schema (the where problem) is processed differently in the central nervous system from the perceptual identification of the features in a body image (the what problem). Hence, the position of body segments or areas may be either registered as location in a sensory-motor mapping of the body space (that can be reached by a movement of the hand, for instance) or perceived as a position in the perceptual representation of a body image.

Proprioceptive information is necessary for updating the postural body frame (or schema), whereas exteroceptive multimodal information, mainly visual, underpins the central representation and percept of the body image (Paillard 1982).

There are several pieces of evidence showing that deafferented patients may have a preserved body image though they have lost their body schema. G.L., for instance, is normally able to perceive a thermal stimulus delivered to a given point on the surface of the skin of her left arm. When prevented from seeing her body and requested to do so, she is unable to point with her right arm to the place of stimulation. Having lost the ability to proprioceptively update her body schema, she cannot locate that place in her sensorimotor body space. However, she can verbally designate this place in the anatomy of her body ("over my left wrist," for instance), and she even indicates it precisely on a schematic body diagram. In other words, she can locate the stimulus in a perceptual representation of her body, knows *where* the stimulus has been delivered within the frame of her body image, but does not know how to get there in her apparently lost sensorimotor frame (Paillard 1991c).

Of interest here is an opposite syndrome described by Paillard et al. (1983) in a patient with a centrally deafferented forearm following a parietal lesion. This patient, otherwise unable to perceptually detect the presence and content of a tactile stimulus delivered to her deafferented hand in a blindfolded condition, was surprisingly able to point automatically with her intact hand to the place of stimulation. This was described as an equivalent of "blindsight" in the tactile modality. Indeed, in this case peripheral information was still available and processed at a subcortical level, hence allowing the computation of a locality in sensorimotor space, whereas the central process that underpins perceptual awareness of the stimulus was lacking.

Finally, several additional observations concerning the permanence of some basic motor synergies in these deafferented patients are worth mentioning. They concern the preservation in these patients of some inbuilt efferent programs for making anticipatory postural adjustments.

For example, when the subject himself unloads a weight held in his outstretched hand, this produces in control subjects an anticipatory postural adjustment that minimizes upward displacement of the arm, whereas when the experimenter himself unloads the weight, the subject cannot avoid upward displacement (Hugon et al. 1982). If a seated subject is asked to forcibly abduct his leg against resistance, the other leg will also automatically move outward as part of a postural reflex to maintain pelvic alignment (Forget et al., submitted). Similarly, every precision grip involving coordination between thumb and index finger is associated with synergic activity of the extensor of the wrist that compensates for the perturbation by a flexion movement of the index finger (a well-known synergy of Duchenne de Boulogne). EMG recordings have shown that G.L. retains the first (Forget and Lamarre 1990), the second (Forget et al., submitted) and the third (Paillard et al., unpublished results) of these automatisms. (Only the first test has been repeated with I.W. thus far.) This suggests that these postural synergies are not reflexes in origin but are centrally predetermined, either as prewired in the efferent circuitry or as present in a repertoire of inbuilt predispositions, and are preserved for years even when they are of no use.

There are nevertheless other broad categories of anticipatory postural reactions that are clearly under voluntary control and subject to learning: neither subject has any reflex responses to unexpected events, and if I.W. trips, he is liable to fall in a incoordinated way. There are also many adapted feedforward programs that tune motor commands in accordance with the expected dynamic constraints of the planned action (Massion 1984). Muscular proprioception normally plays a predominant role in these adaptive pretuning processes. The problem of how far proprioceptive information of visual origin might allow deafferented patients to compensate for their loss of information about the peripheral state of their motor apparatus awaits further experimentation, yet some evidence on this matter comes from analysis of I.W.'s walking. He relates that walking on flat ground now takes about half the intellectual concentration that it did initially, which suggests some automatization in itself. Analysis of the pattern of activation of muscles during his walking shows that, though very abnormal, there is some phasic activation and relaxation of the calf muscles in relation to the gait cycle that cannot be under visual control and so is presumed to be nonconscious. This suggests that it has become embedded in the motor schema (Burnett et al. 1989).

7   The Problem of Morphokinesis versus Topokinesis

Paillard (1991) has suggested, in the context of drawing and writing, that generating a motor form or orienting an activity within a given spatial frame has different goal requirements, and consequently a different mode of motor commands. Drawing a figure eight in the air, for instance, requires an accurate model of the shape to be drawn (morphokinesis), but this does not need to be located at a specific place in extracorporeal space. Moreover, one can easily change the size of the figure eight without altering the shape. In contrast, reaching to a visual target, say to pick up an object, does require a precise specification of the initial and final locations of the moving limb in an egocentric and exocentric frame of reference (topokinesis).

The deafferented subjects have little difficulty in the morphokinetic mode but have great difficulties with topokinetic movements. G.L. is able to produce a precise ellipse drawn out in the air in front of her. Without vision, the shape of the ellipse remains but the spatial coordinates were altered, as were the orientations of the axes of the ellipse (Teasdale et al. 1993).

There are also differences in their writing. Both can write a legible script, but their techniques for maintaining accuracy with their eyes shut appear to differ. G.L. is very slow and, in making the shapes of the letters, tends to place them in the wrong area of the paper—morphokinesis remains, but topokinesis is degraded. I.W., on the other hand, appears to be more aware than G.L. of the topokinetic problem and eager to achieve the spatial requirements of the task. Thus, with his eyes shut, he moves fast across the page in an attempt to preserve both shape and correct framing of his writing space, and consequently sacrifices some accuracy in making the letters. If he is made to slow down or speed up, the topokinetic component degrades.

8   Production of Force and Corollary Discharge?

In the absence of vision, do these subjects have any knowledge of their motor output? Though there is no disagreement among motor physiologists that perception of movement depends on peripherally originating feedback (and I.W. and G.L. have no perception of movement), is there any evidence that these subjects have some knowledge of force produced? There are several different levels at which this knowledge could arise. There may be some remaining afferent information arising from the periphery, since it is known that I.W. has small muscle afferents intact and both subjects have pain and temperature sensation. Or this could arise purely centrally, either as a perception of the motor command as it leaves the motor apparatus (efference copy) or as a perception of the command itself as it is generated and before the efferent command is sent (corollary discharge).

A simple way to investigate force production is with the perception of weight. When different weights are concealed within boxes and I.W. and G.L. are asked to discriminate between them with the eyes open, they can discriminate to an accuracy of around 10 g in 150 g. They do this by picking the weight up in their hand and raising and lowering the forearm while looking at it. This perceptual liminal difference is very close to normal. It is thought that they are coding velocity of movement and using visual feedback to see whether or not the movement is smaller or larger, depending on how heavy the weight is. This hypothesis has been validated recently at the University of Laval in I.W. and G.L. using SELSPOT recording of the weighting movement (Fleury et al., submitted).

With eyes shut, I.W. still has an ability to perceive differences in weight, but his liminal difference increases to 200 g in 400 g. The fact that a perception of difference is still present suggests that the origin of this perception is peripheral. This receives support from the fact that when the perceived weights are suspended from the index finger, which is raised and lowered, the ability to distinguish different weights grossly diminishes if the muscles moving that finger are fatigued.

G.L. too demonstrated an ability to produce accurate output of force over a very short period of time. When asked to produce an isometric force by pressing between finger and thumb, G.L. was able to code forces as a percentage of her maximum. She could also give a fairly accurate description of how close the force she had produced was to the force required. This argues for a central perception of force production, though whether it is an efference copy from the motor apparatus or a perceptual copy of the command to the motor centers cannot be determined.

Stimulation of the brain by a powerful short magnetic pulse delivered to the scalp (magnetic motor evoked potentials) can lead to small movements of the hand or fingers. By means of such stimulation it was possible to move I.W.'s finger, while he was maintaining a small isometric force, in a simple twitch movement of which he was not aware. If there is a perceived efference copy, then under these circumstances it does not appear to be at the level of the motor efferent apparatus activated by magnetic stimulation (Cole and Sedgwick 1992).

In experiments with I.W. there is also evidence that over a longer time course he has no ability to perceive and monitor force. He was asked to press down on typewriter keys with each index finger to produce a maximum key movement of 12 cm with a maximum resistance of 500 g. When asked to press two keys down a half, a quarter, or three quarters of the total distance at the same time or to press one key down and then match that force with a force subsequently on the other key, control subjects were able to do this with relative ease. I.W. found it very difficult either to produce the same force at the same time or to match the force produced by one hand with the other hand. This suggests that he cannot monitor the force he is producing.

There is thus an intriguing difference in I.W.'s inability to maintain forces that he is unaware of and G.L.'s ability to produce calibrated pulses of force quite accurately scaled in a range derived from the production of a series of five maximum forces. The duration of force output may well be crucial here. Both subjects may be able to learn to generate a calibrated pulse of force in an open-loop fashion. However, if the forces have to be altered, they fail. They may have access to some transient corollary signals to regulate the generation of force pulses, whereas information about the sustained maintenance of a given force is lacking.

Additional evidence that there are some interactive visuoproprioceptive processes normally associated with motor programs was obtained from experiments in mirror drawing. When asked to trace around a star of David on a table with the index finger with visual feedback through a mirror, and hence inverted, control subjects find it very difficult to draw oblique lines and turn the corners of the star. This is considered to be because of a mismatch between the visual and muscular proprioceptive feedback. It was therefore expected that deafferented subjects would be able to do this task better than controls. Indeed, G.L. was able to do it first time without any conflict (Lajoie et al. 1992). I.W., in contrast, did have a problem at the corners, though he was slightly better than controls.

We may argue that I.W., as compared with G.L., is in general cognitively controlling his motor output far more. While he has neither feedback from the arm nor any perception of his motor program, he does become aware of a mismatch between that program and the feedback he is using to guide his motor output, (just as we are not aware of walking until we trip). He may have elaborated a more secure system of coding motor acts than G.L., whereas she may be dependent almost entirely on visual feedback. He is permanently trying to analyze and understand the motor problem he has to solve (his comments during and after each task extensively illustrate this), whereas G.L. reacts much more spontaneously to every situation.

9   Some Consequences of Deafferentation on One's Approach to the World

Both patients have to give their mental attention to some aspect of movement for nearly all of their waking life. Sitting in a chair requires attention to avoid falling out of it. On just one occasion in 20 years has I.W. been aware only of what was going on around him rather than actually aware of the process of walking. This has, unfortunately, not become any more frequent. Were he to fall or trip in such a state, however, he would have no awareness of where he was, and this would make the subsequent fall that much worse (when falling, we automatically stretch out our arms; I.W. has no such ability).

I.W. must avoid places which are dangerous to him—dangerous because of the slipperiness of the floor, because of the wind, because of darkness, or because of unpredictability. Crowded places or places where he may not be able to see someone knock him from behind are prohibited. When walking somewhere new, he will map out his next ten yards or so by standing or sitting and studying the area. He progresses by analyzing the way ahead as a mountaineer will work out a pitch up a sheer face of rock. He also has to judge with great care the relation between his size and, say, spaces through which he needs to go. Whereas control subjects may not always attend to this and may rely on reflexes to change direction or stop during a movement, I.W. has to preplan and be alert to the unpredictable.

I.W.'s attentiveness to his surroundings has led him to become in demand by a holiday care service, which uses him to assess hotels for their disability friendliness. He makes sure that a hotel or car park is flat, that the entrances are the right width, that they are protected from wind, etc. His thoroughness is not solely a professional pride but also a personal necessity. For environmental reasons and perhaps because of constitutional differences in the psychological profiles of the two patients, G.L. does not seem to have developed the same alertness as I.W. to potential dangers. Interestingly, when tested in attentional tasks measuring their ability to react to unexpected peripheral cues or to resist distraction, both patients produced astonishing scores that rank them at the highest level of a scale of performance established in well-trained athletes (Nougier et al. 1994), which reflects their need for continual alertness.

10 Body Language

When I.W. and G.L. met recently, it was fascinating to see them together, for they had each independently developed elaborate gestural movements of the forearms during speech. These are possibly some of the most automatic of their repertoire of movements, and are almost entirely morphokinetic. But before I.W. displays this morphokinetic melody, he settles into a posture and calculates how much safe space he has in front of him to gesture within. Then, with minimal visual feedback, he knows how expansive his gestures can be.

They are both well aware of the importance of body language and are strikingly aware that they lost their unconscious ability to communicate through it. Their solution has been to learn a limited repertoire of arm and hand gestures associated with speech that give the impression of an unconscious body language. These movements may not now require constant and complete visual control and are the most automatic of their movements. Both relearned gestural speech under pressure from a social environment that they felt would otherwise complain of their inexpressiveness. To some extent they are using these gestures to deceive others into reacting in terms of an unconscious language: it is an act in more than one sense.

After a decade of living with this neuropathy, I.W. and G.L. have developed a repertoire of gestural movements. It took them several months, however, before they were able to use them in anything like a natural way. G.L. was rather surprised when her attention was drawn to her body language when viewing a video film of herself. She was not really aware of having controlled it at the time. While both subjects' gestures are particularly from the arm and hand, they have also learned to use the fingers to some extent during gestural movements, though not to the same amount as control subjects. They also employ these gestural movements rather more than control subjects.

Both subjects have learned to produce these elaborate movements extraordinarily well. The very fact that they expend so much precious mental energy in learning and reproducing these gestures must reveal something of the importance of expressive body language for us all.

11   Views of Self and of Body Image

One normally considers the body image as being mainly holistic, as being the perception of a gestalt whose components and analytic features are processed largely at an unconscious level. The body image may play a role in organizing and guiding actions as a global percept rather than as a substrate for a sense of local position that allows perceptual awareness of the relations between body parts. It is at the level of the body schema that neural integrations between sensory inputs and motor control translates smooth movement into coordinated movement. Without peripherally originating proprioceptive feedback, I.W. and G.L. have had to use a perceived, visually maintained body image for this purpose. Their use of the body image, and so their perception of it as a concept, may therefore be different from controls' use and perception, since it may operate at two levels: as a holistic gestalt and as a schema replacement.

With this caveat, however, I.W. says that his sense of body image, his sense of his wholeness and configuration, has altered little as a consequence of his deafferentation syndrome. It should be remembered that deafferentation occurred when he was 19. He has little doubt that if the neuropathy had occurred before he had built up an image, then the situation would have been very different. This does not tell us whether the image is built up early in life or it is innate. However, perhaps it is unwise to consider these possibilities as mutually exclusive or to suggest that continued experience does not also play a role. That the body image is built up during early life and then maintained seems unlikely, if only for the simple reason that our size and shape alters during growth. Similarly, our weight and physical prowess may continue to alter during life.

Immediately after the neuropathy I.W. was unable to move, and at that stage, though ill and bewildered, he does remember that he began to think differently about his body: a thing that he could not move had an altered relationship to himself. It was when he began to recover movement that he began to recover a more normal body image, he considers. Though he thinks his body image is normal, he does agree that he finds it difficult to compare with the previous image he had before the neuropathy.

It may be important that G.L. occasionally talks of her body as being a machine on which she imposes commands. It is not clear how literally she feels this. A more accurate description may be that she uses her body as a tool, a passive instrument that can be used to move and to interact with her environment (a machine, though it must be started and controlled, is taken to have some autonomous performance). However, her reduced ability to code accurate movements, because of her additional head and neck deafferentation, does suggest that a normal body image depends to some extent on the ability to move that body. Finally, a tool is not a satisfactory simile in that when we use tools they rapidly become elaborated into a motor schema, and hence are hardly attended to.

I.W. makes the point himself that he has to concentrate more on his body for movement throughout the day than do control subjects. He therefore probably has to be more aware of a body image than do control subjects, and this may have helped him maintain it. Both I.W. and G.L. also have normal senses of pain and temperature. The former was likely very important in avoiding injury, and hence in maintaining a healthy and whole body. Both are useful in determining boundaries. Neither subject has noticed any phantom-limb sensations.

Their body images depend excessively on visual information, and this in itself may suggest it would make such images qualitatively different if they were maintained with both visual and peripheral proprioceptive information. Much proprioceptive and cutaneous information arises from the hand in a way that visual information could not likely mimic. I. W. agrees that his maintained image might fade in time if not updated and that without vision the remaining senses of pain and temperature, together with fatigue, would be insufficient to keep it. It is not clear, however, that this fading would be qualitatively different for controls.

When talking of boundaries between him and the external world, I. W.'s immediate concern was to stress his need to have a larger personal space surrounding him to avoid the danger of unexpected movements by others. He suggests that, in the absence of touch, his personal boundaries are visually maintained, that he has to keep an idea of the positions of his limbs and their relations to external objects in mind all the time and, by this visual monitoring and visual memory, keep alive both a knowledge of where he is and an awareness of body image. In addition, he needs more space around him to remain safe. On meeting women, he will usually thrust out a hand rather than bestow a kiss upon the cheek. When kissing, he cannot see his body sufficiently to maintain a comfortable posture.

Both patients are very aware of the effects of their neuropathy upon them. The need to concentrate on all movements, and to have developed only a relatively small repertoire of movement has restricted them enormously. The spontaneity of life, the subconscious flow of life, has been removed. When performing any complicated motor act, neither I.W. nor G.L. have sufficient concentration to have their mind elsewhere: I.W. has often said that he cannot walk and daydream at the same time. This focusing of concentration must, one imagines, alter the way in which they view the world and the passage of time. In this, their neuropathies are diseases of consciousness as well as of their peripheral nervous systems. Different motor acts require different amounts of energy: it is easier for I.W. to drive 300 or 400 miles in a car than to stop and refuel for petrol. They view each day in terms of the amount of energy required to move through it rather than for its own sake.

All movement is a form of communication, and both subjects are aware of how abnormal they appear with their impoverished movements. Perhaps this may explain, in part, their extravagant gestural language when seated—extravagant in terms of large and frequent use rather than in the sense of involved or complicated in repertoire. The desire to be seen as normal, or not to be noticed at all, has been an huge motivation, in I.W. particularly.

12   Unavoidable Limitations

In I.W.'s case his success in returning to a nondisabled world for much of his existence has brought many satisfactions. However, because of the extraordinarily rare and difficult nature of his problem and the difficulties in conceptualizing it, this has also led to a lack of awareness in those around him. A brother once said that people stopped asking after I.W. once he exchanged an invalid carriage for a car, assuming that he had recovered.

In children, motor skills, such as learning to write or ride a bicycle, once learned, become unconscious, and so not worthy of praise. We may encourage our children to learn to ride a bike or to swim, but we don't continue to encourage them once they are successful. For I.W. and G.L. to have learned a motor task makes it only slightly easier to perform again. The more they do, the more they are expected to do, and some days I.W. just cannot find the mental effort and concentration to perform all the necesssary motor acts. Something he can do perfectly well one day he just cannot be bothered to do the next, and this he finds very difficult to explain to friends or to get people to understand.

He describes the level of functioning he has chosen to exist at as his peak. Every day he tries to do as best he can, in a way in which some athletes might understand but few others. Athletes in turn are asked to peak a few times in their career or a few times a year; I.W. faces such tasks every day. He is concerned that in the future the pace at which he lives may prove unsustainable. It is to be hoped that the experience of meeting physiologists with an interest in his condition might make him realize the exceptional nature of his response to it and make a possible slackening of his activity more acceptable to him.

Neither subject has managed to use their fingers well since the neuropathy, though G.L. has been able to type. They use one or two in apposition to the thumb in a pincer grip. The fine and skillful movements of the hand are lost irreparably, since they depend on fine motor control under constant tactile and proprioceptive feedback. This suggests that fine, skilled movements of the hand are particularly sensitive to the absence of tactile cues. It cannot have been coincidence that Charles Bell called his book first describing proprioception and active touch, *The Hand: Its Mechanism and Endowments as Evincing Design.*

When the two patients met, there was concern that G.L. would consider herself a relative failure, since she had patently not been able to recover as much useful movement as I.W. In fact, rather the reverse occurred: I.W. wondered whether the unremitting mental concentration required to reach the level of rehabilitation that he did was worth it when he saw G.L. so well adapted to a wheelchair. Though hardly apparent to outsiders, I.W. maintains that he has had to become selfish to maintain such a level of functioning. Their differing responses to such similar neuropathies shows, among other things, the importance of treating all people as individuals.

13   Conclusions

There are naturally concerns over the extent to which we can extrapolate from these extraordinary subjects, studied repeated over a long time, to others and to controls. However, with appropriate questions and with results interpreted carefully, their study can be important. Their disability and their experiences have allowed an enormous understanding of the role of the sixth sense (see Cole 1995).

Future work may focus on the extent to which visual "proprioception" has taken over from muscular proprioception to provide visually based kinesthetic engrams. The fate of those areas of the brain involved in touch and movement and sensation of position after being deafferented for so long remains to be studied, though there is some evidence for functional reorganization in these areas from experiments on the distribution of visually induced brain waves in I.W. (Barrett et al. 1989). Real-time neural imaging studies may give us answers both to the question of the fate of the deafferented areas and to the perhaps more interesting one of what areas are used to compensate for the massive deafferentation these patients have suffered.

Acknowledgments

Most of the work described in this chapter has been obtained with the help and interest of the subjects G.L. and I.W. We thank them for their cooperation. It is also a pleasure to thank our colleagues in Quebec and Montreal, listed in Blouin et al's paper, for many discussions and experiments. Finally, Dr. Yves Lamarre, as G.L.'s neurologist, first realized the importance of her case and initiated experimental work with her.

References

Barrett, G., Cole, J. D., Sedgwick, E. M., and Towell, A. D. 1989. "Active and Passive Movement-Related Cortical Potentials in a Man with a Large-Fibre Sensory Neuropathy." *Journal of Physiology* 414:11.

Bell, Charles. 1979. *The Hand: Its Mechanism and Vital Endowments as Evincing Design.* Brentwood, Essex, England: Pilgrims Press. First published by W. Pickering, London, 1833.

Blouin, J., Bard, C., Teasdale, N., Paillard, J., Fleury, M., Forget, R., and Lamarre, Y. 1993. "Reference Systems for Coding Spatial Information in Normal Subjects and a Deafferented Patient." *Experimental Brain Research* 93:324–331.

Burnett, M. E., Cole, J. D., McLellan, D. L., and Sedgwick, E. M. 1989. "Gait Analysis in a Subject without Proprioception below the Neck." *Journal of Physiology* 417:102.

Cole, Jonathan. 1995. *Pride and a Daily Marathon.* Cambridge: MIT Press.

Cole, J. D., and Sedgwick, E. M. 1992. "The Perceptions of Force and of Movement in a Man without Large Myelinated Sensory Afferents below the Neck." *Journal of Physiology* 449:503–515.

Fleury, M., Bard, C., Teasdale, N., Paillard, J., Cole, J., Lajoie, Y., and Lamarre, Y. 1995. "Weight Judgment: The Capacity of a Deafferented Subject." *Brain* 118:1149–1156.

Forget, R., and Lamarre, Y. 1987. "Rapid Elbow Flexion in the Absence of Proprioceptive and Cutaneous Feedback." *Human Neurobiology* 6:27–37.

Forget, R., and Lamarre, Y. 1990. "Anticipatory Postural Adjustment in the Absence of Normal Peripheral Feedback." *Brain Research* 508:176–179.

Forget, R., Lamarre, Y., and Bourbonnais, D. Submitted. "Postural Adjustments Associated with Active Movement: Anticipation and Sensory Feedback Influences."

Gibson, J. J. 1979. *The Ecological Approach to Visual Proprioception.* Boston: Houghton-Mifflin.

Goldberg, G. 1985. "Response and Projection: A Reinterpretation of the Premotor Concept." In E. A. Roy, ed., *Neuropsychological Studies of Apraxia and Related Disorders.* Amsterdam: North-Holland.

Head, H., and Holmes, G. 1911–1912. "Sensory Disturbances from Cerebral Lesions." *Brain* 34:102–245.

Hugon, M., Massion, J., and Wiesendanger, M. 1982. "Anticipatory Postural Changes Induced by Active Unloading and Comparison with Passive Unloading in Man." *Pfluger Archives,* 393:292–296.

James, W. 1890. *Principles of Psychology.* New York: Holt.

Jeannerod, M., Michel, F., and Prablanc, C. 1984. "The Control of Hand Movements in a Case of Hemianaesthesia following a Parietal Lesion." *Brain* 107:899–920.

Lajoie, Y., Paillard, J., Teasdale, N., Bard, C., Fleury, M., Forget, R., and Lamarre, Y. 1992. "Mirror Drawing in a Deafferented Patient and Normal Subjects: Visuo-proprioceptive Conflict." *Neurology,* 42:1104–1106.

Massion, J. 1984. "Postural Changes Accompanying Voluntary Movements: Normal and Pathological Aspects." *Human Neurobiology* 2:261–267.

Nougier, V., Rossi, B., Bard, C., Fleury, M., Teasdale, N., Cole, J., and Lamarre, Y. 1994. "Orienting of Attention in Deafferented Patients." *Neuropsychologica* 32:1078–1088.

Paillard, J. 1980. "Le corps situé et le corps identifie: Une approche psychophsyiologique de la notion de schema corporel." *Revue medicale de la Suisse Romande* 100: 129–141.

Paillard, J. 1982. "Le corps et ses langages d'espace." In E. Jeddi, ed., *Le corps en psychiatrie*. Paris: Masson.

Paillard, J. 1987. "Cognitive versus Sensorimotor Encoding of Spatial Information." In P. Ellen and C. Blanc-Thinus, eds., *Cognitive Processing and Spatial Orientation in Animal and Man*. Dordrecht: Martinus Nijhoff.

Paillard, J. 1991a. "Les bases nerveuses du controle visuo-manuelle de l'ecriture." In C. Sirat, J. Irigoin, and E. Poulle, eds., *L'ecriture: le cerveau, l'oeil et la main*. Paris: Brepols.

Paillard, J. 1991b. "Motor and Representational Framing of Space." In J. Paillard, ed., *Brain and Space*. Oxford: Oxford University Press.

Paillard, J. 1991c. "Knowing Where and Knowing How to Get There." In J. Paillard, ed., *Brain and Space*. Oxford: Oxford University Press.

Paillard J., Michel, F., and Stelmach, G. 1983. "Localization without Content: A Tactile Analogue of 'Blind Sight'." *Archives of Neurology* 40:548–551.

Phillips, Charles. 1985. *Movements of the Hand*. Liverpool: Liverpool University Press.

Rothwell, J., Traub, M. M., Day, B. L., Obeso, J. A., Thomas, P. K., and Marsden, C. D. 1982. "Manual Motor Performance in a Deafferented Man." *Brain,* 105:505–542.

Sanes, J. N., Mauritz, K. H., Dalaka, M. C., and Evarts, E.V., 1985. "Motor Control in Humans with Large-Fibre Sensory Neuropathy." *Human Neurobiology* 4:101–114.

Sterman, A. B., Schaumberg, H. H., and Asbury, A. K. 1980. "The Acute Sensory Neuropathy Syndrome: A Distinct Clinical Entity." *Annals of Neurology* 7:354–358.

Sherrington, C. S. 1900. "Cutaneous Sensation." In E. A. Schafer, ed., *Textbook of Physiology*. Edinburgh and London: Pentland.

Teasdale, N., Forget, R., Bard, C., Paillard, J., Fleury, M., and Lamarre, Y. 1993. "The Role of Proprioceptive Information for the Production of Isometric Forces and for Handwriting Tasks." *Acta Psychologica* 82:179–191.

Bodily Awareness: A Sense of Ownership

M. G. F. Martin

When Descartes denies that he is lodged within his body as a pilot is within a ship, he draws our attention to the special phenomenological relation that each of us bears to his or her own body.[1] For we experience our bodies "from the inside" and not just as one more among the material objects of perception. In this paper I seek to give an account of this special phenomenological relation and the bearing it has on how each of us is related through perception to his or her own body.

I will assume a perceptual account of bodily sensations: the feelings of pain, pleasure, heat, cold and pressure. Rejecting a long tradition that assumes that bodily experiences are nonperceptual states immediately caused by action on the body, I will take having such experiences as being one of the ways in which a subject comes to be aware of events in her body or the state of various body parts. In the first part of the paper I will offer an account of the special phenomenology of the body that is consistent with such a perceptual account of sensation: when one feels a sensation, one thereby feels as if something is occurring within one's body.

In the second part of the paper I will argue for certain consequences of this account. If we take bodily sensation to be perceptual and to have the phenomenological character I suggest, it will turn out that the subject can be aware only of her own body and the parts of her body, and not of things that do not belong to her body at all, through such sensation.[2] The awareness one has of one's body through such experience is therefore distinct among the perceptual modes in providing a way in which one can come to be aware of only one object and its parts.

This feature of bodily awareness has led some philosophers to suppose that in being aware of one's body in this way, one is introspecting the self, albeit in a bodily mode. In the final section of this paper I argue against this assimilation of bodily awareness to self-awareness.

1   A Phenomenological Sense of Ownership

What is it to have a feeling of pain in your left ankle? One traditional view treats such bodily sensations as nonperceptual sensory experiences, in contrast to visual, tactual, and auditory experience. In vision one comes to be aware of how things are in the physical world around one. When you see a vase of roses on the table, you have a visual experience as of the presence of red flowers. We can talk of this visual experience as being correct or veridical, as opposed to illusory or incorrect, depending on whether there are such flowers in front of you. According to the traditional view of bodily sensations, such sensations can be neither veridical nor illusory, for they are "as of" nothing at all in the objective world. In contrast, when one has a feeling of pain, one is aware of some purely subjective state of affairs that obtains just in case one is having such a sensation and that in itself points to nothing outside of the inner mental realm to the physical world beyond.[3]

The traditional view flies in the face of the naive phenomenology of such experience. When you feel an ache in your left ankle, it is your ankle that feels a certain way, that aches. Now ankles are no less components of the physical world than are rocks, lions, tables, and chairs. So at least to first appearance, bodily sensation is no less concerned with aspects of the physical world—in this case one's body—than are the experiences associated with the traditional five senses.

This should lead us to question the traditional idea that sensations are special mental objects of awareness. Philosophers often take our talk of having an ache or feeling a pain as being a commitment to the existence of mental objects—aches and pains—of which we are aware when we feel pain. When one feels an ache in one's left ankle, one is certainly in a mental state, feeling a sensation, just as when one sees something, one is in a mental state, having a visual experience. In the latter case, the object of the visual experience is the physical object one is perceiving. In the former case, the object of a bodily sensation (understood as a state of mind), such as an ache in the ankle, is the body part that feels a certain way, e.g., that aches. The qualities that characterize the experience qualify the part of the body that one is aware of: it is one's ankle that hurts, not some inner mental object.

Some philosophers hold a perceptual theory of sensation because they wish to deny that there are any subjective qualities or qualia belonging to sensations, or to any sensory experience.[4] That is no part of what is assumed here. It may well be that we need to understand the quality that the experience attributes to the body part, the quality of hurting, say, in terms that make reference to subjective qualities of experience, just as Lockean theories of colors make reference to subjective qualities of vision.[5] All that is being claimed here is that the objects to which such qualities are attributed in experience appear to the subject to be body parts and not mere mental objects.[6]

In this paper I will simply assume and not argue for such a perceptual model of bodily sensation.[7] But consider one point in its favor: On such a view, we can easily explain Wittgenstein's observation that one does not feel a sensation simply to be in a particular location within objective space but rather feels it at a location that is primarily that of a body part and only secondarily the objective location of that part. If we think of the objects of such sensory states primarily as mental objects, this fact will seem mysterious— why should a mental object be tied to parts of one's physical body rather than regions in space? But if we think of the phenomenological character of sensation representationally, an unmysterious answer is forthcoming: the experience is as of a certain body part, as warm, for example, and feels to be occupying a certain spatial position relative to other body parts.

Can the perceptual account of bodily sensation accommodate Descartes's observation that there is a distinctive phenomenology of the body? If one perceives one's body through sensation, just as one perceives other objects through the five senses, does this not make one's body just another object among the many that one perceives? And if one's body merely appears to one in all experience as just one more object among the many that one perceives, then there would be no room for the intimate experience of the body that Descartes observed.[8]

To respond to this, we need to look more closely at the feature of sensation mentioned above. When I feel an ache in my ankle, the ankle that feels hurt to me does not just feel like an ankle belonging to some body or other. Rather, the ankle feels to me to be part of my body. This feeling is present even in the case of phantom-limb sensations. It is not as if it feels to the subject as if there is pain at some place in midair. Instead, it feels to her as if a part of her body is located at that place, even though the relevant body part no longer exists.[9] The perceptual account can offer the following explanation of the distinctive phenomenology of the body: in having bodily sensations, it appears to one as if whatever one is aware of through having such sensation is a part of one's body. This contrasts strikingly with the traditional five senses, which can present to one a manifold of objects, one's body being merely one among this manifold.

This phenomenological quality, that the body part appears to be part of one's body—call this *a sense of ownership*—is itself in need of further elucidation. It seems that if any of our bodily sensations include this phenomenological quality, then they all do—at least to the extent that such sensations have a location.[10] Compare Brian O'Shaughnessy's claim to find "it all but impossible to comprehend a claim concerning sensation position that detaches it from actual or seeming limb, e.g. 'A pain to the right of my shoulder and not even in a seeming body part'."[11] Now there appears to be a tension between the claim that sensations have this positive quality and O'Shaughnessy's claim that we can't conceive of how some might lack it. If the sense of ownership is a positive quality of sensation over and above the felt quality of sensation and the location—that there is hurt in an ankle, for example— then it should be conceivable that some sensations lack this extra quality while continuing to possess the other features. That is, we should be able to conceive of feeling pain in an ankle that does not positively appear to belong to one's own body. Just as we conceive of cold as the converse quality of warmth, could we not also conceive of a converse quality of ownership of sensation location such that one might feel pain in an ankle not positively felt to belong to one's own body? If O'Shaughnessy is right, we can make no sense of either possibility.[12] Since there is little difficulty in conceiving that one might have some way of perceiving the parts of others' bodies, the problem here concerns the qualitative sense of ownership that our sensations actually have. A fuller account needs to be given of this phenomenological characteristic.

An answer is indicated by the kind of example that makes the phenomenological feature itself most salient. As Thomas Reid noted, in tactual experience one can shift one's attention from the physical object being felt to the sensations one enjoys while touching it.[13] Reid took this as evidence for the presence of purely subjective sensation in all perception, albeit sensation not normally attended to. However, Reid's interpretation of the phenomenology does not seem to be the correct one. When one attends to the object felt, one is aware of various properties of the object— its surface texture, how solid it is, and its general shape—and one is aware of the object "out there." Shifting one's attention to one's sensations, one comes to be aware of one's bodily sensations elicited in this perception. Bodily sensations are themselves a form of perception, I claim, and not something purely subjective prior to genuine perception. So, in shifting one's attention, one is not moving from the external, physical world to introspective attention of the inner, mental world. Rather, one is shifting one's attention from objects that lie outside one of one's boundaries, the surface of a hand, to what is going on at or beneath that bodily boundary. This invites the following conjecture: for me to feel as if some part of my body occupies a region of space through having bodily sensation is for it to seem to me as if that region falls within one of the boundaries of my body.

This does not yet answer the initial worry. If "falling within one of one's boundaries" is a positive quality of a sensation over and above the qualities and location of sensation, then it should be conceivable that a sensation should lack this feature, and also conceivable that sensations could have the opposing feature of "falling outside of one's boundaries." This is answered by recognizing that the quality of falling within one of one's apparent boundaries is not independent of the felt location of sensation. The sense one has of the location of sensation brings with it the sense that the location in question falls within one of one's apparent boundaries.

This requires us to look to the structure of the spatial content of bodily sensation. Consider first the spatial content of kinesthetic experiences, another example of awareness of one's body. If you raise your hands above your head, you will be aware of the position of both hands in space relative to each other. This awareness of their relative positions is an awareness of how they are displaced across a region of space beyond the space in which your body is located and in which you have neither kinesthetic nor sensational awareness. In this case, to give an adequate account of the spatial content of kinesthesia, we have to make reference to regions of space of which the subject is not currently in a position to have bodily experience. More generally, in having a sense of the shape of your body through kinesthetic awareness, you will be aware of its shape as in a space that extends beyond the limits of your body and encloses it. So the locations where one's hands feel to be are felt to be locations within a space that extends beyond the space one is then aware of. In turn, the sense of falling within a boundary may be no more than the sense that the location in question is within a space that seems to extend into regions that one could not currently be aware of in this way. Any region in which it seems to one that one could now be feeling sensation will thereby feel to one to fall within one of one's boundaries; at the same time, one has the sense that there are locations outside of one's boundaries, whatever these happen to be, since the space one feels these locations to be part of feels as if it extends beyond whatever one does feel.

One may picture this sense of boundedness in the following way. There is no distinction to be drawn between the point from which one is aware of objects and the objects of which one is aware that then stand in some relation to that point. Rather, such awareness seems to extend only to the apparent limits of the body, to each of the body's apparent boundaries. One has a sense that there are such boundaries—a sense one would have even if one was not aware where the boundary was—in virtue of the way in which parts of bodies appear to be located in a space that extends to regions one does not feel in this way. The modal contrast here, between regions where one could currently feel sensation and those where one couldn't, is to be drawn within the content of the bodily experiences themselves. The spatial content of these experiences is such that one is aware of a region as one in which one is aware of things in this manner, in contrast to other regions of space.

While these regions of space will not be occupied by anything that can be felt through bodily awareness, this is not to say that the objects there located are not accessible by any sense experience. They might be, of course, by vision. More interestingly, the objects of touch occupy a space that lies outside the limits of bodily awareness. On a "template" model of touch, it is no accident that tactual perception and bodily sensation coincide, for the two are interdependent: one comes to be aware of the objects of touch through being aware of the properties of one's body and how the two interact. The most basic form of this is the sharing of spatial properties when boundaries of an object and one's body coincide.[14]

Two qualifications need to be added. First, while the simplest such model of a sense of one's body would assume that one's body has one complete boundary within which only parts of one's body are located, no such assumption need be made. We have boundaries falling within other boundaries, and many of our boundaries are not closed. In one sense, an object pressing against the sides of one's esophagus falls within one's boundaries—the place where the object is located falls within the limits of one's skin. At the same time, a fish bone pressing against the walls of the esophagus is felt to be pressing against one of one's boundaries, as lying outside of the boundary of the esophagus walls. Corresponding to the fish bone, one feels sensation at and beneath those walls that feel to lie within one of one's boundaries. A more exact account of the distinction between being felt to be inside or outside is to say that when a tactual object is in contact with one of one's boundaries, one thereby has not only tactual awareness of the object but also bodily sensation at that surface. The bodily sensation has the character of being within one of one's boundaries, and hence the feeling of being internal. The tactual object is thereby felt to be beyond that particular bodily boundary, and hence to be outside of the body. While the location where the fish bone is felt is in fact a location within the body, and a location that falls within what are felt to be the outer boundaries of the body, one's skin, it is not positively felt to fall within those boundaries, and hence is not thereby felt to fall within one's body.

Second, I have offered no account of what it is for the location of a sensation to fall within a reidentifiable or nameable body part, as when the location of a pain is in one's left hand, rather than just in some body part or other at a given position. The fact that locations of sensation are often in nameable parts requires a further complication of the account. It surely seems sufficient that a sensation should feel to be located within the body if it feels to be located within a nameable body part. But this addition does not really alter the main claim. For one can ask what it is for a felt body part to feel as if it is part of one's body. For this too there is the analogous problem that there seems to be no case of feeling a body part to belong to someone else's body. The same form of answer can be applied in this case: that a body part feels to belong to one's body is not independent of the fact that one feels it to be a specific body part. A contrast will remain between parts of my body and other objects in the world if the part is felt to be located within a space that could contain other objects.

This account of the sense of ownership explains how our bodily experiences can have as part of their phenomenological content that the region felt falls within one's body. Furthermore, it explains how all bodily sensation of a determinate location will possess this quality.[15] The mysterious necessity of sensation falling within the apparent body is easily explained: it simply derives from the spatial content that sensations have. Given that bodily sensation has this content, all spatially located sensations will feel as if they fall within the body. This is not to claim that there could not be other ways in which bodily sensation could have been, nor that there could not have been other kinds of phenomenological features that indicate what is within the body. The account here thus starts from the evident but contingent fact that our bodily sensations have a certain character. The account explains what it is for our sensations to have the character they do, and hence explains the Cartesian phenomenological observation that we are aware of our bodies "from the inside."[16]

2 The Sole Object of Awareness

In the last section I claimed that part of the phenomenological character of sensations is that one feels events as occurring not only within body parts, but also within body parts that belong to one's own body, and I argued that we can make sense of this claim in terms of the structure of the spatial content of sensation. I now want to turn to the bearing this has on the question of what objects one can come to be aware of through sensation. Bodily sensations, together with kinesthesia, proprioception, and the vestibular sense, amount to an awareness of one's body that is only of one's own body and its parts. Call this the *sole-object view*.[17]

The sole-object view is not the only account of bodily awareness. I have already noted that there is a long tradition in philosophy of denying that sensation is perceptual awareness of one's body. Even if one grants that sensation does give one an awareness of body parts, one might claim that it is a merely contingent matter that one comes to be aware only of one's own body parts in this way and that it is quite conceivable that one could come to be aware of parts of others' bodies in the same way. Call this the *multiple-object view.* I call this view thus not because it need claim that we are actually aware of more than our own bodies through sensation and kinesthesia but because it claims that it is consistent with the form of awareness we have that more than one body could be presented to a perceiver in this way. Just because everything one feels is felt to be part of one's body, this doesn't yet show that everything one feels must be a part of one's body. So the observations of the last section do not appear to decide between the two views. Here I will argue that on examination those observations do in fact support the sole-object view.

Wittgenstein seems to have been a proponent of the multiple-object view. He thought it quite conceivable that one should feel pain in someone else's tooth, in a piece of furniture, or in empty space.[18] However, it is doubtful that Wittgenstein rejects the traditional view of sensation as purely subjective. For example, according to him, the location of sensation in one's hand amounts to no more than one's being disposed to point to that place and say that the ache is located there. And when we draw out the consequences of a perceptual account of sensation, it turns out that Wittgenstein's own examples are best described in terms of the sole-object view.

Wittgenstein rightly claims that one can easily conceive of a case in which it feels to one as if there is pain in one's left hand and one indicates one's neighbor's hand when asked where it hurts. When we assume that one's neighbor's hand is not also a part of one's own body, the sole-object view must count this as a case of illusion or hallucination. The perceptual account of sensation already gives us reason to endorse this description of the case. Consider again phantom-limb sensation. When an amputee feels a pain three inches below her knee, that location may well fall outside the actual limits of her body. Prima facie, this is a case of being aware of a point outside of one's actual body, even though for the sufferer, it is still a case of being aware of a location as falling within the apparent limits of her body. However, anyone who wishes to adopt a perceptual view of bodily sensation—even if they reject the sole-object thesis—has reason to reject this description of phantom-limb sensation. In having a pain, a sufferer is aware of a part of some body as being some way.[19] In the case of referred pain, the experience is illusory to the extent that it feels to the sufferer as if one part of her body is hurt when in fact another part is. In a phantom-limb sensation, the sufferer feels as if a part of her body is hurt that in fact no longer exists. This is akin to cases of perceptual hallucination, as when someone suffering delirium tremens "sees" a pink rat. In this case we should not say that this person is aware of some object, for there is nothing there. Rather, she is having a visual experience as of a pink rat but is not perceiving anything. So in the phantom-limb example, for the sufferer, it is as if a part of her left leg is damaged but in fact no such part exists, and she is aware of nothing at all but is merely having a hallucination.

Likewise, the Wittgenstein example involves an element of illusion and can be explained without supposing that the subject is positively aware of his neighbor's hand. From the description that Wittgenstein offers, it is at least as natural to suppose that the subject is aware of a hand—not his neighbor's but rather his own left hand. The illusory element in the experience is simply that it feels to him as if his hand is at a location where his hand happens not to be, although coincidentally his neighbor's hand is. The case is one in which the sensation does appear to be located in a part of the subject's own body, and we have been given no reason to suppose that he is wrong about this fact rather than about the location of the body part.

The sole-object view need not claim that the apparent locations of pain and other bodily qualities must be restricted to the actual bounds of one's body. There are plenty of actual counterexamples to this thesis without having to consider the fiction Wittgenstein presents us with. The claim is merely that such experiences can only be genuinely perceptual and count as the awareness of some body part, rather than as a case of illusion or hallucination, if the body part in question is actually part of one's own body. Once we take bodily sensation to be a form of perception, we can see that Wittgenstein's fiction concerns an illusory or hallucinatory experience, and hence offers no challenge to the sole-object view.

However, Wittgenstein's story can be supplemented so as to present more of a challenge. We might suppose that the neighbor's hand has a radiotransmitter attached that is sensitive to activity in nerves associated with pain, pressure, and movement. The sufferer, in turn, has an attached receiver that stimulates him so as to have a corresponding painful sensation when any damage occurs in his neighbor's hand. To avoid any trace of illusion, we must suppose that this new area of pain does not feel to the sufferer as if it is within his own left hand. Rather, it must feel as if it is in some new part of his body, as if he had grown a new hand. We may suppose that the sufferer is able to report both the location and the status of the neighbor's hand in virtue of the sensations produced by the transmitter-receiver when the neighbor is nearby.

Now, it may be argued that the transmitter-receiver acts as a form of prosthetic nervous system: imagine someone having parts of his internal nervous system replaced by such an electronic device; the current fiction merely asks us to extend this to someone else's body. The transmitter is to be thought of as extending the range of bodily sensation in the manner that spectacles and binoculars do for vision. The sensation is no longer fortuitously associated with the other body, and hence is no longer so obviously to be treated as a case of illusion.

This gives the multiple-object account a stronger case. How should one respond? As with the earlier example, it is open to the sole-object view to redescribe the situation as one of illusion: rather than treat the transmitter as a prosthetic extension of the nervous system, this view will claim that it is nothing more than a sophisticated mechanism for causing pains in two people instead of one. Although the damage to the neighbor's hand is a cause of the subject's sensation, the view will deny that it thereby comes to be an object of perception. This claim is coherent—many things can cause sensory experience without thereby being the objects of those experiences: the alcoholic does not see the alcohol earlier imbibed when he has a hallucination of a pink rat caused by that drink—but the claim that the sensation is purely illusory does not follow from the thesis that bodily sensations are perceptions. So why should the sole-object view be justified in insisting on this redescription?

We need to examine more closely the model of perception that underlies the plausibility of this apparent counterexample and any justification the sole-object view can provide for rejecting this model in the case of bodily awareness. The existence of a reliable causal link that can support the transmission of information often seems to be a prerequisite for genuine perception. In the example, just such a link is established between body parts and the subject's experience of them. This undermines at least one explanation of why we should treat the case as an illusion, as the sole-object view dictates. But for the example finally to convince, the materials it supplies must be sufficient for perception, and this involves two assumptions: that in the case of bodily awareness the objects of perception are body-parts and that the kind of causal and informational link set up in the example is sufficient to establish a perceptual link between that object and the subject's experience of it.

This mirrors a certain view of visual perception. One might think that the role of light in vision is to act as a causal route for the transmission of information about the objects of perception to the perceiver, who then has visual experiences of those objects. Which objects one can come to see would then be limited by the distance over which light can still reliably transmit information from objects to us, which turns mainly on the degree of resolution that our eyes can achieve. The latter is a contingent matter, and certain prosthetic devices can be employed to extend the range of one's eyes: we do not tend to think that the use of spectacles, or even the use of binoculars or telescopes, prevents us from genuinely seeing objects through them. In the case of bodily awareness, one's nervous system plays an analogous role to the medium of light. It is a contingent matter that one's nervous system stops at the skin, and we can imagine this contingent limitation being overcome by such prosthetic devices as the radio transmitter.

The sole-object view needs to reject this picture of bodily awareness. It must deny that the existence of a causal/informational link between body parts and perceiver suffices for her perception of those parts. For it claims that a necessary condition for perceiving a body part will be that the part in question is part of the subject's body. On this view, the primary object of bodily awareness is one's body as a whole, so one perceives its parts only because they are parts of that object. Given this, no matter how sophisticated and reliable the transmitting link is between body part and the subject's bodily sensation, the sensation will not count as perception of that body part if it does not belong to her body but will rather be illusory or hallucinatory.

Why prefer one picture over the other? This is where the sole-object view can appeal to the phenomenological characteristics of bodily sensation, discussed above. On the opposing view, perception of the body is a matter of perceiving those body parts with which one has an informational link. That the body parts belong to one body is determined separately from whether the body parts are perceived. Located sensations have the phenomenological feature that the place that one feels to be hurt feels to one to fall within the bounds of one's body. I argued that this sense of ownership, in being possessed by all located sensations, cannot be independent of the spatial content of the sensation, the location of the event. In the alleged counterexample, when the subject feels pain in virtue of damage to the neighbor's hand, it feels to the subject as if the body part belongs to her body, even though it does not. In this respect, bodily experiences of parts of other people's bodies will be illusory.

This gives rise to a further problem. While the sense of ownership is veridical in the usual case, since one happens to feel sensations only within body parts that belong to one's own body, it is a mere accident that this is so: all located sensations possess this feature regardless of whether the locations in question do fall within the subject's body. So there is no reliable mechanism that associates the phenomenological feature, the sense of ownership, with any objective facts concerning actual ownership of the body part. Although phenomenologically it appears to the sufferer as if the body part has a certain property, that of being a part of his body, there is no perceptual connection between the body part seeming so and its actually being so, since perceiving something to have a property depends on there being a reliable link.

There is no problem here for the sole-object view. According to this view, bodily awareness is primarily awareness of one's physical body, and awareness of body parts only in as much as they are parts of that body. Consequently, for any bodily sensation that is genuinely perceptual, the body part in question will be a part of one's body, as it appears to be. Since it is in the nature of bodily experience to be experience of one's body, there need be no further mechanism to track which body it is to which a body part belongs. This is just a corollary of a point made in the last section: that we should think of apparent ownership not as being a quality additional to the other qualities of experience but as somehow already inherent within them.

So the sole-object view can justify its description of the apparent counterexample by appeal to general considerations about what it is for sensations to be perceptions of the body. On the opposing multiple-object view, the phenomenological feature of the experience that the body part appears to belong to the subject's body cannot be a genuinely perceived feature of a body part. In contrast, the sole-object view can respect the appearance that this is a genuinely perceived property of the body part. When we acknowledge the distinctive phenomenology that we are aware of events within the body "from the inside," we are led to the conclusion that if this is a form of perceptual awareness, it is awareness of one object only. This is not to claim that it is impossible to feel sensations to be located in regions that fall outside of the actual limits of the body, but it is to deny that such experiences can then amount to genuine perceptual awareness of whatever is located in those places.

3   Bodily Awareness and Self-Awareness

In the last two sections I have claimed first that, with respect to the phenomenological content of bodily sensation and kinesthesia, body parts are presented as belonging to the perceiver's body and second that a subject, in having such experiences, comes to perceive only one object, his or her body. The apparent counterexamples were explained away as cases of illusion or hallucination, where the subject either misperceives the location of a body part of which she is aware or hallucinates a nonexistent body part. These properties of bodily awareness are reminiscent of features that have sometimes been attributed to self-awareness or introspection (see Frege's comment that "everyone is presented to himself in a special and primitive way, in which he is presented to no-one else").[20]

Hume famously denied that any of us is acquainted with his or her self. Some philosophers following him in this have justified the claim through repudiating a perceptual account of introspection. The principal objection here turns on the thought that were introspection a form of perception, then necessarily it would take only one object, one's self. But, it is sometimes claimed, one can only have genuine perception of objects where one perceives one object among many. If this is true, then either introspection is not the perception of an object, or it is not perception. A correlative objection is that perception could only be of one object, as introspection would have to be, only if the mechanism of perception were in some way magical. Any such arguments against treating introspection as a form of perception would apply equally well against treating bodily awareness as a form of perception that takes one's body as its sole object. I need to defend both the claim that perception can be of something as an object, even when only one object is given, and the claim that perception can latch onto just that one object without requiring a magical mechanism.

We can find the first line of objection to taking introspection to be a form of perception in the work of Sydney Shoemaker. He suggests that "a mode of perception must be such that someone's perceiving something in that way can enter into the explanation of how it is that the person has knowledge of that thing, where part of the explanation is that perceiving the thing provides the person with identification information about it."[21] Shoemaker claims that introspection cannot meet this condition, since no manifold of objects is presented, and hence introspection is not perception. If this objection is a good one, it tells not only against a perceptual account of introspection, but also against any perceptual account of bodily awareness that acknowledges the phenomenological sense of ownership and the sole-object view.[22] My discussion already provides us with sufficient resources to rebut this worry.

For vision, we can distinguish the subject's point of view on the objects of perception from the locations of the various objects of perception, all of which will be perceived to stand in various spatial relations to that origin, as well as to each other. Any visual object of perception will be presented as an object in as much as it is presented as occupying a space adjacent to other objects, all of which are on a par. The structure of the spatial content of bodily awareness is different. There is no distinct point of view that the subject possesses independent of the object, his or her body, that she is aware of in this way.[23] But it does not follow from this that the body cannot be presented in bodily experience as a genuine object. Recall that the subject's body parts are presented as located within a space not all of which the subject can be aware of at the time. It is through this that the subject has a sense of her own boundedness, and hence a sense of herself as a spatial object within a larger world. Although the subject does not have to single out or identify her body as one object among the many presented to her in experience, she does nevertheless have a sense of it as just one object, among the many that there may be within that space.

This leads to the second objection. What singles out just one object, among all those in the world that one could be perceiving, as the sole-object of this kind of awareness? Doesn't this require some kind of magical mechanism?[24]

As with the first claim, we musn't be misled by what is true of other sense modalities. In vision, a distinction needs to be drawn between the ability to perceive an object and the ability to single it out from among the others perceived, or to keep track of it, since a multiplicity of objects may be presented to the perceiver at a time. If one construes bodily awareness as a single-object modality along the same lines, it may seem as if both features—that of presenting an object and that of tracking an object—have to be combined. But in the case of visual attention, it is clear that tracking can break down: the object picked out at one point may be mislaid at the next, and another mistaken for it. This may make it seem that any perceptual ability that involves tracking an object might break down in this way. Hence, the existence of a perceptual ability that cannot so break down is liable to appear magical. But it is simply wrong to think of the way in which one object is singled out in bodily awareness in these terms. That bodily awareness suceeds in latching onto one object results not so much from a superability to track one object as the inability to experience more than one object, or the parts of more than one object, in this way. That the body, in addition to its parts, is experienced through bodily awareness is simply a function of the spatial content of such experience. But no more than one object could be presented in this way.[25]

Nevertheless, the question remains of what makes one particular object the object of bodily awareness. The structure of such experience is that if any object is picked out, there will be just one such object. But this does not yet say which object is picked out in this way. In the argument of the last section I implicitly assumed that the object one perceives through bodily sensation is one's own body and that body parts appear to one to belong to that body. But this claim does not follow from any of the claims made in my earlier discussion of the phenomenology of bodily experience. Undoubtedly, it is natural to assume that if there is a sole-object of bodily experience, the best candidate as the object of perception is one's own body. But there are other candidates: Consider the entity consisting of a subject's physical body minus those parts of her body in which she has lost the power of movement and sensation. Conversely, take the candidate to be the subject's physical body plus any prosthetic limbs and devices over which he has immediate, and not merely instrumentally mediated, control. A further entity is the sum of the body parts causally responsible for the sensations that the subject has at a time. This would include the neighbor's hand and any other body part that the subject might also appear to feel. This is importantly different from the other candidates. For the others, one can specify each part of that object without first determining whether the subject feels any sensation in that part. In the last case, whether or not a body part belongs to the entity in question is determined solely by whether the subject has a sensation for which the body part is responsible. For this entity, sensation apparently in a body part makes the body part part of the entity rather than being a way of perceiving that part as belonging to the entity.

While one might rule out certain candidates by denying them the status of being genuine "natural" objects of the sort that may count as the primary objects of perception, this would not answer the problems raised by the last candidate. For in this case we need not read the challenge as claiming that the candidate entity is perceived through bodily sensation, since the entity is constituted by one's having sensation in its parts, rather than by existing independently of perception and then being alighted on. The challenge is rather to show that this sense of ownership reflects facts about a genuine object in the world, rather than a mere phenomenal construction: an entity whose existence depends solely on one's experience of it, having no independent place in the natural world.

To meet this challenge, we have to give some reason for supposing that some object, given independently of our awareness of it, is the object that bodily experience is about and that bodily experience is about some such entity. One answer is to look for a function of bodily awareness and then to show that this function determines which object is the object perceived. For instance, following a suggestion by Brian O'Shaughnessy, one might claim that conscious bodily awareness plays a central role in controlling and determining intentional action.[26] Given this, the object of bodily awareness would need to be the object with which one most immediately acts. This object, it may be argued, is one's physical body. Since the question of whether one can act with an object or not is fixed independently of whether one has sensation in the object, the awareness in question can be counted as genuinely perceptual, and we have a criterion for deeming the feeling of pain in a neighbor's hand to be illusory.

However, it is not yet clear whether this line of reasoning will succeed. One question about it is whether a clear function can be ascribed to any form of conscious experience. And in the particular case of action control, there is a genuine question of whether successful action requires continuous monitoring of the body. So the explanation above might actually turn out to be a hostage to fortune, depending on the correct empirical account of visuomotor control.[27] An alternative would be to avoid looking for a direct functional role for conscious experience itself and instead look at the explanations of what underlies the content that such experience has. Even if conscious experience of the body is not involved in the coordination of all action, there is reason to think that there are unconscious representations of the body, body schemata, to control at least some action.[28] Furthermore, it is plausible to suppose that such representation is drawn on in determining the content of conscious kinesthesia and hence bodily sensation. One might think of such unconscious representations (themselves posited at a subpersonal level of processing) as in part determining the extent of the object with which an agent can immediately act, since their function is to control this object. This in turn may be taken to be the object of current conscious awareness through kinesthesia and sensation, and its limits will then determine whether such awareness is illusory or veridical.

Note that both of these justifications leave open whether the object of awareness is itself identical with the subject's physical body. In either case one might suppose that permanent loss of use of a body part might lead to its separation from the object with which an agent immediately acts, and hence exclude that body part from genuine awareness. Correspondingly, familiarity with an artificial limb may lead to its inclusion the elements with which a subject can immediately act, and hence include it as something in which the subject can have genuine awareness.[29]

There is no space here to develop either proposal. For my purposes, the important point is just to note that such an account is required to underwrite the claim that bodily awareness is genuine awareness of one's body, and also to indicate that there is no particular reason to suppose that some such account cannot be given. However, the fact that such an account does need to be given points to a significant disanalogy between bodily awareness and introspection, at least as it has commonly been conceived by philosophers.

While it is plausible to suppose that the object of bodily awareness might coincide with various psychological conceptions of the concept of self, such as the Gibsonian notion of the ecological self,[30] among philosophers, self-consciousness and the concept of the first-person, or self, have had a more restricted range of application. Two conditions are often imposed: First, a guaranteed reference. When the subject thinks about herself in the first person, she must be guaranteed to be referring to herself—a tie between the agent of thought and the object thought about. Second, since the guarantee seems to be part of the concept of the first person, when the subject employs the first person concept, it is a priori that she will be thinking about herself.

If self-consciousness is tied to this concept of self, then a given mental episode—thought or experience—will be an exercise of self-consciousness only where the object of that episode is guaranteed to be the self and where the object is presented to the subject as herself. Otherwise, in having this thought or experience, the subject should be able to wonder whether this object of which she is thinking or having an experience is genuinely herself. So a perceptual account of introspection would need not only to explain how only one object can be experienced by the subject in this way but also to show how the object being so experienced by the subject must be experienced by the subject as herself.

It is implausible to claim that this condition is met in the case of bodily awareness, even if it could be met elsewhere. If the arguments of this paper are correct, we should conceive of bodily awareness as a form of perception of a single object. If a thinker thinks about whatever she is aware of through bodily awareness, she is guaranteed to be thinking solely of one object. However, which object bodily awareness presents is not determined solely by phenomenological considerations. Rather, some account needs to be given of what ties the content of bodily awareness to a particular object. This further account does not seem to be one that we can provide purely a priori.

A Cartesian dualist is, of course, unlikely to accept that bodily awareness is a form of introspection, for he will insist that body and self are distinct entities, and hence that awareness of the body is not awareness of the self. But one might reason that showing that bodily awareness is a form of introspection would then form an argument against Cartesian dualism. My concerns here are pressing even if we grant that we are material, living animals and not immaterial egos.

It is not unnatural to describe the sense of ownership associated with body parts as the sense of being aware that the left hand one feels is one's own left hand, that it belongs to oneself. In being aware of one's body, one will be aware of its parts as parts of oneself. It is this thought that an introspective model of bodily awareness will stress. In the account offered here, body parts appear to belong to a particular body, one's own body. There is no need to cash out the claim that the body is one's own by supposing that bodily awareness also involves some further exercise of introspection. For there is no other object presented to one in the way that one's body and its parts are presented, so one's body can be picked out simply as that object so presented when attending to it through bodily awareness.

Now if we are not Cartesians, there is little inclination to distinguish between this object and oneself. But to grant this is not yet to grant that the object in question is presented as oneself, or that its parts are presented as belonging to oneself. It is this further claim that we should reject. As we have seen, a substantive account needs to be given of which object is the object of bodily awareness, an account that turns either on the function of such awareness or possibly on the unconscious representations (together with their function) that such awareness depends on. On such an account, it seems possible that the object in question may turn out to be distinct from what is strictly one's physical body, for two objects can be identical only if they share all and only the same parts. If the primary object of perception is the object with which one most immediately acts rather than one's physical body, then it is arguable that this entity may include artificial limbs and other prosthetic devices if these elements themselves come to be represented within the body schema. In such a case the physical organism and the immediate object of agency will be distinct, since the latter includes parts that the former doesn't. Inasmuch as a body part feels like it belongs to the body that one is aware of through bodily sensation, it will feel like it belongs to the object of agency rather than to one's physical body. So if one is identical with one's physical body, one will still not be aware of it through bodily sensation but rather will be aware only of the object of agency. Of course, the claim that the physical body and the object of agency can come apart is itself speculative. But for the point being made, no more than speculation is required. If it is at least open to the subject to wonder whether the object that she is presented in bodily sensation is not herself but rather only an object closely associated with herself, then that object cannot be presented to her as being the self, and hence bodily awareness cannot be a form of introspection.

One might reply that it is no less an issue which object the self is to be identified with. Perhaps the self should be identified not strictly with the physical organism but rather with the immediate object of agency. Then the prosthetic limb would be no less a part of the self than would her flesh and blood. In this case the debate about the object of bodily awareness and the debate about which object the self is would coincide, which would leave bodily awareness as a form of being aware of the self. But even this would not be enough to meet the conditions needed to show that bodily awareness is self-awareness. Rather, what one needs to establish is that they coincide a priori. Only then would it turn out to be a confusion to wonder whether the object of bodily awareness is oneself rather than an issue to be settled by empirical study. This might follow if our concept of the self was so grounded in bodily awareness that it made no sense to wonder whether the object present in bodily awareness, whatever it might be, must be oneself. But there seems to be no reason to endorse this claim.

To deny that bodily awareness is self-awareness is not to dispute that there is a close connection between the sense we have of our own bodies and the concept we have of ourselves and that the connection warrants more extended discussion. But what I hope I have shown is that bodily awareness is sufficiently worthy of discussion in itself and its character sufficiently distinctive without having to assimilate it to introspection.

Acknowledgments

Various forms of this paper were presented at talks in London, Oxford, and Sussex, and I thank the audiences for comments. Bill Brewer, Malcolm Budd, Tim Crane, Marcus Giaquinto, Lucy O'Brien, David Owens, and Jo Wolff and the editors of this volume all made very helpful suggestions in addition.

Notes

1. Meditation 6, in *The Philosophical Writings of René Descartes,* vol. 2, trans. R. Cottingham, R. Stoothoff, and D. Murdoch (Cambridge: Cambridge University Press, 1984), p. 56.

2. However, where people share bodies, as do Siamese twins, each may be aware of those parts of the other's body that are also parts of their own.

3. For a recent expression of this view, see Colin McGinn, *The Character of Mind* (Oxford: Oxford University Press, 1982), p. 8.

4. See, for example, David Armstrong, *Bodily Sensations* (London: Routledge and Kegan Paul, 1962).

5. See Peacocke's discussion of 'hurt' in "Consciousness and Other Minds," *Aristotelian Society Proceedings,* suppl. vol. 59 (1985): 97–117, and Ayers discussion of pain as a secondary quality in *Locke* (London: Routledge, 1991), vol. 1, pp. 214–216.

6. However, I don't wish to take issue with claims made by P. Wall in "Pain and Placebo Response," *Experimental and Theoretical Studies of Consciousness* (Chichester: John Wiley and Son, 1993), pp. 187–211. He contrasts pain, and bodily sensation in general, with external perception, through being more susceptible to psychological influence and not always requiring peripheral stimuli to determine location of experience. These considerations do not support readopting a subjective account of sensation, being more a matter of degree than kind.

7. For additional comments, see my "Sense Modalities and Spatial Perception," in *Spatial Representation*, edited by N. Eilan, R. McCarthy, and B. Brewer (Oxford: Basil Blackwell, 1993), pp. 206–218, esp. pp. 207–209.

8. However, one who appears to deny that it can, while rejecting the traditional subjectivist view of sensation, is Merleau-Ponty. See *The Phenomenology of Perception*, trans. C. Smith (London: Routledge, 1962).

9. See J. Van Deusen, *Body Image and Perceptual Dysfunction in Adults* (Philadelphia: W. B. Saunders and Co., 1993), chap. 7, for a recent introductory discussion of this phantom limbs and treatment of patients.

10. Not all bodily sensations need possess a felt location. No claims that I make here concerning the sense of ownership should be thought to apply to sensations that lack a felt location.

11. *The Will* (Cambridge: Cambridge University Press, 1980), vol. 1, p. 162.

12. There appear to be empirical counterexamples. See, for example, G. von Békésy's example of extrasomatic sensation in *Sensory Inhibition* (Princeton: Princeton University Press, 1967), pp. 220–226, and M. F. Shapiro et al., "Exosomesthesia, or Displacement of Cutaneous Sensation into Extrapersonal Space," *AMA Archives of Neurology and Psychiatry* 68 (1952): 481–490. Close examination of both cases suggests that it is far from clear that this is so, but proper discussion of these must here be postponed.

13. See his *Inquiry*, chap. 5, in *Inquiry and Essays* (Indianapolis: Hackett, 1983).

14. I discuss this view of touch in more detail in "Sight and Touch," in *The Contents of Experience*, edited by T. M. Crane (Cambridge: Cambridge University Press, 1992), pp. 196–215. A seminal discussion of this view of tactual perception is given in Brian O'Shaughnessy, "The Sense of Touch," *Australasian Journal of Philosophy*, 67 (1989): 37–58.

15. This does not, of course, apply to the case of unlocated sensations.

16. However, it is no part of the claim here that there are no other qualities of sensations that may correspond to what is felt to appear to belong to me or my body. My claim is only that the sense of ownership, as here outlined, is at least present in all such sensation and is more fundamental to explaining the phenomenology of bodily experience than any other such quality.

17. This view has been adopted by Gareth Evans (see *The Varieties of Reference* [Oxford: Oxford University Press, 1982], chap. 7) and in a slightly different form by Michael Ayers (*Locke* [London: Routledge, 1991] vol. 1, pp. 180–192; vol. 2, pp. 285–288).

18. See L. Wittgenstein, *The Blue Book*, in *The Blue and Brown Books*, 2nd ed. (Oxford: Basil Blackwell, 1969), pp. 49–51.

19. Whether a pain experience represents a body part as disordered by representing it as hurt or whether we must conceive of hurt and disorder as distinctly perceived properties is a nice question. For a discussion that bears on this, see Ayers, *Locke*, and Peacocke, "Consciousness and Other Minds."

20. Frege, "Thoughts," in *Logical Investigations* (Oxford: Basil Blackwell, 1977), p. 12. Frege's claim concerning the first person is stronger than my claim concerning bodily awareness. The claim that I am aware of my body in a way in which I am aware of no

other object does not rule out the possibility that another may be aware of my body in the same way, if, for example, two people could share one body.

21. "Introspection and the Self," in *Studies in the Philosophy of Mind*, ed. Peter A. French, Theodore Edward Uehling, and Howard K. Wettstein, Midwest Studies in Philosophy, no. 10 (Minneapolis: University of Minnesota Press, 1986), pp. 101–120, at pp. 116–117.

22. Shoemaker himself does not present his objection as a decisive one, relying instead on the claim that since perceptual acquaintance with the self can't explain all cases of self-awareness, the appeal to such acquaintance is superfluous to the explanation of our possession of self-consciousness.

23. Dominic Murphy pointed out to me that this is reflected in our abilities to imagine situations experientially. When we visualize, we need not place ourselves within a situation (one can be a "fly on the wall"), but in kinesthetic imagining, there is no room to distinguish between the point of view imagined and the object so imagined.

24. Compare some of G. E. M. Anscombe's criticisms of the view that one is presented with a self, in "The First Person," in *Metaphysics and the Philosophy of Mind* (Oxford: Basil Blackwell, 1981), pp. 21–36, especially the comments on p. 31.

25. This account does not rule out the possibility that different bodies could be presented at different times, as long as only one is present at a time. Some might claim that this would point to a disanalogy with self-awareness, since self-awareness may be held to require awareness of oneself over time. My arguments here will not trade on any such alleged difference.

26. *The Will*, 2 vols. (Cambridge: Cambridge University Press, 1980), and "Proprioception and the Body Image," in this volume.

27. For some of the philosophical implications of empirical studies in this area, see Bill Brewer, "The Integration of Spatial Vision and Action," in *Spatial Representation*, edited by N. Eilan, R. McCarthy, and B. Brewer (Oxford: Basil Blackwell, 1993), pp. 294–316.

28. The notion of body schemata originates with Head (see Studies in Neurology, vol. 2 [Oxford: Oxford University Press, 1920]). For recent discussions of the role of representation of the body in motor control, see, for example, the two contributions by Jacques Paillard and by V. S. Gurfinkel and Y. S. Levick in *Body and Space*, edited by J. Paillard (Oxford: Oxford University Press, 1991).

29. So it is consistent with this view that the object of bodily awareness might consist of discrete parts that are distinct "natural" objects in their own right.

30. J. J. Gibson, *The Ecological Approach to Visual Perception* (Boston: Houghton Mifflin, 1979). For a discussion of the different conceptions of the self employed in psychology, see U. Neisser, "The Self Perceived," in *The Perceived Self: Ecological and Interpersonal Sources of Self-Knowledge*, edited by U. Neisser (Cambridge: Cambridge University Press, 1993).

Bibliography

Anscombe, G. E. M. 1981. "The First Person." In her *Metaphysics and the Philosophy of Mind*. Oxford: Basil Blackwell.

Armstrong, D. A. 1962. *Bodily Sensations*. London: Routledge and Kegan Paul.

Ayers, M. 1991. *Locke*, 2 vols. London: Routledge.

Brewer, B. 1992. "Self-Location and Agency." *Mind*. 101:17–34

Brewer, B. 1993. "The Integration of Spatial Vision and Action." In *Spatial Representation*, ed. N. Eilan, R. McCarthy, and B. Brewer. Oxford: Basil Blackwell.

Descartes, R. 1984. *The Philosophical Writings*, vol. 2. Trans. R. Cottingham, R. Stoothoff, and D. Murdoch. Cambridge: Cambridge University Press.

Dretske, F. 1981. *Knowledge and the Flow of Information*. Oxford: Blackwell.

Evans, G. 1982. *The Varieties of Reference*. Oxford: Oxford University Press.

Frege, G. 1977. "Thoughts." In his *Logical Investigations* Oxford: Basil Blackwell.

Gibson, J. J. 1979. *The Ecological Approach to Visual Perception*. Boston: Houghton Mifflin.

Gurfinkel, V. S., and Levick, Y. S. 1991. "The Postural Body Scheme." In *Body and Space*, ed. J. Paillard. Oxford: Oxford University Press.

Head, H. 1920. *Studies in Neurology*, vol. 2. Oxford: Oxford University Press.

Jeannerod, M. 1988. *The Neural and Behavioural Organization of Goal-Directed Movements*. Oxford: Oxford University Press.

Martin, M. 1992. "Sight and Touch." In *The Contents of Experience*, ed. T. M. Crane. Cambridge: Cambridge University Press.

Martin, M. 1993. "Sense Modalities and Spatial Properties." In *Spatial Representation*, ed. N. Eilan, R. McCarthy, and B. Brewer. Oxford: Basil Blackwell.

McGinn, C. 1982. *The Character of Mind*. Oxford: Oxford University Press.

Merleau-Ponty, M. 1962. *The Phenomenology of Perception*. Trans. C. Smith London: Routledge and Kegan Paul.

Neisser, U. 1993. "The Self Perceived." In *The Perceived Self: Ecological and Interpersonal Sources of Self-Knowledge*, edited by U. Neisser. Cambridge: Cambridge University Press.

O'Shaughnessy, B. 1980. *The Will*. Cambridge: Cambridge University Press.

O'Shaughnessy, B. 1989. "The Sense of Touch." *Australasian Journal of Philosophy* 67:37–58.

Paillard, J. 1991a. "Knowing Where and How to Get There." In *Body and Space*, J. Paillard. Oxford: Oxford University Press.

Paillard, J. 1991b. "Motor and Representational Space." In *Body and Space*, ed. J. Paillard. Oxford: Oxford University Press.

Peacocke, C. 1979. *Holistic Explanation*. Oxford: Clarendon Press.

Peacocke, C. A. B. 1985. "Consciousness and Other Minds." *Aristotelian Society Proceedings*, suppl. vol. 59: 97–117.

Reid, T. 1983. *Inquiry and Essays*. Indianapolis: Hackett.

Shapiro, M. F., Fink, M., and Bender, M. 1952. "Exosomesthesia, or Displacement of Cutaneous Sensation into Extrapersonal Space." *AMA Archives of Neurology and Psychiatry* 68:481–490.

Shoemaker, S. 1986. "Introspection and the Self." In *Studies in the Philosophy of Mind*, ed. Peter A. French, Theodore Edward Uehling, and Howard K. Wettstein, Midwest Studies in Philosophy, no. 10. Minneapolis: University of Minnesota Press.

Van Deusen, J. 1993. *Body Image and Perceptual Dysfunction in Adults*. Philadelphia: W. B. Saunders and Co.

Von Békésy, G. 1967. *Sensory Inhibition*. Princeton: Princeton University Press.

Wall, P. 1993. "Pain and the Placebo Response." In *Experimental and Theoretical Studies of Consciousness*, edited by G. Bock and J. Marsh. Chichester: John Wiley and Sons.

Wittgenstein, L. 1969. *The Blue and Brown Books*, 2nd ed. Oxford: Basil Blackwell.

Bodily Awareness and the Self

Bill Brewer

What can we learn about the nature of the self from reflection on bodily experience? I will approach this question by addressing a more specific issue: to what extent does the phenomenon of bodily awareness undermine a Cartesian conception of the self? In other words, what, if anything, can be extracted from the nature of a person's epistemological relation with his body in defence of the commonsense, anti-Cartesian idea of a person as no less basically bodily than mentally endowed?

In *The Varieties of Reference* (1982), Gareth Evans claims that considerations having to do with certain basic ways we have of gaining knowledge of our own physical states and properties provide "the most powerful antidote to a Cartesian conception of the self" (1982, 220). In this paper I start with a discussion and evaluation of Evans's own argument, which is in the end, I think, unconvincing. Then I raise the possibility of a more direct application of similar considerations in defence of commonsense anti-Cartesianism. Progress in this direction depends on a far more psychologically informed understanding of normal and abnormal bodily awareness than is generally found in philosophical discussions of these issues. In the context of my attempt at such an understanding, I go on to assess the potential of this more direct line of argument.

1 Evans's Antidote to Cartesianism

Evans's argument from bodily awareness against the Cartesian conception of the self (1982, 215–222) starts with the observation that certain self-ascriptions of physical properties made on its basis display a particular immunity to error. This is not the claim that any such self-ascriptions are absolutely incorrigible or immediately evident. His point is not that they are necessarily true if sincerely made, or automatically endorsed whenever true. It is rather that a certain special sort of error is not possible, which Shoemaker christens "error through misidentification relative to the first person pronouns," "where to say that a statement '*a* is ϕ' is subject to error through misidentification relative to the term '*a*' means that the following is possible: the speaker knows some particular thing to be ϕ, but makes the mistake of asserting '*a* is ϕ' because, and only because, he mistakenly thinks that the thing he knows to be ϕ is what '*a*' refers to" (1984, 7–8).

Thus self-ascriptions are immune to error relative to the first-person pronouns just in case one cannot express knowledge, in making such self-ascriptions, that *someone* is the way one judges oneself to be, yet be mistaken in judging that it is oneself who is that way because, and only because, one misidentifies the person one knows to be that way as oneself. For example, when I judge that I am thinking about last night's concert in the normal way, it would be nonsense to admit that I do indeed know of some person that he is thinking about last night's concert, yet to query whether that person is really me.

Now it may well be that in the case of every physical self-ascription (in contrast, perhaps, to some mental self-ascriptions) there are ways one might come to know it to be true that leave the judgment open to error through misidentification in this sense. For example, I might judge my arm to be bent at a certain angle by seeing an arm in a mirror, of identical appearance to my own and with a watch just like mine on it, bent at just that angle. Here it is possible that I do know some arm to be bent at that angle but that I am in error in supposing it to be my own, perhaps because it is my identical twin's, which is tangled up with mine as we roll around together. In cases like this in which I judge myself to be physically thus and so on the basis of my perception, from the outside, of the object I take to be my body, the judgement 'I am thus and so' is indeed subject to error through misidentification relative to the first-person pronoun.

Nevertheless, Evans claims, there are ways we have of gaining knowledge of our own physical properties that do issue in judgments immune to this particular kind of error. In particular, this seems to be the case in connection with the cluster of internal senses that go under the general title of "bodily awareness," which includes at least the following: sense of joint position and sense of balance (which inform us of the current configuration of our bodies and limbs); kinesthetic sensation (which tells us about our active and passive bodily movements); and tactual perception, very generally, of body-surface contact, moving stimulation, temperature, and pressure.

As Evans himself puts it,

None of the following utterances appears to make sense when the first component expresses knowledge gained in the appropriate way: "Someone's legs are crossed, but is it my legs that are crossed?"; "Someone is hot and sticky, but is it I who am hot and sticky?"; "Someone is being pushed, but is it I who am being pushed?". There just does not appear to be a gap between the subject's having information (or appearing to have information), in the appropriate way, that the property of being *F* is instantiated, and his having information (or appearing to have information) that *he* is *F*; for him to have, or appear to have, the information that the property is instantiated just is for it to appear to him that *he* is *F*. (1982, 220–221)

Thus it seems that when they are made on the basis of these particular, indeed *normal*, ways of becoming aware of our bodies, physical self-ascriptions are immune to error through misidentification relative to the first-person pronouns. (I will drop the qualification where possible and refer the phenomenon simply as "immunity to error through misidentification" hereafter.)

Evans's argument continues with a diagnosis of this immunity to error through misidentification as symptomatic of a kind of direct demonstrative reference, which is contrasted with indirect, identification-dependent, reference. To refer to a particular object in thought, the thinker must know which object is in question in the following sense. There must be some account of what it is about her thinking in virtue of which how things are with that object determines whether her thought is true or false. One way of meeting this condition is with an explicit identification of the object in question, which might have misfired, so to speak, and latched onto a different object, or possibly no object at all. But this cannot be the only way of meeting the "know which" requirement, on pain either of an infinite regress, which would undermine the possibility of any genuine reference to objects in thought at all, or of an untenable reduction of all knowledge of objects to knowledge by description (Russell 1917).

The suggestion is that every judgment '*a* is ϕ' must rest on some identification '*b*' of *a*, which constitutes the thinker's knowledge of which object is in question, together with the judgment '*b* is ϕ'. This is how the possibility of error enters, for the judgment of identification '*a* = *b*' might be mistaken. But then '*b* is ϕ' must presumably rest in turn on some pair of judgements '*b* = *c*' and '*c* is ϕ', and so on without limit, in which case all such thought is in fact impossible. The only way to halt this fatal regress is to suppose that a thinker's knowledge of which object is in question is always ultimately to be spelled out in terms of some definite description 'the *x*' that is uniquely satisfied by *a*. On this view, every judgment '*a* is ϕ' rests, in effect, on a single pair of judgments '*a* = the *x*' and 'The *x* is ϕ'. But certainly in connection with self-identification, which is our central concern here, and indeed with many other varieties of reference too, this descriptive model is unacceptable. The best way to see this in the case of the first person is to recognize that for any suggested descriptive concept *x*, uniquely satisfied by oneself, one might realize that the *x* is ϕ without realizing that *one* is ϕ oneself, in the sense in which this would give rise to the judgment

'I am ϕ', which might come as further news. For one might not know, or have forgotten, that one is the x. For example, I might be fully aware that the man in green is about to be run over without any inclination to take the avoiding action that would be immediate on coming to realize that *I* am about to be run over. Hence quite generally, the judgment 'I am ϕ' cannot be captured by any descriptive thought to the effect that the x is ϕ (Castañeda 1966; Perry 1979; Evans 1982, 206).

So there must be another, more basic and direct way of meeting the condition on thought about an object that the thinker knows which object is in question. Evans suggests that demonstrative identification in general, and self-identification in particular, instantiate this basic mode of singular reference. The central idea is that the "know which" requirement is met in these cases in part by the thinker's actually being informationally linked with the object, by his propensity to have his judgment immediately controlled by information received in certain special ways *from that object,* and also in part by his disposition to act *in relation to that object* on the basis of his judgment. What makes it the case that a particular object o is identified in thought, what therefore constitutes the thinker's knowledge of which object is in question, is the place of the thought as a suitably sensitive response to information directly from o and as a suitably sensitive controller of dispositions to act in relation to o.

Now suppose that 'a' is a referring expression that can be used in this way. Suppose that it is used in this way in the judgment 'a is ϕ', and that the information that a is ϕ is gained in this special reference-fixing way. Then it follows that the thinker could not possibly be expressing knowledge that some particular thing is ϕ, but yet be mistaken in asserting 'a is ϕ' because, and only because, he mistakenly thinks that the thing he knows to be ϕ is what 'a' refers to. For the question of which object 'a' refers to is settled precisely by appeal to the facts about which object the thinker is being informed is ϕ. His coming to know that something is ϕ just is his coming to know that a is ϕ.

Immunity to error through misidentification is therefore evidence of this direct form of demonstrative reference. Which object is picked out in thought, if any, is determined as the source of the information giving rise to judgments that are immune to error relative to the referring expression in question. (If there is to be an object of thought at all in a given case, then, of course, this criterion must also come together with the determination by the output connections between the judgment and the thinker's dispositions to action.) Although not infallibly, as we have seen, first-person pronouns can be used in making judgments self-ascribing physical, bodily properties, as well as mental properties, that are immune to error through misidentification. Hence the object of such judgments, the self, is not a Cartesian ego but a bodily subject of both mental and physical properties.

'I' is a referring expression. On any occasion of use, it picks out the thinking subject using it. The way things are with him determines whether the judgment made is true or false. Which object this is whose condition determines the truth or falsity of the judgment is itself partly determined as the thing that the thinker comes to know is F in making judgments of the form 'I am F', which are immune to error through misidentification. In some such judgments, 'F' is a predicate ascribing corporeal characteristics. Hence the self, which is the object thus identified in thought by the use of 'I', is not merely a conscious thinking thing but the very thing that is F, that is either hot or cold, with legs crossed or uncrossed, sitting or standing, and so on, from whose mouth the judgment may or may not be expressed: a material, bodily thing. The subject of thought is a physically extended object.

2   A Cartesian Response to Evans

At this point the determined Cartesian will object that two quite different uses of 'I' are being confused.[1] Evans is right that one can make self-ascriptions of both mental and physical properties that are immune to error through misidentification, and also right in his account of the source of this immunity in the reference-fixing role of the knowledge expressed in such judgments. He is mistaken, though, in assuming that the very same object is identified in both kinds of case. In self-ascribing mental properties, I refer to my essential self, the immaterial Cartesian ego; in self-ascribing physical properties, I refer to my body. All this is perfectly in keeping with Evans's general account of object-involving demonstrative identification. And the equivocation is easily explained by the intimacy of the substantial union of mind and body. But it is equivocation all the same. So there is not a single individual to which both mental and physical predicates are equally applicable.

As things stand, I can see no way for Evans simply to rule out this riposte.[2] Nevertheless, there may be a way forward on the basis of a deeper reflection on the content of bodily awareness and the nature of our self-ascription of bodily sensations. Descartes himself is well aware that a partition of self-ascriptions into the mental and the physical, along the lines exploited above, is not as straightforward as it might at first seem. Purely intellectual properties of rational thought are unproblematically mental. There are equally unproblematic purely physical properties that we ascribe to our bodies, such as posture and location, for example. But perceptual and bodily sensations seem essentially to involve ascriptions to both the mind and the body. In particular, when I am aware that I am being prodded painfully just above my right knee, say, I am aware of both a psychological and a material condition. Thus, on the Cartesian line sketched above, my judgment 'I am being prodded painfully just above my right knee' is really a misleading composite of two logically independent "self"-ascriptions: 'I_e am in pain' and 'I_b am being prodded just above the right knee', where 'I_e' refers to my true self, the Cartesian pure ego, and 'I_b' refers to the body that the Cartesian ego is contingently bound up with, and that is therefore mine but is not *me*. Presumably, then, the idea is that direct awareness of, or being subject to, the pain constitutes some kind of indirect perceptual awareness of the physical state of the body part in question, in virtue of being the natural, evolutionarily, or divinely reinforced, and therefore "appropriate," effect of prodding this body here.

The crux of this Cartesian conception is the claim that commonsense ascriptions of both mental and physical properties to a single entity are ultimately misleading. Fundamentally, the entities figuring in mental and physical ascriptions are ontologically quite separate. "All basic subjects [i.e., everything represented as a mental subject in the *philosophically fundamental account* of things] are wholly non-physical" (Foster 1991, 203–204). A particular consequence of this, in its Cartesian form,[3] is the fragmentation of certain apparently unitary "self"-ascriptions, most notably of bodily sensations, into two independent ascriptions to totally different things: one of purely mental properties to the conscious subject of thought, the wholly nonphysical basic subject, the other of physical properties to the bodily object suitably related to it.[4]

Physical "self"-ascriptions like 'I_b am being prodded just above the right knee' are indeed immune to error through misidentification relative to the "personal" pronoun 'I_b'. But Evans is wrong in inferring from this that one and the same single individual is the subject of both pain and prodding, that $I_b = I_e$. For the Cartesian has a perfectly coherent alternative explanation of the immunity, quite consistent with his dualism. Indeed, he seems to have the luxury of a choice between two such accounts. A first might run as follows. Which body is picked out by 'I_b' is determined, in part, as the normal source of the physical information conveyed in bodily sensation, for example, the body that when prodded just above the right knee standardly causes a painful sensation of the experienced type. For the embodiment relation between a given mind and body is simply constituted by a whole system of epistemologically and operationally appropriate causal-functional relations of this kind between the two. Now a subject has *knowledge* on this basis that there is prodding just above the right knee only if his painful experience is a reliable indicator of this fact, and this is so, by definition, only with respect to the body thus constituted as his. So it is impossible that he should know about the prodding just above a right knee but be mistaken that it is prodding just above *his* right knee, because, and only because, he wrongly takes the body involved to be what 'I$_b$' refers to.

Alternatively, a second dualist strategy, which is also in fact a consistent supplement to the first, simply transposes Evans's general account of perceptual-demonstrative reference, given above, into an explanation of the immunity of certain bodily "self"-ascriptions to error through misidentification. The basic idea would be that judgments like 'I$_b$ am being prodded just above the right knee' are effectively of the form '*That* knee is being prodded', where the reference-fixing quasi-perceptual information link is provided by internal bodily experience. Neither account is completely without difficulties. But I want to move on now to consider a rather different line of argument, and I will have to leave the matter here.

3   The Nature and Spatial Content of Bodily Awareness: A More Direct Objection to Cartesian Dualism

We should focus rather more carefully on the intrinsic nature of the painful sensation of which the basic mental subject is directly aware, on the broadly Cartesian account, the aspect of bodily sensation that is genuinely a property of the subject of experience. In particular, we should inquire into its spatial content. In doing this, I will follow quite closely the discussion in O'Shaughnessy 1980. My point is to see whether anything can be made of a strong intuitive contrast between bodily sensation and "external" sense perception. The Cartesian applies very much the same model in both cases. On the Cartesian model, the mind's sensational properties constitute its indirect awareness of their normal and appropriate causes.[5] Yet in bodily awareness, but not in sense perception, psychological properties are themselves located in the physical object of awareness, namely the body. Thus there is some prima facie support for the idea that the body part in which sensation is set is a part, not a mere possession, of the conscious mental subject, that the subject of experience extends physically to encompass the bodily location of sensation.

So we need to ask what exactly the raw data of bodily feeling are. What is the intrinsic nature of the painful sensation that is genuinely a property of the basic mental subject and constitutes the epistemological given in his quasi-perceptual bodily awareness of being prodded painfully just above the right knee? When I am aware of a sharp pain in the back of

my left hand or an itch on the end of my nose, what am I absolutely immediately aware of through which I come, indirectly on the Cartesian's
account, to be aware of some disturbance determinately located at those
parts of my body?

An initial suggestion might be that the direct objects of awareness in
bodily sensation are *purely* sensational.[6] In particular, the idea is that one is
only derivatively presented with a particular spatial location on the basis of
intrinsically nonspatial, purely qualitative dimensions of variation in the
sensational given. On this view, bodily feelings of the kind we are considering come in themselves as if from nowhere. Values on some intrinsically
nonspatial dimension of their qualitative variation nevertheless correspond
with each potential determinate bodily location of sensation, and on the
basis of a sensitivity to this correspondence the subject becomes indirectly
aware of the condition of particular parts of his associated body.

This suggestion is highly problematic though. To begin with, it is impossible to erase the immediate inclination to act in connection with the
particular location of bodily sensation from our conception of the epistemological given in bodily awareness. When I feel a sharp pain in the back
of my left hand or an itch on the end of my nose, the appropriateness of
action concerning these actual bodily locations is written into the very
nature of the experience itself, rather than being something somehow inferred from its prior, intrinsically nonspatial, qualitative essence.[7] Further,
there are no such things as back-of-the-right-hand-ish sharp pains as opposed to back-of-the-left-hand-ish sharp pains; the right/left distinction
need not be matched by any *qualitative* distinction at all. Indeed, the idea of
distinctive qualia associated with every bodily location is absurd. For a
qualitatively unchanging sensation can move, and *change* its location. For
example, the very same burning feeling might be moving gradually down
one's throat. Similarly, qualitatively identical itches might come sometimes
as on the end of one's nose and at other times as (infuriatingly out of
reach) between one's shoulder blades.

I should emphasize here that my claim is certainly not that as a matter
of fact the qualitative and spatial dimensions of bodily awareness vary
completely independently. This is surely false.[8] For example, I have never
had, nor will have, a feeling in my left foot qualitatively like the nervous
sensation of butterflies in my stomach. Given the cases I site, dependence
of this kind must be contingent and quite limited, however. My claim is
rather that the undeniable spatial component in bodily sensation cannot
generally be inferred from an intrinsically nonspatial qualitative given.
Spatial content must be a part of what is epistemologically basic in bodily
awareness.

So there is, over and above the sensational quale of a bodily feeling, an ineliminable presentation of some more or less specific place in egocentric space that is not a mere construct out of any purely sensational qualitative features. Thus bodily awareness is intrinsically spatial. Apparent location is an essential component of the epistemological given in bodily sensation.

Recognizing this might prompt a second suggestion: that the direct objects of awareness in bodily sensation are feelings-apparently-at-a-particular-place-in-egocentric-space. The crucial claim here is that the intrinsic spatiality of bodily awareness is given prior to and independently of any information as to which body part is involved in the awareness at that given location. Feeling is determinately located in a particular part of the body only derivatively, as follows: "We run the tip of a finger along the body-thing until the sensation it produces occupies the same position on the sense 'skin' as does the sensation to be located; and this procedure fixes a point on the body-thing that we call 'the location of the sensation' " (O'Shaughnessy 1980, 163).

This second suggestion is also unsatisfactory. If we propose an epistemological given in bodily awareness of feeling-at-a-point-in-space, then we should be able to make sense of the idea of determinately located yet utterly unattached feeling. But what grip can we get on this idea of a feeling existing "in mid-air *simpliciter*, i.e., not even seemingly in a seeming limb" (O'Shaughnessy 1980, 161)? Certainly phantom-limb sensations are more or less determinately located egocentrically. And they are not in fact set in any part of the subject's body. For there is no actual limb where they seem to be. Nevertheless, they do come immediately as if in a particular body part. That the pain is in a phantom *foot* is not derived from the fact that there is pain that seems to be at a place where the foot would have been if it were still there. It is given directly in the experience of pain-in-the-foot-there. So although the revised suggestion improves on the first by admitting the intrinsic spatiality of bodily awareness, it still falls short of the truth by ignoring the immediate relation between awareness and particular parts of the body.

We cannot get away from the fact that bodily sensations immediately appear as determinately located not only in egocentric space but also in specific body parts filling those locations. Indeed, they come as determinately located egocentrically precisely in virtue of coming as set in particular parts of the body extending to particular places in egocentric space. Again O'Shaughnessy captures this precisely, as follows: "The sensation comes to awareness as at 'a point in physical space'—and not just as at 'the part of the body it is in'—*only to the extent that* the aesthetised subject seems to himself immediately to extend into certain nooks and crannies and the sensation to be cited therein" (1980, 221).

There are two extremely important points here. First, the intrinsic spatiality of bodily awareness is sustained by its directly presenting certain parts of the subject's body as filling particular egocentric locations. Second, this presentation of the body as determinately extended in physical space depends in turn on the bodily sensation itself apparently being set in that body part there.

In sensational bodily awareness of a sharp pain in the back of one's left hand, say, or an itch on the end of one's nose, the experience itself is intrinsically spatial. Furthermore, knowledge where to point to locate the sensation, knowledge of which body part the sensation is in, and knowledge of the egocentric position of that body part are epistemologically on a par as basic. In O'Shaughnessy's terms once again, "The basic 'given' is, not just feeling, not just feeling-in-a-certain-body-part, but *feeling-in-a-certain-body-part-at-a-position-in-body-relative-physical-space*; and so, also, certain-body-part-at-a-position-in-body-relative-physical-space: the latter being disclosed along with and via the former *and* the former being disclosed along with and via the latter" (1980, 165).

Central to the current argument, then, are the following three points.

• Bodily awareness is intrinsically spatial: the apparent location of sensation is as essential to its very nature as its purely qualitative feel and is in no way derived from any intrinsically nonspatial variation in it.
• This spatial location of sensation comes to light only as one is aware of one's body as determinately extending into and filling certain regions of the perceived physical world.
• This awareness of one's body as filling physical space both rests on, and, more important, provides intrinsic spatiality in virtue of, the setting of bodily sensations in particular body parts.

In bodily awareness, one is aware of determinately spatially located properties of the body that are also necessarily properties of the basic subject of that very awareness. In contrast with external sense perception, a psychological property of oneself is physically located in or on the body, as a property of the body. Therefore, rather than any mere possession, the animal body *is* the conscious mental subject of bodily awareness.

4   Extending the Argument

The case against a Cartesian conception of the self can, I think, be strengthened by considering further the precise spatial content of bodily awareness.[9] We can begin with a comparison between ourselves and a bodily deafferented patient studied by Jacques Paillard.[10]

Below her nose G.L. has no sense of touch or kinesthetic sensation. She is unable to detect light-to-normal pressure or vibration, but shows some sensitivity to temperature and deep pain (e.g., when prodded with a needle or pressed firmly with a finger or thumb). Her motor fibers are un-affected, and she can certainly make willed movements. With respect to the minimal bodily awareness she has of a hot or painful stimulus, say, her sense of spatial location is extremely interesting. She is quite unable imme-diately to act in connection with the location of the sensation by pointing, protecting, rubbing, scratching, or whatever. But she can point to the cor-rect location on a drawn diagram or model of her body. She can mimic our normal ability to reach immediately and without reflection for the place of bodily stimulation only indirectly, by groping around for the rele-vant body part and moving along it to the right location. This is presum-ably done on the basis of her representation of this location on a detached, third-person image of her body of precisely the kind serving her discrimi-nation of the location on a diagram. (Indeed, she will go to the equivalent place on the examiner's body if his body part is placed in her groping path.) Given such a representation, she has a kind of knowledge of where the sensation is on her body and where, in relation to other body parts, this place is likely to be, which makes no *immediate* contact with any ability to act in connection with that location yet which explains her actual perfor-mance. Compare this with a case where I know that my key is in a red box under a blue cushion between the chair and the window—perhaps a child has hidden it and tells me only this. Both here and in G.L.'s case, what is required is a search around the relevant area, homing in on the goal loca-tion by using the cues encountered along the way.

So G.L. has knowledge of the location of those very few bodily sen-sations of which she is aware that is quite different in kind and content from our own. It may still be true that this minimal awareness in some sense satisfies O'Shaughnessy's tripartite description of "feeling-in-a-certain-body-part-at-a-position-in-body-relative-physical-space." For she may well know that the pain is in her left hand somewhere out by her hip. But this has no immediate significance for the control and coordination of her action in connection with that location. She has at first simply a disen-gaged, descriptive grasp of which body part is in pain, along with, perhaps, an approximate sense, again purely descriptive, of where that body part stands in relation to other parts. Yet neither of these components of the spatial content of her awareness has any direct implications for how she

should act so as to point to, protect, rub, or scratch the location of sensation. This can only be discovered by an unreliable trial-and-error investigation of herself with continual reference to the detached, third-person
image of where the pain is on her body.

G.L.'s relation to her body is rather like that of a sailor in a ship
(Descartes 1984, 56). When it is damaged, a red light flashes on an electronic diagram of the ship at the place corresponding to the location of
the damage. The pilot must then send out the mechanics to hunt around
the relevant area for anything that looks as if it might be responsible for the
alert, and try to put it right. What is missing in the spatial content of her
impoverished bodily awareness is the first-person or egocentric element in
the way sensations are given location in our case by their setting in particular body parts. All she has is something like a detached, third-person description.

Our own position, as we have seen, is quite different. The spatial content of our "feeling-in-a-certain-body-part-at-a-position-in-body-relative-
physical-space" is given indexically in terms of its implications for our direct
action in connection with that location. Which bodily location is involved is
given, at least in part, as a kind of practical demonstrative: 'there', said as one
reaches for the place in question. Knowledge of how to point to, protect,
rub, or scratch the location of sensation is not so much discovered by some
comparison of the consequences of one's flailing movements with an external picture of a bodily target as immediately present as part of what it
amounts to for the sensation to seem to be where it is.

The intrinsic spatial content of normal bodily awareness is given directly in terms of practical knowledge of how to act in connection with
the bodily locations involved. The connection with basic action is absolutely not an extrinsic add-on, only to be recovered by experiment and
exploration from a detached map of the vessel that the subject of awareness happens to inhabit. It is rather quite essential to the characterization
of the spatiality of bodily sensation. This spatiality is, as we have seen, ineliminable from the nature of normal bodily awareness. So the subject of
such awareness is necessarily an embodied agent. Furthermore, the properties of the body of which one is aware in bodily awareness are sensational
properties of the subject of that very awareness. Therefore, the subject of
awareness is the physically extended body.

Location on a certain body part in egocentric space cannot be detached from the given in our bodily awareness without loss. This spatial
content cannot normally be characterized independently of the practical
knowledge of how to act in connection with that location on the body
part. The spatial content is partially specified in these practical terms and

cannot correctly be specified otherwise. For on any nonpractical, third-person specification, it follows that the knowledge of how to act in connection with the relevant bodily location is a subsequent experimental achievement, of the kind that G.L. has to make, or that I have to make in retrieving my key in the situation described above. But we are not related to our bodies as a sailor is present in a ship in this way. So the subject of normal bodily awareness is itself a subject of both mental and physical properties.[11]

In normal bodily awareness the experiencer is presented as extended, because the sensational property of which he is the subject seems physically located as a property of a given (seeming) body part at a certain location in egocentric space. This spatial content is in turn given, at least in part, in terms of its immediate implications for his basic physical action in connection with that location. Of course, all this may on occasion be illusory in all sorts of ways. Nevertheless, it is normally veridical, when things in fact are how they seem. In these cases the extended physical body that provides the determinately located setting for the psychological sensation must *be* the subject of sensation. The basic subject is therefore a mental and physical subject-object physically extended in space. Hence, Cartesian dualism is inconsistent with a correct account of the nature and content of bodily awareness.

Let me restate my argument once again, though in a slightly different form, stressing two points:

• The direct object of bodily awareness is intrinsically spatial, not purely sensational. The object of awareness itself is spatially located—a property of a given body part at a particular location in egocentric space.
• The direct object of bodily awareness is genuinely psychological, not merely spatial. The object of awareness is itself a mental item—a psychological property of the basic subject of experience.

Together these imply that the psychological subject is a spatially extended object. The ascribed property is a property of the spatially extended body but is also essentially a property of the subject of consciousness itself.

5 A Cartesian Last Stand

Again the determined Cartesian has a response here. She will insist that our physical location of bodily sensation is, although quite natural, strictly in error: the result of some kind of projection. She may well admit that we have no awareness of what is projected prior to projection. In other words, she might accept that the epistemological given in bodily awareness is intrinsically spatial, just as I characterize it. Nevertheless, she will insist, this physical location is always mere appearance. In so-called veridical cases, the illusion of a certain kind of sensation set in a particular body part might inform us about the physical state of that part. Yet any idea that sensation itself is physically located, or that any property of the body we thereby come to know about is a psychological property of the conscious subject, as it appears to be, is in error. Sensation proper is correctly ascribed to the wholly immaterial mind, and any appearance of bodily location is part of the close epistemological relation between mind and body that constitutes contingent embodiment. Illusory cases that we are inclined to describe in terms of a sensation actually being somewhere other than where it seems to be would have to be regarded as some further, deviant breakdown in the normal suitability of this relation for the subject's acquisition of knowledge about how things are with the body with which he is (temporarily) associated.

This line of reply seems to me quite untenable, even on the dualist's own terms, and is straightforwardly inconsistent with the basic motivation for the dualist position. The driving force behind the Cartesian conception of the self as a wholly nonphysical mind is a commitment to take as authoritative what is epistemologically given as basic in introspection. Yet in normal bodily awareness, this is an immediate presentation of oneself as a spatially extended material subject of experience. Nothing less does justice to the phenomena. Spatiality cannot be stripped away from bodily sensation without significant loss. What remains is nothing remotely recognizable as our experiential awareness of our bodies. On its own terms, then, the dualist conception of the self is undermined by a proper account of our bodily awareness.

In response it might be suggested that this is a bit too quick.[12] For Descartes himself notoriously distinguishes between what is clear and distinct in our sensations and what is merely obscure and confused (1985, 216–217). The point is then that we have clear and distinct knowledge of bodily sensations only when we consider them as purely qualitative, nonspatial features of an immaterial mind. Any purported conception of them as properties of located body parts is really obscure confusion. I think there are two possible grounds for this response, both of which are highly problematic. First, what is epistemologically basic, and so authoritative, might be restricted to those things of which a person is in principle infallible. Perhaps this succeeds in creating some disanalogy between the qualitative and spatial components of bodily awareness, although the infallible introspectible base would surely shrink dramatically under pressure. But the real price of defining clarity and distinctness in terms of infallibility in this way is the total collapse of Descartes's foundationalism into extreme skepticism. If we acquire basic knowledge only by absolutely infallible methods and all nonbasic knowledge is to be derived by deductive inference from basic knowledge, then we know almost nothing: we lose all epistemological contact with the real world in which we live. Second, the case for obscurity in our grasp of properties of our bodies that are necessarily properties of ourselves, the subjects of awareness, may rest on an unfair presumption of what is required. If we take a completely detached view of our bodies as physical objects totally on a par with any inanimate lump of matter, other than in respect of their complexity perhaps, then it will indeed be difficult clearly and distinctly to conceive of any of their properties as necessarily properties of a conscious subject of thought and experience. But why is this point of view obligatory? As I argue in the final section, the difficulty disappears if we allow ourselves the internal perspective on our bodies *as ours,* as our spatially extended selves.

Although my own line of argument is rather different from Evans's, I think he is quite right that we have, in the epistemology of bodily awareness, a most powerful antidote to the Cartesian conception of the self. The picture that emerges is one of the conscious self as a materially embodied organism, a subject of experience in which this realm of the psychological itself extends physically into the extremities of the animal body. The traditional idea of the true, mental self as an extensionless inner sanctum, a control center for the dispensable bodily machine, is an illusion, unsupported even by the nature of the psychological phenomena themselves. In particular, this idea fails to do full justice to the intrinsic first-person, *spatial* content of bodily experience.

6 Experience of Ownership and the Subject as Object

The anti-Cartesian line of argument I have been presenting also suggests a direction for resolving Nagel's (1970) worry about how we are to conceive of ourselves as both subjects of experience and elements of the objective order. For in bodily awareness, the subject of awareness is presented to himself precisely as a physically extended body in the spatial world of other material things.

A good way to bring out this thought is in connection with the question how we experience our bodies *as ours.* Clearly, this is not, and cannot be, an external perceptual phenomenon. For when we perceive it from the outside, our body has no indelible stamp of ownership. It appears just as one object among many, although it is one whose features we know very well. Yet its being ours strikes us far more forcefully than the transferable contingency of anything we simply recognize perceptually as ours in this external way. Erwin Straus puts the distinction like this: "In the phrase 'my house', *my* stands for something owned by me [something I might recognize in a glance as mine and know intimately, but which I can sell or trade, something which can go from *one* owner to *another*]. In the phrase 'my hand', the same word refers to me, the owner, as a live body" (1967, 112).

The position I have been developing allows us to see how this distinctive sense of ownership might have its source in bodily sensation.[13] In bodily awareness, I have argued, the subject is aware of *himself* as a spatially extended body. So bodily ownership is experienced in this extension of the subject of experience into the material world. The peculiarly intimate sense in which my body parts seem to be mine is just that in which they seem to be parts of the spatially extended physical body that I seem to be. Experienced bodily ownership, then, is awareness of *oneself* as extended in space.

Furthermore, we can now see how Nagel's problem is misguided. The difficulty is supposed to lie in a person's identifying himself, the subject of thought and experience, with a physical thing. In fact, Sartre presents the very same problem, and he already has a sense of how it is made quite unmanageable in the formulation: "Actually if after gasping 'my' consciousness in its absolute interiority and by a series of reflective acts, I then seek to unite it with a certain living object composed of a nervous system, brain, . . . whose very matter is capable of being analysed chemically . . . , then I am going to encounter insurmountable difficulties. But these difficulties all stem from the fact that I try to unite my consciousness not with *my* body but with the body of *others*" (1969, 303; quoted in Evans 1982, 266).

If, on the other hand, the problem is supposed to be for me to unite myself as a conscious subject with *my* body, then there is really no difficulty at all. For in bodily experience I am aware of parts of my body precisely as physical parts of myself, the material subject of that experience. Experienced embodiment just is a presentation of the subject as a spatially extended body.[14] Again, as with the explicitly anti-Cartesian reflections above, we come a long way simply by recognizing the absolute inseparabilty of the mental and the physical in bodily awareness.

Acknowledgments

Many thanks to José Bermúdez, John Campbell, Quassim Cassam, David Charles, Bill Child, Naomi Eilan, Elizabeth Fricker, Jennifer Hornsby, Tony Marcel, Mike Martin, Paul Snowdon, Helen Steward, Rowland Stout and Timothy Williamson for their helpful comments on earlier versions of this paper.

Notes

1. I have been helped in formulating this response by discussions with Mike Martin.

2. He does suggest a possible line of reply (1982, 221–224), but this is unsuccessful in my view. His idea is that the Cartesian conception of 'I' as equivocal introduces an unacceptable sophistication into our thoughts about our bodies: bodily self-ascriptions can be made only indirectly via the descriptive identification 'the body from which I hereby have information' (1982, 221). It is not clear to me, though, why the Cartesian has to employ a descriptive model rather than a perceptual-demonstrative model for reference to the body. Yet on the latter type of model, Evans's worry about indirectness, at least, is surely unfounded.

3. See Foster 1991, secs. 7.1 and 7.3, for the contrast between Cartesian and Humean forms of dualism. I agree with his central contention in section 7.3 that "there is no escaping from what initially strikes us as self-evident, that mental items can only occur as the token states and activities of subjects, and that this ontological dependence on subjects forms part of our fundamental understanding of their nature" (1991, 219). Thus the Cartesian (rather than Humean) version of this dualist thesis is really the only alternative to the commonsense view that even on a philosophically fundamental account of things, persons are bearers of physical as well as mental properties.

4. In fact, there is a serious tension in Descartes's own writings about the relation between mind, body, and person, particularly in connection with bodily sensation. Two incompatible positions have strong textual support. First, there is the official dualism, on which a human being is a concoction of two ontologically separate substances: a mind and a body. Everything there is to say about such a person consists in some combination of independent ascriptions of radically different properties to these two quite distinct entities. The relation of embodiment that obtains between them over a given period of time is then to be construed as wholly reducible to a set of quite contingent causal-functional relations obtaining between those ascriptions over this time. Second, there is a substantial personal unionism, on which a human being is an integrated individual substance in whom the intermingling and coextension of the mental and the physical explain the experience of embodiment given in bodily awareness. Bodily sensation can be properly understood only as predicated of a single unified entity with both mental and physical properties.

The Cartesian that I am concerned with here is the more standard exclusive proponent of the former. My argument is that Descartes is right to move toward the latter in his discussion of bodily awareness. Given their incompatibility, this constitutes an objection to the official dualism. The only alternative is to suppose that there are really three distinct substances on the scene: the immaterial mind that is the subject of pure thought and its modifications, the material body that is the subject of pure extension and its modifications, and the integrated person that is the subject of phenomenological sensation and its modifications. Descartes does sometimes suggest this view, but a distinction between the subject of thought and the subject of sensation, over and above any standard mind-body dualism, seems to me quite unacceptably to overstep the mark of ontological excess, although I cannot argue the point here. For commentary on Descartes's views in this area, see Wilson 1978, chap. 6, sec. 6; Cottingham 1986, chap. 5, secs. 4 and 5; Schmaltz 1992, 281–325.

5. I mean this model of both sense perception and bodily awareness to be neutral on the question whether the Cartesian spells out the fact that a given immaterial mind has a particular sensational property in terms of its apprehension of some kind of sensation-object or in terms of its sensing with a certain intentional content.

6. Here and throughout this discussion of the epistemological given in bodily awareness, I mean to include as direct objects the properties of things of which one is immediately aware. In the end, my view is that the only *object* of bodily awareness, strictly speaking, is the animal body that is the subject of awareness. The basic form of the direct anti-Cartesian argument I am interested in is as follows. The properties of which we are immediately aware in bodily awareness are spatially located properties of the body that are also necessarily properties of the subject of that very awareness. Therefore, the subject is a material object. Quassim Cassam and Michael Martin are concerned with closely related issues in their contributions to this volume.

7. See section 4 herein for a development of this point.

8. Tony Marcel brought this home to me.

9. Again I have profited from O'Shaughnessy's (1980, 224–226) discussion of these issues here.

10. In 1992 Paillard reported on his patient G.L. in detail to the King's College Cambridge Research Centre Project on Spatial Representation.

11. I do not mean to imply that things are any different for G.L. in this respect. It is just that her status as a subject of both mental and physical properties cannot be inferred from the spatial content of her bodily awareness in the way I suggest.

12. I am grateful to Quassim Cassam for pressing this point.

13. It would, however, be a one-sided account of our sense of bodily ownership that focused *solely* on the contribution of bodily sensation and left out our capacity for basic, noninstrumental physical action.

14. As Evans is reported as remarking (1982, 266), this knowledge of my own body from the inside is an essential ground for my identification of myself as an element of the objective order, rather than a full account of it. Certainly, some capacity for self-location is an additional requirement. For more on this very important topic, see Evans 1982, 222–224; Cassam 1989; Brewer 1992.

References

Brewer, B. 1992. "Self-Location and Agency." *Mind* 101:17–34.

Cassam, Q. 1989. "Kant and Reductionism." *Review of Metaphysics* 43:72–106.

Castañeda, H.-N. 1966. " 'He': A Study in the Logic of Self-Consciousness." *Ratio* 8:130–157.

Cottingham, J. 1986. *Descartes*. Oxford: Basil Blackwell.

Descartes, R. 1984. *Philosophical Writings*, vol. 2. Translated by J. Cottingham, R. Stoothoff, and D. Murdoch. Cambridge: Cambridge University Press.

Descartes, R. 1985. *Philosophical Writings*, vol. 1. Translated by J. Cottingham, R. Stoothoff, and D. Murdoch. Cambridge: Cambridge University Press.

Evans, G. 1982. *The Varieties of Reference*. Oxford: Clarendon Press.

Foster, J. 1991. *The Immaterial Self*. London: Routledge.

Nagel, T. 1970. *The Possibility of Altruism*. Oxford: Clarendon Press.

O'Shaughnessy, B. 1980. *The Will*, vol. 1. Cambridge: Cambridge University Press.

Perry, J. 1979. "The Problem of the Essential Indexical." *Noûs* 13:3–21.

Russell, B. 1917. "Knowledge by Acquaintance and Knowledge by Description." In his *Mysticism and Logic*. London: George Allen and Unwin.

Sartre, J.-P. 1969. *Being and Nothingness*. Translated by H. E. Barnes. London: Methuen.

Schmaltz, T. M. 1992. "Descartes and Malebranche on Mind and Mind-Body Union." *Philosophical Review* 101:281–325.

Shoemaker, S. 1984. "Self-Reference and Self-Awareness." In his *Identity, Cause, and Mind*. Cambridge: Cambridge University Press.

Straus, E. W. 1967. "On Anosognosia." In *Phenomenology of Will and Action*, edited by E. W. Straus and D. Griffith. Pittsburgh: Duquesne University Press.

Wilson, M. D. 1978. *Descartes*. London: Routledge.

Introspection and Bodily Self-Ascription

Quassim Cassam

1   Introduction

Hume claimed that when he introspected, he was unable to catch himself without a perception or observe anything but perceptions. He concluded that the self is nothing but a "bundle or collection of different perceptions, which succeed each other with an inconceivable rapidity, and are in a perpetual flux and movement" (Hume 1978, 252). If the self is a bundle of perceptions and we are introspectively aware of our perceptions, then we are, in a sense, aware of ourselves. What we lack, on Hume's view, is awareness of what Kant was later to describe as a "fixed and abiding" self (Kant 1929, A107). Kant, who defined the "soul" as the object of "inner sense"—a quasi-perceptual faculty by means of which the mind "intuits" its thoughts, feelings, and desires—put this point by saying that everything in inner sense is in "constant flux" and that inner sense therefore yields "no intuition of the soul itself as an object" (Kant 1929, A22/B37).

Hume took it for granted that mental "subjects" are nonphysical. Would the claim that the self cannot be encountered "as an object" still be defensible on the "materialist" view that the self is a physical thing? It might be thought that if the self is a physical thing, then it is perceivable in the way in which physical things in general are perceivable. As Roderick Chisholm puts it, "If we are identical with our bodies and if, as all but sceptics hold, we do perceive our bodies, then, whether we realize it or not, we also perceive ourselves" (Chisholm 1994, 94). Since bodies are, and are perceived as being, "fixed and abiding," awareness of one's body is not only awareness of what is in fact the subject but awareness of it "as an object," in Kant's sense.

One reaction to the position outlined by Chisholm would be to argue that although mental subjects have corporeal characteristics, they are not identical with their bodies. For example, suppose that subjects of experience include *persons*, in Strawson's sense (1959, chap. 3). Strawson claims that persons are physical things, but that the criteria of personal identity are not the same as those for bodily identity. In this sense, a person is not identical with his or her body. Nevertheless, this does not affect the point about the perceivability of the self. It is still the case that a Strawsonian person is "a corporeal object among corporeal objects" (Strawson 1966, 102) and encounterable as an object of what Kant called "outer" sense.[1] If human beings are perceivable as "fixed and abiding," then so are at least some subjects. The suggestion, then, is that a materialist view of the self calls into question the Humean idea that the self is "elusive."

It might be objected that this suggestion misses Hume's point. Even if the self is a physical thing, and so an object of outer sense, it remains true that it is not an object of *introspective* awareness, which is what Hume is concerned with.[2] As Sydney Shoemaker puts it on Hume's behalf, "Someone who thinks that selves have some intrinsic physical properties . . . could hold that a self could be perceived in virtue of its physical properties, and even that it could be so perceived by itself—as when one sees oneself in a mirror, or in a foreshortened view. But it would still be ruled out that the self could be an object of *introspective* perception" (Shoemaker 1994b, 123). This argument rests on what Shoemaker himself identifies as the common assumption that "we are not presented with ourselves in introspection as bodily entities" (Shoemaker 1994b, 132). This may create the illusion that we are nonbodily entities, but for Shoemaker the point is that "when one is introspectively aware of one's thoughts, feelings, beliefs and desires, one is not presented to oneself as a flesh and blood person, and one does not seem to be presented to one as an *object* at all" (Shoemaker 1984a, 102). I will refer to this as the elusiveness thesis (ET).

One response to ET, proposed by M. R. Ayers, has been to argue that it is utterly implausible, since certain forms of sensory and bodily awareness "from the inside," such as proprioceptive awareness and awareness of bodily sensations, constitute *introspective* awareness of oneself as being "a material object among others" (Ayers 1991, 285). I will describe someone who argues in this way as a *materialist opponent* of ET. For this proposal to constitute a genuine threat to ET, a number of conditions have to be fulfilled. First, the forms of bodily awareness to which the proposal appeals must be, in Shoemaker's sense, awareness of oneself "as an object." Second, they must be genuinely introspective. This is related to the point that the forms of bodily awareness to which the materialist opponent of ET appeals are, unlike the example of seeing one's body in a mirror, supposed to be not just awareness of what is in fact the self but awareness of the self "*qua* subject of experiences" (Shoemaker 1994b, 119; see also Brewer 1992). This raises the question of how the conditions on awareness of oneself qua subject relate to the conditions that a form of awareness must fulfill to count as introspective. I will come back to this.

I will argue that bodily awareness "from the inside" does *not* fulfill all of these conditions. Although some forms of bodily awareness are, in the relevant sense, "introspective," they are not awareness of oneself "as an object," in *Shoemaker's* sense. There is also a Kantian reading of the phrase 'awareness of oneself qua subject' where bodily awareness—even "introspective" bodily awareness—cannot be awareness of oneself qua subject. Why does any of this matter? On the face of it, there is likely to be more than one way of understanding the notions of introspection, awareness of something as an object, and awareness of oneself qua subject. On Shoemaker's understanding of these notions, the materialist objection to ET may be unsuccessful, but the materialist will no doubt reply that given what *she* understands by them, bodily awareness *does* constitute "introspective" awareness of oneself "as an object." Unless it can be shown that one or the other reading of these notions is arbitrary or unmotivated, there cannot be a simple answer to the question of whether ET is undermined by reflection on the nature of bodily awareness.

It would be a mistake to conclude that discussion of the materialist objection to ET serves no purpose. In the first place, discussion of the nature of bodily awareness in the context of ET promises to bring several important features of such awareness, as well as different ways of understanding ET, into sharper focus. Since ET, or, to be more precise, a certain misunderstanding of it, is represented by Shoemaker (1984a, 103) as motivating the Cartesian dualist account of the self, it is important to establish precisely what this thesis amounts to.[3] Second, although a given reading of ET may be not be arbitrary or unmotivated in absolute terms, it may nevertheless be inappropriate in a given context. The question, then, is whether it is possible to give the materialist's objection more weight by locating the dispute over ET in the context of a larger philosophical debate.

On one view, one cannot be said to *know* that one is a material object among others unless one is introspectively aware of oneself as such. This is an echo of Kant's idea that knowledge of the nature of the self needs to be grounded in "an intuition of the subject as object" (Kant 1929, B421). So one way of understanding the significance of bodily awareness in connection with ET would be this: the issue is whether the sense in which bodily awareness "from the inside" does (arguably) constitute introspective awareness of oneself as being a material object among others grounds or underpins one's introspective *knowledge* that one is such an object, on what might be called a *broadly* Kantian conception of self-knowledge.[4] The suggestion, then, is that although one may not be introspectively aware of oneself "as an object" in Shoemaker's sense, bodily awareness amounts to introspective awareness of oneself as an object in the sense that matters most in this epistemological context.

This suggestion will not cut any ice with someone who maintains that there is *no* substantive sense in which knowledge that one is a material object among others requires introspective awareness of oneself as being such an object. It might be objected, for example, that if one were not *already* persuaded by other considerations that the self is material, one would have no grounds for describing bodily awareness as a genuine form of *self-awareness*, introspective or otherwise. I will return to this point in section 4. Nor will the suggestion cut any ice with someone who agrees with Kant himself *both* that self-knowledge requires "an intuition of the subject as object" *and* that one cannot possibly be aware of oneself "as an object" in the sense required for knowledge of the nature of the "I or he or it (the thing) which thinks" (Kant 1929, A346/B404). For Kant and other transcendental idealists, the self that one knows to be a material object among others is not the "philosophical self." The latter cannot be identified with a human being, a human body, or anything else (such as a Strawsonian person) that is a part of the world (Wittgenstein 1961, 5.641).

These objections cannot be assessed other than in the context of a theory of self-knowledge. In particular, an account needs to be given of how the "broadly Kantian conception of self-knowledge" differs from Kant's actual conception, and of the sense in which, according to the former, knowledge of the nature of the self needs to be grounded in self-awareness. Kant appears to assume that if self-knowledge were possible, it would have to take the same form as knowledge of objects distinct from the self.[5] As will be seen below, this is an assumption that the materialist opponent of ET must reject, but it might still possible for the materialist opponent of ET to remain faithful to the spirit, if not the letter, of Kant's account. Since it is beyond the scope of my discussion here to propose a detailed theory of self-knowledge, my suggestion that bodily awareness, in the sense required for self-knowledge, is introspective awareness of oneself as being a material object among others will have to remain somewhat speculative.[6]

2   The Elusiveness Thesis

A potentially powerful line of argument in support of ET would be to show that (1) a form of awareness must fulfill certain conditions to count as introspective, (2) self-awareness must fulfill certain conditions to count as awareness of oneself as an object, and (3) no form of self-awareness can satisfy both sets of conditions. I will focus on a Shoemakerian version of this argument.

In connection with (1), it might be held that introspective awareness, properly so called, is a form of awareness that serves as the basis for making first-person statements in which the first-person pronoun is used as subject. First-person statements in which 'I' is used in this way are those that, in Shoemaker's terminology, are immune to error through misidentification relative to the first-person pronoun. To say that a statement '*a* is *π*' is immune to this kind of error is to say that the following is not possible: the speaker knows some particular thing to be *π* but makes the mistake of asserting '*a* is *π*' because, and only because, he mistakenly thinks that the thing he knows to be *π* is what '*a*' refers to (Shoemaker 1994a, 82).

Next, consider Shoemaker's account of what it is for one to be aware of oneself as an object. Shoemaker concedes that there can occur something describable as "being an object to oneself" (1994a, 86) but proposes that awareness of oneself as an object must be a form of perceptual awareness and that perceptual awareness of oneself (in a mirror, for example) requires an identification of the presented object as oneself (1984a, 105). Combining this with the preceding account of the notion of introspective self-awareness explains why one cannnot be introspectively aware of oneself as an object. Identification "necessarily goes together with the possibility of misidentification" (Shoemaker 1994a, 87), so awareness of oneself as an object cannot be the basis of first-person statements that are immune to error through misidentification relative to 'I'. Therefore, although awareness of oneself as an object is possible, it cannot be a form of *introspective* awareness.

This argument for ET only carries weight to the extent that there are good grounds for accepting the proposed conditions on introspection and awareness of objects. A complication is that there are several different notions of immunity to error through misidentification. One distinction (in Shoemaker 1984b, 46) is that between "logical" and "de facto" immunity to error through misidentification. Another (in Shoemaker 1994a, 82) is the distinction between "absolute" and "circumstantial" immunity. Below I will briefly discuss the second of these distinctions. The first distinction may be illustrated by contrasting self-ascriptions of past and present experiences. Present-tense self-ascriptions of pain, for example, are logically immune because when one ascribes pain to oneself on the basis of feeling pain, it is not possible that one should be mistaken because, and only because, the person that one knows to be in pain is not oneself. Consider, in contrast, self-ascriptions of past experiences based on apparent memories of them from the inside. If *a*'s brain were divided into two halves and each half transplanted into distinct debrained bodies, the resulting offshoots, *b* and *c*, might both wake up seeming to remember *a*'s past experiences and actions from the inside. The fact that neither *b* nor *c* is identical with *a* is a reason for denying that they literally *remember* *a*'s experiences, but both *b* and *c* might be said to "quasi-remember" them. Quasi memory is supposed to be "just like" ordinary memory except that it is not confined to one's own past (Shoemaker 1984b, 23). Ordinary memories are a subclass of quasi memories. Since it is logically possible that there should be quasi memories that are not ordinary memories, self-ascriptions of past experiences based on apparent memories of these experiences from the inside are not logically immune to error through misidentification. On the other hand, given that all quasi-remembering is in fact remembering, such judgments "can be said to have *de facto* immunity to error through misidentification" (Shoemaker 1984b, 46). If a distinction along these lines between logical and de facto immunity to error through misidentification is viable, then it raises the question of whether it is logically immune or merely de facto immune first-person statements that *introspective* self-awareness needs to be capable of grounding. I will come back to this.

The most obvious difficulty with Shoemaker's defence of the view that one cannot be introspectively aware of oneself as an object is this: he concedes that perceptually based demonstrative judgments such as 'This is red' do not involve an identification of the presented object and are immune to error through misidentification relative to the demonstrative pronoun. As he writes, "normally it is not the case that I say 'This is red' because I find that something is red and identify that thing as 'this'" (Shoemaker 1994b, 130). Yet the awareness on which such judgements are based is the best possible example of perceptual awareness of something as an object. At any rate, if this is not an example of awareness of something "as an object," then it is utterly mysterious what this notion is supposed to amount to. So it is not true *in general* that there is any incompatibility between the idea that a form of awareness is awareness of something as an object and the idea that this sort of awareness yields judgments that are immune to error through misidentification. Therefore, the fact that introspectively based first-person statements are immune to error through misidentification is not enough *on its own* to establish that the awareness on which such statements are based is not perceptual, and so not awareness of oneself as an object, any more than the fact that demonstrative judgments are immune to error through misidentification shows that the awareness on which they are based is not perceptual.

Shoemaker maintains that it is a mistake to assimilate self-reference to demonstrative reference, because there are important differences between them that do not come out if one confines one's attention to present-tense judgments. Crucially, "the immunity to error through misidentification of first-person judgements is preserved in memory, whereas that of demonstrative judgements is not" (Shoemaker 1994, 130). How can this be reconciled with the concession that self-ascriptions of past experiences based on apparent memories of them are not logically immune to error through misidentification? It will not be enough in this connection to point to the de facto immunity of such judgments, since it is plausible that past-tense demonstrative judgments (e.g., 'This was red') can also be de facto immune to error through misidentification.[7] Shoemaker's response is that this does not affect his main point, since the possibility of quasi memories that are not memories does not show that first-person memory judgments involve "a perceptual tracking of a self over time" (Shoemaker 1994b, 131). In contrast, past-tense demonstrative judgments do rest upon the ability to keep track of an object.

It is certainly plausible to suggest that self-reference differs from demonstrative reference in that the latter, but not the former, involves the ability to keep track of an object,[8] although much more needs to be said about the notion of keeping track. What is less clear is the bearing of this difference on the earlier argument for ET. If past-tense demonstrative judgments as well as past-tense first-person judgments can be de facto immune to error through misidentification, then both judgments that do and those that do not involve keeping track of an object can be de facto immune.[9] So there still seems no reason in principle why awareness of oneself as an object—where this is now understood as involving some form of perceptual self-tracking—cannot yield judgments that are de facto immune to error through misidentification and so that count as *introspective* awareness.

One response to this argument on behalf of ET would be to deny that where a form of awareness involves keeping track of an object, judgments based on such awareness can be immune to error through misidentification. Since this amounts to a denial of the de facto immunity of all past-tense demonstrative judgments, there are strong reasons for not responding to the doubts about ET in this way.

Another response is this: introspective awareness is, by definition, a form of awareness on the basis of which it is possible to make first-person statements in which the first-person pronoun is used as subject. If the awareness on which a first-person statement is based involves keeping track of a presented object, then the statement is not one in which 'I' is used as subject. Another way of making this point would be to say that it is necessary but not sufficient for awareness of oneself to count as introspective that it ground first-person statements that are (de facto) immune to error through misidentification. A further condition is that introspective self-awareness must not involve "keeping track" of the self, in a sense that requires further elaboration. This suggests the following restatement of the argument for ET: (a) introspective awareness, properly so called, must be capable of grounding first-person statements that are immune to error through misidentification, and must not involve the "perceptual tracking of a self over time"; (b) awareness of oneself as an object must be perceptual and so must involve the perceptual tracking of oneself over time; (c) therefore, one cannot be introspectively aware of oneself as an object.

What is the significance of bodily awareness for this argument for ET? Ayers claims that Shoemaker's argument for ET is "evidently fallacious" (Ayers 1991, 287), since bodily awareness is awareness of oneself as being a material object among others. There is, however, no question that the argument is valid, given Shoemaker's *own* understanding of the notions of introspection and awareness of oneself as an object, for it is a tautology that no form of awareness can both involve and not involve the perceptual tracking of a self. This confirms the suggestion made at the end of section 1 that rather than trying to show that Shoemaker's argument is invalid in its own terms, a better approach would be to argue that some forms of bodily awareness satisfy better grounded and, *in the present context*, more relevant criteria for counting as awareness of oneself as an object.

The first question, then, is whether first-person judgments based on awareness of one's body from the inside can be shown to be immune to error through misidentification. Consider the case of bodily sensations such as pain. Since pains are necessarily felt to have a bodily location (see O'Shaughnessy 1980, chap. 5), our awareness of them is, in this sense, "bodily." Yet self-ascriptions of pain are paradigm first-person judgments that are immune to error through misidentification. So bodily awareness can be the basis of first-person judgments that are immune to error through misidentification.

Awareness of bodily sensations such as pain is not the only form of bodily awareness that satisfies the immunity condition on introspection. Another form of bodily awareness that does so is proprioceptive awareness of the position of one's limbs. In part 3, I will attempt to bring out the special status of proprioceptive awareness. I will focus on proprioceptively based self-ascriptions of limb position, such as 'My legs are crossed', and will refer to such self-ascriptions as 'L-ascriptions'. It might be wondered what bearing my discussion of proprioceptive awareness has on ET, for the latter is concerned with introspective awareness of thoughts, feelings, beliefs, and desires, rather than awareness of limb position. It might also be objected that bodily awareness is not properly described as awareness of oneself qua subject, or awareness of oneself as an object. I will consider these objections in section 4.

3 Proprioception and Appropriation

Are L-ascriptions immune to error through misidentification? It has been claimed that although each of us is normally proprioceptively aware only of his or her own body, one can envisage this restriction as not obtaining. As Armstrong put it, "We can conceive of being directly hooked-up, say by a transmission of waves in some medium, to the body of another. In such a case we might become aware e.g. of the movements of another's limbs, in much the same sort of way that we become aware of the motion of our own limbs" (Armstrong 1984, 113). If one can be aware of someone else's body in the same sort of way that one is normally aware of one's own, then one might be mistaken in thinking that the body one is aware of from the inside is one's own. So L-ascriptions are not immune to error through misidentification.

According to Evans, for examples such as Armstrong's to threaten the immunity of L-ascriptions, one's judgment 'My legs are crossed', based on proprioceptive, or if one prefer "quasi-proprioceptive," awareness of someone else's limbs, would have to express *knowledge* that *someone's* legs are crossed. If this condition is not met, then such examples do not establish the liability of L-ascriptions to error through *misidentification* (Evans 1982, chap. 7).

I will not discuss this argument here. Instead, I want to examine the possibility of showing that L-ascriptions are immune to error through misidentification by appealing to what might be called an *idealist* account of body ownership. Consider the following analogy: If one asks what makes a pain one's own pain, one answer, which might be described as idealism about pain ownership, would be that what makes it one's own is the fact that one is aware of it in the appropriate way. This would explain why one cannot be aware, in the appropriate way, of a pain that is not one's own. Suppose next that one asks what makes a particular body or limb one's own. A parallel answer would be that one's own body just is the one that one is aware of in the appropriate way, that is, "from the inside." If one's own body is, by definition, the one that one is aware of from the in- side, then it is no more possible for one to be mistaken in thinking that the body that one is aware of from the inside is one's own than for one to be mistaken in thinking that the pain that one feels is one's own. Hence, L-as- criptions are not just de facto immune but also logically immune to error through misidentification.

Even for the idealist, however, there would remain the following asym- metry between L-ascriptions and self-ascriptions of pain: although L-ascrip- tions are logically immune to error through misidentification when based on awareness of a pair of legs from the inside, the idealist must grant that there are ways of knowing one's legs to be crossed (looking in a mirror, for example) that do *not* generate logical immunity to error. In contrast, it might be held that there is no way of knowing that one is in pain that does not generate logical immunity to error through misidentification. If there is no way of knowing that one instantiates a given property that does not generate logical immunity to error through misidentification, then self-ascriptions of that property are, in Shoemaker's terminology, *absolutely* immune to error through misidentification. If there are ways of knowing that one instantiates a given property that do, and ways that do not, generate logical immunity, then those self-ascriptions of that property that *are* logically immune to error through misidentification are *circumstantially* immune.

Although it is possible to draw such a distinction between absolute and circumstantial immunity, it is unclear what the point of the distinction is supposed to be (see Evans 1982, 220). As far as my discussion of idealism is concerned, the crucial issue is whether L-ascriptions are logically immune to error through misidentification. If they are logically immune, the fact that it is *also* possible to ascribe bodily properties to oneself in ways that leave open the possibility of misidentification appears to be of little significance. The proposal to be examined is that L-ascriptions are logically immune to error through misidentification because the awareness on which they are based has the "appropriating" function claimed for it by idealism.

One example of an idealist conception of body ownership is Locke's account of what makes a limb a part of one. In the context of a discussion of how personal identity is compatible with a change of substance, Locke writes,

That this is so, we have some kind of evidence in our very bodies, all whose particles, whilst vitally united to this same thinking conscious self, so that we *feel* when they are touched, and are affected by, and are conscious of good or harm that happens to them, are a part of our *selves* i.e. of our thinking conscious *self.* Thus the limbs of his body are to everyone a part of himself; he sympathizes and is concerned for them. Cut off an hand, and thereby separate it from that consciousness he had of its heat, cold, and other affections; and it is then no longer a part of that which is *himself,* any more than the remotest part of matter (Locke 1975, book 2, chap. 27, sec. 11).

The argument, in other words, is as follows:

a. To experience a limb as a part of oneself is to feel when it is touched, to be conscious of its temperature and other "affections," and to have sympathy and concern for it.
b. To experience a limb as a part of oneself is necessary and sufficient for it to be a part of one.

The idea, then, is that the peculiar awareness one has of one's limbs, not to mention one's thoughts and actions, appropriates them to oneself.

This is not to rule out the possibility of phantom-limb experiences, the possibility that one might be mistaken in thinking that there is a limb there at all, but if there is a limb one is conscious of in the "appropriating" way, then, in virtue of this fact, the limb is a part of one. This argument is difficult to assess without seeing how the reference to "other affections" in (a) is spelled out, but there certainly seem to be grave difficulties with it as it stands. On the one hand, it cannot be necessary for a body part to be a part of one that one should experience it as such, for one has many bodily parts that one does not experience at all. Locke's reply to this would presumably have been to appeal to his animal/person distinction (Locke 1975, book 2, chap. 27): insensitive internal organs and limbs without feeling are a part of the animal in which one is "realized," but not of the person one is. If, however, the animal/person distinction is unsustainable, the necessity component of (b) remains problematic.

The sufficiency component of (b) is more difficult to assess. Someone influenced by Armstrong's example might wish to press the question of why one's brain might not be connected by wave transmission in some medium to some other person's legs in such a way that one is conscious of heat or cold in them, feels when they are touched, and is, as a result, concerned for them. Clearly, Locke is committed to rejecting this description of the case: it would not be some other person's legs that one is conscious of but one's own. Is such a stipulation be justified? One reason for thinking that it is not is that Locke's account of what it is to experience a limb as a part of one is inadequate. The less demanding the conditions on experiencing a limb as a part of one, the easier it is to construct examples in which all of Locke's conditions are met with respect to a particular limb, but in which it would nevertheless be counterintuitive to insist that the experienced limb really is a part of one. This suggests that what is required to strengthen the idealist's position is a richer account of what it is to experience a limb as a part of one. The idea is that the conditions on experiencing a limb as a part of one must be strong enough that if all the conditions were really met with respect to a particular limb, then there would be no good case for continuing to insist that it might nevertheless not belong to one.

It is not difficult to think of ways in which (a) needs to be enriched. An important aspect of one's awareness of a limb as a part of one that Locke does not mention is one's proprioceptive awareness of its spatial position and movement. It also seems to be part of one's appropriating awareness of one's limbs that one does not experience them in isolation from each other and the rest of one's body; rather, they are experienced as integrated with each other and the rest of one's body as part of an integrated totality (see O'Shaughnessy 1980, 146). This condition may be referred to as the *unity* condition on bodily awareness. Suppose, then, that to experience a limb as a part of one is to have feeling in it, to be concerned for it, to be proprioceptively aware of its position and movement in space, and to experience it as an integrated part of a bodily totality. A limb that meets all these conditions is, in O'Shaughnessy's terminology, "immediately present" to one (1980, 145). So instead of speaking somewhat vaguely of one's experience of a limb "from the inside," one may speak of a limb or body part as being immediately present to one. With the notion of immediate presence in place, Locke's conditions may be revised as follows:

a'. To experience a limb or body part as a part of one is for it to be immediately present to one.
b'. The immediate presence to one of a limb or body part is necessary and sufficient for it to be a part of one.

Despite this enriching of Locke's notion of "appropriating" bodily awareness, the necessity component of (b') remains problematic, for many of one's internal organs are not immediately present to one, and one's limbs might cease to be present to one as a result of illness or injury. What of the sufficiency component? Suppose that the immediate presence of a limb to one is indeed a sufficient condition for it to be one's own. The question now is whether L-ascriptions are or are not immune to error through misidentification. For the idealist, this question is easy to answer. If a pair of crossed legs is immediately present to one and if their immediate presence to one is sufficient for them to be one's own legs, then in judging 'My legs are crossed' on the basis of their immediate presence, one cannot be mistaken because, and only because, the immediately present limbs are not one's own. The L-ascription comes out as not merely de facto immune to error through misidentification but also as logically immune.

Is it plausible that the immediate presence to one of a limb or body part is a sufficient condition for it to be one's own? Once again the idealist must confront the question of why it cannot happen that the crossed legs that are immediately present to one and that one takes to be one's own actually belong to one's twin on the other side of the room. This version of Armstrong's example may be referred to, somewhat question-beggingly, as the *alien limb* example. To simplify matters, I will assume that the alien limb is not immediately present to one's twin, although in a fuller discussion it would be necessary to address the question of whether one and the same limb might be immediately present to, and therefore, according to (b'), belong to, two people. If the alien-limb example is coherent as described, it is conceivable that one's L-ascription 'My legs are crossed' is mistaken because, and only because, the person whose legs are immediately present to one is not oneself.

Another example that might be thought to threaten the sufficiency component of (b'), although it has no direct bearing on the issue of immunity to error through misidentification, is the example of a prosthetic limb. Is it not conceivable that a suitably sophisticated prosthetic limb should be immediately present to one? Yet even a sophisticated prosthetic limb would surely not be a part of one. To make it plausible that an immediately present prosthetic limb may fail to be a part of one, consider the following admittedly outlandish example suggested by O'Shaughnessy: one's hand and forearm have been amputated without one's knowledge. Suspended in midair behind a screen is a metal hand with mechanisms exactly duplicating those of an ordinary hand attached to one's wrist. If one is asked to move one's index finger, "certain brain events then occur which transmit an electrical 'message' to the nerve endings of my arm, this current is then transmitted across space to the copper wires in the metal hand, the mechanical muscle then contracts and the metal finger moves!" (O'Shaughnessy 1980, 134). We might also be able to reproduce the postural messages that an ordinary hand sends to the brain, and even import tactile and other sensations. At this point it would not be implausible to claim that the detached hand is immediately present to one, but it would not be correct to say that it is a part of one. So here is another counterexample to the sufficiency component of (b').

An idealist who is committed to the sufficiency component of (b') has two options in the face of the alien-limb and prosthetic-limb examples. The first would be to deny that the "alien" and prosthetic limbs would not be a part of one. The other would be to accept that they are not a part of one, but to argue that they do not fulfill all the conditions on immediate presence. The first of these options will have to contend with the intuition that a limb with which one is not materially united cannot be a part of one.[10] Because one's being materially united with a limb is a necessary condition for it to be a part of one, its immediate presence to one cannot be a sufficient condition. The idealist could reply to this argument by simply rejecting the material-unity condition, but this would be somewhat dogmatic. A better response would be to accept the material-unity condition but to interpret it in such a way that it poses no threat to idealism. So the two questions that now need to be addressed are these: (1) What is to be understood by material unity? (2) Is there a plausible interpretation of the material-unity condition that would allow the idealist to say, without laying himself open to the charge of gerrymandering the notion of material unity, that the alien and prosthetic limbs are not only immediately present to one but also materially united with one?

In connection with (1), consider Ayers's remark that a bullet embedded in the flesh of an animal is not materially united with it, because material unity is not the same as mere local conjunction. The difference between the two may be brought out by considering what happens when water freezes solid:

> If there had been a stone in the water, then, however firmly it is now wedged in the ice, it is still proper to think of it as a distinct individual rather than as part of a materially unitary whole. Its parts are causally and historically related as they are not related to the parts of the lump of ice. It is in broadly the same way that a bul-let or, for that matter, a plastic hip-joint remains distinct from the animal in which it is embedded, a tree from the rock enclosed in its roots. (Ayers 1991, 232)

The use to which the idealist might hope to put these remarks is this: the essence of material unity is not local conjunction but causal and histor-ical connection. Above I said that the idealist is going to have to contend with the intution that the alien and prosthetic limbs are not a part of one, because they are not materially united with one. Given the distinction be-tween material unity and local conjunction, it is possible to redescribe this intuition as the intuition that such limbs are not locally conjoined with the rest of one's body. It does not follow, however, that one is not materially united with them. For a limb to be immediately present to one, one must be causally related to it, and the idealist may claim that the causal connec-tions between oneself and a limb necessary for it to be immediately present to one are at the same time sufficient for one to be materially united with it. The claim, then, is that though one's being materially united with a limb is a necessary condition for it to be a part of one, this does not show that its being immediately present to one is not a sufficient condition.

There are many objections to this argument. The most obvious is that there seems to be no good reason to accept that the connections between oneself and a limb that result in its being immediately present to one also ensure that one is materially united with it. For example, if the immediate presence to one of the legs of one's twin were the result of the propriocep-tive and sensory feedback being fed into one's brain and nervous system by a Cartesian malicious demon, it is difficult to believe that this would be enough for one to count as materially united with the immediately pres-ent limb. This is related to the point that even if material unity is not the same as local conjunction, it does not follow that local conjunction is not necessary for material unity. To this extent, the idealist is guilty of misun-derstanding Ayers's distinction between material unity and local conjunction. It should be said, of course, that the notion of local conjunction is not entirely straightforward, but no sane account of local conjunction should allow one to count as locally conjoined with the limbs in the earlier examples. If one is not locally conjoined with the distant prosthetic or alien limbs, one is not materially united with them. Hence, they are not a part of one. If they are nevertheless immediately present to one, then the immediate presence to one of a limb is not a sufficient condition for it to be a part of one. In those cases in which material unity and immediate presence come apart, then, it is material unity that matters, according to what might be called *realism* about the body. This suggests the following way of fleshing out the realist alternative to idealism: for a limb or body part to be a part of one, it is both necessary and sufficient that one is materially united with it.

Before examining the consequences of realism for the immunity to error through misidentification, or otherwise, of L-ascriptions, there is another idealist move to consider. Instead of claiming that the earlier examples do fulfill the material-unity condition, the idealist would be better advised to deny that they fulfil all the conditions on immediate presence. The condition that seems to be violated in the examples is the unity condition, the condition that an immediately present limb must be experienced as integrated with the rest of one's body. The question that the idealist should press is this: how can a limb that is spatially distant from the rest of one's body be experienced as a part of the totality that is one's body? Since normal bodily awareness is not the experience of oneself as something scattered, the distance between the alien limb and the rest of one's body is scarcely compatible with the limb's being experienced as integrated with one. So the fact that one is not locally conjoined with a limb not only shows that one is not materially united with it; it also casts doubt on the idea that it could be immediately present to one.

All of this has a bearing on the earlier suggestion that one might become aware of the movements of another's limbs in much the same sort of way that we become aware of the motion of our own limbs. If experiencing someone else's limbs in the same sort of way as one experiences one's own means experiencing them as integrated with the rest of one's body, then this not as easy to imagine as the alien-limb example suggests. This line of argument might prompt the response that the unity condition on immediate presence is not as clear-cut as I have assumed. For example, Gallagher argues that although one's body appears in one's field of consciousness in an "owned" way, as one's conscious attention is directed toward one's body, it becomes "disintegrated, consciously articulated into parts" (1986, 545). If *normal* bodily awareness is disintegrated, then it may be a mistake to impose a strong unity condition on immediate presence in the hope of keeping the conditions of material unity and immediate presence together. Much will depend on whether it is correct to understand the notion of immediate bodily presence as having to with the directing of one's conscious attention toward one's body.

These are all questions that the idealist needs to address at some point, but a much simpler point will suffice for present purposes. This is the point that even if there is a strong unity condition on immediate presence, this is not enough for the idealist's purposes. If idealism aims to establish the *logical* immunity of L-ascriptions, then it needs to show not just that it is hard to imagine cases of immediate presence without material unity but also that it is logically impossible for a limb with which one is not materially united to be immediately present to one. There is no plausible and nongerrymandering reading of "immediate presence" and "material unity" that entitles the idealist to such a claim. Hence idealism fails to demonstrate the L ascriptions are logically immune to error through misidentification.

The moral of the discussion so far appears to be that the concession that a limb must be materially united with one for it to be a part of one is fatal for idealism, since it would be quite futile for the idealist to try to demonstrate that the conditions of material unity and immediate presence cannot come apart. Realism, in contrast, claims that a limb belongs to one, in the sense required for the "my" in a bodily self-ascription to be justified, if and only if one is materially united with it. It might be objected that this can only mean that it belongs to one if it is materially united with one's body, and that this cannot be an adequate answer unless the realist has a substantive account of what makes a given body one's *own* body. If the only way that one can be materially united with something is for one's body to be materially united with it, then realism is surely in trouble, for one's body cannot belong to one in virtue of being materially united with one's body. So the realist has got to show either that the question of what makes one's body one's own is improper or that she has the resources to answer it.

Consider, to begin with, the second of these options. One possibility would be to argue that what makes a particular body one's own is the fact that it is materially united with one's brain. If the realist is required to give an account of what makes one's body one's own, then will not the realist also have to explain the fact that a particular brain is one's own brain? If so, then one explanation might be that my brain is the brain in which my thoughts are tokened. Is the last 'my' irreducible, as it were? On one view, even this last 'my' can be eliminated in favor of a demonstrative such as 'this'. For example, Parfit claims that "when I think of my present thought as being mine . . . , my identifying reference essentially involves an *indexical* word, or a *demonstrative*, rather than the ascription of a unique property. . . . Since I can use the self-referring use of 'this', I do not need to use 'mine' " (1984, 517–518). So the thesis that is beginning to emerge is this: what makes a particular body mine is that it is materially united with the brain in which *this* very thought is tokened.

One question is whether this account of body ownership is successful. A prior consideration, however, is that it is far from obvious that the realist should go down this particular road. What seems to be motivating the account is what might be called *reductionism about ownership*, the idea that there should be no irreducible use of 'my' in an account of what makes one's body one's own. In reply, the realist should point out that it is not even clear that the 'my' in 'my body' needs to be given a substantive explanation, let alone that the explanation should take the particular reductive form just proposed. For example, it may be that talk of subjects "having" bodies is, in part, a reflection of the belief that we are, as the Cartesian claims, separately existing entities, distinct from our brains and bodies. As Wittgenstein put it, "There is a criterion for 'this is my nose': the nose would be possessed by the body to which it is attached. There is a temptation to say that there is a soul to which one's body belongs and that my body is the one that belongs to me" (1979, 24). Clearly, this is a temptation to which the realist should refuse to succumb. Here I will not pursue the question of whether the realist is in a position to disarm demands for a substantive account of body ownership not motivated by specifically Cartesian considerations (e.g., Shoemaker 1984c).

The position at which we have arrived in this: on Shoemaker's conception of introspective awareness, for proprioceptive awareness to count as introspective, it must *at least* ground L-ascriptions that are immune to error through misidentification. If the required form of immunity is logical immunity and one also agrees with the realist that for an L-ascription to be correct the self-ascribed limb must be materially united with one, then L-ascriptions are not logically immune, and the awareness on which they are based is not introspective. This invites the question of why it would not be enough for bodily awareness to count as introspective that L-ascriptions should be de facto immune. It is unacceptable simply to stipulate that introspective awareness must be capable of yielding logically immune first-person judgements. The demand for logical immunity must be properly grounded and not simply based upon a prior commitment to ET. Since it is not clear what grounds there could be for insisting on logical immunity, it would be more pertinent to ask whether L-ascriptions are even de facto immune for the realist.

The following observations make it plausible that realism is entitled to claim that L-ascriptions are de facto immune to error through misidentification: In the first place, the intelligibility of the supposition that the body immediately present to one might not be one's own should not be taken to show that the idea that people "have" bodies in a natural sense is compatible with the thought that it might be true *in general* that the bodies immediately present to them are not their own. Secondly, although it is conceivable that a limb with which one is not materially united, and hence that is not a part of one, should nevertheless be immediately present to one, one's being materially united with a limb is, in normal circumstances, a *causally* necessary condition of its being immediately present to one. This is why bodily self-ascriptions based on immediate presence of a limb are de facto immune to error through misidentification. To this extent, proprioceptive awareness remains a candidate for being a form of introspective awareness.

4   The Body and the Self

At the end of section 2, I raised the question of whether the fact that proprioceptive awareness is introspective has any bearing on ET. After all, what has introspective awareness of where one's limbs are in space got to do introspective awareness of thoughts, feelings, beliefs, and desires? This invites the following response: The objects of introspective awareness are supposed to be "inner" states or occurrences, and these include sensations such as pain. It is intrinsic to such sensations, however, that they present themselves as located in parts of one's body. For one to experience a body part as a part of one's body is for it to be immediately present to one, and at least in the case of limbs, their immediate presence to one requires that one is proprioceptively aware of them (see above). So introspective awarenes of at least some inner occurrences is bound up with introspective awareness of where one's limbs are in space.

An objection to this line of argument is that it has no bearing on those inner occurrences, such as thinking, that are not experienced as having a bodily location. The claim that thinking is not experienced as having a bodily location is open to dispute, but I will not pursue this point here. It is enough to cast doubt on ET that introspective awareness of at least *some* inner states or occurrences requires awareness of oneself as being a material object among others. This suggests that the supporter of ET should explore the other options set out at the end of section 2. On this approach, the appeal to bodily awareness "from the inside" does nothing to undermine (ET), not because it is not introspective or has nothing to do with one's awareness of inner occurrences but because such awareness is (1) not awareness of oneself "as an object," or (2) not a genuine form of self-awareness or, at any rate, awareness of oneself qua subject.

Suppose, for the sake of argument, that bodily awareness is admitted to be a genuine form of introspective self-awareness, introspective awareness of what Ayers (1991, 287) calls the "bodily self" qua subject. The question raised by (1) is this: if bodily awareness "from the inside" is introspective self-awareness, can it also be awareness of the presented bodily self "as an object"? Earlier I extracted from Shoemaker's discussion the proposal that for a form of awareness to count as introspective, it must (a) yield judgments that are de facto immune to error through misidentification and (b) not involve the perceptual tracking of a self. The argument of section 3 shows that bodily awareness meets the first of these conditions, but nothing has been said so far about whether it also meets the second condition. If it meets the first but not the second condition, then bodily awareness may be awareness of the "bodily self" as an object but it is not be introspective, despite the de facto immunity of L-ascriptions. If bodily awareness meets both conditions, then it is introspective but is not awareness of the bodily self "as an object," on the assumption that awareness of something as an object must involve keeping track.

To understand the force of (b), I need to say more about the notion of tracking. Shoemaker writes that the past-tense demonstrative judgement 'This was red,' "might be grounded in part on an observed similarity between the thing one sees now and the thing one remembers seeing to be red in the past" (1994b, 130). If this is what keeping track of an object involves, then it would be quite implausible to suppose that past-tense L-ascriptions are based upon an ability to keep track of one's body or body parts. There is no question of the judgment being based upon an observed similiarity between the body immediately present to one now and the body immediately present to one in the past. As Evans stresses, keeping track requires "*skill* or *care* (not to lose track of something) on the part of the subject" (1982, 237). Victims of "proprioblindness" might be said in some sense to to be exercising "skill or care" in keeping track of their bodies, but it is not plausible that normal bodily awareness requires such skill or care.[11] To this extent, the awareness on which past-tense L-ascriptions are based satisfies the second condition on introspective awareness as well as the first.

The conclusion that the supporter of ET draws from all of this is that (introspective) bodily self-awareness is not awareness of oneself as an object. But how well grounded is the assumption that awareness of something as an object must involve keeping track of it? It would be a mistake for the materialist opponent of ET to dismiss as arbitrary or unmotivated the idea that straightforward *perceptual* awareness of something as an object is connected with a capacity to keep track of it. The question is whether awareness of *oneself* as an object must be, in *this* sense, perceptual.[12] If the materialist insists that there is a sense in which bodily awareness is awareness of oneself as an object despite the fact that it differs from other forms of perceptual awareness, he needs to explain not only what this sense is but also why the sense in which bodily awareness constitutes awareness of oneself as an object matters more in the present context than the sense in which it does not constitute awareness of oneself as an object.

One account of the sense in which bodily awareness is awareness of the bodily self as an object despite the fact that it does not involve keeping track might be the following: Material objects are not only spatially located but also possessors of "primary" qualities such as shape and solidity. To experience something *as* a material object is to experience it *as*, among other things, having shape and solidity. One way in which one might be aware of the presence of something solid at a certain location is to discover that one cannot push one's body through it when it is in tactile contact.[13] To experience the solidity of another object in this way is at the same time to be aware of the solidity of one's own body, to be aware of it as a solid object competing with other solid objects to occupy space. In O'Shaughnessy's words, "the space and solidity of our bodies provides the access to the space and solidity of other bodies" (1989, 38; see also Martin 1993, 213). To the extent that the body one is introspectively aware of is experienced not only as subject (see below) but also as the bearer of properties whose possession by an object makes it a material object, one is aware of oneself as being a material object among others.

Another way of bringing out the force of the idea that one is aware of oneself as an object is suggested by Merleau-Ponty's remark that the presence of an object "is such that it entails a possible absence" (Merleau-Ponty 1989, 90). Merleau-Ponty himself described the presence of one's body as being absolute rather than de facto, but reflection on the possibility of proprioblindness casts doubt on this claim. More generally, awareness of something as an object might be thought to involve awareness of it as something to which there is, or might be, more than meets the eye. Bodily self-awareness would then count as awareness of oneself as an object to the extent that it is awareness of the bodily self as having "secret recesses" (Leder 1990, chap. 2), in the form of internal organs and other body parts, which only come into view in special circumstances, such as illness or injury.

I remarked in the introduction that the answer to the question of whether introspective bodily awareness counts as awareness of oneself as an object depends on the context in which the question is asked. Suppose that one is interested in the question because one is interested in the nature of self-knowledge and is influenced by the Kantian thesis that self-knowledge requires an intuition of the subject as an object. One would then have to ask whether the sense in which one is aware oneself as an object in bodily self-awareness constitutes intuitive awareness *of the kind required to underpin a claim to self-knowledge.* This is the point at which the difference between Kant's own conception of self-knowledge and what was described as the "broadly Kantian conception" does important work. If one assumes that the fundamental source of self-knowledge must be intuition in *Kant's* sense and that intuitive awareness of something in his sense must be perceptual, and so involve keeping track, then bodily self-awareness fails to count as awareness of oneself as an object in the sense that matters most. According to the broadly Kantian conception, however, although self-knowledge needs in *some* sense to be grounded in awareness of oneself as an object, such awareness need not be straightforwardly perceptual. As long as one rejects the assumption that knowledge of the self has to take the same form as perceptual knowledge of objects distinct from oneself, there is room for the idea that the respects in which bodily self-awareness is awareness of oneself as an object grounds introspective self-knowledge.[14]

There is little doubt that bodily awareness is, by Kantian lights, awareness of one's *body* as an object to the extent that it is awareness of it as (relatively) "fixed and abiding" (see Cassam 1993). As (2) suggests, the really difficult question for Kant is not whether one is aware of one's body as an object but whether introspective bodily awareness is a genuine form of self-awareness, or awareness of the self qua subject. One objection to the idea that bodily awareness is self-awareness is that it makes what must here be the question-begging assumption that the self *is* something bodily. In reply, the materialist might argue as follows: it is true that the initial discussion of the materialist objection to ET proceeded on the assumption, which Shoemaker endorses, that the self is bodily. On the other hand, it is also possible to understand the materialist opponent of ET as simply claiming that one's body *presents itself* as the subject of some of one's inner states. This would help to explain the idea that bodily awareness is awareness of oneself qua (embodied) subject. It is, a further question however, whether the nature of the subject is as it appears to be. Talk of one's being aware of one's body *qua* subject need not *presuppose* the bodily nature of the self. Rather, according to the broadly Kantian conception of self-knowledge, it is one of a range of considerations that helps to *motivate* a nondualist conception of the self.

If the conditions on awareness of oneself qua subject are the same as the conditions on introspective awareness, then, on the assumption that bodily awareness is introspective, such awareness must also be awareness of oneself qua subject. By Kant's lights, however, it is scarcely intelligible to say that a spatial object or "outer appearance," such as one's body, might be, in Ayers's words (1991, 286), the "*presented* subject of experience." The Kantian subject is, by definition, an object of inner sense (see Kant 1929, A342/B400). What is represented by us as an object of inner sense cannot be an object of outer sense, so a spatial object such as one's own body cannot *appear* or present itself to one as the possessor of one's thoughts, feelings, and desires. As Kant, who describes his dualism as "empirical" (1929, A379) rather than "transcendental," puts it, "thinking beings, *as such*, can never be found by us among outer appearances" (1929, A357). This is claimed to be distinct from "transcendental" (Cartesian) dualism because it leaves open the possibility that what appears to us in spatial form "is (in itself) internally a subject" (1929, A360).

Is Kant's empirical dualism acceptable? There are several reasons for thinking that it is not.[15] First, the fact that bodily awareness satisfies Shoemaker's conditions on introspective awareness cannot simply be dismissed, since it is plausible that the conditions on introspective awareness and those on awareness of oneself qua subject are, if not identical, at least closely related. Second, it is also unclear what someone who thinks that inner states are perceived by means of inner sense, which "has to do neither with shape nor position" (Kant 1929, A33/B49-50), can make of the fact that some inner states present themselves as located in parts of one's body. There may be a gap between the idea that sensations present themselves as having a bodily *location* and the idea that one's body presents itself as their *subject*, but the two ideas are surely not unconnected. Third, the body is the subject's point of view on the world. One's own location, which determines what one can perceive,[16] is the location of one's body, and perceived objects are perceived as standing in spatial relations to one's body.[17] In these and in other respects, one apprehends one's body as "a natural self, and, as it were, the subject of perception," in Merleau-Ponty's phrase (1989, 206). The spatial content of bodily awareness might show that such awareness is not a form of "inner sense" in Kant's sense, yet the various respects in which one is aware of one's body as a "natural self" calls into question Kant's empirical dualism.

If this line of argument is to be persuasive, more needs to be said in general terms about what it means to describe something as the "presented" subject of experience. It is not obvious, however, why one should accept an account of this notion that excludes the possibility of a physical thing appearing to one qua subject of one's inner states. It is instructive in this connection to contrast Descartes's approach with Kant's. As I remarked at the outset, Shoemaker presents the thesis that "one is not presented to oneself in introspection as a *bodily* object" (Shoemaker 1984a, 103) as a consideration that has (mistakenly) been thought to support a Cartesian dualist view of the self. Far from endorsing this thesis, however, Descartes went out of his way to draw attention to the respects in which one is introspectively aware of oneself as something bodily. His claim was rather that the experienced unity of mind and body embodies an illusion about the true nature of the "I" that thinks. Since it is plausible that this claim can only be disarmed by broadly conceptual or metaphysical considerations, it would be a mistake to suppose that the fact that one is introspectively aware of oneself as a material object is enough to refute Cartesian dualism. Nor is this fact enough to refute the transcendental-idealist thesis that the self that one knows to be an object in the world can only be the empirical self and not the "transcendental" subject. What the materialist opponent of ET is right to emphasize, however, is that it is the Cartesian, rather than the materialist, whose conception of the true nature of the "I" is at odds with how it presents itself as being, both to others and to itself in introspection. If materialism is correct and the "I" that thinks is a corporeal object among corporeal objects, then things are just as they seem.

Acknowledgments

Michael Ayers's remarks on the nature of self-consciousness in Ayers 1991 provided the initial stimulus for this paper. I am grateful to Michael Ayers, Bill Brewer, Naomi Eilan, and an anonymous reader for the MIT Press for detailed written responses to an earlier draft, and to audiences in Berkeley, Oxford, and Cambridge for many other helpful comments.

Notes

1. Kant describes "outer sense" as a property of our mind by means of which we represent objects as "outside us, and all without exception in space" (Kant 1929, A22/B37).

2. Chisholm is well aware of this. See Chisholm 1994, 94.

3. See the introduction to Cassam 1994 for a more detailed account of the historical importance of various versions of the elusiveness thesis.

4. For further discussion of this issue, see the introduction to Cassam 1994, especially pp. 7–9.

5. This is made explicit in Kant 1929 at B158.

6. See the papers in Cassam 1994 for an overview of some of the issues that a theory of self-knowledge must address.

7. Shoemaker claims that the judgment 'This *was* red then' "involves an identification that could be mistaken" (Shoemaker 1994b, 130). As Evans points out, however, although a past-tense judgment of the form 'This was *F*' might be based on 'That was *F*' and 'This = that' when made after a long enough period of observation, "we cannot apply this procedure generally, supposing our demonstrative Ideas of objects to cover only momentary slices of the objects' histories" (Evans 1982, 175). This brings out the importance of the thesis that not all past-tense demonstrative judgments are subject to error through misidentification.

8. The importance of this aspect of "I-thinking" is emphasized in Evans 1982, chap. 7, and Cassam 1992, sec. 3.

9. As Evans points out in effect. See Evans 1982, chaps. 6, 7.

10. For more on the notion of "material unity," see Ayers 1991, chap. 20.

11. "Proprioblindness" is Sacks's term (1991) for whole-body loss of touch and proprioception. Cole 1991 contains a moving and fascinating account of an actual case of proprioblindness.

12. This question is pressed in the introduction to Cassam 1994, especially pp. 12–13. As Martin also points out, although the fact that one does not encounter one's body as one among others in bodily awareness may show that such awareness is not perceptual in Shoemaker's sense, this is compatible with maintaining that one is nevertheless aware of one's body "as an object in a world which can contain other objects" (1993, 209).

13. I am indebted at this point to O'Shaughnessy 1989, 41.

14. This approach to introspective self-knowledge is defended at greater length in the introduction to Cassam 1994.

15. In the following account of the respects in which bodily awareness is awareness of oneself qua subject, I am indebted to Bell's exposition of the phenomenological characteristics that help to define Husserl's notion of the "living body." See Bell 1990, 209–210. There is more on Kant's conception of bodily awareness in Cassam 1993.

16. See Evans 1982, chap. 7, and Cassam 1989 for further discussion of the connection between perception and self-location.

17. As Bell puts it (1990, 210), the "living body" is the "absolute point about which all spatial relations are experienced as orientated." See Evans's notion of "egocentric space" in Evans 1982, 153–154.

References

Armstrong, D. M. 1984. "Consciousness and Causality." In D. M. Armstrong and N. Malcolm, *Consciousness and Causality*. Oxford: Basil Blackwell.

Ayers, M. R. 1991. *Locke*, vol. 2. *Ontology*. London: Routledge.

Bell, D. 1990. *Husserl*. London: Routledge.

Brewer, B. 1992. "Self-Location and Agency." *Mind* 101:17–34.

Cassam, Q. 1989. "Kant and Reductionism." *Review of Metaphysics* 43:72–106.

Cassam, Q. 1992. "Reductionism and First-Person Thinking." In D. Charles and K. Lennon, eds., *Reduction, Explanation, and Realism.* Oxford: Clarendon Press.

Cassam, Q. 1993. "Inner Sense, Body Sense, and Kant's Refutation of Idealism." *European Journal of Philosophy*, 1:111–127.

Cassam, Q., ed. 1994. *Self-Knowledge.* Oxford: Oxford University Press.

Chisholm, R. 1994. "On the Observability of the Self." In Cassam 1994.

Cole, J. 1991. *Pride and a Daily Marathon.* London: Duckworth.

Eilan, N., R. McCarthy, and B. Brewer, eds. 1993. *Spatial Representation.* Oxford: Basil Blackwell.

Evans, G. 1982. *The Varieties of Reference.* Edited by J. McDowell. Oxford: Clarendon Press.

Gallagher, S. 1986. "Body Image and Body Schema: A Conceptual Clarification." *Journal of Mind and Behaviour* 7:541–554.

Hume, D. 1978. *A Treatise of Human Nature.* Edited by L. A. Selby-Bigge. Oxford: Clarendon Press.

Kant, I. 1929. *Critique of Pure Reason.* Translated by N. Kemp Smith. London: Macmillan.

Leder, D. 1990. *The Absent Body.* Chicago: University of Chicago Press.

Locke, J. 1975. *An Essay Concerning Human Understanding.* Edited by P. Nidditch. Oxford: Clarendon Press.

Martin, M. 1993. "Sense Modalities and Spatial Properties." In Eilan, McCarthy, and Brewer 1993.

Merleau-Ponty, M. 1989. *Phenomenology of Perception.* Translated by C. Smith. London: Routledge.

O'Shaughnessy, B. 1980. *The Will: A Dual Aspect Theory*, vol 1. Cambridge: Cambridge University Press.

O'Shaughnessy, B. 1989. "The Sense of Touch." *Australasian Journal of Philosophy* 67: 37–58.

Parfit, D. 1984. *Reasons and Persons.* Oxford: Clarendon Press.

Sacks, O. 1991. Foreward to Cole 1991.

Shoemaker, S. 1984a. "Personal Identity: A Materialist's Account." In S. Shoemaker and R. Swinburne, *Personal Identity.* Oxford: Basil Blackwell.

Shoemaker, S. 1984b. "Persons and Their Pasts." In S. Shoemaker, *Identity, Cause, and Mind.* Cambridge: Cambridge University Press.

Shoemaker, S. 1984c. "Embodiment and Behavior." In S. Shoemaker, *Identity, Cause, and Mind.* Cambridge: Cambridge University Press.

Shoemaker, S. 1994a. "Self-Reference and Self-Awareness." In Cassam 1994.

Shoemaker, S. 1994b. "Introspection and the Self." In Cassam 1994.

Strawson, P. F. 1959. *Individuals: An Essay in Descriptive Metaphysics*. London: Methuen.

Strawson, P. F. 1966. *The Bounds of Sense*. London: Methuen.

Wittgenstein, L. 1961. *Tractatus Logico-philosophicus*. Translated by D. Pears and B. McGuinness. London: Routledge and Kegan Paul.

Wittgenstein, L. 1979. *Wittgenstein's Lectures, Cambridge, 1932–1935*. Edited by A. Ambrose. Oxford: Basil Blackwell.

Consciousness and the Self

Naomi Eilan

As the title of this paper suggests, the problems I want to discuss lie at the intersection of two questions. The first is the question of how we explain what it is for perceptions to yield consciousness of the environment, in what does the *consciousness* of conscious perceptions consist. The second is the question of what is the concept of *self* needed for explaining what it is to be a subject of experiences. To anticipate, I will be suggesting, first, that an explanation of perceptual consciousness rests on an explanation of what it is for an organism to be a subject of experiences. Second, I will be suggesting that the concept of a subject we need here must make essential appeal to the subject's actual movements in her actual environment. It is not merely the representation of oneself as embodied but the fact of one's embodiment that will be doing the work in the account of perceptual consciousness that emerges.

I begin with a few brief remarks about the relation between explanations of perceptual consciousness and those of subjecthood. For this we need before us a passage from Gareth Evans's *Varieties of Reference* and a very brief summary of the way Evans goes on to develop the questions raised in this passage:

However addicted we may be to thinking of the link between [perceptual] input and behavioural output in information processing terms . . . , it seems abundantly clear that evolution could have thrown up an organism in which such advantageous links had been established long before it had provided us with a conscious subject of experience. (Evans 1983, 158)

Evans goes on to suggest that if this is not immediately obvious, the point is brought home by consideration of the kinds of cases that Weiskrantz has labeled blindsight, in which information is evidently processed but consciousness is prima facie lacking (see Weiskrantz 1986 for a comprehensive study of such cases). He then argues that what such cases show is that for an information-processing system to be a conscious subject of experiences, perceptual information, which is, on Evans's account, essentially nonconceptual (and very similar to the kinds of contents ascribed by Gibson to perceptions) must be input to a concept-using system. When we have a system that counts as a subject in virtue of the use of concepts, then the perceptual-input states are conscious experiences.

I will later come back briefly to Evans's own positive account of perceptual consciousness. At this point I want to focus on, and help myself to, the way he sets up the problem of explaining consciousness, which brings us directly to the topic of this paper. This is the idea that, to put it at its strongest, explaining what it is for perceptual states to be conscious just is a matter of explaining what it is for an information-processing system to be a subject. Now there are three ways in which such a claim might be read. The first two are reductive. On one of these, the concept of a subject of experience is explanatorily prior to that of perceptual consciousness, and we can give an exhaustive account of what it is for a perceptual state to be conscious by appeal to materials we use in explaining what it is for an information-processing system to be a subject. The alternative reductive claim is that the concept of perceptual consciousness is explanatorily prior and we can give an exhaustive account of what it is for an information-processing system to be a subject by appeal to the materials yielded by an explanation of perceptual consciousness. On the third reading, the claim is a no-priority interdependence claim. On this view, the notions of a subject of experience and of perceptual consciousness are interdependent. Explaining either of them must rest on picking out the points of intersection between the two.

In what follows, I will be adopting, without argument, the first reductive reading of the claim, namely that we get everything we need for explaining what it is for perceptual states to be conscious once we have explained what it is for a system to be a subject. I do not pretend that doing so can, of itself, disqualify the alternatives. However, I hope that the substantive account of consciousness it yields will illustrate the rationale for adopting this position, even if it does not serve, as it stands, to dissolve the attractions of the alternative accounts of the relation between explanations of consciousness and of what it is to be a subject.

1 Points of View

If we are looking for an explanation of perceptual consciousness by appeal to an account of what it is to be a subject of experiences, the natural place to turn is to the notion of a point of view. When we ask what is needed for the perceptual input to an information-processing system to yield consciousness of the environment, we naturally reach to the metaphor of a field of consciousness and to the idea of such a field originating in, or converging on, a point of view. And the notion of a point of view has, of course, a long history in debates about the self and self consciousness, though not always under this description. On the reductive strategy that we are examining it is natural then to suggest, something along the following lines. First, perceptual states are conscious just when they are representations from the subject's point of view. Second, an explanation of perceptual consciousness just is an explanation of what it is for perceptual representations to be from the subject's point of view.

Two ways in which the notion of a point of view enters into accounts of the self and self-consciousness are of particular relevance to such a strategy. On the first, the way the notion of a point of view is introduced gives it no independent explanatory force in accounting for self consciousness. One example of this way of introducing the notion of a point of view would be to suggest, first, that self-consciousness is essentially linked to the capacity to employ what Evans called a primitive theory of self location, a theory that provides the subject simultaneously with an objective conception of her environment and with a detached, and in this sense objective, grip on her own position in it as one object among others (Evans 1983, 222–223). I will refer to the kind of self consciousness involved in the capacity to employ such a theory as substantive self consciousness, understood as requiring, at the very least, a grip on oneself as one physical object among others and, at the most, a grip on oneself as one person among others. The notion of a temporally extended point of view, or a subjective route through the world, Strawson's terms, might then be introduced as one of the by-products of the capacity to employ such a theory in the course of explaining one's perceptions to oneself. More specifically, we may say, again borrowing from Strawson, that when we have such a primitive theory of self location in play, we can draw a distinction between how things seem to the subject and how they objectively are, where how things seem to a subject over time just is the extended point of view, the subjective route (Strawson 1966, 105–106).

On this way of introducing it, the notion of a point of view has no role in *explaining* either what the self is or what it is to be self-conscious. Selves are empirical persons, and self-consciousness is a matter of having a detached grip on oneself as one object among others. These notions are given explanatory priority over the notion of a point of view in the sense that the latter floats out of, is an abstraction from, an explanation of the interdependence between having a detached grip on oneself (substantive self-consciousness) and a detached grip on the environment.

We get to the second, explanatorily richer appeal to the notion of point of view when we turn to the idea that such empirical self-consciousness does not exhaust the nature of self-consciousness, to the idea that we must, in addition, recognize a transcendental form, and, moving from Kant to Wittgenstein's *Tractatus*, to the claim that we must, in addition to the empirical human subject, recognize the existence of a metaphysical ego.

Now, very crudely indeed, on Wittgenstein's account, the metaphysical ego can be equated with the point of view from which, he says, all thought is entertained (Wittgenstein 1961b, 5.641). Something of the flavor of the claim can be made vivid by bringing in the analogy Wittgenstein uses between such an ego and the geometrical point of origin of the visual field. Just as the latter is not an object represented in the visual field but rather an unrepresented mathematical point of origin of all representations in the field, so consciousness at large or, more generally, all thought is entertained from a point of view that is not, and cannot be, represented in thought as an object. This point of origin or, if you like, this essentially elusive point of view from which all thought is entertained, just is the metaphysical ego (Wittgenstein 1961b, 5.633, 5.6331; for an illuminating discussion of the analogy, see Pears 1987, 179–183). Now, whatever else it is, this way of using the notion of a point of view to explain the nature of the self and of self consciousness is not merely an explanatorily empty way of describing the product of one's perception being embedded in a primitive theory of empirical self location. (Indeed, it is not clear whether it need, or even can, have any connection at all with any particular thesis about substantive self-consciousness.) If one believes in metaphysical egos, then one intends such belief to have very profound and far-reaching consequences for how we conceive of the contents of thoughts and, more generally, of the relation of mind and world.

I don't pretend that these brief remarks do anything like justice to either way of appealing to the notion of a point of view in connection with explanations of the nature of the self and of self-consciousness. But for present purposes, they will have to do. For I would like to suggest that, however much they are developed and expanded, neither will do if our interest is to explain perceptual consciousness on the reductive strategy that says that perceptual-input states are conscious just so long as they are representations from the subject's point of view.

To begin with what I will call the *explanatorily-empty* notion of a point of view, doubts might be directed at both the necessity and the sufficiency of this notion for an explanation of perceptual consciousness. One kind of doubt about its sufficiency might go as follows. The notion of a point of view offered on this theory is the product of the exercise of conceptual abilities; it is the seeming side of the distinction between how things seem and how they are when such conceptual abilities are in play. The notion of seeming, as it is used in this connection, applies equally to thought; it does not single out a specifically perceptual form of seeming. If we want to explain perceptual consciousness by appeal to the notion of the subject's point of view, however, we want a notion of a point of view that *will* engage directly with what distinguishes perceptual seemings from mere thinkings. In this connection, it is natural to reach for the idea of an extra- or nonconceptual element in perceptual experience as that which distinguishes perceptual consciousness from pure thought, and then to demand of explanations of perceptual consciousness by appeal to the notion of a point of view that they engage directly with this aspect of experience.

Doubts about the necessity of the link with a primitive theory of self-location for perceptual consciousness may turn on the wish to allow for some continuity between ourselves and other animals, animals for which we seem to have no grounds to ascribe the capacity for the kind of detachment needed for substantive self-consciousness in particular and for concept use more generally. This, incidentally, is one reason for entertaining doubts about Evans's own positive account of perceptual consciousness. For Evans, nonconceptual perceptual information must be input to a concept-using system for it to be right to speak of a subject at all, and hence for it to be right to speak of perceptual consciousness. If the system we are considering has states with only nonconceptual content, the system is not a subject, and its perceptual input states are not conscious. True, Evans's appeal to informational content is motivated partly by the wish to do justice to our continuity with other animals. But if having such perceptions with nonconceptual content does not yield consciousness, then the continuity being registered can barely be called psychological continuity. And it is this that the objector wants. Crudely, the objection is that perceptual consciousness is a more primitive phenomenon than both concept use and self-consciousness.

Now the difficulty with the sentiments underpinning both kinds of objections, as they are often voiced and developed, is that they fail to make a clean break from the very powerful grip of the claim that perceptions (intuitions) without concepts are blind, that the world becomes accessible to consciousness precisely in virtue of the link with concepts. Why should this idea of a necessary link between consciousness and concepts hold such sway, even *after* a distinction of whatever kind between conceptual and nonconceptual contents has been introduced? At least one, often implicit, reason, it seems to me, is a very strong intuition to the effect that consciousness of the environment requires some minimal form of substantive self consciousness; it is only when we have such minimal substantive self-consciousness that we can begin to talk of subjects at all, and hence of subjects' points of view. The link with concepts, on this route, lies in the fact that *however* we draw the distinction between conceptual and nonconceptual contents, we want the kind of reasoning constitutive of substantive self-consciousness (e.g., the kind of reasoning constitutive of grasp of a primitive theory of self-location) to manifest conceptual structure. (If such reasoning doesn't manifest conceptual structure, what does?)

If this is right, and if we are to take seriously such objections as we have been considering to an explanation of consciousness by appeal to the explanatorily empty link between the notion of a point of view and the capacity to employ a primitive theory of self-location, as I think we should, the very least we need is a notion of a subject of experience where being a subject and having a point of view are independent of any capacity for substantive self-consciousness. And once we do this, it also opens up a far more promising route for the reductive strategy to follow.

Thus, suppose we want to allow fish and kangaroos, say, to be subjects of experience, or at least not to rule them out solely on the grounds that we believe they are not capable of substantive self-consciousness. Now we don't to lose Strawson's idea that possession of a point of view of the kind needed for being a subject in some way reflects the interaction between building up a picture of the environment and locating oneself in it, for it gets to the heart of what we think of as a subjective point of view on the environment. What we want, then, is a way of using this idea that does not imply the capacity for substantive self-consciousness. One way to get this is to think of the spatial contents of such creatures as merely implicitly self-relational. For example, to a creature capable of self-consciousness we ascribe perceptions with contents such as, the chair is to the left of me, the ball is heading in my direction, I am in front of the chapel, and so forth. For a creature without such self-consciousness we want the second relatum to be merely implicit in the contents, so that we, in giving the truth conditions of the representation, must refer to the perceiver, but the creature itself does not.

What we need here can be set in relief by considering a proposal made by John Perry. His question is, How should we explain the contents of a subject's perceptions when she sees a ball coming toward her and ducks, or when she keeps track of an object she is looking at as she moves relative to it? The natural verbal expression of such perceptions is, 'The ball is coming towards me', 'The object that was on my left is now on my right', and so forth, and such expression suggests that the contents of the perceptions contain a detached grip on oneself as an object. Perry, however, has argued that the contents of such perceptions should be thought of in terms of a propositional function whose argument place is supplied not by any representation of the subject but rather by the subject herself. In such cases he speaks of the contents "concerning," rather than being about the subject (Perry 1993, 205–226).

The idea of the subject herself popping up in the argument place of a propositional function, in place of a representation of her, is one very vivid way of explaining what it is for the truth conditions of a perception to be essentially linked to an unrepresented subject. However, I do not think it will do as it stands. The kind of amending it needs, both in general terms and relative to the purpose of linking contents to consciousness, can be brought out by considering the following two objections to it.

The first objection is this. The very least needed for a subject to have some kind of grip on her physical environment as a connected space is that she be able to reidentify places as she moves relative to them. The very least this requires is some kind of grip on the fact of her movement through these places, which in turn, the claim goes, requires some kind of grip, however minimal, on herself as a physical object. All of this requires, in Perry's terms, that the argument place be filled by some kind of representation of the subject as an object.

The second objection can be brought out by considering the directional vectors that are partially constitutive of the spatial phenomenology of perception: up, down, left, right, in front of, behind, and so forth. These may be used to represent both the direction of objects from the subject (as in 'This house is to my left') and the relations among other perceived objects (as in 'The house is to the left of the tree'). On Perry's account, such terms as 'to the left' are used uniformly in both cases, the difference being that in the first case, when one of the relata is the subject, the subject is left unrepresented. The objection, briefly stated, is that if it is correct to discern such relational structure when the subject is one of the relata, then it must surely be correct to ascribe to the subject the capacity to think of the relation as an instance of the relation in which the tree, say, can stand to the house. And this, as Evans argues, requires that the subject have "the idea of himself as one object among others; and he must think of the relation between himself and objects he can see and act upon as relations of exactly the same kind as those he can see between pairs of objects he observes" (Evans 1983, 163). (This kind of reasoning is a local exemplification of the requirement that thoughts meet what Evans calls the Generality Constraint [Evans 1983, 100–105].)

There is something right about both types of objection, but as far as they go, neither should make us give up what seems to me to be an important insight of Perry's, though I want to link it, as he does not, to explaining the notion of a point of view needed for an account of perceptual consciousness. What we need to meet both objections is an account of the spatial contents of perceptions that shows them to be simultaneously (a) *implicitly* self-relational in such a way as to give the subject an implicit grip on herself as an object (so as to meet the first objection, but without bringing in the representation of the subject as an object) and (b) of a more basic, primitive kind than conceptual contents, of a kind that shows such primitiveness to be constituted by the absence of the detachment needed for substantive self knowledge (so as to meet the second objection).

In a moment I will turn to fleshing out the way I think these very abstract and programmatic requirements should be met. Before that, let us have the full proposal before us. Suppose we call the contents of such implicitly self-relational, primitive representations of the environment *essentially perspectival* contents. We can then introduce a notion of a nonreflective point of view where perceptions of the immediate environment are from such a point of view just in case their contents are essentially perspectival. One is a nonreflective subject, on this account, when one's perceptions yield such a nonreflective perspective on the environment. And, turning now to the explanation of perceptual consciousness, on the reductive strategy we are examining, we can say that what distinguishes perceptual seemings from mere thinkings is that their content is, at least partially, essentially perspectival. (So, on this account, perceptions being from, or reflecting, a subject's point of view is a feature of the *content* of the perceptions, unlike on the explanatorily empty way of introducing the notion of a point of view.)

To generalize, the proposal I want to consider is as follows. First, the distinctive feature of conscious perceptions is that whatever other contents they have, their contents will always include a layer of such essentially perspectival contents, always include a layer of contents that makes the perceptions representations from a nonreflective point of view. Second, this fact explains what makes perceptual input yield consciousness of the immediate environment. The consciousness of conscious perceptions consists in such essential perspectivalness.

This, in very programmatic and abstract form, is, I believe, the most promising first, as yet very crude, move to make on the reductive strategy we are now examining. It is high time to make it all less programmatic and abstract, which I now want to try to do by bringing in some psychological work that can, I think, begin to put some substantive flesh on this idea of essentially perspectival representations. Before that, however, a few brief words about the second, explanatorily rich appeal to the notion of a point of view in an account of the self and of self-consciousness.

The notions of a nonreflective point of view and of essentially perspectival representations borrow much from the explanatorily rich way of introducing the notion of a point of view into discussions of the self but deprive it of its metaphysical implications or bite. Or rather, this is the intention. Instead of a subject who is not an object *tout court* (but rather a point of view), the appeal is to a subject who does not think of herself as an object or whose capacity to do so plays no part in making her a subject of this kind. And instead of the idea of *all* thought being from a point of view unrepresentable by thought itself, I am suggesting the idea of specifically perceptual representations that are essentially perspectival in that intrinsic to a specification of their contents is that the subject is a merely implicit relatum. One question I will return to in the last section of this paper is whether we can have representations with essentially perspectival contents thus defined without the metaphysical price (or prize, depending on one's perspective) of some form of idealism, that is, without the metaphysical bite that arguably comes with the explanatorily richer appeal to the notion of a point of view in explaining self consciousness. For the moment I will simply register the fact that this is the intention.

2   The Ecological Self and Consciousness

I turn now to some remarks about Gibson's account of the way perception simultaneously informs subjects about the environment and about themselves, his account, that is, of the way in which, as he puts it, "egoreception accompanies exteroception like the other side of the coin" (Gibson 1987, 418), and about Neisser's suggestion that the kind of responsiveness to self-specific information described by Gibson gives us the most primitive notion of a self, the "ecological self," as he calls it (Neisser 1988). The suggestion I want to pursue, very generally put, is that development of the notion of an ecological self gives us the materials for explaining what it is to be a nonreflective, unselfconscious subject of experiences and, on the reductive strategy I am pursuing, that we can then put this notion to use in explaining what it is for perceptions to be conscious.

Before beginning, two caveats especially important for those familiar with the work I will be referring to.

• Although there are interesting discussions in the psychological literature about whether and how Gibson's account of perception should be thought of as engaging with perceptual consciousness, none of these discussions, to my knowledge, make any appeal to Gibson's account of the relation between the pick-up of self-specific and environmental information as having any bearings on this. Similarly and again to my knowledge, discussions of the ecological self and ecological self-perception are conducted without consideration of any bearings on explanation of consciousness. So here I will be putting Gibson's and Neisser's ideas to a use to which they were not intended, as far as I know. That said, I don't think I am distorting the actual claims about ecological self-perception in any way, though I will be adding further constraints on the relation between egoreception and exteroception to those explicitly considered by Gibson or Neisser, because of the use to which I will be putting it.

• This is a warning that must accompany any appeal to Gibsonian ideas, and it is brief. In appealing to some important insights of Gibson's, I mean to be committed to nothing other than what I explicitly refer to in the Gibsonian approach to perception.

In his discussion of Gibson's ideas, Neisser (1988) distinguishes between two ways in which egoreception (ecological self-awareness, in Neisser's terms) is constantly conjoined to perception of the environment. First, there is information in the *optical flow* that specifies various features of one's own *movement* relative the environment. Second, there is the idea that what we perceive are *affordances* for action, which, as Neisser says, involve the notion of the subject as an *agent*, rather than merely as a mover.

Let us begin with the first way in which self-perception and environmental perception are said to be linked, namely to the way in which optical-flow is said to provide the perceiver with information about the perceiver's movements. Very roughly indeed, when the perceiver moves, this is invariably accompanied by flow in the optic array. Gibson's idea is that by and large, the world being as it is, there is a correlation between particular patterns of flow and particular properties of the perceiver's movement, so the flow pattern can sufficiently specify for the perceiver both that she is moving and various properties of her movement: its direction, speed, and so forth. Many of his suggestions about specific correlations have been artificially induced. One famous example is the swinging or moving room. The room is a bottomless box suspended from the ceiling, with patterned walls. The subject stands on the floor, and the room is moved backward and forward. When the room is moved toward the subject, this produces the same optic-flow patterns as would be produced if the subject were swaying toward the wall. Adults and infants, in slightly different conditions, sway backward and forward, correcting or compensating, as it were, for illusory changes in their own posture (Lishman and Lee 1973, Lee and Aronson 1975).

Can appeal to the many ways in which information in the ambient array provides subjects with information about their own movements be used to fill in the idea of how a temporally extended point of view can be constructed? The crucial question here is what is involved in the subject's pick up of such self-specific information, how is the self-specific information used by the subject. Consider, for example, a creature with a flight mechanism not unlike that of the housefly. This creature maintains stability in flight with a mechanism referred to as an optomotor response, and this mechanism exhausts the creature's responsiveness to self-specific information. Crudely, the mechanism works in such a way that every global change in optic flow is compensated for by moves in the opposite direction of that indicated by the flow, and we may imagine that the computations underlying such compensations are fairly complex. Suppose now that we want to know how the creature does something other than maintain a stable path of a flight. Suppose that we want to ascribe to it movements generated by the aim of making contact with or avoiding surfaces in its environment. The problem is that any movement thus generated will be automatically corrected for by the optomotor-response mechanism. Now one solution, proposed in fact for flies, is to introduce a separate mechanism, sensitive to features in the environment, that causes very fast changes of direction, for example, that are too fast for the optomotor mechanism to pick up and correct for. Generalizing, imagine a creature which is such that its mechanisms for detecting and responding to self-specific optic-flow patterns, i.e., patterns generated by its own movements, operate completely independently from mechanisms for detecting environmental features, and that these are somehow synchronized so as to enable the creature to survive.

I do not know whether Neisser would say that such a creature should be credited with being an ecological self in virtue of this way of responding to self-specific information. There is certainly nothing like an extended point of view here. If being an ecological self is to be equated with possessing a nonreflective point of view, we must add some restrictions to the former notion. A nonreflective point of view was introduced as the product of the build-up of an implicitly self-relational representation of the environment. If self-specific information is to contribute to generating a nonreflective point of view, it must be exploited in generating such an implicitly self-relational representation of the environment. Such exploitation is precisely what is excluded from the psychological makeup of the creature we have been describing. The mechanisms for detecting environmental and self-specific information operate completely independently of each other.

The question now is, can anything in Gibson's account of perception help in cashing in the idea of an essentially perspectival representation of the environment, into which optic-flow information must be input if it is to contribute to the generation of a point of view? Here we come to the importance, for present purposes, of the claim that what we perceive are affordances, where in this context, affordances are relativized to properties of the particular observer, as when objects are represented as liftable, places within reach or to the left, shapes as graspable, ditches as leapable, and so forth.

The notion of affordances as used by Gibson and his followers is somewhat loose. I want to propose a tightening up of it that is in keeping with the best of what Gibson says on this score but, more important, is absolutely vital, in my view, for considering Gibson's approach to perception as potentially explanatory of consciousness on the strategy we are now pursuing. I suggest that we read Gibson's idea that what we perceive are affordances for action as the claim that our perceptions are egocentric, in the sense developed by John Campbell (Campbell 1992, 82–88; 1994, 41–51). Representations of the environment are egocentric for Campbell just in case their contents are causally indexical, that is, just in case the causal (and hence physical) significance of these contents is cashed, for the subject, exclusively in terms of implications for her own actions or perceptions. It is important here that the subject's capacity to reflect on herself as an agent or perceiver plays no part in giving perceptions their causally indexical content. What introduces their causal content is their use in the planning and executing what are in fact the agent's actions and generating what are in fact her perceptual expectations. It is this feature in Campbell's notion of egocentricity that makes egocentric representations subjective or immersed, on his account, in contrast with objective or detached representations of the environment, which are explained as representations that employ forms of causal reasoning that essentially exploit the subject's capacity to think of herself as one object among others (for example, the kind of reasoning involved in a primitive theory of self-location).

Returning now to the idea of a nonreflective point of view, an essentially perspectival representation of the environment, I want to suggest the following account of it. First, the frame of reference used in such a representation for individuating places should be thought of as egocentric, in Campbell's sense (i.e., it will individuate places in casually indexical terms, such as right and left, within or without of reach, and so forth). Second, we get the minimum needed for a point of view when self-specific information in the ambient array is exploited by a psychological structure that displays what Peacocke calls "perspectival sensitivity" (1983, 66–78). Displaying perspectival sensitivity is, very roughly, a matter of sustaining aims with respect to features in the environment over changes in position relative to them, and on the account I am proposing, this is a matter of being able to update the egocentric identification of places in response to changes in position so as to sustain one's aims relative to places as one moves. For those familiar with Peacocke's account, one central difference between his account and the use to which I appropriate it turns on the way such sensitivity is explained. On his account, such sensitivity is a matter of being responsive to changes in the sensational (nonrepresentational) properties of experiences. Here the suggestion is that such sensitivity is a matter of being sensitive to self-specific information in the ambient array.

Suppose that such a proposal is developed in more detail. On the reductive strategy we are pursuing, the claim is that this kind of explanation of what it is for an information processing system to be a (nonreflective) subject gives us everything we need for explaining consciousness. More specifically, on this strategy, the claim is that for a perceptual–input state to yield consciousness of the environment, it is necessary and sufficient that at least part of its contents be essentially perspectival (where the latter notion is now given substance by appeal to egocentricity and perspectival sensitivity). Doubts may be raised both about whether there is enough here for an explanation of consciousness and about whether there is enough here for even a glimpse of the external world. In the next section I want to say why I think the first doubt is justified, and in the last section I turn to some issues raised by the second doubt.

3 Perceptual Consciousness and Attention

It is one question whether for perceptual information to be conscious it is a necessary and sufficient condition that its content be essentially perspectival. It is another question whether the materials we have availed ourselves of to explain consciousness are sufficient to show whether, and explain why, this account is either true or false. It seems to me clear that the answer to the second question must be negative. For reasons of space, I now turn to some work on split-brain patients both to illustrate the explanatory insufficiency of the way the notion of essentially perspectival contents has so far been linked to perceptual consciousness and to suggest how this link must be deepened by appeal to work on attention.

Split-brain patients are patients whose left and right neocortices have been disconnected by surgical transection of the corpus callosum. Philosophical attention to work on commissurotomy has focused, naturally enough, on the implications for explaining the unity of consciousness of the resulting segregation of visual input from the right and left hemifields. But no less interesting is work on humans and other animals that has examined the visual–information uptake that remains unified or unsegregated in such patients and is presumably to a large extent mediated by phylogenetically more primitive midbrain structures unaffected by the surgery (see, for example, Holtzman, Volpe, and Gazzaniga 1984;

Trevarthen and Sperry 1973; Trevarthen 1974). There are two points I want to make about this integrated vision.

• By and large there is a convergence of opinion, based on both positive and negative evidence, that the content of visual information mediated by these more primitive unaffected structures is the kind of information that Gibson ascribed to perception and that fits everything I have said about essentially perspectival content. For the purpose of the points I will be making, I will assume that this is how we should describe the content of the unaffected, integrated visual input.

• Almost all researchers in this area describe these unified perceptions as non- or preconscious. This in itself suggests that ascribing perspectival contents to perceptions does not compel one to think of such perceptions as conscious, and that there is at least a chink in the explanatory armor of the reductive strategy as so far elaborated. One question here is whether there is an implicit or explicit account of consciousness that underpins such denials of consciousness to the unified, perspectival contents in the split brain. And the answer is that there is. In many such cases of denial, we find the idea that if the spatial information available to each hemisphere is conscious, then it must be available for making comparisons across the hemispheres. For example, if one is perceptually conscious of two shapes, one must be in a position to judge (though not necessarily to get right) whether or not they are the same. As is well known, split-brain patients fail on a wide range of interhemispheric spatial comparisons. Therefore, the reasoning goes, whatever spatial information is unified across the fields, is used in directing integrated locomotion, and so forth, it is not conscious. If it were conscious, it could be put to use in making such explicit judgments.

The conception of consciousness that underpins this line of reasoning is very similar to Evans's. What makes perceptual information conscious is its being input to a concept-using, rational system. The next question is, Is there anything in the work on split-brain patients to which we can appeal to overcome the grip of this account of consciousness? Here too I believe that the answer is positive and is to be found in work on attention in the integrated field of vision in commisurotomy patients. To illustrate this claim, I will focus on work reported in Holtzman, Volpe, and Gazzaniga 1984, a paper in which the assumption just sketched about what is required for consciousness is more or less explicit and in which the term 'consciousness' is certainly reserved for cortically dependent vision.

The paper is concerned with the question of whether attention gets divided when the brain is split, and it reviews evidence for delivering a negative answer, especially with respect to the allocation of spatial attention. Two examples of their work will suffice to extract the general point I want to make.

• Normal subjects cannot divide attention between two locations in space separated by more than a certain distance. Beyond a certain range, subjects cannot attend to two places at once. It turns out that exactly the same is true of split-brain subjects when each of the two locations is in a separate hemifield. If splitting the cortices had resulted in the generation of two spatial-attention systems, there should be no difficulty in simultaneously attending to two widely separated locations, one in each hemifield.

• In normal subjects the speed with which they attend to a place in their visual field is greatly affected by information provided by previously flashed "precues" about the location of the imminent target. For example, suppose your task is to press a button as quickly as possible if a number flashed up in front of you is odd. The speed with which you attend to the target, measured by reaction time, is significantly affected by prior information or misinformation about the location of the to-be-shown target. If the information is correct (this might consist of an arrow pointing you in the right direction), this is termed a valid cue. If it is false (e.g., an arrow pointing in the opposite direction), it is called an invalid cue. In experiments with normal subjects, valid cues speed up reaction times, and invalid cues retard them.

• If commissurotomy yields two attentional systems we should expect no cueing effects across the hemifields. Holtzman et al. (1984) found many such effects, including ones that exploit quite sophisticated spatial information. Here is one example. Split-brain patients are presented with two 3 by 3 grids, one in each hemifield. The task is to press a button if a number that may occur in any one of the squares of the grid in one hemifield is odd. The valid precue in the other hemifield is an x in the square homologous to the one in which the target will appear in the other field. The invalid cue is an x is the wrong square. Generally, valid cues speeded up response times, and invalid cues retarded them.

To someone not immersed in the vast and often quite technical psychological literature on attention, it will seem extraordinary that these results should not be thought of as having a direct bearing on consciousness. For raising the question of whether or not attention is divided across the hemifields just seems to be a case of raising the question of whether there is one perceptual consciousness here or two. My attending to a bit of space has no effect, one way or another, on whether you can do so, or on the speed with which you attend to other bits of space. If there are such effects, there is one perceptual consciousness. Or so it would appear.

Now it seems to me that this uninformed response must be the right one. To make it good, what is needed is a definition of perceptual consciousness, somewhat along the following lines. Suppose that we think of the spatial representations that structure attention in a single attentional system and determine where attention can fall as yielding something I will call the *attentional field*. We can then appeal to the spatial structure of the field to define perceptual consciousness as follows. Perceptions are conscious just so long as they are the possible contents of focal attention, where being a possible content of focal attention just is a matter of being within the attentional field.

Now it is generally agreed that the contents of the field in perceptual attention represent the space around the perceiver on an egocentric frame.

So this explanation of perceptual consciousness would be appealing to exactly the same essentially perspectival contents as were appealed to in explaining what it is to have a nonreflective point of view on the environment. The fact that we get this result by defining perceptual consciousness in terms of its link with the attentional system may make the detour through the notion of a point of view seem redundant in the explanation of the link between perspectival contents and consciousness. However, I think appeals to attention and to the notion of a point of view need each other for bringing out why it is true, if it true, that for perceptions to be conscious, it is necessary and sufficient that they have essentially perspectival contents.

On the one hand, any explanation of perceptual consciousness must appeal to the concept of spatial attention. Such attention is *the* psychological mechanism of perceptual consciousness. This requires of the philosopher in particular to appeal selectively to the extraordinarily rich empirical literature on the workings of perceptual attention. More strongly, if having a particular kind of content, e.g., content that I have described as essentially perspectival, is necessary and sufficient for perceptual representations to be conscious, then this must be because we have to appeal to such content to explain the spatial structure of an attentional field and to explain what is meant by a single, unified system of attention.

On the other hand, if work on the spatial structure of attention is immediately relevant to an explanation of consciousness, then this must be because the kind of contents appealed to in explaining this structure just are the contents needed for explaining what it is for a spatial representation to be a representation from a subject's point of view. More specifically, one often gets the impression that for many psychologists who work on spatial attention, consciousness is seen as a wholly separate problem, one that has to be explained independently of any particular theory of attention. This cannot be right. Surely attending to something is sufficient for being conscious of it, and we are owed an explanation of why this is so. The missing link here, it seems to me, is the link between the spatial structure of the attentional field and the notion of a single point of view. More specifically, the link that has to be made explicit is the link between what are generally agreed to be the egocentric axes of the attentional field and the idea of egocentric representations being representations from the subject's point of view.

4   Implicit Self-Consciousness and Externality

Earlier I said that the notion of an essentially nonreflective point of view shares several features with the notion of a point of view as it used, for example, by Wittgenstein in explaining the nature of the metaphysical ego.

The question I now return to, briefly, is whether the way the notion of a nonreflective point of view has been developed and the use to which it has been put allow one to insist that essentially perspectival representations can be thought of as providing subjects with a grip on an external, mind-independent world. I approach this question via a brief comparison with Merleau-Ponty's version of the claim that perceptual consciousness must be explained by appeal to a subject who does not think of himself as one object among others.

Although Merleau-Ponty rejected Husserl's full-blown phenomenological reduction in giving the basic contents of consciousness, and with it Husserl's appeal to a transcendental ego as the subject of conscious experience, he did advocate a modified form of reduction or bracketing, and with it an appeal to a subject who, in an important sense, is not an object. The limited form of bracketing he advocated in giving the basic contents of perceptions involved a hiving off of all objective science, a bracketing that will return us to the "pre-scientific life of consciousness." An essential ingredient in this bracketing is a bracketing off of our conception of ourselves as physical objects, as "objective bodies." Thus he writes, "If I can, with my left hand, feel my right hand as it touches an object, the right hand as an object is not the right hand as it touches; the first is a system of bones, muscles, and flesh brought down at a point in space, the second shoots through space like a rocket to reveal the external object in its place. Insofar as it sees or touches the world, my body can therefore be neither seen nor touched. What prevents it ever being an object, ever being 'completely constituted' is that it is that by which there are objects. . . . The body therefore is not one more among external objects with the peculiarity of always being there" (Merleau-Ponty 1989, 92).

I want to focus on three distinguishable ideas in Merleau-Ponty's conception of the relation between the subject of experience and the basic contents of perceptual consciousness.

• First, there is the idea that in explaining the basic contents of experience, we must appeal to a subject who is not an object to himself. Everything that Merleau-Ponty says is consistent with treating the basic contents of perceptual experiences as he conceives of them as, at the very least, essentially perspectival in my sense.
• The contents of the essentially perspectival perceptions are autonomous, in a sense of autonomy introduced by Peacocke (1992, 90) with respect to nonconceptual contents. To say they are autonomous is to say that creatures can have perspectival representations without any capacity for nonperspectival representations.
• The third ingredient is a much headier doctrine, developed at length throughout Merleau-Ponty's writings, to the effect that perspectival contents are not only autonomous but also explanatorily basic in such a way as to yield frank idealism. Here we find the idea that objective, scientific reasoning is derivative and ultimately refers

back to our prescientific consciousness. Our conception of an objective space is ultimately to be explained in terms of a potential-action space. Physical objects, for example, are explained essentially in terms of the possibility of actions directed at them. In effect, then, Merleau-Ponty is denying that we have a disengaged and, in this sense, objective conception of the external world.

Everything I have said about essentially perspectival representations and the idea of a nonreflective point of view commits me to the autonomy of such contents. The challenge I now want to consider is a challenge to the possibility of holding onto autonomy while simultaneously insisting that such perspectival representations provide the subject with a grip on an external world, nonidealistically conceived. The challenge, succinctly put, is this. The only route out of Merleau-Ponty's idealist egocentric predicament requires one to deny autonomy to perspectival representations.

Some such line of thought, though not precisely in these terms, may be attributed to Tom Baldwin, who in his generous, illuminating, but brooking-no-nonsense paper "Phenomenology and Egocentric Thought" (1988) suggests the following corrective to the egocentric predicament. First he suggests an equation between Merleau-Ponty's phenomenal prescientific space with Evans's egocentric space, that is, with an egocentric or essentially perspectival way of representing space (Evans 1983, 153 ff.). Second, Baldwin goes on to deny the autonomy of such egocentric contents. In particular, he thinks that one cannot be credited with an egocentric grip on the world independently of the capacity for objective thought. He argues that the objective and the egocentric are interdependent and that you cannot have one without the other—an idea he rightly attributes to Evans (Evans 1983, 161). More specifically, he writes, "There is no way to hold a phenomenal conception of one's body without also recognising that the objective conception applies to it. In grasping a cup I do not think of my arm as a detachable instrument, and I do not think of it as a system of bones, muscles and flesh; nonetheless, I cannot but think of it as interacting causally with the cup. One's understanding of action would be wholly mysterious unless intrinsic to one's conception of oneself as an agent was an understanding of oneself as located within objective space and interacting causally with objects in the environment." And he goes on to makes similar remarks about one's conception of oneself as a perceiver.

I think it is undeniable that one's *conception* of oneself as an agent or perceiver would be mysterious unless one thought of oneself as one physical object among others. But that, in a sense, is irrelevant to the issue of autonomy. What is needed for denying a realist interpretation of autonomy is a claim to the effect that a subject's perceptions can provide him with a grip on the external world *only* if he does have such a conception of himself. More specifically, Campbell's notion of causally indexical contents suggests that we should distinguish between two ingredients in our conception of an external world. First, there is the idea that the external world is the physical world, in particular, a world of causal process and connections. Second, there is the idea of the objective world, the world as it is independently of our interaction with it. One way of rephrasing Baldwin's claim about the interdependence of the egocentric and the objective would be to say that we cannot have a grip on a physical world without having, at the same time, an objective conception of the world. This just is to deny the autonomy of causally indexical contents.

My main response to this kind of objection is that it seems to me to underestimate seriously the depth and acuteness of the egocentric predicament, both of which can be brought out as follows. Suppose that you explain the consciousness of your current perceptions in the way I have been sketching. In doing so, you will be using a detached representation of yourself as one object among others. It would be nice if you could use the account you give of the content of your perceptions to anchor your detached representation of yourself to the world. But the essence of the account you have given makes the way you figure in the account, as the focal point of your experiences, representationally silent. There is a yawning chasm between your detached representation of yourself as an object and your representationally silent occurrence as an extended of point of view. Asserting a constitutive link between egocentric representation of the environment and the capacity to represent yourself as an object will not of itself eliminate this chasm, nor will it begin to explain how this might be done. This, I venture, is at least part of the source of the sense of a deep elusiveness of the self captured by Wittgenstein in his entry in the *Notebooks* when he wrote, "The I, the I, is what is deeply mysterious" (1961a: 5 August 1916). And it is here that the idea of the metaphysical subject may be felt to emerge with full force.

It seems to me that the only route out of this predicament without appealing to the metaphysical subject—and I think there must be such a route—rests on distinguishing a genuinely reflective, nonperspectival level of consciousness and recognizing that it requires separate explanation. By 'reflective consciousness' I mean a kind of consciousness that essentially involves the representation of one's mental states. Explaining what this involves in turn requires, I suggest, an account of the way in which temporal concepts structure the phenomenology of mature human consciousness so as to entail the representation of mental states, in particular, of first-order conscious perceptions. And we need an account of how such reflectivity is linked to the capacity for detached representation of oneself as one object among others. The hope must be that an account of the relation between consciousness and the self on this detached, reflective level will provide the materials for beginning to understand the relation between being the point of view from which one has first-order experiences and the capacity for detached reflection on oneself and the world, and thus for beginning to bridge the gap between them.

Acknowledgments

A version of this paper was read to the Philosophical Society, Oxford. I am greatly indebted to John Campbell for his response. My thanks also go out to Bill Brewer, Christopher Peacocke, and my coeditors for comments on earlier versions.

References

Baldwin, Tom. 1988. "Phenomenology and Egocentric Thought." *Aristotelian Society Proceedings*, suppl. vol. 62:27–44.

Campbell, John. 1993. "The Role of Physical Objects in Spatial Thinking." In *Spatial Representation: Problems in Philosophy and Psychology*, edited by N. Eilan, R. McCarthy, and B. Brewer. Oxford: Basil Blackwell.

Campbell, John. 1994. *Past, Space, and Self*. Cambridge: MIT Press.

Dimond, S. J., and Beaumont, J. G., eds. 1974. *Hemisphere Function in the Human Brain*. London: Elek Books.

Evans, Gareth. 1983. *The Varieties of Reference*. Oxford: Clarendon Press.

Gibson, E. 1993. "The Ontogenesis of the Perceived Self." In *The Perceived Self: Ecological and Interpersonal Sources of Self Knowledge*, edited by U. Neisser. Cambridge: Cambridge University Press.

Holtzman, J. D., Volpe, B. T., and Gazzaniga, M. S. 1984. "Spatial Orientation Following Commissural Section." In *Varieties of Attention*, edited by R. Parasuraman and D. R. Davies. New York: Academic Press.

Humphrey, N. K. 1974. "Vision in a Monkey without a Striate Cortex." *Perception* 3:241–255.

Gibson, J. J. 1979. *The Ecological Approach to Visual Perception*. Boston: Houghton Mifflin.

McCarthy, Rosaleen. 1993. "Assembling Routines and Addressing Representations: An Alternative Conceptualisation of What and Where in the Human Brain." In *Spatial Representation: Problems in Philosophy and Psychology*, edited by N. Eilan, R. McCarthy, and B. Brewer. Oxford: Basil Blackwell.

Merleau-Ponty, M. 1989. *Phenomenology of Perception*. Translated by C. London: Routledge.

Nagel, Thomas. 1979. "What Is It Like to Be a Bat?" In his *Mortal Questions*. New York: Cambridge University Press.

Nagel, Thomas. 1986. *The View from Nowhere*. Oxford University Press.

Neisser, U. 1993. "The Self Perceived." In *The Perceived Self: Ecological and Interpersonal Sources of Self Knowledge*, edited by U. Neisser. Cambridge: Cambridge University Press.

Peacocke, Christopher. 1983. *Sense and Content*. Oxford: Clarendon Press.

Peacocke, Christopher. 1992. *A Study of Concepts*. Cambridge: MIT Press.

Pears, David. 1988. *The False Prison*, vols. 1 and 2. Oxford: Clarendon Press.

Perry, John. 1993. *The Problem of the Essential Indexical and Other Essays*. New York: Oxford University Press.

Reed, E. 1987. "Why Do Things Look As They Do? The Implications of J. J. Gibson's *The Ecological Approach to Visual Perception*." In *Cognitive Psychology in Question*, edited by A. Costall and A. Still. Brighton: Harvester Press.

Strawson, P. F. 1966. *The Bounds of Sense*. London: Methuen.

Trevarthen, C. 1974. "Analysis of Cerebral Activities that Generate and Regulate Consciousness in Commissurotomy Patients." In *Hemisphere Function in the Human Brain*, edited by S. J. Dimond and J. G. Beaumont. London: Elek Books.

Trevarthen, C., and Sperry, R. W. 1973. "Perceptual Unity of the Ambient Visual Field in Human Commissurotomy Patients." *Brain* 77:1–17.

Weiskrantz, L. 1986. *Blind Sight: A Case Study and Implications*. Oxford: Oxford University Press.

Wittgenstein, L. 1961a. *Notebooks, 1914–1916*. Edited by G. von Wright and G. E. M. Anscombe. Translated by G. E. M. Oxford: Basil Blackwell.

Wittgenstein, L. 1961b. *Tractatus Logico-philosophicus*. Translated by D. Pears and B. McGuiness. London: Routledge.

Contributors

Thomas Baldwin is a Fellow of Clare College and a lecturer in the Faculty of Philosophy at Cambridge University. He is the author of *G. E. Moore* (Routledge, 1990). He is currently working on the theme of naturalism in twentieth-century philosophy.

José Luis Bermúdez is currently a British Academy Research Fellow in the Philosophy Faculty of the University of Cambridge. He was a member of the Spatial Representation Project at King's College, Cambridge. His publications include journal articles on the history of philosophy and the philosophy of psychology. He is writing a book on the structure and development of self-consciousness.

Bill Brewer is CUF Lecturer in Philosophy at Oxford University and a Tutorial Fellow of Saint Catherine's College. He was formerly a Research Fellow on the Spatial Representation Project at King's College, Cambridge. He has published on issues in epistemology and the philosophy of mind, was an editor of *Spatial Representation* (Blackwell, 1993), and is currently working on the book *Perception and Reason* (Oxford University Press) on the role of spatial content in the justification of perceptual knowledge.

George Butterworth is a Professor of Psychology at the University of Sussex, England. From 1988 to 1994 he was editor of the *British Journal of Developmental Psychology*. With Margaret Harris he is coauthor of *Principles of Developmental Psychology* (Erlbaum, 1994). His research interests are in perception and cognitive development in human infancy and early childhood.

John Campbell is Fellow and Tutor in Philosophy at New College, Oxford. He works on philosophy of mind, philosophy of language, epistemology, and metaphysics. He is the author of *Past, Space, and Self* (MIT Press, 1994).

Quassim Cassam is a Lecturer in Philosophy at Oxford University and a Fellow of Wadham College, Oxford. He has published articles on Kantian metaphysics and the first person, and is the editor of *Self-Knowledge* (Oxford University Press, 1994). He is currently writing a book on the self.

Jonathan Cole is a Clinical Neurophysiologist at Poole Hospital in Britain. His research interests have focused on the neurophysiology of movement. *Pride and a*

Daily Marathon, his first book, was published by Duckworth in 1991. At present he is working on a study of the culture and neurology of the face for the MIT Press.

Naomi Eilan is a Jacobsen Fellow at University College, London. She was previously Senior Research Fellow at King's College, Cambridge, and Director of the joint philosophy-psychology project Spatial Representation at the King's College Research Centre. She works on problems in consciousness, self-consciousness, and spatial thought. She is currently working on the book *Consciousness and the Self* (Oxford University Press).

Shaun Gallagher is a Professor of Philosophy at Canisius College in Buffalo, New York. He is the author of *Hermeneutics and Education* (State University of New York Press, 1992), and has published articles on a variety of issues related to contemporary continental philosophy. He is coeditor of *Merleau-Ponty, Hermeneutics, and Postmodernism* (SUNY Press, 1992) and editor of *Hegel and Hermeneutics* (SUNY Press, in press). As a recent invited Visiting Scholar, he studied issues related to self-consciousness and body awareness at the Medical Research Council, Applied Psychology Unit, at Cambridge, England.

Marcel Kinsbourne is Research Professor of Cognitive Studies at Tufts University and Consultant Neurologist at the Boston Veterans Administration Medical Center. He is a behavioral neurologist and experimental psychologist. His published research addresses a range of issues from normal and abnormal development to neuropsychological analysis of focal brain damage. He is currently studying the organization of brain systems that underlie consciousness.

Anthony Marcel is a Research Scientist currently working for the Medical Research Council, Applied Psychology Unit, in Cambridge. He was joint editor of *Consciousness in Contemporary Science* (Oxford University Press, 1988). His main research is on aspects of consciousness.

M. G. F. Martin is a Lecturer in the Department of Philosophy, University College, London. He has published a number of articles on perception, including work on the sense of touch and its relation to our awareness of our own bodies. He is currently working on a book on naive realism.

Andrew N. Meltzoff is a Professor of Psychology at the University of Washington. His primary interests are in developmental cognitive psychology, particularly children's understandings of mind. His current research concerns body imitation, the object concept, and the ontogenesis of folk psychology in infants and young children.

M. Keith Moore is a Research Scientist at the University of Washington. His interests are in cognitive development in infancy. His research concerns the nature of thought without language, as manifest in the development of object identity and permanence and in the origins of imitation.

Brian O'Shaughnessy is a Reader in Philosophy in the University of London and teaches at King's College, London. He has been Visiting Professor at the University of California at Los Angeles on a number of occasions, as well as at the University of California at Berkeley. He is the author of *The Will,* vols. 1 and 2 (Cambridge University Press, 1980), as well as of numerous articles in journals. He is currently working on the book *Consciousness and Perception.*

Jacques Paillard is an Emeritus Professor at the University Aix-Marseille, where he taught behavioral neurosciences. He was Director of the Brain Research Institute of the National Center of Scientific Research (CNRS) in Marseille and one of the founder of the European Brain and Behaviour Society. His primary interests were proprioception and visuomotor control. He published many papers and book chapters and recently edited *Brain and Space* (Oxford University Press, 1991). For the last few years he has collaborated with Yves Lamarre at the Centres de Recherches Neurologiques de Montreal and with Chantal Bard at the University Laval in Quebec.

James Russell is with the Department of Experimental Psychology, Cambridge University. He is the author of *The Acquisition of Knowledge* (Macmillan, 1978) and *Explaining Mental Life* (Macmillan, 1984), and is the editor of *Philosophical Perspectives on Developmental Psychology* (Basil Blackwell, 1987). His recent empirical research has focused on executive functioning in normally developing children and in persons with autism.

Paul F. Snowdon is a Fellow and Lecturer in philosophy at Exeter College, Oxford, and a University Lecturer in philosophy at Oxford University. He has written about perception, personal identity, and the mind-body problem. He is currently working on a book about personal identity.

Index

Self-coherence, in Stern's analysis, 101
Self concept, in Neisser's analysis, 89
Self-consciousness, 205, 217. *See also*
Substantive self-consciousness thesis
body image in, 36, 40
and body schema, 33
and ecological self, 95
fully fledged, 153, 156
and imitation experiments, 33
levels of, 10–11, 153
nonconceptual, 167–173
of oneself as an object, 3, 6–7, 11–12,
21–22
ontogenesis of, 10–12, 167–168
and ownership of sensations, 23–24
and perceptual origins of self, 102
primary vs. higher-order, 89
primitive, 11, 163–173
self as object of, 283
Self history, in Stern's analysis, 101
Self-knowledge
and imitation, 99
Kantian conception of, and bodily
awareness, 313–314, 331–332
kinds of (Neisser), 88–89
self-perception as foundation for, 87
Self-perception, self-knowledge founded
on, 87
Self-reference vs. demonstrative
reference, 316–317
Self-world dualism, 8–12, 127, 129–131
and agency, 129, 131–137
and object permanence, 139
and other minds, 141–146
Sensations, bodily, 267, 268–278, 286. *See
also* Bodily awareness
and Cartesian model, 297–298
experienced location of, 16–17,
19–20
in deafferented subjects, 24–25
kinesthetic and postural, 184, 187,
190–200
nonrepresentational role of, in
proprioception, 191–192, 198, 200
ownership of, 23–24
role of, in proprioceptive awareness of
posture and movement, 18–20
and sense of ownership, 306
spatial content of, 19–20, 23–24

spatial location of, 269–273, 286 (n. 10),
297, 298–304, 308 (n. 6), 332
Sense of ownership, 281, 305–306
phenomenological, 268–273, 277–278,
279
Shatz, Carla, 236
Sherrington, C. S., 88
Shoemaker, Sydney, 22–23, 25–26
on awareness of self, 312, 313, 315–317,
318, 327, 331, 332, 333
on brain zaps, 74, 76–77, 83, 84–85 (n. 4)
on concept of person, 80
on error through misidentification,
291–292, 315, 320
on introspection, 279
on tracking, 329
Shontz, F. C., 227–228, 235, 239
Short-term body image
cause of, 183–184, 187, 193–196
concept independence of, 186
content of, 176–177, 184–186, 203
vs. long-term body image, 15–18,
21–22, 34–35, 183–184, 187
as a phenomenal reality, 183–187
as the potentially proprioceptively
perceptible, 185–187
as the proprioceptively perceived,
184–187
as the proprioceptively perceptible,
185–187
raw material of, 186
three different varieties of, 183–187
Siamese twins, "belongingness"
experiment with, 92
Simulation of gestures, 50, 54, 60–65
Single mind and split brain, 78
Singular terms, reference, and conceptual
roles of singular terms, 29–30
Size estimation, 230, 235
Skills, infant's acquisition of, 95–96
Skrinar, G. S., 238
Sneezing, 250
Snowdon, P. F., 6–7
Social interaction
and body image, 36
and direct perception, 96–101
and other minds, 145
and psychological states, 36, 39–40
and self-awareness, 144–145